THREE DECADES OF ENGENDERING HISTORY

THREE DECADES OF ENGENDERING HISTORY

Selected Works of Antonia I. Castañeda

EDITED BY

Linda Heidenreich with Antonia I. Castañeda
Original Interviews by Luz María Gordillo and a
Conclusion by Deena J. González

Number 9 in the Al Filo: Mexican American Studies Series

Roberto Calderón, Series Editor

Denton, Texas

Printed in the United States of America.

10 9 8 7 6 5 4 3 2 1

Permissions:
University of North Texas Press
1155 Union Circle #311336
Denton, TX 76203-5017

The paper used in this book meets the minimum requirements of the American National Standard for Permanence of Paper for Printed Library Materials, z39.48.1984. Binding materials have been chosen for durability.

Library of Congress Cataloging-in-Publication Data

Castañeda, Antonia, author editor interviewee.
[Works. Selections]

Three decades of engendering history : selected works of Antonia I. Castañeda / edited by Linda Heidenreich with Antonia I. Castañeda ; original Interviews by Luz María Gordillo and a conclusion by Deena J. Gonzáles. -- Edition: First.

pages cm -- (Number 9 in the Al Filo: Mexican American studies series)

Includes bibliographical references and index.

ISBN 978-1-57441-568-1 (cloth : alk. paper)

978-1-57441-569-8 (pbk. : alk. paper) -- 978-1-57441-582-7 (ebook)

1. Mexican American women--History. 2. Mexican American women--Social conditions. 3. Mexican American women--Ethnic identity. 4. Mexican American women--Intellectual life. 5. Gender identity--Cross-cultural studies. 6. Women political activists--United States. 7. Feminism--United States. 8. Chicano movement. 9. Castañeda, Antonia--Interviews. I. Heidenreich, Linda, 1964- editor. II. Gordillo, Luz María, 1962- interviewer. III. González, Deena J., 1952- writer of supplementary textual content. IV. Title. V. Series: Al filo ; no. 9.

E184.M5.C36782 2014

305.48'86872073--dc23

2014027845

Three Decades of Engendering History: Selected Works of Antonia I. Castañeda is Number 9 in the Al Filo: Mexican American Studies Series

The electronic edition of this book was made possible by the support of the Vick Family Foundation.

For Our Mothers:
Irene R. Castañeda
Dolores del Carmen Heidenreich
Luz María de los Cobos Torres.

TABLE OF CONTENTS

List of Figures ix

Foreword and Acknowledgments xi

Introduction: Three Decades of Engendering History 1

Introduction to the Interviews: Tres Entrevistas/Tres
Pláticas 25

**Part One: Speaking Back, Critiquing the Dominant
Discourse** 35

Chapter 1: The Political Economy of Nineteenth-Century
Stereotypes of Californianas 37

Chapter 2: Malinche, Calafia y Toypurina 65

Plática I: El Cuerpo y El Baile 89

**Part Two: Remapping a Tradition: Critical
Historiographies** 99

Chapter 3: Women of Color and the Rewriting of Western
History 103

Chapter 4: Gender, Race, and Culture 143

Plática II: "Pero No Somos Princesas ni Príncipes" (But We're
Neither Princesses nor Princes) 187

**Part Three: Writing Mestiza and Indigenous Women into
History** 197

Chapter 5: Sexual Violence in the Politics and Policies of
Conquest 201

Chapter 6: Engendering the History of Alta California, 1769–
1848... 229

Plática III: Birthing Chicana History................................... 273

Part Four: Embodied Histories...................................... 291

Chapter 7: "Que Se Pudieran Defender (So You Could Defend
Yourselves)"... 295

Chapter 8: Language and Other Lethal Weapons..................... 331

Chapter 9: Lullabies y Canciones de Cuna........................... 349

Chapter 10: "La Despedida".. 371

Conclusion to *Three Decades of Engendering History*................. 379

Permissions Acknowledgments.. 387

Bibliography.. 389

Index.. 439

LIST OF FIGURES

Figure 1: Drs. Antonia Castañeda and Luz María Gordillo, San
Antonio, TX 2011 90

Figure 2: Dr. Castañeda in Crystal City at the Mexican Cemetery,
2011 97

Figure 3: Antonia Castañeda in Puebla, Mexico, 2011 188

Figure 4: Young Huchnom woman with the characteristic facial
tattooing of their people 231

Figure 5: A page dated April 1781 from the San Carlos Borromeo
"First Book of Matrimony." 234

Figure 6: The Wife of a Monterey Soldier 244

Figure 7: A California Wedding Party of 1845 248

Figure 8: The Anza Expedition, 1775-1776 253

Figure 9: Doña Mariana Coronel grinds corn on a *metate* 255

Figure 10: The famed southern California ranchero Juan Bandini
and his daughter 258

Figure 11: Dr. Antonia Castañeda, San Antonio 2011 274

Figure 12: Romana Raquel Rodríguez, Crystal City's midwife and
healer, c. 1926 311

Figure 13: Troca enlonada (tarp-covered flatbed truck) with
            migrant workers leaving for beet fields in the north,
            taken at San Antonio, Texas, May 1946 313

Figure 14: Irene R. Castañeda, Crystal City, Texas 317

Figure 15: Irene R. Castañeda, in the middle, stands with
            coworkers in front of a hop kiln 318

FOREWORD AND ACKNOWLEDGMENTS

Anthologies, it seems, have so many pieces that acknowledgements are a near impossibility; far too many debts are incurred in the course of the project. This project, because it was collaborative, owes a great debt to many people. It is a labor of love and respect, from myself, Luz María Gordillo, and Deena J. González for Antonia Castañeda, a scholar who continues to inspire. Once I mustered the courage to approach such a project, I immediately thought of Deena and Luz María as co-conspirators. We emailed and made sure we were on the same page before approaching Antonia, knowing she might be hesitant to have her work featured in such a way. We brain-stormed on the articles we wanted to include and consulted with her. Initially we were going to do the editing labor as a team but then two very good things happened: Deena González had an opportunity to serve in upper administration (she is now a vice provost at Loyola Marymount), and Luz María Gordillo, with her expertise in visual arts, dreamed a movie. Last year, it was realized in the production of *Antonia: A Chicana Story* (co-produced with Dr. Javier Pescador).The movie has been shown at the annual conferences of the National Organization for Chicana and Chicano Studies (NACCS) and the Latina American Studies Association (LASA) and will soon be available to university libraries and departments. This project, of course, continued to be collaborative, with Luz María contributing not only the interviews, but their introductions, and Deena González, as one of the "MALCS generation," crafting the conclusion. I want to thank Antonia Castañeda for her assistance and patience with this project and for her great heart in allowing us to offer it to you. As a first-time editor to a project of this size, I relied on her for input on introductions and framing, verifying dates and numerous other details. Finally, Dr. Roberto Calderón was a support from the project's very inception. Without his encouragement and advocacy it would not have seen print. The first thank you, then goes to "Team *Three Decades*."

At Washington State University so many people were generous with their time that I face the risk of missing someone. Dr. Lisa Macintyre, in the department of Sociology put up with my very basic questions about optical scanning, editor's notes, and more. Initially the department (the only one on campus with the software we needed), was going to loan use of the scanner, but it broke the week before I was able to start the scans. Rose Smetana, our program director in the Department of Critical Culture, Gender, and Race Studies walked me through the basics of removing section breaks and other technical editing feats. Trevor Bond with our manuscripts collection helped chase images and scan public domain materials. Thank you as well to Dr. Tanya Gonzales, a recent graduate of our American Studies program, for helping me chase down articles at the beginning of the project, and for proofing the manuscript as it came to a conclusion. Support from the Chicana/o Studies Colectiva at WSU was and is critical to all the work I do at WSU. Lizeth Gutiérrez, Jorge Moraga, Veronica Sandoval and Joaquín Chapar continue to support me, as we support each other in developing Chicana/o Studies curriculum for Chicana/o Latina/o Freedom School, helping the next generation with their projects, and inspiring each other on projects such as this. Thank you as well to Drs. Jerry García and Brian McNeill of the Inland Northwest Coalition for Chicana/o Latina/o Studies for friendship and support, and faith that we can realize the dream of Aztlán in the inland northwest. These are the friends and colegas who make labor at a predominately white institution such as WSU survivable, even while working to shift the demographics and the discourse of the space. Washington State University, Pullman, is a relatively small institution located in the rural space of the Washington/Idaho border. A work like this is only possible in our space because of the generosity of all who work here.

Finally, and perhaps most importantly, this work could not have been done without the support of family. My family at Sacred Heart parish, especially "what's left of the Catholic left" supported me with prayer throughout the project, as did my mother, who worries when I stay up too late writing, and reminds me to take care of myself. My partner, Karen Gallaghar, who so values the work that I do that she makes it a family priority.

This work is dedicated to our mothers: Irene R. Castañeda, whose life and mentoring weaves in and out of Dr. Castañeda's work in so many ways; Dolores del Carmen Heidenreich, my own mother who continues to teach me strength, love and listening through her own life; and Luz María de los Cobos Torres, who inspired and supported Dr. Gordillo's commitment to 'Other' feminisms and who unfortunately passed while we labored to bring forth this work. These are the women who taught us strength in struggle, they make our work possible.

THREE DECADES OF
ENGENDERING HISTORY

Introduction

Three Decades of Engendering History

One sunny day in 1995, three Chicana/o graduate students at the University of California, San Diego stood outside their building waxing poetic on their yet-unrealized dissertations. When I, the newest of the threesome asked Greg Rodríguez what he "wanted to do" with his dissertation, he replied, "I want to do what Antonia Castañeda did, take on the big guys." Thus began my introduction to the work of Dr. Antonia Castañeda. Appalled that I was not familiar with her work, one of my colleagues immediately loaned me a copy of her dissertation, and my writing and research was forever changed.

My experience is not unique. In writing of the rich and interdisciplinary origins of Chicana history, another Chicana historian, Miroslava Chávez-García noted that it was Dr. Castañeda's work that inspired her; Dr. Juan Gómez Quiñones had handed her a copy of the now classic *Between Borders: Essays in Chicana/Mexicana History*. In it she found Castañeda's "Political Economy of Nineteenth Century Stereotypes of Californianas," and "through that piece... [she] found [her] calling."[1]

Dr. Castañeda's work shaped and influenced two generations of Chicana/o historians and will undoubtedly shape many to come. Reference to it can be found in the footnotes of established scholars such as Albert Hurtado, Susan Lee Johnson, and Deena González. It is foundational for Chicana historians of my generation, such as Bárbara O. Reyes, Miroslava Chávez-García, María Raquél Casas, Maylei Blackwell and Luz María Gordillo.[2] It is also found in the dissertations of a new generation of scholars such as Margo Tamez, Erika Pérez, Jennifer Mata, and Tanya Gonzales.[3] A survey of Google Scholar found over 150 citations of her work for the articles included in this volume alone.

The influence of her work in press and in person reshaped the fields of Chicana/o Studies and Western History. The impact of her professional mentoring on Chicana/o historians was felt nationally. It was Dr. Castañeda who pulled us together at conferences, introduced us to each other and made sure we knew each other's work. She read drafts of work—essays and conference papers, dissertations and manuscripts—and asked questions that brought our analysis to the place it needed to be. Equally important, her publications and her stature told us that our work mattered; Chicana histories are critical, they can empower our communities; they can change the way people understand our national past.

While the pláticas/interviews included in the volume address the work of Antonia Castañeda in mentoring a generation of Chicana/o academics, the primary focus of this volume is her publications, from "Political Economy of Nineteenth Century Stereotypes of Californianas" to her later work challenging the very categories in which so many of us continue to work. Earlier texts such as her widely circulated dissertation, or the now classic *Literatura Chicana*, remain important for understanding the breadth and impact of her work but will need to be reprinted at a later date. For it was in "Presidarias y Pobladoras" that Castañeda challenged an established cannon which, at that time, continued to portray California's past in one-dimensional terms with mestizo peoples effectively erased from the drama of the past. "Presidarias Y Pobladoras" put flesh and blood on our mestiza/o past and the gendered interactions of españoles, mestizas/os and indigenous peoples in California's violent, rich and resilient history.[4]

Antonia Castañeda's earliest scholarly work appeared in the 1970s. In 1971, in *El Grito*, one of the first refereed journals in Chicana/o Studies, she published Irene Castañeda's history of the family in Crystal, Tejas, and their journey to Washington State.[5] One year later Prentice Hall published *Literatura Chicana: Texto y Contexto/Chicano Literature: Text and Context*, which she, with Joseph Sommers and Tomás Ybarra-Frausto, co-edited.[6] Like the Chicana/o Studies journals of the time, *Literatura Chicana* was more than a work of excavation and exposure; it was a work of decolonization—moving our texts to the center of cultural discourse, making our histories and literatures available for future generations, and placing it within a broader hemispheric context, which we would now term transnational. And it accomplished its goal; at the turn of this century, playwright Cherríe Moraga wrote that the "first paragraph" she ever read on La Llorona, was in *Literatura Chicana*.[7] The text has become a classic, referenced by scholars and theorists of Chicana/o histories and literatures as they map the development of the field. *Literatura Chicana* was followed by "Comparative Frontiers: The Migration of Women to Alta California and New Zealand," which drew attention to the centrality of women and gender to the colonial project and the lessons of class and gender analysis to be learned from comparative studies.[8] These important works could not be included in this collection.

Dr. Castañeda's historical articles, the bulk of which are collected in this volume, excavated the lives and struggles of mestiza and indigenous women in eighteenth and nineteenth-century California. They were published in prestigious journals including *Frontiers*, the *Pacific Historical Review*, and the *Chicano-Latino Law Review*. Other articles appeared in anthologies published by the University of Minnesota Press (1996), Indiana University Press (2000) and Arte Público (1993). In widely circulated articles, such as "Engendering the History of Alta California, 1769-1848:

Gender, Sexuality, and the Family," Castañeda took a direct and honest look at sex and gender relations in colonial California. Demonstrating that there is no romantic past to which we can turn, she excavated stories of violence against women, as well as stories of survival and resistance. It is articles such as "Engendering History" and "Sexual Violence and the Politics of Conquest," as well as "Presidarias y Pobladoras" that remind each new generation of Chicana/o scholars that our struggles are not new—inequalities run deep.

Dr. Castañeda's writings taught us that history is a tool with which we can speak back—challenge stereotypes, create new narratives and new futures. As my generation moved through our own professional careers, we assigned her work to our students and we built upon her work in our own research. Eventually, so many of our students complained of "hunting down" and "chasing" Dr. Castañeda's work, and suggested the need for a collected volume, that we stopped and listened. What you have before you is not the total of Dr. Castañeda's work. Rather, it represents the work we most often use in our own scholarship as well as those articles we most frequently assign to our students. We believe it will prove a valuable resource for many generations to come.

The MALCS Generation: Mapping a Usable Past

Castañeda's generation of scholars came from communities of workers and self-identified Chicanas/os. Like so many of us, they were the first in their families to attend university, often the first to graduate high school. MALCS, then, emerged out of a "politics of necessity."[9] In the words of Adaljiza Sosa-Riddell, one of the key founders of Mujeres Activas en Letras y Cambio Social (MALCS):

> Chicana/Latina women were an integral part of the activities collectively recognized as the Chicano Movimiento, most active and visible from 1964 to 1975. By the early 1980s their contributions were barely acknowledged. Sensing this collective loss of voice, feeling highly isolated, eager to extend their knowledge to other

women, and desiring to change society's perceptions, a group of Chicana/Latina academic women gathered at the University of California, Davis, in spring 1982. Mujeres Activas En Letras Y Cambio Social (MALCS) was established at this first meeting.[10]

In 1983 the Chicana scholar-activists who founded this new Chicana-centered organization (and who, with the exception of two professors, were graduate or even undergraduate students) boldly articulated the influence of their home communities on their scholarship:

> We are the daughters of Chicano working class families involved in higher education. We were raised in labor camps and barrios, where sharing our resources was the basis of survival. Our values, our strength derive from where we came. Our history is the story of the working class people—their struggles, commitments, strengths, and the Chicano/Mexicano experience in the United States. We are particularly concerned with the conditions women face at work, in and out of the home. We continue our mothers' struggle for economic and social justice. The scarcity of Chicanas in institutions of higher education requires that we join together to identify our common problems, to support each other and to define collective solutions. Our purpose is to fight the race, class, and gender oppression we have experienced in the universities.[11]

Mujeres en Marcha, from Berkeley: Teresa Córdova. Margarita Decierdo, Adela de la Torre, Denise Segura, Lupe Frias, Deena González, Beatriz Pesquera, Patricia Zavella, Gloria Cuádraz and Prof. Sylvia Lyzár-raga, among others joined with Adaljiza Sosa-Riddell, Antonia Castañeda, Helen Lara Cea, Emma Pérez and others to create a sitio for Chicana Scholars throughout Greater Mexico.[12] Historian Emma Pérez, then still a graduate student, would later map the theory of *sitio y lengua*, explaining boldly how such spaces are critical to Chicana survival.[13]

The scholarship and activism of this generation created a "turning point" in Chicana Studies and Chicana history. Mujeres en Marcha had organized a panel focusing on Chicana issues at the National Association for Chicano Studies conference in Tempe, Arizona, earlier that spring

(1982). Teresa Córdova was the moderator with Margarita Decierdo, Gloria Cuádraz, Deena González, Elisa Facio, and Adela de la Torre as panelists. At the conference there was push-back, with many Chicano scholars making accusations with which Chicana feminists are all too familiar: feminism is a white ideology, women's issues are divisive, feminists are Malinchistas, etc.[14]

Yet, because of the spaces created by this generation, the struggle moved forward and two years later the theme for the 1984 National Association for Chicano Studies (NACS) conference was "Voces de la Mujer."[15] In the words of Teresa Córdova, "The 1984 conference, 'Voces de la Mujer,' was a hallmark in the Chicana struggle for voice and presence."[16] *Chicana Voices*, the anthology which grew out of the conference, was also a "historic first," as the first publication of NACS to focus on Chicana issues and Chicana Studies.[17] That volume included the work of many of the scholars who became foundational to the fields of Chicana Studies and Chicana History: Norma Cantú, Cynthia Orozco, Alma M. García, Denise Segura, Teresa Carrillo, Yolanda Julia Broyles, and more.

The MALCS generation of scholars was fierce, in part, because interest in, as well as resources and support for their work were scarce; in relation, their work was oppositional—to the dominant US historical cannon, as well as to Chicano and Euro-American women's historical scholarship on the West, and to feminist scholarship more generally.[18] The battles they fought were within the academy and without, within multiple traditional disciplines including history, and within the growing interdiscipline of Chicana/o Studies.

PRELUDE TO A REVOLUTION: THE OPPOSITIONAL TRADITION OF CHICANA/O STUDIES[19]

The work of the MALCS generation, Dr. Castañeda's generation, was possible because of the generations of scholars whose previous struggles paved the way. Before there was a field of Chicana History, before the

Euro-Americans who dominated and structured the field of history could even conceive of Chicanas/os as subjects, barriers had to be struck down, and doors pushed open. And so it was that in the early decades to the mid-twentieth century, at about the time that the women of Mujeres en Marcha, NACS, and MALCS were born, a small group of Mexican-American scholars were able to gain access to higher education. Taking an oppositional stance in academia, they researched, published, taught, and lay the groundwork for challenging the discourse about Chicanas/os in the US. Their work: to insist on Mexican Americans as historical subjects. George I. Sánchez, Carlos Castañeda, Jovita González, and Ernesto Galarza left a solid foundation on which to build.[20]

Among women scholars, it was Jovita González whose work was passed down. Earning her MA in history, from the 1920s through the 1940s González published folklore and cultural history in periodicals as diverse as the *Southwest Review* and *LULAC News*.[21] Her work of collecting and documenting the folklore of Tejanos and Mexican descent people of the Rio Grande Valley lacked the class analysis of the later fields of Chicana/o history and Chicana/o Studies, yet it also contained thinly veiled critiques of the US Invasion; as José Limón points out in *Dancing with the Devil*, such critiques were less veiled in her later work.[22] Likewise, while female characters are not always prominent in her work, at times her stories and essays problematized patriarchy—a critique that would later become central to Chicana Studies in general and Chicana history in particular.[23]

Yet in order for the work of Chicana historians to flourish pivotal political, education, and intellectual shifts still needed to happen. In addition to the Chicana/o Movement itself, a strong Chicana feminist movement had to emerge and with it a flourishing of Chicana feminist cultural production. Concomitantly, an increase in the numbers of Chicanos and especially Chicanas in graduate programs, and the formation of groups within and without the academy—La Colectiva, Mujeres en March, Third World Women, and more, had to be realized. These scholars, emerging from the Chicana/o movement, directly challenged and revised the nationalist, triumphalist narratives of the dominant culture.

As Chicana scholars González, Alma M. García, Miroslava Chávez-García, and Maylei Blackwell have noted, the 1960s and 70s established interdisciplinary Chicana feminist roots from which new fields of study, including Chicana History flourished.[24] Scholars and activists founded periodicals that centered Chicanas/os as subjects in all fields: literature, history, sociology, psychology, education, and more. Chicana Feminist periodicals such as *Encuentro Feminil* took the lead in centering Chicana experiences and challenging patriarchy, especially when publications founded by males failed to do this work. Scholars and activists (and scholar-activists) challenged academic boundaries as well as the masculinist, often sexist and homophobic discourse of the Chicano Movement.[25] Political Scientist Adaljiza Sosa-Riddell critiqued masculine narratives of colonization, and argued that machismo was/is a myth of the colonizer.[26] Scholar-Activist Anna NietoGómez excavated the histories of early Mexicana revolutionary organizations, including Club Las Hijas de Cuauhtémoc, mobilizing these histories to inspire their own generation as well as the generations to come.[27]

Regeneración, Encuentro Feminíl and *El Grito Del Norte*, were all critical to this work.[28] In 1973 the Chicana feminist journal *Encuentro Feminil* published Adelaida R. Del Castillo's "Malintzín Tenepal," reclaiming Malintzín as a survivor and taking the offensive in an age-old war of position.[29] The interdisciplinarity of this work laid the foundation for the anthologies that followed and continue to influence the production of Chicana history to-date. A sub-genre of literature and history critiquing and reclaiming Malintzín would soon evolve, including Norma Alarcón's "Chicana Feminist Literature: A Re-Vision through Malintzín or Malinche: Putting Flesh Back on the Object," and Shirlene Soto's "Tres modelos culturales: la Virgen Guadalupe, La Malinche y La Llorona."[30]

Marta Cotera's *Diosa y Hembra: The History and Heritage of Chicanas in the United States, Profile on the Mexican-American Woman*, and *The*

Chicana Feminist, were part of this interdisciplinary and historically grounded tradition. All three collections published in the 1970s, became foundational works for placing Chicanas at the center of Chicano history and discourse.[31] "Our Feminist Heritage," published in *The Chicana Feminist,* excavated the activism of the Liga Feminista, the Liga Feminil Mexicanista and more as foremothers to the Chicana activists of the 1960s and 70s.[32] Such pioneering work inspired young historian Vicki L. Ruiz to go on to produce the first Chicana history monographs, but that would be in the ensuing decade.[33]

Chicana scholars continued to fight for recognition of their work and their history both in white academic journals and those journals published by Chicanos.[34] The first refereed Chicana/o studies journals, *El Grito* and *Aztlán,* founded in 1969 and 1970, respectively, slowly integrated Chicana history into their publications. In 1972, a year after publishing Irene Castañeda's "Crónica de Cristal," *El Grito* published a historical excavation of Teresa Urrea, the Mexicana healer whom Porfirio Díaz exiled to the US.[35] In 1973, prompted by Chicana feminists, it published a special focus issue on Chicanas. The volume contained no history articles, but was instead a rich volume of art and literature, including Adaljiza Sosa Riddell's poem mobilizing the icon of Malinche to critique the double standard and the construction of Malinche as traitor to "her" people.

Pinche, como duele ser Malinche

Pero sabes, ése,

what keeps me from shattering into a million fragments?

It's that sometimes

you are muy gringo, too.[36]

Similarly, throughout the 1970s very little Chicana history would be published in the pages of *Aztlán.* There were some exceptions. Laura E. Arroyo published a demographic study of Chicana labor. In volume five Sosa Riddell's "Chicanas and El Movimiento" traced the roots of sexism to the Spanish conquest, mapping race stratification and status among Spanish, Mestiza, and Indigenous women.[37] One year later Maxine Baca Zinn's article on political familism appeared in volume 6. In tracing the history of Chicana struggle and survival she built directly on Sosa Riddell's earlier work, calling attention to her mapping of Chicana sex and race subordination in Spanish and then US colonization.[38] For Chicanas, by the 1970s, the intersection of race and sex was central to both interdisciplinary and disciplinary work.

The predominance of male-centric scholarship in Chicano journals was reflected in the history monographs produced and published in the 1970s and into the 80s. While centering Chicano histories was indeed critical to disrupting the white frames that continued to structure both higher education and popular discourse, for this decade, Chicano monographs were just that: Chicano history. In 1972, Rudy Acuña, a Latin Americanist, shattered the ice with his now classic *Occupied America* dismantling myths of manifest destiny and labeling the US Invasion for what it was; other pithy and layered texts exposed stereotypes and lay bare the structural shifts that established and maintained white supremacy in the US West.[39] Albert Camarillo mapped the process of barrioization in Santa Bárbara, both its debilitating effects and the resistance to cultural genocide which emerged from such segregated spaces; Ricardo Romo mapped similar processes for the city of Los Angeles, and the list goes on and on.[40] What these monographs held in common was a critical Chicano approach to history where Chicanos were subjects not objects, where capitalism was not taken for granted but interrogated as a distinct economic system, and where the white supremacy that had come to structure the Southwest was marked and deconstructed as a social system.

While Chicano historians produced monographs and scholarly arti-cles focused on Chicano history, gender analysis and Chicana histories remained confined to anthologies and journals. During the decade of the 1970s, it would be two graduate students, María Linda Apodaca, in the Program in Comparative Culture at the University of California,

Irvine, and Marta Cotera at the University of Texas, Austin, who would publicly challenge Chicano historians on the erasure of Chicanas from the historical record. Consistent with the Chicano scholars excavating and reclaiming our histories in the 1970s, Apodaca's article contained a strong critique of capitalism. Yet "The Chicana Woman: An Historical Materialist Perspective" diverged from and complicated Chicano historians' monographs and scholarly articles by arguing that romanticizing the pre-conquest and pre-invasion past erased Chicana realities and Chicana histories; the socio-economic systems prior to 1846 and prior to 1521 absolutely had to be mapped, interrogated and critiqued.[41] According to Apodaca, a materialist analysis across time would allow historians to map various historical realities: "the expropriation of [Chicana] labor power and that of their families; 2) man's supremacy in the home and in society and; 3) society's denial of their importance in social production."[42] Equally important, she articulated a theme that continued (and continues) to influence and drive Chicana scholars to do the work at hand, "We must have histories that can be the basis for future social action."[43] At the time that Apodaca published her article, a small cohort of Chicanas were completing their PhDs in the field of history: Luisa Año Nuevo Kerr, Shirlene Soto, and Yolanda Romero earned their PhDs in history between 1970 and 1980, a time when, if you were a Chicana in a PhD program, you were the only Chicana in the PhD program.[44]

Into the 1980s Chicana scholars excavated and published Chicana stories and histories in anthologies by coalitions of feminists of color such as *This Bridge Called My Back*.[45] In the 1980s as well, Gloria Anzaldúa published the interdisciplinary *Borderlands/La Frontera: La Nueva Mestiza*, introducing foundational concepts such as mestiza consciousness. She gendered the border using the ancient past, colonial past, and violence of the US Invasion to claim it as a Chicana homeland.[46] From the 1970s and through the 1980s Chicana scholars built a field that mapped gender, power and difference. As Ramón Gutiérrez and Miroslava Chávez-García remind us, Chicana history was both central to the broader field of Chicana studies and shaped by it.[47]

By the 1980s a small but growing number of Chicana/o historians was active in academe, teaching in colleges and universities and publishing refereed work. As Castañeda and González have noted, many of the early Chicana/o historians received their degrees in Latin American History. Chicana historians Ana Macías, Luisa Año Nuevo Kerr, Raquel Rubio Goldsmith, and Shirlene Soto, like their male counterparts, received their degrees in Mexican and Latin American History.[48] Their work crossed borders; it was transnational before that concept and term became part of contemporary discourse. Chicana historian Magdalena Mora worked with Anthropologist Adelaida R. Del Castillo to edit *Mexican Women in the United States: Struggles Past and Present.*[49] Del Castillo's *Between Borders: Essays on Mexicana/Chicana History* contained work by Chicana historians including Antonia Castañeda, Emma Pérez, and Raquel Rubio Goldsmith, as well as Mexicana historians, Chicano historians, literary scholars Rosaura Sánchez and José Limón, and scholars from other fields. The anthology, like the symposium out of which it grew, stands as a testimony to the critical work of the 1980s, the decade when Chicana/o Studies diversified, and scholars who made connections between gender, culture, sexuality, and political economy introduced frames and tools of analysis that forever changed not only the field of Chicana/o Studies, but also traditional disciplines such as History and Linguistics. As Deena González notes, by the 1980s, these professional academics, as well as activist scholars such as Enriqueta Vásquez and Elizabeth (Betita) Martínez were opening doors and inspiring a new generation.[50]

By the time of the MALCS generation, then, we were beginning to see a generation of Chicana scholars staking claims in graduate programs across the disciplines —and Chicana historians emerging within PhD programs in US history. Like the Chicana historians emerging from the fields of Mexican and Latin American history, they often took a hemispheric approach to their research and scholarship.[51] Like the Chicana historians of the generation before them, their work was strongly feminist and materialist, bringing a critical, intersectional and gendered lens to their sources. As Deena González argues, a distinctive field was emerging...

texts produced by Chicano and Chicana writers and historians in the 1980s laid a foundation for revisionist insights and created a discourse community that continues to serve our study of the twentieth-century experiences of Mexican-origin people in the far West as in the Midwest, and increasingly in the South and Northeast United States.[52]

In graduate schools they fought for the right to write the Chicana past; to do so they had to directly confront the practiced ignorance of professors and advisors.[53] They worked across fields to found MALCS and to establish a Chicana Caucus within the National Association for Chicana and Chicano Studies. Building on the work of the generations before them, they gendered and sexed the discourse of the fields of Chicano history and Labor history, and challenged the white supremacy embedded in the field of Women's history—they created a new subfield: Chicana history. They prevailed, and in doing so they shifted the very categories in which historians study, research, think. Yet as Antonia Castañeda argued in "Women of Color Rewriting History," there is still much work to do.

OVERVIEW:

The articles chosen for this volume are rooted in the mestiza past and in the discipline of writing the past. They also represent structural shifts and attempted structural shifts—calls to historians to think about the categories in which we labor. And so we have organized the articles thematically, to highlight the structural shift that each set of articles represents. There are four parts to the volume, with pláticas interspersed between each of the parts. Part One includes writing on types and stereotypes. Both "The Political Economy of Nineteenth Century Stereotypes of Californianas," and "Malinche, Calafia y Toypurina: Of Myths, Monsters and Embodied History," map the evolution and deployment of gendered stereotypes wielded against indigenous and mestiza women throughout colonial histories. The sections that follow are organized in a similar manner.

Part Two includes Castañeda's most frequently used historiographies. "Gender, Race, and Culture: Spanish Mexican Women in the Historiography of Frontier California" has already been republished twice, in different editions of *Unequal Sisters*; but because historians so frequently utilize it, and because the problems it maps continue to exist in various guises, it is included here. The prize-winning "Women of Color and the Rewriting of Western History: The Discourse, Politics and the Decolonization of History" is included for similar reasons. We include both of these essays for their utility and in the hope that the next generation of historians will learn from and build upon Castañeda's work, rather than reinventing the wheel—or even worse, spinning it.

Part Three's articles are the foundational texts that shifted the way so many of us write about indigenous and mestiza women in greater Mexico. "Engendering the History of Alta California, 1769-1848: Gender, Sexuality, and the Family" engendered gender and the family as critical institutions in colonial processes. Likewise, "Sexual Violence in the Politics and Policies of Conquest," mapped the function of sexual violence in eighteenth-and-nineteenth century California, as well as resistance to it. Both articles excavate, gender and problematize the history of Alta California, and were/are pivotal to the re-periodization of Chicana/o history.

Part Four consists of two recent articles, "'Que Se Pudieran Defender': Chicanas, Regional History, and National Discourse" and "Language and Other Lethal Weapons: Cultural Politics and the Rites of Children as Translators of Culture," and two new articles, "Lullabies y Canciones de Cuna: Embodying Chicana History" and "La Despedida." All four articles address the body as a site of history, challenge "the West" as a category, and call a new generation of historians to bring the discipline into a new, complex, more nuanced age; the last two of these articles comprise a portion of Dr. Castañeda's most recent work excavating, mapping and bringing forth the long and strong post WWII history of Tejanas —women who labored and raised their families in the migrant circuit from the Lower Rio Grande valley of Texas to the agricultural valleys of Washington State in the Pacific Northwest.[54] Finally, the volume concludes with an essay by another founder of the field, Dr. Deena González, speaking to the state of the field and the role of Dr. Castañeda and her generation of Chicana Historians in getting us to this place.

Three pláticas, all organized, orchestrated and made reality by Dr. Luz María Gordillo, are interspersed throughout the volume. Gordillo, associate professor at Washington State University, Vancouver, is author of *Mexican Women and the Other Side of Immigration*, winner of the National Association for Latina and Latino Anthropologists Book Award (2011). Using oral histories and interviews for that work, as well as articles appearing in the journal of *Chicana/Latina Studies*, and the anthology *Hidden Lives and Human Rights: Understanding the Controversies and Tragedies in Undocumented Immigration*, she was the perfect scholar for the task at hand.[55]

Initially, we had conceived of the volume containing a solitary interview. But the work of our generation, as that of the generation before us, continues to be very interdisciplinary. Dr. Gordillo, in addition to earning her degree in History, also trained in Cultural Anthropology at the New School for Social Research in New York City. In approaching the entrevistas, then, she used the skills developed in some of her earlier work to construct charlas/pláticas—discursive spaces that could then become discursive texts, where she introduced questions to fuel conversations, thus producing new primary material for you, our readers.

As the knowledges that we bring with us from our homes and communities continue to break into and shape our academic work, the tools with which we approach our sources, including our human sources, remain rooted in the very interdisciplinary roots of Chicana history. And so the pláticas found in this volume weave in and out of the articles, establishing a dynamic where the articles signal text/product and the pláticas, context/process. Thus Plática I is between Drs. Luz María Gordillo and Antonia Castañeda, discussing the relationship between the body, labor and knowledge; Plática II is between Dr. Thomas Ybarro-Frausto and Dr. Castañeda; and Plática III is a conversation between three foundational scholars of Chicana History: Drs. Emma Pérez, Deena González, and Antonia Castañeda. Dr. Luz María Gordillo will address the talks in greater detail in her *Introduction to the Interviews* that follows this introduction.

The historical context of these essays, as well as the pláticas, demonstrates how critical it is that scholars come together to share their research, critique each other's work, support each other. "The Political Economy of Nineteenth-Century Stereotypes of Californianas" which opens this volume, was, in part, a product of the "Mexicana/Chicana Women's History International Symposium" organized by Prof. Juan Gómez Quiñones and Adelaida R. Del Castillo in the winter of 1982. Consistent with the historical reality, and with the early transnational trend of Chicana/o Studies, the symposium brought together scholars and activists and scholar-activists from both sides of the border, to share their new and emerging scholarship—scholarship that was changing the way that historians and other Chicana/o and Mexican studies scholars interpreted the past.[56]

Today's scholars continue to flourish at such conferences; Chicana scholars still gather at MALCS, present their work, critique each other's research, and mentor another generation of fierce scholar-activists. The National Association for Chicana and Chicano Studies serves a similar function for Chicana/o Studies scholars as well. As NACCS celebrates its 40th anniversary (2012) and MALCS its 30th (2013), in a contemporary political climate of renewed attacks against Chicanas/os and Latinas/os, it is vitally important to recall these critical legacies. For today there is a significant difference from the conferences of the '80s. Today, when our generation gathers, it has the privilege of building on the work of earlier generations of Chicana/o historians and other Chicana/o scholar-activists. We came to the field with the foundation laid for us. It is our hope, in putting this volume forward, that it will facilitate and expedite development of the field. In your hands you have a collection of essays which helped to get us where we, as historians and as Chicana/o Studies scholars, are today. Use it, build on it, pass it on to the next generation.

Linda Heidenreich
Pullman, Washington 2012

NOTES

1. Miroslava Chávez-García, "The Interdisciplinary Project of Chicana History: Looking Back, Moving Forward," *Pacific Historical Review* 82, no. 4 (November 2013): 542-543.
2. See, for example, Albert L. Hurtado, *Intimate Frontiers: Sex, Gender, and Culture in Old California* (Albuquerque: University of New Mexico Press, 1999); Susan Lee Johnson, "A Memory Sweet to Soldiers: The Significance of Gender in the History of the American West," *Western Historical Quarterly* 24, no.4 (November 1993): 495-517; Johnson, *Roaring Camp: The Social World of the California Gold Rush* (New York: W. W. Norton, 2000); Deena González, *Refusing the Favor: The Spanish-Mexican Women of Santa Fe, 1820-1880* (New York: Oxford University Press, 1999); González, "Gender on the Borderlands; Re-Textualizing the Classics," *Frontiers* 24 (2003). For recent scholarship see Bárbara O. Reyes, *Private Women, Public Lives: Gender and the Missions of the Californias* (Austin: University of Texas, 2009); Miroslava Chávez-García, *Negotiating Conquest: Gender and Power in California, 1770s to 1880s* (Tucson: University of Arizona Press, 2004) ; María Raquél Casas, *Married to a Daughter of the Land: Spanish-Mexican Women and Interethnic Marriage in California, 1820-1880* (Reno: University of Nevada Press, 2007); Luz María Gordillo, *Mexican Women and the Other Side of Immigration: Engendering Transnational Ties* (Austin: University of Texas Press, 2010); Maylei Blackwell, *¡Chicana Power! Contested Histories of Feminism in the Chicano Movement* (Austin: University of Texas, 2011.)
3. Jennifer Mata, "Creating a Chicana Narrative: Writing the Chicanas at Farah into Labor History (PhD diss., Washington State University, 2004). Erika Pérez, "Colonial Intimacies: Interethnic Kinship, Sexuality, and Marriage in Southern California, 1769-1885" (PhD diss, University of California, Los Angeles, 2010); Margo Tamez, "Nádasi'né' ndé' isdzáné begoz'aahí' shimaa shiní' gokal gowa goshjaa ha'áná 'idlí texas-nakaiyé godesdzog: Returning Lipan Apache Women's Laws, Lands, and Power in El Calaboz Ranchería, Texas-Mexico Border" (PhD diss., Washington State University, 2010). Indeed, the number of new scholars utilizing Castañeda's work continues to grow. A search, via ProQuest recovered five dissertations citing her work for each of the years 2009 and 2010,

yet the search did not locate the work of T. Gonzales or M. Tamez, both of whom made extensive use of Castañeda's work.

4. Antonia Castañeda, "Presidarias y Pobladoras: Spanish-Mexican Women in Frontier Monterey, Alta California, 1770-1821" (PhD diss., Stanford University, 1990).

5. Irene Castañeda, "Crónica de Cristal"/Chronicle of Crystal," *El Grito* 4 no. 2 (Winter 1971): 42-52. During this time, Dr. Castañeda was a contributing editor at *El Grito*.

6. Antonia Castañeda, Tomás Ybarra-Frausto, and Joseph Sommers, *Literatura Chicana: texto y contexto* (Englewood Cliffs: Prentice-Hall, 1972).

7. Cherríe Moraga, *Loving in the War Years: lo que nunca pasó por sus labios*, 2d ed. (1983; Cambridge: South End Press, 2000), 145.

8. Antonia Castañeda, "Comparative Frontiers: The Migration of Women to Alta California and New Zealand," in *Western Women: Their Land, Their Lives*, eds. Lillian Schlissel, Vicki L. Ruiz, and Janice Monk (Albuquerque: University of New Mexico, 1988). The article was published while Castañeda was still in graduate school.

9. Cherríe Moraga, Introduction to *This Bridge Called My Back: Writings by Radical Women of Color*, eds. Gloria Anzaldúa and Cherrie Morag (San Francisco: Aunt Lute Press, 1981). Moraga introduces her concept of theory in the flesh as born of a "politics of necessity."

10. Adaljiza Sosa-Ridell, *Reader's Companion to US Women's History*, quoted in "History of MALCS," http://www.malcs.org/history/.

11. Mujeres Activas en Letras y Cambio Social, "June 1983 MALCS Declaración," accessed 6 January 2011. http://malcs.net/.

12. Correspondence Deena González, 28 January 2014. See also Vicki Ruiz, *From Out of the Shadows: Mexican Women in Twentieth-Century America* (New York: Oxford University Press, 1988): 122-123.

13. Emma Pérez, "Sexuality and Discourse: Notes from a Chicana Survivor," in *Chicana Lesbians: The Girls Our Mothers Warned Us About*, ed. Carla Trujillo (Berkeley: Third Woman Press, 1991), 161-171.

14. González, 17-18; Teresa Córdova, "Letter to the Chicana Caucus," 28 January 2014.

15. At this point in time the organIzation was still NACS. It was not renamed the National Association for Chicana and Chicano Studies until 1995 (see History of NACCS, http://www.naccs.org/naccs/History.asp).

16. Teresa Córdova, Foreword, in *Chicana Voices: Intersections of Class Race, and Gender,* eds. Córdova et al. (1986; Albuquerque: University of New Mexico, 1990), xiii.

17. Córdova, *Chicana Voices*, xix.
18. Not only in the 1980s but into the early 1990s.
19. Per the concept of oppositional consciousness developed by Chéla Sandoval. See Sandoval, "US Third World Feminism: The Theory and Method of Oppositional Consciousness in the Postmodern World," *Genders* 10 (Spring 1991), 1-24.
20. For historiographies addressing this foundational generation, see Richard A. García, "Turning Points: Mexican Americans in California History: Introduction to the Special Issue," *California History* 74, no. 3 (Fall, 1995): 226-229; Deena González, "Gender on the Borderlands: Re-Textualizing the Classics," *Frontiers* 24 no. 2/3 (2003): 15-29; David G. Gutiérrez, "Significant to Whom?: Mexican Americans and the History of the American West," *Western Historical Quarterly* 24, no.4 (Nov. 1993): 519-539.
21. Sergio Reyna, Introduction to *The Woman Who Lost Her Soul and Other Stories*, by Jovita González (Houston: Arte Público, 2000), xi, xxii.
22. José E. Limón, *Dancing with the Devil: Society and Cultural Poetics in Mexican-American South Texas* (Madison: University of Wisconsin, 1994), 67-68, 74.
23. Limón, 74; María Cotera, Epilogue to *Caballero: A Historical Novel*, by Jovita González and Eve Raleigh (College Station: Texas A&M, 1996): 339-346.
24. Alma M. García, ed. *Chicana Feminist Thought: Basic Historical Writings* (New York: Routledge, 1997); Miroslava Chávez-García, "The Interdisciplinary Project of Chicana History: Looking Back, Moving Forward," *Pacific Historical Review* 82, no.4 (Nov. 2013): 542-565; Maylei Blackwell, *¡Chicana Power! Contested Histories of Feminism in the Chicano Movement* (Austin: University of Texas, 2011). See also Deena González, "Gender on the Borderlands: Re-Textualizing the Classics," *Frontiers* 24, no. 2/3 (2003): 15-29; Ramón A. Gutiérrez, "Community, Patriarchy and Individualism: The Politics of Chicano History and the Dream of Equality," *American Quarterly* 45, no. 1 (March 1993): 44-72. Note that González's work was published in *Gender on the Borderlands*, a special double issue of the journal *Frontiers*. The volume grew out of a conference (July 2001) of the same name. Castañeda, who then held the O'Connor Chair in Borderlands History at St. Mary's University, organized the conference under the auspices of a NEH Institutional Grant; she then edited the anthology that grew from it, with Susan H. Armitage, Patricia Hart, and Karen Weathermon. The double issue was subsequently published as

Gender on the Borderlands: The Frontiers Reader (Lincoln: University of Nebraska Press, 2007).

25. Alma M. García, 4.

26. Blackwell, 97-99. Sosa-Riddell would go on to become the first Latina to earn a doctoral degree in Political Science (see the American Political Science Association: http://www.apsanet.org/content_53751.cfm).

27. Blackwell, 102-109, 133; Introduction to *Encuentro Feminil*," 1, no.2 (1973): 3-7, in García, 113-116.

28. Alma M. Garcia, 8. See also the Chicano Periodical Index for 1969-73. *Regeneración* and *Encuentro Feminíl* were both Chicana Feminist journals, *El Grito Del Norte* the newspaper edited by Enriqueta Longeaux Vasquez and Elizabeth Martínez.

29. Blackwell, 145-146-156. Adelaida R. Del Castillo, "Matlintzín Tenepal: A Preliminary Look into a New Perspective," in Alma M. García, 122-126.

30. Adelaida R. Del Castillo's "Malintzín Tenepal: A Preliminary Look into a New Perspective," *Encuentro Feminil* (December 1973), served as the opening salvo in this battle. See also Norma Alarcón, "Chicana Feminist Literature: A Re-Vision through Malintzín or Malinche: Putting Flesh Back on the Object," in *This Bridge Called My Back: Writings by Radical Women of Color* (New York: Kitchen Table, 1983); Shirlene Soto, "Tres Modelos Culturales: La Virgen de Guadalupe, La Malinche y la Llorona," *Fem* 10 (1986): 13-16. See also Cordelia Candelaria, "La Malinche, Feminist Prototype, *Frontiers* 5, no.2 (1980): 1-6.

31. Alma M. García, 8.

32. Marta Cotera, "Our Feminist Heritage," in *Chicana Feminist Thought*, ed. Alma M. García (New York: Routledge, 1997), 41-44.

33. Vicki L. Ruiz and Leisa D. Meyer, "Ongoing Missionary Labor": Building, Maintaining, and Expanding Chicana Studies/History, an Interview with Vicki L. Ruiz," *Feminist Studies* 34, no. 1/2 (Summer 2008): 23-45; Vicki L. Ruiz, *Cannery Women, Cannery Lives* (Albuquerque: University of New Mexico, 1987).

34. García, 8.

35. García, 8; Richard and Gloria L. Rodríguez, "Teresa Urrea: Her Life as it Affected the Mexican-US Frontier," *El Grito* 5, no.4 (Summer 1972): 48-68.

36. Adaljiza Sosa Riddell, n.t., *El Grito* 7, no.1 *Chicanas en la Literatura y el Arte* (September 1973): 76.

37. Laura E. Arroyo, "Industrial and Occupational Distribution of Chicana Workers," *Aztlán* 4, no.2 (Fall 1973): 343-382. Arroyo's article included a narrative and analysis of the Farah strikes.

38. Maxine Baca Zinn, "Political Familism: Toward Sex Role Equality in Chicano Families," *Aztlán* 6, no.1 (Spring 1975): 13-26.

39. Rodolfo Acuña, *Occupied America: The Chicano's Struggle Toward Liberation* (San Francisco: Canfield Press, 1972). Acuña's first edition was widely and unevenly reviewed. While some, such as Mario Trinidad García (for the *Pacific Historical Review*, 43 no. 1) lauded the long-needed economic analysis of the US Invasion, others, such as Victor Dahl, writing for the *Western Historical Quarterly*, were upset by the tone and berated its "angry statement of charges..." (4, no. 3, 340).

40. Albert Camarillo, *Chicanos in a Changing Society: From Mexican Pueblos to American Barrios in Santa Barbara and Southern California, 1848-1930* (Cambridge: Harvard, 1979); Ricardo Romo, *East Los Angeles: History of a Barrio* (Austin, University of Texas Press, 1983); See also Matt A. Meier and Feliciano Rivera, *The Chicanos: A History of Mexican Americans* (New York: Hill and Wang, 1972); and Richard Griswold del Castillo, *La Familia: Chicano Families in the Urban Southwest, 1848 to the Present* (Notre Dame: University of Notre Dame Press, 1984); Richard Griswold del Castillo, *The Los Angeles Barrio, 1850-1890: A Social History* (Berkeley: University of California Press, 1979); Arnoldo de León, *They Called them Greasers: Anglo Attitudes toward Mexicans in Texas, 1821-1900* (Austin: University of Texas Press, 1983); Gilberto Miguel Hinojosa, *A Borderlands Town in Transition: Laredo, 1775-1870* (College Station: Texas A&M, 1983); Mario T. García, *Desert Immigrants: The Mexicans of El Paso, 1880-1920* (New Haven: Yale University, 1981).

41. María Linda Apodaca, "The Chicana Woman: An Historical Materialist Perspective," *Latin American Perspectives* 4, no.1/2 (Spring 1977): 70-89.

42. Ibid., 73.

43. Ibid,. 72.

44. Mary Pardo, "Honoring and Remembering One of the First Chicana Historians: Shirlene Soto," *Noticias de NACCS* December 2009, 2, 15; "Chicana Historians," List compiled by Antonia Castañeda with Vicki Ruiz, 1.

45. González, "Gender on the Borderlands,"17, 27.

46. Gloria Anzaldúa, *Borderlands/La Frontera: The New Mestiza* (San Francisco: Aunt Lute Books, 1987).

47. Chavez-García; Ramón A. Gutiérrez, "Community, Patriarchy and Individualism: The Politics of Chicano History and the Dream of Equality," *American Quarterly* 45, no. 1 (March 1993): 44-72. Interestingly, Gutiérrez's article takes an interdisciplinary approach to mapping and critiquing the field.

48. Author correspondence with Antonia Castañeda, Deena González. See also, Pardo, "Honoring and Remembering One of the First Chicana Historians."

49. Magdalena Mora and Adelaida R. Del Castillo, eds. *Mexican Women in the United States: Struggles Past and Present* (Los Angeles: UCLA Chicano Studies Research Center, 1980).

50. González, "Gender on the Borderlands, 17.

51. Castañeda, "Gender, Race, and Culture: Spanish-Mexican Women in the Historiography of Frontier California," and ""Que se Pudieran Defender," in this volume. Deena González, "Gender on the Borderlands."

52. González, "Gender on the Borderlands; Re-Textualizing the Classics," *Frontiers* 24 (2003): 15.

53. Castañeda, "Que Se Pudieran Defender," in this volume.

54. "Comino Chronicles: A Tale of Tejana Migration," *Chicana/Latina Studies* 9, no. 1 (Fall 2009), is also part of this larger project.

55. Luz María Gordillo, *Mexican Women and the Other Side of Immigration: Engendering Transnational Ties* (Austin: University of Texas, 2010); Gordillo, "Engendering Transnational Social Networks: Mexicanas and Community Formation in San Ignacio-Detroit," *Chicana/Latina Studies* 10, no.1 (Fall 2010): 28-59.

56. Adelaida R. Del Castillo, ed., *Between Borders: Essays on Mexicana/Chicana History* (Encino: Floricanto Press, 1990), iii.

TRES ENTREVISTAS/
TRES PLÁTICAS

So here we go as feminists wanting to be practical and wanting to make a difference and wanting to make some changes, and we're looking at everything that gives us strength: having roots, having a historical past that we can connect with and say, "This is the route that my particular group has walked and I can see how what happened in the past has affected the present and therefore affected me and who I am and how I feel about myself."

Gloria Anzaldúa[1]

I was a graduate student at Michigan State University when Antonia Castañeda gave a captivating presentation; the minute I saw her she mesmerized me. Her presence—a balance of humility, modesty and strength—combined with the ease with which she delivered an engaged poetic and inspirational presentation on Chicana feminism profoundly absorbed the students attending the talk. What a powerful experience to have one of the founders of Chicana history and an established scholar-activist giving a talk in the Midwest.

It was the first time I experienced theory and praxis in one text; Dr. Antonia Castañeda's creativity and academic discourse were not mutually exclusive but instead wove an intense and complex narrative of struggle, resistance and success. This was a different approach to research—it was a Chicana Studies approach to history, one that would come to frame my own work. Castañeda's work along with that of other Chicana historians, and my then advisor, Dr. Juan Javier Pescador, provided a base from which I could develop my own perspective. As with so many Chicana historians of my generation, their generation offered me the freedom to do the work that mattered to me, to my communities; this work culminated in my first book *Mexican Women and the Other Side of Immigration: Engendering Transnational Ties* published in the prestigious Chicana Matters series at the University of Texas Press co-edited by Deena González and Antonia Castañeda.[2]

After years of reading her work, incorporating her theories, and having the pleasure of befriending Antonia Castañeda, I find myself honoring her many years of activism and intellectual contributions to the Chicana/ Mexicana community by collaborating with historians Linda Heidenreich and Deena González in putting together this much needed collection. When I heard the proposal for the collective work, I decided that an interview with the author would not only give us her presence and strength as an intellectual but cement her position as an auteur dictating the structure of her work, not just her articles, which are many and influential, but her mentoring of the next generation and her co-founding of critical institutions such as the Chicana Matters Series.

The project almost immediately grew and expanded into two projects: a book manuscript of her most influential articles, with interviews conducted by myself, and a film project mapping not only her work, but also her life. Inspired by theories of filmmaking and the prospect of re-building a visual text that narrated Antonia's story, the idea of shooting a documentary while conducting the interview came to its fullness while discussing the topic with my once advisor, now colleague,

Dr. Juan Javier Pescador from Michigan State University.[3] In November
of 2010 Dr. Javier Pescador flew from Michigan and I from Portland to
meet Dr. Castañeda in San Antonio, Texas. We stayed for a week, talking,
listening, filming, and following her through her workday. Months after
that, we re-united again in Pasadena, California, where we filmed with
Antonia and other Chicana colleagues at the national conference of the
National Association for Chicana and Chicano Studies (NACCS). Our
shooting and recording continued one more time in Portland, Oregon,
where Antonia, Linda Heidenreich, Javier and I convened to finalize the
shooting. We spent days and hours with Antonia and I cherished every
minute of our conversations both in public and in private. I thank her
and all the colleagues who participated in this arduous process of filming
and recording; in particular Linda Heidenreich, Emma Pérez, Deena
González, Tomás Ybarra Frausto, Antonia Castañeda and Juan Javier
Pescador. Also, thanks to Sara Morris and Laura Philpot who helped
transcribe some of the interviews.

My experiences taking notes for the written interview while shooting
video for the documentary were, at times, surreal. One evening I would
find myself outside the Esperanza Peace and Justice Center in San Antonio,
shooting images of Antonia Castañeda while she climbed up on the thin
edge of a wall balancing her body carefully to pose next to a life-sized
black and white photograph of an immigrant family—part of a larger
photographic project of Mexican-Americans and Chicanas/os producing
culture in the early twentieth century in Texas. In sharp contrast, the
next day I would be in Antonia's and her partner Arturo's spacious living
room celebrating Thanksgiving with their family and close friends. New
hardwood floors and elegant white walls with paintings from diverse
Chicana/o artists framed the familial portrait of people sharing food,
news and some of us making new acquaintances.

Whether in private or public, Antonia opened up and allowed me to
be a part of her life for a bit of time, enough to write many volumes. In as
much as I would love to do that, however, my co-editors have given me a

limit of pages. As such, I will transcribe these pláticas the way I perceived the voices, the intonations, the stories, the moods and sentiments, the politics, and the way Antonia Castañeda and other colleagues narrated their stories and thus the story of a whole community's struggle and formidable resilience.

CONTEXTO: THE THREE INTERVIEWS/PLÁTICAS

Plática I "El Cuerpo y El Campo: The Body as Site of Knowledge," is a conversation between Antonia and myself, where she shares her experiences working in the fields and the connections this labor pushed her to make about knowledge and the body. We filmed at a junkyard, on our way back from Crystal City—where Antonia was born—to San Antonio—where she currently resides. I remember Antonia's reaction when I asked her to climb into the abandoned tireless, old, rusty colored, troca (pick-up truck) that we used as a prop while we shot our film. It was difficult to guess the original color of that troca though we speculated that the year of its glory must have been the 1950s. Antonia remained calm despite her leg continuously hurting and never complained even though we had been shooting since early morning.[4] She did not hesitate to say "terrífico!" when I prudently asked, "Antonia would you mind getting into the troca so that you may read your Comino piece?" Once inside, she had to find a safe place to sit among so much junk including rusted cables and sharp steel rods, an enormous tractor tire that served as Antonia's chair, and an assortment of stubborn irrepressible weeds and flowers, in order to read aloud her piece entitled "Comino Chronicles: A Tale of Tejana Migration."[5] It was in this context that she shared with us memories of her own travels in trocas during her long and arduous journeys from Texas to the Pacific Northwest and within Washington State.

Later on that same evening, in a vast empty field with the sun rapidly submerging West in the flat landscape mid-way between Crystal City and San Antonio—representing her past and present—Antonia and I engaged in discussions about the body and its movement while working the crops.

I watched Antonia mimic the movements her body so clearly remembered of years picking in the fields. Disconnected from the landscape and wearing jeans and a matching jacket, Antonia with perfect synchronicity and out of context, performed what I call the "labor dance" or "danza del jale" conjuring up a form of cleansing of re-birth with every muscle she moved. Unlike the universality of the "dance macabre" which leads everyone to an inevitable death regardless of race, class or sexual orientation, the castigating "labor dance" is particular to working class bodies that also represent strength and collaborative resilience; the "labor dance" forces the body to withstand different levels of repetitious movements and body conditions.[6] Like the "dance macabre" it has death and danger present in its definition, but at the same time the body re-invents itself within the new forms of movements and thus transforms the violence. Clearly the "danza del jale" has many health repercussions particular to these movements (for example back complications for bending over while carrying heavy sacks, breathing pesticides, and living in unhealthy conditions), but, how does this "labor dance" affect working class bodies when creating community? How do synchronic repetitive movements influence young growing bodies? Antonia and other children necessarily labored alongside adults in the fields because survival depended on the labor of all: the family was an economic unit.[7] The interstice where forced metrical body contortions meet sensuality and dignity, resilience, resistance, and survival are key variables in analyzing the performance of the body while laboring in the fields. In the fields, the "dance macabre" together with the "labor dance" creates a dialectic that spirals around working class bodies laboring for sustenance, survival, and the creation of different sexualities.

An analysis of the transnational body and its movement within systems of oppression is an unknown territory that becomes tenuous and fragile. Antonia and I, when discussing the topic wanted to be careful not to exoticize the fields and diminish or minimize the intensity and exploitative impacts of the labor, but on the other hand we needed to recognize the influence that field labor and labor camp life had on the body itself and on the experience of growing up. Antonia was able to articulate it so that we could both patiently deconstruct the thoughts, the images and the words together. Plática II, "Pero no somos princesas ni príncipes (But We're Neither Princesses nor Princes)," took place in the home of Tomás Ybarra-Frausto and his partner Dudley Brooks. As we entered their living space in downtown San Antonio I was immediately taken into a New York-like world; after walking a few feet through a narrow hallway, a fantastic space opened up before us. It was a beautiful loft with different open rooms: each one with a particular mood, sense, color, and even smell. On the left I saw a small private reading room surrounded by magnificent paintings and shelves upon shelves of books that smelled marvelous— old and musty. Outside and right in front were more shelves that turned into rows and rows of books leading into a formal living room. Adorning the middle of the living room was a large round coffee table and on it, a wooden handcrafted bowl filled with colorful crystal marbles. Facing the living room and across the bookshelves, there were two windows framed by a collection of masks, many from Mexico, but others from different parts of the world. Plants surrounded the loft everywhere giving the space a cozy intimate mood. Both Tomás and his partner Dudley embraced all of us and delightful conversations began to unfold.

While we were surrounded by this wonderful world of works of art and Chicana/o literature, Tomás and Antonia began to reminisce, unnoticed, and like old friends they questioned the beginning of their encounters with one another. In the midst of laughs and some uncomfortable silences, Castañeda and Ybarra-Frausto narrated their story along with the story of thousands of Tejanos who were forced to migrate West in hopes of not only better economic futures for their families, but perhaps most importantly in the hopes of building on their resistance and communal dignity. This second plática is a personal story, but also a story about community, about the founding of the first Calmecac in the Yakima Valley[8], and about a generation of Chicana/o workers, who found their way to the university, and then struggled to bring resources to the next generation.

Plática III, "Birthing Chicana History," came about in the context of the thirty-eighth annual NACCS Conference in Pasadena, California. Amid our busy schedules of panels, events, meetings, and award luncheons, I had coordinated a time when Drs. Emma Pérez, Deena González, and Antonia Castañeda were all available to film.

I was happy to witness such a historical meeting of the minds, surrounded by the founders of what we now know as the field of Chicana History: Deena González, Emma Pérez and Antonia Castañeda. Chicana feminism is a lonely academic journey despite the many strides we have accomplished in recruiting and retaining Chicanas/Mexicanas in academia. Building community has been a necessary survival skill for Chicanas/Mexicanas and other women of color, and Emma Pérez, Deena Gónzalez and Antonia Castañeda began constructing the intellectual networks that are now the nexus of the Chicana Historian's community. They took active roles in the creation of organizations like MALCS (Mujeres Activas en Letras y Cambio Social) and NACCS (National Organization for Chicana and Chicano Studies); they carved out spaces in academic presses previously dominated by Euro-American scholars.

In this third plática they address how allying themselves with one another and their entire community became their life story; they shared their different experiences of growing up, in the fields or in urban surroundings, in the hallways of academia, and in their community. Life-experiences and political activism heavily influenced their scholarly work—an important intellectual production that has inspired many to carry on with the Chicana/Mexicana project.

The conversation provided insight into the arduous task of excavating and reinventing the way history is written. How they rescued female's statements from archives tinted with bias and racism, and created a new gendered history. This new history brought an origin tale to Chicanas and re-created the meaning of the word "archive." The archive now had female voices that demanded to be accounted for. In recalling some of the horrors but also some of the triumphs of academic life, these historians allow readers to learn from their challenges but also from their success stories. Their encounter with archival bias and academic discrimination fueled their courage to continue and interpret the lives of Chicanas/Mexicanas while they constructed community within and outside of the halls of academe.

While I listened to these three Chicana historians I reminded myself how we all came to encounter our own political, social and cultural struggles. I remembered again Antonia's repeated questions: "Why Me?" Then I think, "Why work on a collection of her work and why shoot a film about Antonia Castañeda?" And I conjure up Gloria Anzaldúa's possible answer in the introductory epitaph, "[because] I can see how what happened in the past has affected the present and therefore affected me and who I am and how I feel about myself."[9] Historians build stories, we put together vignettes of life experiences and piece them into narratives that give life and make sense to our communities and also provide alternative theoretical frameworks to people beyond the academic fields that we populate. With this in mind, I turn the lens toward Historian and Activist Antonia Castañeda; she is the protagonist of many stories. These three pláticas evolve around the building of an academic field, but so much more. They are stories of the self, of building, creating and excavating of community's memories; they are stories of strength, political and spiritual growth. They evoke snippets of life stories that belong to all of us. I share these pláticas with excitement and anticipation—moments shared with Antonia Castañeda that I will always cherish. "Luz María, nunca nos desaparecemos," she said to me in an interview while sitting on a bench in the 'Mexican section' of the segregated cemetery in Crystal City.[10] These interviews give life to her words.

Luz María Gordillo
Barcelona, Spain 2012

NOTES

1. AnaLouise Keating and Gloria Anzaldúa, "Writing, Politics, and Las Lesberadas: Platicando con Gloria Anzaldúa," *Frontiers: A Journal of Women Studies* 14, no. 1 (1993): 113.

2. Luz María Gordillo, *Mexican Women and the Other Side of Immigration: Engendering Transnational Ties* (Austin: University of Texas Press, 2010).

3. He and I had extensive experience collaborating; we had worked together on a photographic installation in 2001 at Michigan State University and Oberlin College as well as filmed numerous interviews in Mexico and in the US both for his work and mine on Mexican immigration to the United States focusing on the immigrant experience.

4. Antonia Castañeda had been suffering from chronic back pain for years. Months after the shoot, she had to have back surgery to alleviate some of that pain.

5. Castañeda, "Comino Chronicles: A Tale of Tejana Migration," *Chicana/Latina Studies: The Journal of Mujeres Activas en Letras y Cambio Social* 9, no.1 (Fall 2009): 62-69.

6. The "dance macabre" is an allegory that represented the universality of death while emphasizing the vulnerability of life regardless of class status in the late middle ages. In Mexico, "la danza macabra" is translated in the worshiping of the day of the dead with the same significance, that death and life are part of the same continuum. Currently there's a strong cult for the veneration of La Santa Muerte (Death) in Mexico that has become very popular among working class Mexicans. What I mean by "labor dance" is also an allegory representing the universality of the body's castigating movements in the world of working class subjects but also its adaptability and re-interpretation of those movements at a more intimate and personal level.

7. Antonia Castañeda, interview by the author, San Antonio, Texas, 2010.

8. A Calmecac was a school for Aztec nobles. Chicana/os from Seattle and throughout Greater Mexico founded cultural centers sometimes named them after these Aztec schools representing their indigenous past.

9. AnnLouise Keating and Gloria Anzaldúa, "Writing, Politics, and Las Lesberadas: Platicando con Gloria Anzaldúa," *Frontiers: A Journal of Women Studies* 14, no. 1 (1993): 113.

10. Antonia Castañeda, interview by the author, Crystal City, TX, 2010. "We never disappear."

PART ONE

SPEAKING BACK, CRITIQUING THE DOMINANT DISCOURSE

...colonizing males constructed Indian women's bodies, both symbolically and materially, as a site to effect territorial and political conquest[;]women constructed and used their bodies, both symbolically and materially, as instruments of opposition, resistance, and subversion of colonial domination.

"Malinche, Calafia y Toypurina"

"The Political Economy of Nineteenth Century Stereotypes of Californianas" (1990)

"Malinche, Calafia y Toypurina: Of Myths, Monsters and Embodied History" (2005)

"The Political Economy of the Nineteenth-Century Stereotypes" and "Malinche, Calafia y Toypurina" stand as bookends of sorts.Written over a decade apart, the two articles are brought together here because of their strong critiques of dominant discourses, and the bold way in which both essays map the role of political economy in constructing the very stereotypes that feed popular (white) culture.

First presented at the "Mexicana/Chicana Women's History International Symposium" in Santa Monica, California (1982), "Political Economy" represents some of Dr. Castañeda's earliest published work. As with other essays presented at that symposium, the work has proven foundational. In it Dr. Castañeda maps the power of gendered stereotypes in fueling Manifest Destiny and corollary nineteenth-century ideologies. By focusing on three proponents of Manifest Destiny: Richard Henry Dana, Thomas Jefferson Farnham, and Alfred Robinson, she demonstrates how stereotypes of Californianas shifted as the socio-political and economic needs of Euro-Americans shifted over time; what remained and remains consistent, is the manner in which the stereotypes functioned to negate the lived realities and histories of nineteenth-century Mexicanas and Californianas not only in their own time, but in the histories produced by the Euro-American male historians who followed them.

Written almost two decades later, "Malinche, Calafia y Toypurina" brings textual analysis back to the Spanish colonial era and forward into our own time. Mapping the development of colonial stereotypes of indigenous women, Castañeda argues that popular literature, particularly the novelas de caballería (novels of chivalry) fed the colonial project, justifying violence against indigenous women, communities, and peoples. Thus the popular fictions written and circulated of Calafia, preceded the "myth and paradigm of the historical Malinche," but served a similar function, normalizing conquest in the mind of the colonizer, while eroticizing and demonizing the bodies of indigenous women. Critical to this later article, as to all of Castañeda's later work, is her attention to resistance and the many ways that indigenous and mestiza women have resisted colonial domination. Women resisted with their bodies, in day-to-day practices, and in overt uprisings. In this context, renowned women such as Toypurina are part of a long and rich history of indigenous women's resistance.

CHAPTER 1

THE POLITICAL ECONOMY OF NINETEENTH-CENTURY STEREOTYPES OF CALIFORNIANAS

Recent scholarship in Chicano and women's history has challenged the limited, stereotypic images of Mexicanos and women prevalent in the contemporary and historical literature of nineteenth-century California and the American west.[1] In studying North American imperial expansion, Chicano and other scholars have concluded that pejorative, racist stereotypes of Mexicanos, in particular, were an integral part of an ideology that helped justify the Mexican-American War as well as subsequent repression in the conquered territory. One scholar persuasively argues that the notion of Manifest Destiny, which a priori assumed the inferiority of Mexicanos, was "the product of a campaign of ideological manipulation."[2]

In addition, studies in women's history, which tend to focus on the changing material reality and developing ideology of the United States, conclude that the constrictive, stereotypic molds into which women have been cast in the literature are sex- and class-based. The literature of the period was generally written by middle class, Anglo males who interpreted women's experiences from their own gender and class perspective of women's proper roles. In this way, these authors created sexist and unidimensional portrayals of women. Recent work has shown that even in the literature of the American West—where greater sexual equality allegedly existed—women are stereotyped into four sexually defined roles: gentle tamers, sun-bonneted helpmates, hell-raisers and bad women.[3]

According to these studies, sexually defined stereotypes of women are rooted in the material changes which occurred in the nineteenth century when the United States was moving from an agricultural economy to mercantile capitalism. This transition from a pre-industrial economy physically removed the workplace from the household. In the process, many of women's traditional economic functions disappeared and the social relations of production were transformed. Women began to be defined primarily by their sexual function as reproducers of the species, and by the social roles ascribed to wife and mother. During the nineteenth century, the view that women's proper place was in the home formed a central part of the ideology of an industrializing America—an ideology which came to enshrine women in the cult of true womanhood.[4]

However, these studies have not yet examined the portrayal of Mexican women and the relationship between stereotypes and ideology. Furthermore, these discussions have altogether ignored the intersection of sex, race and class in the development of America's ideology in the nineteenth century. Although Mexican women in California—Californianas—have never been the subject of any major historical work, they do appear in three kinds of North American literature which presents them in a contradictory, but nevertheless, stereotypic light. This literature—which spans both the nineteenth and twentieth centuries—includes contemporary travel, journalistic, and biographical works; nineteenth- and twentieth-century novels; and general histories, both academic and popular, of California.[5]

This paper examines contemporary North American literature on early California and the stereotypes it presents of Mexican women.[6] The effort here is to examine the literature within the framework of mid-nineteenth century America's system of beliefs and ideas, and to suggest how the images of Mexicanas fit into that system. The discussion focuses on Richard Henry Dana's *Two Years Before the Mast* (1840), Thomas Jefferson Farnham's *Travels in California and Scenes in the Pacific Ocean* (1844) and Alfred Robinson's *Life in California* (1846). As an integral part of nineteenth-century American, but particularly Californian, literary culture, these works have served as primary sources for historical, novelistic, and popular accounts of provincial California. Dana and Robinson's works in particular have long influenced perceptions and interpretations of Mexicanos in California.

While the contemporary and historical literature purports to present accurate descriptions of Mexican women's experience and condition, it actually constructs stereotypic images which serve ideological purposes. The stereotypes manifest the polarities of "good" and "bad" women applied to women generally. This simplistic dichotomous portrayal is further complicated by stereotypical notions of gender, race, and class. While these prejudices are evident in most accounts of Mexicanas, and while all the descriptions purport to present transhistorical or timeless images, the descriptions do, in fact, vary considerably across time in terms of the particular aspects of these stereotypes which are emphasized. These variations correlate with the changing needs of the capitalist and imperialist system, its shifting relations to Mexicano culture and economy in California and the evolving ideology of the nature of women.[7]

The earliest images of Mexican women in North American literature appeared in contemporary travel, journalistic, and biographical accounts written in the 1830s and 1840s.[8] The authors were Anglo men—merchants, sailors and adventurers—engaged in the hide and tallow trade and/or America's westward expansion. Some arrived in the early 1820s when the newly-independent Mexico opened its borders to foreign trade. They brought their wares from Boston to Valpariso to California. In this remote province, recently freed from the grasp of Spain's stringent regulations and mercantilist economic policies, Yankee and English traders found a ready market for the Chinese, European, and American goods crammed into the holds of their ships. They soon established a brisk, lucrative trade, exchanging their cargo for hides and tallow, often at a 200 percent profit.[9]

The next two decades—the 1830s and 1840s were years of escalating conflict between the young Mexican Republic and an expanding United States. The conflict, which culminated in the Mexican-American War, raged hot and cold in California prior to the actual outbreak of war in 1846.[10] The three narratives discussed in this paper appeared during the height of this rising conflict.

Richard Henry Dana in *Two Years Before the Mast* (published anonymously in 1840), presented the first major image of Mexican women in California. Dana, the scion of a cultivated patrician family in Cambridge, Massachusetts, sailed to California on the *Pilgrim*, a ship belonging to Bryant, Sturgis, and Company, the major American firm engaged in the hide and tallow trade. In this work, Dana recorded his experiences as a sailor as well as his impressions of the country, the land, and the people he saw on his journey during his two years aboard ship.

Dana has little to say of a positive nature about Mexican people in general. His views of Mexican women, which center on virtue, are moralistic and judgmental. According to Dana, "The fondness for dress among the women is excessive, and is sometimes their ruin. A present of a fine mantel, or a necklace, or pair of earrings gains the favor of a greater part. Nothing is more common than to see a woman living in a house of only two rooms, with the ground for a floor, dressed in spangled satin shoes, silk gown, high comb, gilt if not gold, earrings and necklace. If their husbands do not dress them well enough, they will soon receive presents from others."[11] Therefore, Dana points out, "the women have but little virtue," and "their morality is, of course, none of the best." Although the "instances of infidelity are much less frequent than one would at first suppose," Dana attributes this to "the extreme jealousy and deadly revenge of their husbands."[12] To this Yankee patrician, Mexican women are profligate, without virtue and morals, whose excesses are only kept in check by a husband's vengeful wrath. In this narrative Mexican women are seen as purely sexual creatures.

Dana's work, which had immediate success in the United States and England, set the precedent for negative images of Mexican women in California. He created the image of Mexicanas as "bad" women. This condemnation of Mexican women's virtue appears again and again in subsequent works. The view of Mexicanas as women of easy virtue and latent infidelity easily led to the stereotype of the Mexicana as prostitute in the literature of the gold rush.

While Dana's writing attempted to convey the impression of an interested but rather detached objective observer of California's people and life, Thomas Jefferson Farnham's *Travels in California and Scenes in the Pacific Ocean*, published in 1844–45, was sensationalistic and vituperative. Farnham, a lawyer, came to California from Illinois by way of Oregon. He arrived in Monterey in 1841 and immediately took up the cause of Isaac Graham and his band of sixty foreigners. Governor Alvarado had shipped the group to jail in Mexico on charges of conspiracy to overthrow the government.[13] Farnham described his travels on the Pacific Coast and detailed the Graham side of the political affair. Throughout his account Farnham consistently derided the Californianos. In his words, "the Californians are an imbecile, pusillanimous race of men, and unfit to control the destinies of that beautiful country."[14] In clear, direct, and hostile terms, Farnham echoed the same sentiment that Dana and others had expressed with more subtlety, replacing passionate partisanship for the previous pretense of objectivity.

The Californiano's mixed racial background is a constant theme in Farnham's narrative. It is also the focus of his blunt comment on women, of whom he states "The ladies, dear creatures, I wish they were whiter, and that their cheekbones did not in their great condescension assimilate their manners and customs so remarkably to their Indian neighbors."[15] Unlike Dana, who was, at times, ambivalent about the racial characteristics and beauty of the elite Californianas, Farnham was clear about their racial origins and his own racial views.

Like Dana, Farnham was also concerned with the Californiana's dress and appearance. While Dana focused on the extravagance of dress, Farnham centered on the looseness of the clothing and the women's "indelicate" form. "A pity it is," notes Farnham, "that they have not stay and corset makers' signs among them, for they allow their waists to grow as God designed they should, like Venus de Medici, that ill-bred statue that had no kind mother to lash its vitals into delicate form."[16] Since Californian women do not lash their own or their daughter's "vitals into delicate form," they obviously are neither proper themselves nor are raising proper daughters for California. Farnham would have women's dress hide their form in the multiple layers of clothing that simultaneously hid the bodies of middle-class women in the United States and severely limited their physical mobility. Although Farnham made few additional direct statements about women, he did relate the woeful tale of a Southern lad's romance with a Californiana. The young man, who was ready to bequeath her all his worldly goods, was left bereft by the infidelity of his Californiana sweetheart.[17] For Farnham, whose work justified the filibustering efforts of foreigners in California, Mexican women had no redeeming qualities.

Alfred Robinson, while no less concerned than Dana or Farnham with Californianas' virtue, morality, race and appearance, countered his countrymen's negative image by presenting the polar opposite view —albeit only of upper-class women—in his work, *Life in California*, published in 1846. Unlike Dana, who spent only a short time in California, or Farnham, who came in 1841, Robinson had been in California since 1829 and was on intimate terms with the Californianos. As resident agent for Bryant, Sturgis, and Company he had extensive business dealings with the province's largest landowners.[18]

In 1837, at the age of thirty, Robinson converted to Catholicism and married fourteen-year-old Ana María de la Guerra of the elite de la Guerra y Noriega family of Santa Barbara. The de la Guerras were one of the very few families in California who could truthfully claim Spanish ancestry. Life in California was written from the viewpoint of an observer who "sought to refute the inaccuracies of itinerant travelers like Dana."[19]

Robinson interspersed descriptions of women's physical appearance, dress, manners, conduct and spiritual qualities throughout his work.[20] In this book, Californianas are universally chaste, modest, virtuous, beautiful, industrious, well-bred aristocratic Spanish ladies. "With vice so prevalent amongst the men," Robinson states in his most explicit passage, "the female portion of the community, it is worthy of remark, do not seem to have felt its influence, and perhaps there are few places in the world where, in proportion to the number of inhabitants, can be found more chastity, industrious habits, and correct deportment, than among the women of this place."[21] Robinson defended the morals, virtue and racial purity of elite Californianas. By making racial and class distinctions among Californianas he transformed the image of immoral, bad and sexual women into the image of the sexually pure, good Californiana.

Dana and Farnham cast Mexican women into molds of the women of easy virtue, no morals and racial inferiority. Robinson cast elite Californianas into the stereotype of a genteel, well-bred Spanish aristocrat with virtue and morals intact. Her European ancestry and aristocratic background, to say nothing of her economic value, made her worthy of marriage. Dana and Farnham, in their concern with the Californiana's race, virtue and morals set the parameters of the stereotype. Robinson accepted the parameters and addressed the same issues.

Recently, these nineteenth-century narratives have attracted the attention of scholars and others working in Chicano, Women's, California and Southwestern history and culture. While Chicano historians and other scholars have noted the existence of contradictory stereotypes of women, few have examined the nature of these dual images. Generally, these scholars have attributed Mexicano stereotypes to historical Hispanophobia, anti-Catholicism, racial prejudice and to the economic and political issues involved in the Mexican-American War. More recently, David Langum and Janet LeCompte have specifically addressed the image of Californianas and Nuevo Mexicanas in nineteenth-century works written by Anglos.[22]

Langum, who recognizes the existence of contradictory views and their focus on the issues of morality and virtue, argues that the negative image was the minority view. And this image, he further argues, was class-based. That is, it not only derived from upper-class Yankees like Dana, but more importantly, the subjects of the image were lower-class Mexican women, the only group of Californianas with whom Dana, as a sailor, had any contact. According to Langum, Dana had neither access to nor interaction with upper-class women. He could not, like Robinson, form an opposite view, and therefore generalized his observations of lower-class Californianas to all women. Ignoring the sexist bias in these works, Langum not only attributes the dichotomous images of Californianas to the class prejudice of the writers and the class origin of the subjects, he further assumes that the stereotypes were accurate for lower-class women.[23]

While class was most certainly an issue in the development of dichotomous stereotypes of women, Langum's argument does not entirely hold up. Although Dana was not, like Robinson, on intimate terms with the Californiano elite, he did have the opportunity to observe them at close hand, and on occasion, he attended their social functions. In fact, he attended the festivities and dance celebrating Robinson's marriage to Ana María de la Guerra. As he develops it, Langum's class explanation is merely an extension of Cecil Robinson's earlier interpretation of pejorative Mexicano stereotypes in American travel literature immediately preceding the Mexican-American War.[24] Robinson argued that Anglos formed a mistaken perception of all Mexicanos on the basis of contact with relatively few Mexicans in the border area. This interpretation has been challenged and refuted as the basis for the development of stereotypes of the Mexicanos.[25]

LeCompte, whose main interest is the independence of Nuevo Mexicanas during Mexico's Republican period, also notes Anglo writers' comments about the dark skin of New Mexican women, their idleness, boldness of demeanor, revealing clothing and deplorably low standards of female chastity. She attributes Anglos' negative views of the Nuevo Mexicana's morality to the sexism inherent in Anglo norms for proper female behavior. And these norms, LeCompte continues, were conditioned by the more constrictive position of women in North American society and culture, and by the corollary view of womanhood as the upholder and symbol of American morality. Unfortunately, LeCompte does not develop the argument. The article is devoted to an exposition of the economic and social independence of New Mexican women. it generalizes about the nature of their independence without substantive research.[26]

Despite the limitations of Langum and LeCompte's work, both essays are suggestive and raise the issue of class, women's economic dislocation and sexism as relevant to American stereotyping of Mexican women.[27] However, for the historian attempting to reconstruct the history of Mexican women in nineteenth century California, the ideological and historical significance of these particular dichotomous stereotypes remains to be clearly confronted.

My research leads me to concur with the conclusions of earlier studies that nineteenth-century North American literature on California expressed an ideological perspective reflecting an economic interest in California, that the stereotypes of Mexicanos, including those of women, functioned as instruments of conquest, and thus served the political and economic interests of an expanding United States.[28] However, I would further argue that the stereotypes of women were not static; they changed across time—from the pre-War period, through the War, the gold rush and the late Victorian era.[29] The changing images of Mexicanas in California, I further assert, were consistent with the economic and socio-political needs of a changing U.S. capitalist and imperialist system.

Initially, the pejorative images of Mexican people, which derived from the authors' firm belief in Anglo America's racial, moral, economic and political superiority, served to devalue the people occupying a land base the United States wanted to acquire—through purchase if possible, by war if necessary. The values of supremacy, including male supremacy, expressed in the creation of negative stereotypes and embedded in the notion of Manifest Destiny, were central to America's ideology—an ideology based on the exclusion of non-whites from the rights and privileges of American democratic principles and institutions. Thus, the early negative stereotypes of Mexican people focused on their racial characteristics and alleged debased condition. These stereotypes appeared regardless of class or circumstance of the writers. Their writings uniformly portrayed the same image of Mexicanos whether the latter were encountered in the Mexican interior or in Mexico's northernmost provinces.[30]

The material basis of nineteenth-century racist ideology and stereotypes of Mexicanos has been addressed by other scholars. However, these stereotypes have not been examined specifically within the framework of an ideology in transition.[31] Nor have these studies examined ideas about women in America's ideological structure, or the stereotypes of women in relation to war, conquest and ideology. In short, the dimension of sex, as well as the interaction of sex, race and class, have been ignored. In this regard I would argue the following four points: (1) nineteenth-century stereotypes of Mexican women revolved around the issue of women's virtue and morality; (2) these stereotypes were both sexually and racially defined; (3) judgments of Mexicanas' morality were one of the indices used to judge the moral fiber of the Mexican people; and (4) women's economic value and class position in California were pivotal to the dichotomous stereotypes cast in the 1840s and varied across time.

In addition to its racial bias, American ideology of the mid-nineteenth century reflected the economic, social and cultural changes attendant in the transition from commercial to industrial capitalism and the nation's concomitant movement towards continental imperialism. Certain aspects of America's ideology were in process of reformulation as values consistent with changing economic and social relationships increasingly being shaped by the entrepreneurial and rising industrial classes. Among the most important ideological reformulations accompanying the economic transformation was the redefinition of the role and position of women in American society.[32]

The changing image of Mexican women, I contend, derived from America's unfolding system of beliefs and ideas about sex and race, as well as about economic and political expansion. With reference to Mexicanas, these images functioned on two levels: first, as rationalization for war and conquest and, second, as rationalization for the subordination of women.

In the mid-nineteenth century, capitalist ideology was defining womanhood in terms of specific gender roles that excluded the dimension of economic production. Women's social worth was increasingly constricted within proscribed norms around her home, her only power base. A woman's value and power were determined by possession and exhibition of certain cardinal virtues: piety, purity, submissiveness, and domesticity. All four virtues were central to a woman's moral strength and character that were largely judged by her sexual conduct. With sexual purity her only form of power and the home her only sphere of influence, womankind was now only supposed to produce children and a moral, virtuous culture, a culture she inculcated in her progeny along with the appropriate gender roles.[33] Thus, in the developing bourgeois ideology, the American woman held her country's morality in her hands. By the mid 1840s, when Anglo Americans were publishing their impressions of California, ideas and definitions of women's role derived from the ethos of the bourgeois class whose hegemony extended to the definition and production of culture. Within that culture, women were expected to act within the proscribed norms of what one scholar has called "the cult of true womanhood."[34]

Although the image of woman sheltered from the competition of the marketplace was generally appropriate only for middle-class women, by the mid-nineteenth century the notion of woman as the purveyor of a people's morality was being applied to all women in general. The American woman became the symbol of the country's innocence, morality, and virtue; she was held almost solely responsible for the morality and virtue of the nation. Thus, in the 1840s, women's value was not only determined by her newly defined gender-specific roles, but she represented the moral strength of her country.[35] This view of women was part of the ideological framework within which North American authors, most of whom were from the middle class, perceived, interpreted and judged the Mexican female in California.

Anglo American male writers assigned to Mexican women the same social value based on gender specific norms and roles they assigned to white womanhood in the United States. However, for Mexican women, the dimension of race was also integral to the judgment of their virtue and morality. Nineteenth-century Anglo Americans' views of Mexican people as racially inferior are well-documented and need not be elaborated here.[36] What does need to be understood is that in terms of women, America's racial bias against Mexicanos coalesced with the moral judgment of women and hardened into a stereotype of Mexicanas as both racially and morally inferior, with one reinforcing the other in a most pernicious way. In her study of Nuevo Mexicanas, LeCompte further underscores this point by arguing that Anglo "... visitors from the land of the double standard, blamed New Mexicans' sexual freedom entirely on women."[37] Thus, the most salient stereotype of Mexicanas in the pre-War literature is that of the racially inferior sexual creature—the "bad" woman of easy virtue and no morality.[38] In America's ideological framework, racially inferior people found wanting in moral strength deserved to lose their country. Stereotypes of Mexican women's morality not only encompassed both the sexual and racial dimensions, but were also the basis for moral judgments about Mexican people as a whole.

While Anglo women in industrializing North America were being economically displaced and entombed in the virtues of domesticity, Mexican women in agro-pastoral California were an economic asset. Hispanic law protected women's property rights and gave them equal inheritance rights with males. Mexicanas held an economic power their North American sisters were rapidly losing.[39] Mexican women's economic significance did not escape the Anglos' perception or appropriation, and it clearly affected the creation of a new image—a counter to the pejorative stereotype of the "bad" woman.

From the mid-1820s to the end of Mexican rule, a number of intermarriages between elite Californianas and Anglo males were celebrated in California.[40] Most of the Anglos who married Californianas prior to the North American occupation acquired land through their marriage. The land grants often became the basis for vast wealth.

Californiana-Anglo marriages were occurring at the moment that commercial capitalism of international proportions was penetrating the developing agro-pastoral economy of Alta California.[41] The nascent economy, based on the rise of private property and the corollary rise of an elite ranchero class of large landowners, was tied through the hide and tallow trade to European, Latin American, and North American markets. Manufactured goods and products from these markets were being rapidly introduced into this remote Mexican province.[42] At the same time, Mexican women, particularly elite women, held significant economic power as large property owners in their own right, as conveyors of property to others, and as consumers in a nascent but expanding market.[43] Most of the Anglos who married Californianas were merchants and traders who were directly related to the development of commerce in California. Marriage to an elite Californiana, in addition to landed wealth, also established family and kinship ties with the largest Californiano landowners.[44] Marriage solidified class alliances between Anglo merchants and the Californiano elite, who were jointly establishing control of California's economy. The image of Californianas as "good" women emerged from these marriages and economic alliances on the eve of the Mexican-American War.

The positive image portraying Mexican women as aristocratic, virtuous Spanish ladies directly contradicted the negative view of Californianas—but it did so by singling out elite Californianas, denying their racial identity, and treating them as racially superior to Californiano males and the rest of their people. Further, the new, positive image was no less a stereotype than the negative portrayal. With few exceptions, women in California, including women of the elite ranchero class, were neither Spanish nor aristocratic by birth. They, like their male counterparts, were of mixed-blood or mestizo origin. Whether of military or poblador (settler) families, their grandparents or parents migrated to California from the impoverished classes of Mexico's Northern frontier provinces.[45] Further, the positive portrayal of these elite women in the literature of the 1840s did not extend to the Californiano male, including the male members of the women's families. In this literature, while the women were transformed into Spanish ladies the men remained Mexicans.[46]

While the accounts written by Anglo husbands of elite Californianas attempted to refute the pejorative images of Californiana womanhood, both sets of writing treated Californiano males in equally contemptuous, racist terms.[47] Thus, although the corrective image made racial and class distinctions in its treatment of women, it did not make the same distinctions in its treatment of males.[48] In the corrective literature, elite and non-elite Californiano males were viewed as racially inferior, and the rancheros' class aspirations (higaldismo) were ridiculed. In Europeanizing Californiana *mestizas* and *mulatas* and proclaiming them industrious, moral and chaste, the corrective image justified and rationalized the union of a racially, morally superior Anglo man to a woman of an inferior racial and moral stock. Robinson's Europeanization of Californianas fulfilled Thomas Jefferson Farnham's racist wish that: "the ladies, dear creatures," be made whiter. Finally, the new image transformed elite Californianas into the epitome of the ideal woman enshrined in the cult of True Womanhood. Once the conquest was at hand, the portrayal of Californianas shifted from a negative to a positive image and severed her from her racial, cultural and historical reality.

In this paper I have tried to outline the sexual, racial and economic dimensions of the dichotomous images of Mexican women by focusing on three narratives which defined the stereotypes. I have suggested that this literature and the stereotypes it presents reflected an ideology which not only excluded non-whites from American principles and institutions, but that the stereotypes of women, which represent the intersection of sex, race and class, functioned as instruments of imperialism, conquest and subordination. I will conclude this paper by discussing more precisely how the literary images of Mexican women in California derived from and served the ideological interests of the changing political economy in the United States.

The stereotypes of Californianas cast in the early 1840s, coincident with the period leading to and encompassing the Mexican-American War, presented the polarities of the "bad" and "good" stereotypes of Mexicanas in California.[49] The former set the precedent for pejorative stereotypes of Mexicanas in the North American mind. The latter effectively separated elite women from their history, gave them a new history, and thus made them acceptable to Americans. Both stereotypes revolved around sexual definitions of women's virtue and morality. Both dealt with race but with a crucial difference. The elite Californianas were deemed European and superior while the mass of Mexican women were viewed as Indian and inferior. On the other hand, the contemporary literature, which other scholars have concluded played an ideological role in the justification of war, contained negative images of Mexican women who were seen as caretakers of their own and their peoples' morality.[50] These images formed part of the belief and idea system that rationalized the war and dispossession of the land base. On the other hand, the positive image of Californianas, who were also considered caretakers of morality, legitimized Anglos' marriage to them and provided the necessary validity for their new roles as American wives and mothers. The positive image facilitated the assimilation of these upper-class women into American society.[51]

As the United States consolidated its conquest of California and the Southwest in the post-War period, the negative and positive images of Mexicanas and Californianas hardened into stereotypes of the Mexican prostitute and the romantic, but fading Spanish beauty that still plague us today. In the literature of the gold rush, the negative views of women's morality were generalized to Mexicanas and Latinas who migrated to California during the period. These views found continued expression in the almost singular depiction of Mexicanas/Latinas as fandango dancers, prostitutes, and consorts of Mexican bandits.[52] The pejorative stereotype of Mexicanas as women of easy virtue was cemented into the image of the volatile, sensuous, Mexican prostitute. It is significant that Juanita (Josefa) of Downieville, the only woman hanged during the gold rush era, was Mexicana. For her, the image, the beliefs and the ideas that manufactured them, had dire consequences.[53]

The commonly advanced notion that women, due to their scarcity in the Mother Lode, were afforded moral, emotional and physical protection and respect by Anglo miners, does not hold for Mexican women.[54] Mexicanas, as part of the conquered nation and as part of the group of more knowledgeable, experienced, and initially successful miners competing with Anglos in the Placers became one object of the violence and lawlessness directed against Mexicanos/Latinos. Mexican women's gender did not protect them from the brutality of racism or the rapacity attendant in the competition for gold. Virulent anti-Mexican sentiment combined with economic interest led to the First Foreign Miners' Tax of 1849, which technically levied a tax on all foreign miners but was inspired by the desire to eliminate Mexican competition from the mines.[55] For Mexicanas in the gold rush era, the combined force of sexism, racism and economic interest resulted in a hardening of pejorative stereotypes which further impugned their sex and their race.

The image of the woman of easy virtue, firmly fixed in the literature in the years preceding the war, easily transformed into the Mexican prostitute. It further helped to justify the exclusion of Mexicanos/Latinos from the mines and rationalized their subordination in California. With specific reference to women but also inclusive of men, the literature of the post-War/gold rush era further cemented the earlier shift that divided Mexican women along racial and class lines.

Negative stereotypes of women from the post-War period to the end of the nineteenth century were specifically applied to Mexicanas and Latinas who migrated to California from Mexico and Latin America. Newspaper accounts make a distinction between Mexicanas/Latinas and Californianas. Mexicanas are prostitutes and would remain so for the rest of the century—Californianas are not.

In the literature of the late nineteenth century, Robinson's positive image of Californianas as aristocratic Spanish ladies was picked up, further elaborated and generalized to women living in California prior to the Mexican-American War. And in the pre-War period, now romanticized as the "splendid idle forties," and the "halcyon days of long ago," Californianas are depicted as gentle reposing souls sweetly attending to the sublime domestic duties of ministering to large households of family and Indian servants on their caballero husband's baronial estate. If single, these gay and beautiful Spanish señoritas are in a constant flurry of girlish activity and preparation for the next fiesta and the next beau —a dashing American, of course.[56]

The important point here is that this image not only negates Californianas' mestizo racial origins, ignores or denies the existence of any kind of work and assigns them all the attributes of "True Womanhood," it also locates their existence in a remote, bygone past. They were, but they no longer are. In this representation, the Mexican prostitute and the Spanish Californiana are totally unrelated by race, culture, class, history, or circumstance. In the former there is immorality, racial impurity, degradation, and contemporary presence. In the latter there is European racial origins, morality, cultural refinement, and historical distance.

Irrespective of the view, the end result was the same. Mexicana or Californiana, both representations rendered women in California ignorant, vacuous and powerless. In both cases, her Catholicism and culture made her priest-ridden, male dominated, superstitious and passive. Undemocratic Spanish and Mexican governance made her ignorant. If Mexicana, however, her immorality and racial impurity established her lack of value and exacerbated her ignorance. As part of the conquered Mexican nation, the War confirmed her powerlessness. If Californiana, on the other hand, her racial purity, morality and economic worth elevated her status, making her worthy of marrying an Anglo while dispossessing her of her racial, historical, cultural and class roots. With marriage and a husband's possession of her property, elite Californianas forfeited their economic power. Finally, the Californiana's presence was abstracted to an era long past, her person romanticized. In either case, Mexicana or Californiana, the conquest was complete.

In removing Californianas and their existence from the present, North American writers and their public could rationalize the violence perpetrated against Mexicanos throughout the post-War period to the end of the nineteenth century. One scholar attributes the romanticization of the Californianos—for the romantic, nostalgic view now reincorporated males—to the sympathy the victor has for the vanquished.[57] I would argue that the nostalgic, romantic stereotype of the Californianos projected in late-nineteenth-century literature served specifically to rationalize the dispossession of the elite ranchero class.

Finally, the early narratives which set the parameters for the dichotomous images of Mexican women were written during the brief Republican period of Mexican California. Yet, these dual images have become the standard view of Californianas for the entire nineteenth century in the historical, as well as the novelistic, poetic and popular literature. The dichotomous stereotypes cast in the 1840s have not only frozen Mexican women into a specific, exceedingly narrow time frame and effectively obscured her historical reality for the nineteenth century, they have also exacerbated the notion of discontinuity between nineteenth- and twentieth-century Mexican women and their history.[58]

In view of the consistency of the stereotypes, Mexican women appear not to have an historical presence prior to the 1840s, and to exist only as romantic, but fading Spanish beauties after the Mexican-American War. By the turn of the century, Californianas, like their brethren, cease to exist historically. Within this perspective there is no continuity with women prior to the 1840s, nor any room for continuity between Mexicanas who were here during the 1840s and those who migrated from Mexico during the gold rush or who were part of the Mexican migration in the latter part of the century. In the literature, Mexican women's historical existence is defined out of all but a few short years of the nineteenth century. Her historical presence is confined to the 1840s and left to the assumptions, perceptions and interests of Anglo-American entrepreneurs and filibusters who wrote about California in a period of American continental imperialism that resulted in the Mexican-American War.

NOTES

1. For an important historiographical essay see Juan Goméz-Quiñones and Luis L. Arroyo, "On the State of Chicano History: Observations on its Development, Interpretations and Theory, 1970-1974," *Western Historical Quarterly* 7 (April 1976): 155-185. For a general survey of Chicano history see Rodolfo Acuña, *Occupied America: A History of Chicanos,* 2d ed. (New York: Harper & Row, 1981). For theoretical interpretations see Tomas Almaguer, *Interpreting Chicano History: The "World-System" Approach to 19th Century California* (Berkeley: Institute for the Study of Social Change, Working Paper Series, no. 101, University of California, 1977) and Mario Barrera, *Race and Class in the Southwest* (Notre Dame: University of Notre Dame Press, 1979). For a discussion of the economic motives behind the Mexican-American War see Glen W. Price, *Origins of the War with Mexico: The Polk-Stockton Intrigue* (Austin: University of Texas Press, 1967). For a description of the Mexican-American War in California and subsequent displacement of Mexicanos see Leonard Pitt, *The Decline of the Californios: A Social History of the Spanish-Speaking Californians, 1846-1890* (Berkeley: University of California Press, 1970). For a discussion of post-war displacement in a specific California community see Albert Camarillo, *Chicanos in a Changing Society: From Mexican Pueblos to American Barrios in Santa Barbara and Southern California, 1848-1930* (Cambridge: Harvard University Press, 1979). For specific discussion and varied analysis of stereotypes of Mexicanos in North American literature see James H. Lacy, "New Mexico Women in Early American Writings," *New Mexico Historical Review* 34 (1959): 41-51; James Hart, *American Images of Spanish California* (Berkeley: Friends of the Bancroft Library, 1960); Cecil Robinson, *With the Ears of Strangers: The Mexican in American Literature* (Tucson: University of Arizona Press, 1963); Beverly Trulio, "Anglo American Attitudes Toward New Mexican Women," *Journal of the West* 12 (1973): 229-239; Harry Clark, "Their Pride, Their Manners, and Their Voices: Sources of the Traditional Portrait of Early Californians," *California Historical Review* 52 (Spring 1974): 71-82; Raymond A. Paredes, "The Mexican Image in American Travel Literature, 1831-1869," *New Mexico Historical Review* 52 (January 1977): 5-59; Raymond Paredes, "The Origins of Anti-Mexican Sentiment in the United States," *New Scholar* 6 (1977): 139-165; Doris L. Meyer, "Early Mexi-

can American Responses to Negative Stereotyping," *New Mexico Historical Review* 53 (January 1978) 75-91; David Langum, "California Women and the Image of Virtue," *Southern California Quarterly* 59 (Fall 1977): 245-250; David J. Weber, "'Scarce More than Apes': Historical Roots of Anglo-American Stereotypes of Mexicans," in *New Spain's Far Northern Frontier*, ed. David J. Weber (Albuquerque: University of New Mexico Press, 1979), 293–304; Janet LeCompte, "The Independent Women of Hispanic New Mexico, 1821-1846," *Western Historical Quarterly* 12 (January 1981): 17-35.

2.   Barrera, in *Race and Class in the Southwest*, 12, is one of the few scholars who discusses manifest destiny specifically in terms of ideology. Hart, Paredes, and Clark discuss American attitudes and the literature in terms of justification and rationalization for war and dispossession but do not fully develop an ideological interpretation. See also Ronald Takaki, *Iron Cages: Race and Culture in 19th-Century America* (New York: Alfred A. Knopf, 1979).

3.   For an excellent series of historiographical essays see Part 1: Historiography on Women, in *Liberating Women's History: Theoretical and Critical Essays*, ed. Berenice A. Carroll (Urbana: University of Chicago Press, 1976), 1-92. See also Ann D. Gordon, Mari Jo Buhle, and Nancy Schrom Dye, *Women in American History* (Somerville: New England Free Press) an undated pamphlet of an article first published in *Radical America* 5 (July-August 1971); Barbara Sicherman, "Review Essay: American History," *Signs: Journal of Women in Culture and Society* 5 (1975): 461-485; Joan M. Jensen and Darlis A. Miller, "The Gentle Tamers Revisited: New Approaches to the History of Women in the American West," *Pacific Historical Review* 44 (May 1980): 173-213. For treatment of specific themes see Julie Roy Jeffrey, *Frontier Women: The Trans-Mississippi West. 1840-1880* (New York: Hill & Wang, 1979); Angela Y. Davis, *Women, Race, and Class* (New York: Random House, 1981); Alice Kessler-Harris, *Women Have Always Worked* (New York: The Feminist Press, 1981), 2-101; Carolyn Ware, "Introduction" in *Class, Sex and the Woman Worker*, eds. Milton Cantor and Bruce Laurie (Westport, CT: Greenwood Press, 1979), 3-19.

4.   Ann D. Gordon et. al., *Women in American History*; Ann D. Gordon and Mari Jo Buhle, "Sex and Class in Colonial and Mid-19th-Century America," in *Liberating Women's History: Theoretical and Critical Essays*, ed. Berenice A. Carroll (Urbana: University of Chicago Press, 1976), 278-300; Barbara Welter, "The Cult of True Womanhood," *The American Quar-*

terly 18 (1966): 151-174; Barbara Welter, *Dimity Convictions* (Athens: Ohio University Press, 1976).

5. While there is as yet no major historical study of Mexican women in California, several conference papers have made important contributions to the developing scholarship. See Anita Abascal, "Parteras, Llaveras y Maestras: Women in Provincial California," paper presented at the Conference of the West Coast Association of Women Historians, Los Angeles, California, May 1976; Helen Lara Cea, "Preliminary Conclusions in the Reconstruction of Chicana History in San Jose, 1777-1850," in *Between Worlds: Interpreters, Survivors, Guides*, ed. Frances Karttunen (New Brunswick: Rutgers, 1994); and Cynthia Orozco, "Mexican Elite Women in the 19th-Century: Work, Social Life, and Intermarriage," paper presented at "Mexicana/Chicana Women's History Symposium," Santa Monica, California, March 1982; Gloria E. Miranda, "Family Patterns and the Social Order in Hispanic Santa Barbara, 1784-1848" (PhD diss., University of Southern California, 1978); and Langum, "Image of Virtue," 245-250.

6. The three nineteenth-century works treated in this paper are Richard Henry Dana, Jr., *Two Years Before the Mast* (New York: Harper & Brothers, 1840; reprint ed., New York: Airmont Publishing Company, Inc., 1965); Thomas Jefferson Farnham, *Travelers in California and Scenes in the Pacific Ocean* (New York: Saxton & Miles, 1844; reprint ed., Oakland: Biobooks, 1947); and Alfred Robinson, *Life in California* (New York: Wiley & Putnam, 1846; reprint ed., Santa Barbara: Peregrine Press, Inc., 1970).

7. While this analysis is largely based on my close reading of the contemporary literature, I also drew upon the theoretical analysis in Davis, *Women, Race, and Class*; Gordon et al., *Women in American History*; Gordon and Buhle, "Sex and Class in Colonial and Mid 19th-Century America"; and Marion S. Goldman, *Gold Diggers and Silver Miners: Prostitution and Social Life in the Comstock Lode* (Ann Arbor: University of Michigan Press, 1981).

8. See note 6.

9. Pitt, *Decline of the Californios*, 12. For the development of commerce in California see Hubert Howe Bancroft, *History of California* (San Francisco: H. H. Bancroft & Company, 1885), vol. 2, chapters 13 and 19; vol. 3, chapters 5 and 13. For private ranchos to 1830 see Bancroft, *History of California*, vol. 2, 63 and footnote 24; 63. For development of the hide and tallow trade see Bancroft, *History of California*, vol. 2, 668. For presence

of foreign residents in California, see Bancroft, *History of California*, vol. 3, chapter 6. For land and private ranchos see W. W. Robinson, *Land in California* (Berkeley: University of California Press, 1949; paperback edition, 1979), chapters 4-6.

10. Pitt, *Decline of the Californios*, 26-27.

11. Dana, *Two Years Before the Mast*, 66.

12. Ibid., 136.

13. Pitt, *Decline of the Californios*, 20.

14. Farnham, *Travels in California*, 148.

15. Ibid.

16. Ibid.

17. Ibid., 23-24.

18. A. Robinson, *Life in California*, v-xii.

19. Ibid., vii; See also Langum, "Image of Virtue," 246.

20. A. Robinson, *Life in California*, 13, 30, 32, 37, 41, 50, 51, 62.

21. Ibid., 51.

22. See note 3 for citation of studies dealing with nineteenth century narratives and their portrayal of Mexicanos including articles that focus on women. See note 5 for citations of articles specifically treating Mexican women in nineteenth century California.

23. Langum, "Image of Virtue," 245-250.

24. Cecil Robinson, *With the Ears of Strangers*.

25. See Paredes, "Origins of Anti-Mexican Sentiment"; Paredes, "The Mexican Image"; and Weber, "'Scarce more than Apes.'"

26. LeCompte, "Independent Women," 17-35.

27. See also Trulio, "Attitudes towards Mexican Women," 229-239.

28. Almaguer, *Interpreting Chicano History*, 10-16; Barrera, *Race and Class in the Southwest*, 7-33; and Weber, "'Scarce More than Apes," 293-304.

29. The statement is based on my close reading of the contemporary literature.

30. For a discussion of racial stereotypes see Paredes, "The Mexican Image"; Paredes, "Origins of Anti-Mexican Sentiment"; and Weber, "'Scarce More than Apes.'"

31. See Barrera, *Race and Class in the Southwest*; and Acuña, *Occupied America*. Both works address the material basis of racism.

32. Gordon and Buhle, "Sex and Class"; Gordon et.al., *Women in American History*; Kessler-Harris, *Women Have Always Worked*, 22-51.

33. Gordon and Buhle, "Sex and Class," 283-288; Welter, "The Cult of True Womanhood," 151-174; and Welter, *Dimity Convictions*.

34. Welter, "The Cult of True Womanhood."
35. Ibid.
36. Paredes, "Origins of Anti-Mexican Sentiment," 139-165; Weber, "'Scarce More Than Apes'"; and Hart, *American Images of Spanish California.*
37. LeCompte, "Independent Women," 22.
38. This portrayal of Mexicanas is typical of Dana's *Two Years Before the Mast,* and Farnham's *Travels in California.*
39. E. N. Van Kleffens, *Hispanic Law* (Edinburgh: Edinburgh University Press, 1968).
40. My research on intermarriage is in the early stages. From the secondary literature we only know about a few of the more publicized marriages between Californianas and Anglos, including the following: 1820 - María Lugarda Castro to Thomas Doak; 1822 - Guadalupe Ortega to Joseph Chapman; 1825 - Teresa de la Guerra y Noriega to William Edward Petty Hartnell; 1825 - Josefa Carrillo (San Diego) elopement and marriage to Captain Henry Delano Fitch; 1827 - Marcelina Estudillo to Captain William A. Gale; 1829 - Josefa Carrillo (Santa Barbara) to Captain William Goodwin Dana; 1831 - María Francisca Butron to William Robert Garner; 1837 - Ana María de la Guerra y Noriega to Alfred Robinson; 1847 - María Estudillo to William Heath Davis, Jr.; Also married before the North American occupation were: Arcadia Bandini to Abel Stearns; Rosalía Vallejo to Jacob Leese; Adelaida Estrada to David Spence; Encarnacion Vallejo to John Rodgers Cooper.
41. Almaguer, "Interpreting Chicano History," 10-16; Andrew Rolle, "Introduction" to Robinson, *Life in California,* vi-ix, xi, he notes that "Robinson's generation helped to provide the precedents for Americanizing California," xi.
42. See note 9.
43. Mexican Archives, Civil Records, 1821-1848, Office of the Monterey County Clerk, Salinas, California, volumes 6-16. My research in these archives reveals that Mexican women were engaged in various kinds of property transactions in the Monterey District. Preliminary research reveals that these transactions included twenty-five petitions for and awards of land; six suits for rights of succession; five civil suits regarding property; three sales of houses; two transactions regarding ownership of herds of horses; one woman used property as a dowry; and three petitioned for and received cattle/horse brands. I have not calculated the acreage involved. My research of probate records in Monterey County has yielded few wills left by women in Spanish/Mexican

California. However, in the three wills that I have located, the women all left property to family members. Bowman, who defines prominence for women as property ownership, uses the records of the private land grant cases before the Board of Land Commissioners to discuss women property owners in provincial California. He located sixty-six women grantees who were directly or indirectly connected with the provincial land grants and listed twenty-two women who "carried the operation through from concession to patent for over 355,000 acres of land, or over 41 percent of the patented land grants to women." See J. N. Bowman, "Prominent Women of Provincial California," *Historical Quarterly of Southern California* 39 (June 1957): 149-166.

44. Rolle, "Introduction," to Robinson, *Life in California*, vii, refers specifically to Robinson, but the same generalization applies to Anglos marrying into the Bandini, Carrillo, Castro, Estudillo, Pico, and Vallejo families, who along with the de la Guerras, were large landowners and politically powerful. See also Henry Lynch, "Six Families: A Study of the Power and Influence of the Alvarado, Carrillo, Castro, de la Guerra, Pico, and Vallejo Families in California, 1769-1846" (MA thesis, California State University, Sacramento, 1977).

45. The census and mission registers recording population, births, marriages and deaths during the Spanish period clearly indicate the racial (for both men and women) and class (occupations, for men only) origins of the people who came as military personnel or as settlers. While people often elevated their racial status in these records by designating themselves "Español" even though it was physically evident that they were of mixed blood, the records nevertheless reveal the population was largely mestizo, which included various racial mixtures. The following list of census records includes only those censuses which listed race and/or occupation for the Monterey District. Unless otherwise indicated these records are all in the Bancroft Library, Provincial State Papers, Benicia Military: Real Presidio de Monterey, Lista de la compañia del referido presidio, 30 julio de 1782, Vol. IV, 663-694; Lista de la compañia, 23 mayo de 1791, Vol. XV, 10-12; Lista de los individuos de esta jurisdiccíon que se consideran aptos para el servicio en la compañia de militia ... que se hallen en este presidio, 1805, Monterey; Padrón del Real Presidio de Monterey, 1816, vol. 49, 894; Mission of San Carlos Borromeo, *Book of Marriages*, vol. 1, 1772-1855 (Monterey: Archdiocese of Monterey). The Book of Marriages that researchers work with at the Archdiocese is a photocopy of the original *Libro de matrimonios.*

46. Hart, *American Images of Spanish California*, 21-22.
47. Langum, "Image of Virtue," 246.
48. Robinson, *Life in California.* A dichotomized view of Californianos and Californianas runs throughout Robinson's book. See also, Clark, "Their Pride, Their Manners and Their Voices," who states "... many writers commented on the cruelty of the Spanish spurs. The tradition has had to allow the Californians a streak of cruelty, so that a picture of an oddly dichotomized society of tender-hearted women and bestial men has sometimes appeared in the Californians created by later writers, and this dichotomy may be inferred from the passages on each sex in *Life in California;* and Pitt, *Decline of the Californios,* 15, 17.
49. Dana, *Two Years Before the Mast;* Farnham, *Travels in California;* Robinson, *Life in California.*
50. See Barrera, *Race and Class in the Southwest,* 12; Paredes, "Origins of Anti-Mexican Sentiment"; Paredes, "The Mexican Image"; and Clark, "Their Pride, Their Manners, and Their Voices."
51. Historically, through intermarriage, common law marriage, or concubinage, women have been central to the process of assimilation and acculturation of the conquered group. Often the first level of this process occurs among the elite of both societies, or at least between the elite of the conquered society and the earliest arrivals of the conquering group. The issue of Californianas and assimilation will be treated more extensively in an expanded version of this paper.
52. For a relatively recent scholarly work that recognizes the significance of the issue of sex and Mexicanas in the gold rush era but which accepts, and thus maintains the standard, stereotypic view of Mexicanas as prostitutes, see Pitt, *Decline of the Californios,* 71-73.
53. William B. Secrest, Juanita: *The Only Woman Lynched During Gold Rush Days* (Fresno: Saga-West Publishing Company, 1967); Pitt, in *Decline of the Californios,* 73, accepts the standard view that Juanita (Josefa) of Downieville was a prostitute even though extensive documentation does not prove her prostitution.
54. Julie Roy Jeffrey, *Frontier Women,* 107-146, presents a well-balanced description and discussion of women on the mining frontier. For an excellent analysis of prostitution in the mining frontier and the issue of "respectable" and "non-respectable" women, see Marion Goldman, *Gold Diggers and Silver Miners.* For a discussion of the literature describing the elevated status of women due to their scarcity in the Mother Lode see Jensen and Miller, "The Gentle Tamers Revisited."

55. Pitt, *Decline of the Californios*, 60-65.
56. See Hart, *American Images of Spanish California*, 33; Hunt Jackson, *Ramona: A Story* (Boston: Roberts Brothers, 1892).
57. Clark, "Their Pride, Their Manners, and Their Voices," 72, 81. Most of the historical literature on California directly or indirectly reflects an interpretation of discontinuity between Californianos and Mexicanos.
58. The most succinct statement is by Moses Rischin, "Continuities and Discontinuities in Spanish-Speaking California," in *Ethnic Conflict in California History,* ed. Charles Wollenberg (Los Angeles: Tinnon-Brown Publishers, 1969), 43-60; see also John Womack, Jr., "Who Are the Chicanos?" *The New York Review of Books,* 19 (August 1972): 12-18; and Arthur Corwin, "Mexican American History: An Assessment," *Pacific Historical Review* 42 (August 1973): 269-308.

CHAPTER 2

MALINCHE, CALAFIA Y TOYPURINA

OF MYTHS, MONSTERS AND EMBODIED HISTORY

"Péinate que pareces India."

(Comb your hair, don't be looking like an Indian.)

"Arreglate, que te toman por India."

(Fix yourself up, lest you be mistaken for an Indian girl.)

Do this, that, or the other to your appearance to avoid being perceived as Indian—familiar, familial admonitions for Mexicana/Chicana (meaning mestiza), women and girls on the nineteenth- and twentieth-century Borderlands. Unspoken, but understood, in exhortations to mestizas to erase all cultural, and wherever possible, "racial," traces of Indigenous ancestry, is the underlying equation of Indian womanhood with devalued sexuality.[1]

This equation, as historians, feminist theorists, and other scholars have shown, is rooted in the gendering of the "New World" as female, in the sexualizing and eroticizing of its exploration and conquest, and in the erasing of its subjugated indigenous populations.[2] This equation is equally grounded in the gendered, sexualized, racialized, cultural, and economic violence of colonial domination. It is fixed in the history of Indian-woman-hating that Gloria Anzaldúa, Norma Alarcón, Deena González, and Inés Hernández-Avila theorize.[3] It is premised in the multi-layered strategies of Mestizas' survival, and in the practice of everyday life under conditions in which the Indian in us, always subject to attack, is to be denied, erased, extirpated.

My work, which moves indigenous and mestiza women's bodies and sexuality in eighteenth- and nineteenth-century Alta California to the center of historical inquiry, draws on scholarship that theorizes gender and sexuality as dimensions of subjectivity that are both an "effect of power and a technology of rule," and that analyzes colonial domination in relation to the construction of subjectivities —meaning forms of personhood, power, and social positioning.[4] Relying too on studies analyzing the body as a trope that is key to the configuring of domination, subjugation, and resistance, I explore how women articulated their subjectivity and identity/ies within the confines, conflicts, and contradictions of a frontier colonial order—where Indias were under colonial domination, and Mestizas, initially among the colonizing forces, also became the colonized in the post-U.S. Mexican War era.[5] Mestizas, then, are both dominated and dominating historical subjects whose multiple identities, polyvalent locations, and agency I examine as part of the ongoing debate in Chicana/o Studies about our indigenous identities and selves.[6]

CALAFIA: THE BODY OF MYTH

In California, the myth and paradigm of the historical Malinche has significant antecedents in the myth of Calafia, the beautiful but wild and ferocious black Amazon Queen of the *novelas de caballería,* from which the name California is derived.[7] Though initially a construct of the medieval Spanish literary imaginary, Calafia and the Amazons, the monstrous women of medieval Europe's mythic geography, formed an integral part of the New World historical imaginary and imperial archives from the sixteenth through the eighteenth centuries.[8]

The myth of Calafia and California first appeared in *Las Sergas de Esplandián,* the chivalric novel by Garcí Rodríguez (Ordóñez) de Montalvo, published in 1510 for distribution in America, and had significant currency at the beginning of the subjugation of Mexico.[9] In this male fantasy, the Amadís de Gaula and his son Esplandián, the Christian heroes of the novel, first meet Calafia in combat, when the Amazons join Aramato's struggle to capture Constantinople from the Emperor's Christian allies.

In the fashion of Amazons everywhere, Calafia rules a tribe of women without men in California, a remote island next to the earthly paradise. Calafia and her army of black women warriors tame and mount fearsome flying griffins, wield weapons of pure gold, and battle their male opponents while mounted atop the backs of these fearsome creatures. The women feed the enemy men captured on the battlefield to the griffins, sparing a few for purposes of procreation. When the children are born, Amazon mothers keep the females and immediately kill the males. In this myth of women living with women who kill their male infants at birth, Western constructs of the polluting female body, the "monstrous feminine," converge with fears and fantasies of New World monsters.[10]

Calafia's Amazons and Amadís's Christian troops (male Europeans) fought a ferocious battle. For a while it seemed that the magnificently wild, black warrior-women would triumph; but the wild beasts turned on their mistresses and devoured them. At tale's end, the mighty Calafia is subdued, tamed, dominated. Like infidel queens in most other *novelas,* Calafia converts to Christianity and offers herself—body, soul, and worldly goods—to the hero-object of her desire, even though he rejects her. Moreover, she resignedly accepts Espandián's marriage to the *infanta* Leonorina, and weds Talanque, another victorious Christian, whom the splendid hero bestows upon her.[11]

In this story, published ten years before the conquest of Mexico and the appearance of the historical Malinche, the black Amazonian queen

Calafia, like the land that is named for her, is militarily conquered, Christianized, and married to one of her captors. She relinquishes her authority, sovereignty, religion, and her life among women without men. In the male imaginary, Calafia/the land is tamed, husbanded, seeded.

MYTH AND HISTORY: ARCHIVING THE BODY

Mythic legends of Amazons, and the quest for women reigning in a land of untold riches, ripe to be dominated, who offer themselves to their conquerors, existed not only in the *novelas de caballería,* or "Books of the Brave."[12] Rather, these accounts persisted in the journals and reports of Spanish explorers, *conquistadores,* and colonizing expeditions. The myth, and search for the Amazons, traveled with the explorers, from the Yucatán in the South to far northern waters in the futile search for the Northwest Passage to India. The search for the Amazons, and near sightings, were consistently documented, mapped, and archived.

From Juan de Grijalva's expedition of 1518, one account notes "This Isle of Women is a small island north of Cozumel off the east coast of the Yucatán that, according to López de Gómara, . . . was named for the women-like dolls or idols supposedly found there."[13] A Spanish map of 1526-30 identifies an islet lying off the northwest tip of the "island" of Yucatán, as "Amazonas." A similar map shows both an islet of "Amazonas," and an "isla de mujeres," named Ciualtán (also spelled Cigualtán, Igualtán).[14]

In the North, the myth begins with Hernán Cortés, who sent out the exploring expedition that first landed in Baja California and who came to the peninsula himself in 1535. Cortés writes, in his fourth *Carta de relación* to the Catholic monarchs, "... he [Cristóbal de Olid] likewise brought me an account of the chiefs of the province of Ciguatán who affirm that there is an island inhabited only by women, without any men. . . and that this island is ten days travel from this province. . . ."[15]

Nuño de Guzmán, Cortés' bitter rival and sadistic explorer of Nueva Galicia, also competed to be the first to find the Amazons. In his letter-report, Guzman writes that: "From then [Azatlán] ten days further I shall go to find the Amazons which some say dwell in the sea, some in an arm of the sea, and that they are rich, and accounted of the people for goddesses, and whiter than other women. . . ."[16] Here, Guzman invokes Aztlán, the ancient homeland of the Aztecs, and skin color, both themes which I discuss in other essays.

Peter Martyr, who interviewed Juan de Rivera, Cortés' representative at the Royal Court in 1522, quotes Rivera's discussion about "a region inhabited only by women, in the mountains situated toward the North. . . [by] the name of Igualtán, which in the language of the country, means "region of women," from "iguatl," "woman" and "Lan," "Lord."[17] In his recounting, Martyr fixes the virgin-whore binary for American Amazons —noting that in one account the companies of women are reputedly a group of vestal virgins, and "a pack of harlot amazons" in another.[18]

Literary and historical fusions are evident in another stock female character from the chivalric novels, including *Las Sergas de Esplandián* and its multiple sequels, the *maga enamorada*—the enamored woman.[19] This deceiving, lustful woman uses magic and witchcraft to ensnare the hero—who, finding her neither attractive nor desirable, if not downright repellent, rejects her. Invariably, the *maga enamorada* is a pagan and most often, is Muslim. *La mora encantada,* the enticing Moorish enchantress, is but another representation of the lusting, complicitous, alien-female Other.[20]

Thus, the sexualization, eroticization, racialization, and devaluation of Indian women's bodies symbolized by the Malinche myth during the conquest of Mexico, is here seen within the discourse of the Crusades —the Reconquest of the Peninsula from Muslim rule that ended in 1492 —and of Christian orthodoxy of the Inquisition with its extirpation of the religious and racial Other.

In sixteenth-century Spain, black was a symbol for non-Christian. Calafia, as a non-Christian woman of dark skin and a politico-military-religious foe, is the consummate symbol of the alien "Other." These are political representations of women native to the contested land—the space of war, conquest, and nation building. In the Western imperial gaze, the women of the enemy, of the land under attack or conquest, are anxious to be delivered from their own men, to deliver themselves unto the conqueror, and to be complicit in the conquest.[21]

These politics inform the military-religious conquest and colonization of Alta California in the latter third of the eighteenth century. Though the myth of Calafia and the Amazons faded from the historical record, eventually to be replaced by the Malinche paradigm, the archival record documenting this conquest consistently constructs Indian women in sexual, erotic, and racial terms.[22]

Mexico's independence from Spain in 1821, and the liberalization of trade and colonization policies launched a new *entrada* (incursion), of single males—especially of Euro-American entrepreneurs, merchants, traders, and trappers—into the borderlands region (Alta California, Nuevo Mexico and Tejas).[23] Their arrival, and corollary discourse of U.S. political, national, and capitalist formation, set in motion a new wave of sexualized, eroticized and racialized representations of Californian Indian women, and of Californiana mestizas.

In Euro-American fiction, memoirs, historical documents, and interpretive histories of nineteenth-century California, Californianas, particularly those of landed families, appeared as anxious accomplices to the Euro-American takeover. Their greatest desire, according to Bancroft and echoed by Bolton, was to "marry a blue eyed stranger."[24] Thus, Californiana marriages to Euro-Americans have, until recently, been interpreted within the terms of one aspect of the Malinche *paradigm—traidoras, vendepatrias* (traitors) who gave themselves over to the conquest. While elite mestizas, or Californianas, were deracinated and represented as eagerly complicit with the conquering white males, non-elite mestizas were constructed as Mexican-Indian prostitutes, monte-dealers, and fandango-dancers in another battlefield, now between Catholicism and Protestantism.[25] They represented the other side of the Malinche paradigm—the "conquered," sexually, racially, and socially devalued Indian woman.

INDIA/MESTIZA BODIES: LA HISTORIA ENCARNADA

The arrival of Euro-Americans from the new Protestant nation initiated still another re-enactment of the ongoing ideological/epistemological contest in which native women's bodies were the battlefields. In Alta California the battle began in 1769, when, on arriving here, Spanish colonial authorities (church, military, colonial state), confronted the reality of Amerindian societies in which women not only controlled their own resources, sexuality, and reproductive processes, but also held religious, political, economic, and sometimes, military power.[26] The patriarchal church and state sought to eradicate native traditions that were centered on and controlled by women

In the confessional, priests queried both women and men about their sexual lives and activities and meted out punishment accordingly. While prohibitions against fornication, adultery, masturbation, sodomy, incest, bestiality, and coitus interruptus applied to all, abortion and infanticide—violations of the Fifth Commandment which condemned killing—applied specifically to women and were harshly punished.[27] Hugo Reid writes that the priests at Mission San Gabriel attributed all miscarriages to infanticide and that Gabrielino women were punished by "shaving the head, flogging for fifteen subsequent days, [wearing] iron on the feet for three months, and having to appear every Sunday in church, on the steps leading up the altar, with a hideous painted wooden child *(a monigote)* in her arms" representing the dead infant.[28]

The imperative to control and remake native sexuality, in particular to control women's procreation, was driven as much by material interest as by doctrinal issues. California needed a growing Hispanicized Indian population as both a source of labor and as a defense against foreign invasion, and thus missionaries might take extraordinary measures to assure reproduction.

Father Olbes at Mission Santa Cruz ordered an infertile couple to have sexual intercourse in his presence because he did not believe they could not have children. The couple refused, but Olbes forcibly inspected the man's penis to learn "whether or not it was in good order" and tried to inspect the woman's genitalia.[29] She refused, fought with him, and tried to bite him. Olbes ordered that she be tied by the hands, and given fifty lashes, shackled, and locked up in the *monjero* (women's dormitory). He then had a *monigote* made and commanded that she "treat the doll as though it were a child and carry it in the presence of everyone for nine days."[30] While this woman was beaten and her sexuality demeaned, the husband who had been intimate with another woman, was ridiculed and humiliated. A set of cow horns was tied to his head with leather thongs, thereby converting him into a "cuckhold," and he was "herded" to daily Mass in cow horns and fetters.[31]

Franciscan priests also prohibited initiation ceremonies, dances, and songs in the mission system. They sought to destroy the ideological, moral, and ethical systems that defined native life. They demonized non-complying women, especially those who resisted openly, as witches. Indeed, Ramón Gutiérrez argues that, in the borderlands of New Spain, "One can interpret the whole history of the persecution of Indian women as witches . . . as a struggle over [these] competing ways of defining the body and of regulating procreation as the church endeavored to constrain the expression of desire within boundaries that clerics defined proper and acceptable."[32]

Until recently, literary and historical writings about native women in California history, meaning Indias and mestizas, were informed by the Calafia and Malinche myths, and variations on this theme. More recently, cultural and oral historians, feminist theorists, religious scholars, and cultural critics, among others, are examining the daily lives of California Indian women.[33] They are, to quote feminist theorist Emma Pérez, "excavating words and their inherited meanings," digging in the silences, gaps, and interstitial spaces, of historical documents and other sources for the thoughts, words, actions and forms native women used in shaping multiple, complex, and changing identities across time and space."[34]

These works have concluded that while colonizing males constructed Indian women's bodies, both symbolically and materially, as a site to effect territorial and political conquest, women constructed and used their bodies, both symbolically and materially, as instruments of opposition, resistance, and subversion of colonial domination.[35] In California, as elsewhere in the Americas, indigenous women countered the everyday violence inflicted upon them with gender-centered strategies that authorized them to speak, to act, to lead, and to empower others. They fought the ideological power of the colonial church and state, which subordinated women to men and sought to control their bodies and their sexuality, with equally powerful ideologies that vested women with power and authority over their own sexuality.[36]

Accordingly, historian Nancy Shoemaker concludes that the central signifier of gender identity among native societies was the kind of work one performed. Religious scholars Inés Talamantes and Mary Rojas Muñoz analyze puberty ceremonies and ritual menstrual seclusion to theorize how Apache and Yurok women fit into the symbolic order of the sacred in their respective cultures.[37]

Native systems of gender included gender parallelism, matriarchal sociopolitical organization, and matrilineal forms of reckoning and descent. Some Indian societies had an institutionalized acceptance of gender variation, which scholars refer to as a third gender, or more commonly *berdache,* and which Native Americans refer to as "Two Spirit."[38] Within these diverse cultures, women's power and authority could derive from one or more elements: the culture's basic principle of individual autonomy that structured political relationships, including those between men and women; women's important productive or reproductive role in the economy; and the authority accorded women by their bearing and raising of children.[39] Further, women's power and authority were integral to, and also derived from, their people's core religious-spiritual beliefs, values, and traditions, which generally accorded women and men equivalent value, power, and range of practices.

As part of the natural world, sexuality, for many indigenous peoples, was related to the sacred and, as such, was central to the religious and cosmic order and was celebrated in song, dance, and other ritual observances. Accepted practices included premarital sexual activity, polygamy, polyandry, homosexuality, transvestitism, same-sex marriage, and ritual sexual practices. In general, consent, not contractual obligation, defined marriage, and divorce was easily attainable.[40]

Woman—the female principle—was a pivotal force in Native American origin stories, cosmologies, and world views. Woman, whether in the form of Grandmother, Thought Woman, White Buffalo Calf Woman, or other female being, was at the center of the originating principle that brought the people into being and sustained them. Muñoz recontextualizes the origin myth of the Yurok in which women "in payment for all the things that humans were going to gather from the land . . . offered to menstruate as a way of making payment for all the blood human beings were going to have to spill in order to feed the people."[41] Interpreting Apurowak ritual menstrual seclusion within the concept of balanced reciprocity and rites of reciprocity, Muñoz concludes that women chose self-isolation in order that they might shape the symbolic order established in the beginning. In doing so she calls up a new subject position that decenters Christian concepts of the body as base and vile, of menstruation as a signifier of societal ills, and corollary anthropological interpretations of the "menstrual taboo."[42]

TOYPURINA'S LINE: OPPOSITIONAL BODIES

Toypurina, the medicine woman of the Japchavit *ranchería,* used her power and authority to lead Gabrielino armed opposition to Spanish colonialism.[43] In 1785 she recruited 6 of the 8 villages that attacked mission San Gabriel, an attack she and two male companions organized and led. Toypurina, the other two leaders, and twenty other warriors were captured. After a three-year imprisonment at San Gabriel, in 1788 she was exiled to the far northern regions of Alta California to Mission San Carlos Borromeo. The twenty warriors captured with her were sentenced to between twenty and twenty-five lashes plus time already served. This punishment was levied as much for following the leadership of a woman as for rebelling against Spanish domination. Governor Pedro Fages stated that their public whippings were "to serve as a warning to all," for he would "admonish them about their ingratitude, underscoring their perversity, and unmasking the deceit and tricks by which *they allowed themselves to be dominated by the aforesaid woman"*[44] (emphasis added).

Toypurina's power and influence derived from a non-Western religious-political ideological system of power in which women were central to the ritual and spiritual life of the tribe.[45] California Indian women continued to resist colonial domination with a range of actions and activities, including a religious-political movement that vested power in a female deity and placed the health and well-being of the community in the hands of a female visionary.

In 1801, at the height of an epidemic ravaging the Chumash in the missions and the *rancherías,* a Chumash woman at Mission Santa Barbara launched a clandestine, large-scale revitalization movement.[46] Drawing her authority from visions and revelations from Chupu, the Chumash earth goddess or deity, this neophyte woman—who remains unnamed in the documents—called for a return to the worship of Chupu. Almost all the neophytes, Alcaldes included, went to the visionary's house to present beads and seeds and to go through the rite of renouncing Christianity.[47]

While historical documents portray both Toypurina and the Chumash visionary of 1801 as "witches and sorceresses"—and ecclesiastical and civil officials dismissed, discredited, exiled, or sometimes put to death non-white women charged with witchcraft—women themselves used witchcraft as a means of subverting the sociosexual order sanctioned by religion and enshrined in the colonial honor code as an ethical system.[48] Ruth Behar argues that women used sexualized magic to control men and subvert the male order by symbolically using their own bodies and bodily fluids as a source of power over men.[49]

Other women resisted in less visible, day-to-day practices: they poisoned the priests' food, practiced fugitivism, worshipped their own deities, had visions that others believed and followed, performed prohibited dances and rituals, and refused to abide by patriarchal sexual norms, as well as continued to participate in armed revolts and rebellions against the missions, soldiers, and *ranchos*.[50] Participants cited the priests' cruelty and repression of traditional ceremonies and sexual practices among primary reasons for the attacks on the missions, for the assassination of the friar Andres Quintana at Mission Santa Cruz in 1812, and for the great Chumash *levantamiento* of 1824.[51]

That colonialism, for all its brutal technologies and distorted narratives, could not completely destroy native women's historical autonomy is something native peoples have always known, but scholarly researchers are just beginning to learn.[52] Through oral and visual traditions, and other means of communicating counter-histories, native women's power, authority, and knowledge have remained part of their peoples' collective memory, historical reality, and daily struggles of "being in a state of war for five hundred years."[53] Tribal memory and what anthropologist Ana María Alonso terms "ideology of resistance based on social memory," preserve and reinscribe native women's subjectivity."[54] Elaborating the concept of third space feminism, subjectivity, and women of color, Chela Sandoval, in *Methodology of the Oppressed,* theorizes the state of being in resistance and opposition as a

> . . . mapping of consciousness. . . a topography of consciousness in opposition. . . [that] represents the charting of psychic and material realities that occupy a particular cultural region. This cultural topography delineates a set of critical points within which individuals and groups seeking to transform dominant and oppressive powers can constitute themselves as resistant and oppositional citizen-subjects![55]

Thus, Vera Rocha, a Gabrielino elder whom I interviewed in 1996, related how her own and other Gabrielino children's resistance to the educational systems' unrelenting efforts to de-Indianize them, led to their dropping out of school at very early ages.[56] Rocha, who lived the terrors of the federal government's post-World War II Indian policies, known as the "termination laws" of the Truman and Eisenhower administrations, had received the story of Toypurina and the Gabrielinos as a very young girl from her great-grandmother, who received it from her mother.[57] Rocha, in turn, transmitted the story to her children and grandchildren and, more recently, to the world in general in the form of a public monument—a prayer mound dedicated to Toypurina developed in conjunction with Chicana artist Judith F. Baca.[58] In preserving and retelling the history of Toypurina and her people, Rocha claims and embodies her "right to history," her authority and sources to claim and to speak come not from Western academic fronts.

> The Great Spirit has given me the right to say what comes through my ancestors. My genes are from my ancestors and on to my children . . . The history is coming through me ... That's why I honor Toypurina. Toypurina has given me the instrument to fight.

The histories remain archived in tribal, family, and individual memory, as well as in other texts—some written, most not. Drawing on literary, linguistic, and performance methodologies and theories, feminists and other scholars are learning to read and interpret the ways in which American Indian women, and their mestiza daughters, have constructed identities in daily opposition to assaults on their sexual, social, and cultural bodies within the gendered, sexualized, and racialized politics of colonial and nationalist domination and histories.

MALINCHE'S TONGUES

Let me return to Malintzín/Marina/Malinche/La Lengua, the young Mexican multilingual translator/diplomat who entered the Valley of Anahuac with Cortés in 1519–1521 and who bore Cortés's son.[59] Chicana scholars and writers, whose research and writing has re-membered Malintzín/Malinche since the early 1970s, have reclaimed this symbolic mother of mestizo peoples from the opprobrium of patriarchal Mexicano/Chicano history that condemned her sexuality, devalued and dismissed her as Cortés' "Indian whore."[60]

Most recently, linguist Frances Karttunen extends literary critic/Conchero dancer Inés Hernández's early discussion of Malintzín as the symbolic path-opener, the vanguard, the person in command who leads the way in "La danza de la Conquista," a reenactment in dance performed in native communities since the conquista itself.[61]

Karttunen examines the representation of Malintzín in codices, dance and other cultural representations. She draws on the long Mesoamerican tradition of two-headed and two-faced figures and the Aztec tradition of IXIPTLAYOTL, "representation," in which chosen human beings served as temporary embodiments of deities, providing them a conduit through which to speak and act in the world inhabited by humans, to rethink Malinche. Noting that much has been made of the notion that the indigenous peoples perceived the Europeans as Gods, she inverts the position of deity—or representation of deity (European and male)—and argues that the Aztecs may have perceived Malintzín/the interpreter as an IXIPTLA of a supernatural force. Faced with circumstances unlike any other in the history of her people, Malintzín/Malinche, here interpreted as the embodiment of a IXIPTLA, used the language and skills she needed to live each day, performing her role to perfection.[62]

CONCLUSION

Having gone unspoken and unthought in Borderlands historiography until very recently, to recover, claim and re-member the historical bodies of Indias y Mestizas is critical to researching, writing, and interpreting Chicana history. As recent scholarship reveals, Native Women's bodies —their gender, race, and sexuality—are pivotal to the politics, policies, and cultures of colonialism, nationalism, and transnationalism—from the basic core of family life to contemporary structures of globalization.[63] We need only to read the politics and policies of gender, sexuality, and reproduction in the 1996 immigration law and in the draconian "Welfare" reform measures of 1996-1997 to know the contemporary significance of these politics and policies. The horrendously brutal unsolved murders of over three hundred Mexican women, and disappearance of over five hundred, on the U.S.-Mexico border—most of whom worked in the U.S.-owned *maquiladoras* (assembly plants)—tells us that Malinche's daughters can still be viciously raped, sexually tortured, mutilated, and killed with impunity.[64] It tells the world that young, poor, brown-skinned Mexican women have no value. The sexual nature and utter viciousness of these murders is, I argue, part of a historical continuum of unrelenting sexualized violence against Indian/Mestiza on the Spanish/Mexican/U.S. borderlands from the sixteenth century to the present.[65]

It is within these historical and contemporary contexts that we historicize, analyze, theorize, and interpret the gendered, racialized, and sexualized meanings of oft-heard exhortations, "péinate, que pareces India;" "arréglate que te tienen por India." It is from historical memory of Malinche and Toypurina among countless others, and examination of how native women have deployed their bodies across time, space, condition, and location, that we reconstitute the female body and knowledge of history. It is from knowledge of native women's resistance that Chicanas affirm their oppositional legacy and refuse familial and others' exhortations to disavow our India/Malinche selves with "Si mamá somos!" Or, in Chicano Spanish, "Si mamá semos!"

NOTES

1. Antonia I. Castañeda, "Sexual Politics in the Politics and Policies of Conquest: Amerindian Women and the Spanish Conquest of Alta California," eds. Adela de la Torre and Beatriz M. Pesquera, *Building with Our Hands: New Directions in Chicana Studies* (Berkeley: University of California Press, 1993) 15-33.

2. Virginia Marie Bouvier, *Women and the Conquest of California, 1542-1840: Codes of Silence* (Tucson: U of Arizona P, 2001); Richard C. Trexler, *Sex and Conquest: Gendered Violence, Political Order and the European Conquest of the Americas* (Ithaca: Cornell UP, 1995); Louis Montrose, "The Work of Gender in the Discourse of Discovery," *New World Encounters*, ed. Stephen Greenblatt (Berkeley, Los Angeles, London: University of California Press, 1993), 177-217.

3. Deena J. González, "Lupe's Song: On the Origins of Mexican/Woman-Hating in the United States," in *Race in 21st Century America*, eds. Curtis Stokes, Theresa Meléndez, Genice Rhodes-Reed (East Lansing: Michigan State University Press, 2001) 143-158; Inés Hernández-Avila, "An Open Letter to Chicanas: On the Power and Politics of Origin," *Without Discovery: A Native Response to Columbus*, ed. Ray Gonzales (Seattle: Broken Moon P, 1992), 153-166; Norma Alarcón, "Chicana Feminism: In the Tracks of 'The' Native Woman," *Cultural Studies*, 4-3, (October, 1990): 248-256; Gloria Anzaldúa, *Borderlands/La Frontera: The New Mestiza* (San Francisco: Aunt Lute Press, 1987).

4. Chéla Sandoval, *Methodology of the Oppressed* (Minneapolis and London: University of Minnesota Press, 2000); Deena J. González, *Refusing the Favor: The Spanish-Mexican Women of Santa Fe, 1820-1880* (New York, Oxford: Oxford UP, 1999): Deena J. González, "Juanotilla of Cochin, Vecina and Coyota: Nuevomexicanas in the Eighteenth Century," *New Mexican Lives: Profiles and Historical Stories*, ed. Richard Etualain (Albuquerque: University of New Mexico Press, 2002); Teresa de Lauretis, *Technologies of Gender: Essays on Theory, Film, and Fiction* (Bloomington: Indiana UP, 1987); Rosaura Sánchez, *Telling Identities: The Califomio Testimonios* (Minneapolis: University of Minnesota Press, 1995).

5. For feminist theories of the body and subjectivity, see: Barbara Brook, *Feminist Perspectives on the Body* (London and New York: Longman, 1999); Radhika Mohanram, *Black Body: Women, Colonialism and Space*

(Minneapolis and London: University of Minnesota Press, 1999); Janet Price and Margrit Shildrick, eds., *Feminist Theory and the Body: A Reader* (New York and London: Routledge, 1999); Paula M. Cooey, *Religious Imagination and the Body: A Feminist Analysis* (New York and Oxford: Oxford UP, 1994); Elizabeth Grosz, *Volatile Bodies: Toward a Corporeal Feminism* (Bloomington and Indianapolis: Indiana UP, 1994); Elizabeth Grosz, "Bodies and Knowledges: Feminism and the Crisis of Reason," in *Feminist Epistemologies,* eds. Linda Alcoff and Elizabeth Potter (New York, London: Routledge, 1993): 187-216.

6. Emma Pérez, *The Decolonial Imaginary: Writing Chicanas into History* (Bloomington: Indiana UP, 1999); Linda Tuhiwai Smith, *Decolonizing Methodologies: Research and Indigenous Peoples* (New York and London: Zed Books Ltd., 1999); Florencia E. Mallon, "The Promise and Dilemma of Subaltern Studies: Perspectives from Latin American History," *American Historical Review* 99 (1994): 1491-1515; "Founding Statement: Latin American Subaltern Studies Group," *Boundary* 2, 20 (Fall 1993): 110-21; Hernández-Ávila, "Open Letter to Chicanas"; Jack D. Forbes, *Aztecas del Norte: The Chicanos of Aztlán* (Greenwich, CT: Fawcett Publications, 1973). For discussion of Latinos and indigenous identity relative to the 2000 US Federal Manuscript Census, see: Jack D. Forbes, "2000 Census Will Effect All Persons of Pre-Columbian American Ancestry," and Patrisia Gonzales and Roberto Rodríguez, "On the Census of Being," *Column of the Americas,* 15 October 1999 Xcolumn@aol.com.

7. The myth of Calafia is related in *Las Sergas de Esplandián,* whose author is sometimes identified as Garcí or García Ordóñez de Montalvo and at other times as Garcí or García Rodríguez de Montalvo. See Garcí Ordóñez de Montalvo, *Las Segos Del Muy Esforzado Caballeo Esplandián,* in *Biblioteca de autores españoles, Libros De caballerías,* Don Pascual de Gayangos, ed., vol. 40 (1857; reprint, Madrid: M Rivadeneyra, 1874/1880): 403-561. In this essay, which uses English translations, the author of *Las Sergas de Esplandián* is referred to as Garcí Ordóñez de Montalvo when I cite Dora Beale Polk, *The Island of California: A History of the Myth* (Spokane: The Arthur H. Clark Company, 1991); Irving I. Leonard, whom I also cite, identifies the author of as Garcí Rodríguez de Montalvo, see Irving A. Leonard, *Books of the Brave: Being an Account of Books and of Men in the Spanish Conquest and Settlement of the Sixteenth Century New World* (1949; Berkeley, Los Angeles: University of California Press, 1992). See also Irving Leonard, *Romances of Chivalry in the Spanish Indies* (Berkeley: University of California Press, 1933). See also, Bouvier, 3-17.

8. Leonard, *Books of the Brave*, 38-41. For sustained discussion of medieval mythology and the conquest of the Americas, see Luis Weckmann, *The Medieval Heritage of Mexico*, trans. Frances M. Lopez-Morillas (New York: Fordham UP, 1992), 46-71.
9. Weckmann, 51.
10. Weckmann 46-7; María Helena Sánchez-Ortega, "Woman as a Source of 'Evil' in Counter-Reformation Spain," Anne J. Cruz and Mary Elizabeth Perry, eds. *Culture and Control in Counter-Reformation Spain, Hispanic Issues 7* (Minneapolis: University of Minnesota Press, 1992). I draw upon feminist film criticism for the concept and term "the monstrous feminine." See Barbara Creed, *The Monstrous Feminine: Film, Feminism, Psychoanalysis* (New York: Routledge, 1993). For feminist theories of the body, see Note 5.
11. Ordóñez de Montalvo, 554-56.
12. Irving Leonard used this term to refer to the chivalric novels, or books of fiction, with which Christopher Columbus, Hernán Cortés, Bartolomé de las Casas, and their contemporaries would have been familiar as they stepped ashore in the "New World." See, Leonard, *Books of the Brave*, xlii–xlvii.
13. As quoted in Polk, *The Island of California*, 77.
14. Polk, 78.
15. As quoted in Leonard, *Books of the Brave*, 48-49.
16. As quoted in Polk, 93.
17. Polk, 83.
18. Polk, 78.
19. For gender theory and interpretation of the image of women in the novels of chivalry, most particularly non-Christian women, see Judith Whitenack, "Don Quijote y La Maga: Otra Mujer Que `No Parece,'" ed. Juan Villegas, *La Mujer y su representación en las literaturas hispánicas, Actas Irvine-92: Asociación Internacional de Hispanistas* (Irvine: Regents of the University of California Press, 1994): 82-96; Judith Whitenack, "Conversion to Christianity in the Spanish Romance of Chivalry, 1490-1524," *Journal of Hispanic Philology* 13 (Autumn, 1988): 13-39. For discussion of medieval mythology and the conquest of the Americas, see Weckmann 46-71.
20. George Mariscal, "The Role of Spain in Contemporary Race Theory," *Arizona Journal of Hispanic Cultural Studies* 2 (1998): 7-22.
21. For a discussion of native women (California Indian and Mestiza women) and the issue of complicity in eighteenth and nineteenth century Califor-

nia, see: Antonia I. Castañeda, "Gender, Race, and Culture: Spanish-Mexican Women in the Historiography of Frontier California," *Frontiers: A Journal of Women Studies* XI (1990): 8-20; Antonia I. Castañeda, "The Political Economy of Nineteenth Century Stereotypes of Californianas," ed. Adelaida R. Del Castillo *Between Borders: Essays on Mexicana/ Chicano History* (Los Angeles: Floricanto, 1990): 213-236.

22. Antonia I. Castañeda, "Sexual Violence in the Politics and Policies of Conquest: Amerindian Women and the Spanish Conquest of Alta California," eds. Adela de la Torre and Beatriz M. Pesquera, *Building with Our Hands: New Directions in Chicana Studies* (Berkeley, London, Los Angeles: University of California Press, 1993): 15-33.

23. For nineteenth-century New Mexico and California, respectively, see: González, *Refusing the Favor,* and Sánchez, *Telling Identities.*

24. Castañeda, "Spanish Mexican Women in the Historiography of California."

25. Castañeda, "The Political Economy of Nineteenth Century Stereotypes of Californianas."

26. Weckmann, 49-50; Antonia I. Castañeda, "Engendering the History of Alta California, 1769-1848: Gender, Sexuality, and the Family," eds. Ramón A. Gutiérrez and Richard J. Orsi, *Contested Eden: California before the Gold Rush* (Berkeley: University of California Press, for The California Historical Society, 1997), 230-259.

27. Harry Kelsey, ed., *The Doctrina and Confesionario of Juan Cortés* (Altadena, CA: Howling Coyote, 1979), 112-16, 120-23; Madison S. Beeler, ed., *The Ventureno Confesionario of José Senan, O. EM., U of California Publication in Linguistics* 47 (Berkeley: University of California Press, 1967), 37-63.

28. As quoted in Castañeda, "Engendering," 234-356.

29. Castañeda, "Engendering," 235.

30. As quoted in Edward D. Castillo, "The Native Response to the Colonization of Alta California," Edward D. Castillo, ed., *Native American Perspectives on the Hispanic Colonization of Alta California, Spanish Borderlands Sourcebook 26* (New York: Garland, 1991), 426; Edward D. Castillo, "Introduction," Castillo, ed., *Native American Perspectives on the Hispanic Colonization of Alta California,* xvii–xlv.

31. Bouvier, 127-28.

32. Ramón A. Gutiérrez, "Sexual Mores and Behavior: The Spanish Borderlands," Jacob Ernest Cooke, et. al., eds., *Encyclopedia of the North Amer-*

ican Colonies, vol. 2 (New York: Charles Scribner's Sons, 1993): 700-710. Quote is from 701.

33. See Greg Sarris, *Mabel McKay: Weaving the Dream* (Berkeley: University of California Press, 1994); Greg Sarris, *Keeping Slug Woman Alive: A Holistic Approach to American Indian Texts* (Berkeley: University of California Press, 1993); Greg Sarris, "'What I'm Talking about When I'm Talking about My Baskets: Conversations with Mabel McKay," Sidonie Smith and Julia Watson, eds. *De/Colonizing the Subject: The Politics of Gender in Women's Autobiography* (Minneapolis: University of Minnesota Press, 1992); Castillo, Victoria Brady, Sarah Crome, and Lyn Reese, "Resist! Survival Tactics of Indian Women," *California History* 63 (Spring 1984).

34. Perez, xviii.

35. Castañeda, "Engendering" 237.

36. See Laura F. Klein and Lillian A. Ackerman, eds., *Women and Power in Native North America* (Norman: University of Oklahoma Press, 1995); Nancy Shoemaker, ed., *Negotiators of Change: Historical Perspectives on Native American Women* (New York: Routledge, 1995); Kevin Gosner and Deborah E. Kanter, eds., *Women, Power, and Resistance in Colonial Mesoamerica*, spec. issue of *Ethnohistory* 42 (Fall 1995); Carol Devens, *Countering Colonization: Native American Women in the Great Lakes Missions, 1630-1900* (Berkeley: University of California Press, 1992); Gretchen M. Bataille and Kathleen Mullen Sands, eds., *American Indian Women: Telling Their Lives* (Lincoln: University of Nebraska Press, 1984); Beatrice Medicine and Patricia Albers, eds., *The Hidden Half: Studies of Plains Indian Women* (Lanham: University of America Press, 1983).

37. Shoemaker; Inés Talamantez, "Images of the Feminine in Apache Religious Tradition," *After Patriarchy: Feminist Transformations of the World Religions*, eds. William R. Eakin, et. al. (Orbis Books, 1991) 131-145; Mary Virginia Rojas Muñoz, "'She Bathes in a Sacred Place': Rites of Reciprocity, Scratching Sticks and Prestige in Alta California," MA thesis, U of Santa Barbara, 1997.

38. Sabine Lang, *Men as Women, Women as Men: Changing Gender in Native American Cultures* (Austin: UT Press, 1998).

39. Klein and Ackerman, see especially Klein and Ackerman's introduction and essays by Victoria D. Patterson, Mary Shepardson, Sue-Ellen Jacobs, and Daniel Maltz and JoAllyn Archambault; Shoemaker, especially Shoemaker's introduction, and essays by Lucy Eldersveld Murphy

and Carol Douglas Sparks; Gosner and Kanter, especially the essays by Alvis E. Dunn, Martha Few, and Irene Silverblatt.

40. Antonia I. Castañeda, "Marriage: The Spanish Borderlands," *Encyclopedia of the North American Colonies,* eds. Jacob Ernest Cooke, et al., 3 vols. (New York: Charles Scribner's Sons, 1993), 2:727-38.

41. Muñoz, 18-19.

42. Muñoz.

43. "Ynterrogatorio sobre la sublevación de San Gabriel, 10 octubre de 1785," Archivo General de la Nación, Provincias Internas, tomo I (Californias): 120, Microfilm Collection, Bancroft Library, Berkeley, California; See also, Castañeda, "Engendering," 235-238.

44. "Ynterrogatorio."

45. Alvis E. Dunn, "A Cry at Daybreak: Death, Disease, and Defense of Community in a Highland Ixil-Mayan Village," and Martha Few, "Women, Religion, and Power: Gender and Resistance in Daily Life in Late-Seventeenth-Century Santiago de Guatemala," *Women, Power; and Resistance in Colonial Mesoamerica,* spec. issue *Ethnohistory,* eds. Gosner and Kanter, 595-606 and 627-637, respectively.

46. Robert F. Heizer, "A California Messianic Movement of 1801 among the Chumash," *American Anthropologist* 43 (1941, reprint, 1962): 128-29; Dunn, "A Cry at Daybreak." For discussion of the warrior woman tradition, women's councils, religion, and spirituality as a source of women's power and resistance, and of women's cultural mediation and resistance in Native American history, see Elizabeth Salas, *Soldaderas in the Mexican Military* (Austin: UT Press, 1990), 1-10; Clara Sue Kidwell, "Indian Women as Cultural Mediators," *Ethnohistory* 39 (Spring 1992): 97-107; Beatrice Medicine, "'Warrior Women'—Sex Role Alternatives for Plains Indian Women," *The Hidden Half,* eds., Medicine and Albers, 267-80.

47. Heizer, "Chumash visionary."

48. Antonia I. Castañeda, "Witchcraft on the Spanish-Mexican Borderlands," *The Reader's Companion to US Women's History,* eds. Wilma Mankiller, et al. (New York: Houghton Mifflin Company, 1998), 638-39; Ruth Behar, "Sexual Witchcraft, Colonialism, and Women's Power: Views from the Mexican Inquisition," *Sexuality and Marriage in Colonial Latin America,* ed. Lavrin, 178-206; Ruth Behar, "Sex and Sin, Witchcraft, and the Devil in Late Colonial Mexico," *American Ethnologist* 14 (February 1987): 344-54; Ruth Behar, "The Visions of a Guachichil Witch in 1599: A Window on the Subjugation of Mexico's Hunter-Gatherers," *Ethnohistory* 34 (Spring 1987): 115-38; see also Solange Alberro, "Herejes, brujas, y

beatas: Mujeres ante el Tribunal del Santo Oficio de la Inquisición en la Nueva España," *Presencia y transparencia,* ed. Escandón, 79-94; Henry Kamen, *Inquisition and Society in Spain in the Sixteenth and Seventeenth Century* (Bloomington: Indiana University Press, 1985); Henry Kamen, "Notes on Witchcraft, Sexuality, and the Inquisition," *The Spanish Inquisition and the Inquisitorial Mind* ed. Angel Alcala (Boulder: Social Science Monographs, 1987), 237-47; Sánchez-Ortega, "Woman as a Source of 'Evil' in Counter-Reformation Spain," *Culture and Control in Counter-Reformation Spain;* Marc Simmons, *Witchcraft in the Southwest: Spanish and Indian Supernaturalism on the Rio Grande* (Lincoln: University of Nebraska Press, 1980).

49. Behar, "Sexual Witchcraft, Colonialism, and Women's Power."

50. Bouvier, 133-39; Edward D. Castillo, trans. and ed., "The Assassination of Padre Andres Quintana by the Indians of Mission Santa Cruz in 1812: The Narrative of Lorenzo Asisara," *California History* 68 (Fall 1989): 117-25; Edward D. Castillo, "Introduction" and "The Native Response to the Colonization of Alta California," in ed. Castillo, *Native American Perspectives on the Hispanic Colonization of Alta California,* xvii-xlv and 423-40; Antonia I. Castañeda, "Comparative Frontiers: The Migration of Women to Alta California and New Zealand," *Western Women: Their Land, Their Lives,* eds. Lilian Schlissel, Vicki L. Ruiz, and Janice Monk (Albuquerque: University of New Mexico Press, 1988) 283-300, especially 292-94; James Sandos, "Levantamiento! The 1824 Chumash Uprising," *The Californians* 5 (January-February 1987): 8-11; Bruce Walter Barton, *The Tree at the Center of the World: A Study of the California Missions* (Santa Barbara: Ross-Erickson Publications, 1980), 185; Sherburne F. Cook, *Conflict between the California Indian and White Civilization* (Berkeley, Los Angeles: University of California Press, 1976), 56-90.

51. Sandos.

52. Greg Sarris, "What I'm Talking about When I'm Talking about My Baskets."

53. Paula Gunn Allen, *Spider Women's Granddaughters: Traditional Tales and Contemporary Writing by Native American Women* (New York: Fawcett Columbine, 1989), 2.

54. Alonso, 7.

55. Sandoval, 53.

56. Vera Rocha, personal interview, 5 July 1996.

57. Laurence M. Hauptman, "Congress, Plenary Power, and the American Indian, 1870 to 1992," *Exiled in the Land of the Free: Democracy, Indian*

Nations, and the US Constitution, eds. Oren Lyons, et al. (Santa Fe: Clear Light Publishers, 1992), 318-36.

58. Judith F. Baca, personal interview, 8 October 1995.

59. Sandra Messinger Cypess, *La Malinche in Mexican Literature: From History to Myth* (Austin: University of Texas Press, 1991).

60. Cordelia Candelaria, "La Malinche, Feminist Prototype," *Chicana Leadership: The Frontiers Reader,* eds. Yolanda Flores Niemann, et al. (Lincoln and London: University of Nebraska Press, 2002) 1-14; Deena J. González, "Malinche as Lesbian," *Culture and Conflict in the Academy: Testimonies from the War Zone,* 14 spec. issue *California Sociologist,* (Winter/Summer 1991): 90-97; Adelaida R. Del Castillo, "Malintzín Tenepal: A Preliminary Look into a New Perspective," in *Essays on La Mujer,* eds. Rosaura Sánchez and Rosa Martínez Cruz, (University of California: Chicano Studies Center Publications, 1977) 124-149; Hernández-Ávila, "Open Letter to Chicanas"; Alarcón, "Chicana Feminism: In the Tracks of 'The' Native Woman," *Cultural Studies;* Anzaldúa, *Borderlands/La Frontera.* For an excellent cross-section of Chicana poets writing on Malinche, see: Lucha Corpi, "Marina," Carmen Tafolla, "La Malinche," Angela de Hoyos "La Malinche a Cortez y Vice Versa/La Malinche to Cortez and Vice Versa," Margarita Cota-Cárdenas, "Malinche's Discourse," Erlinda Gonzales-Berry, "Malinche Past: Selection from Paletitas de guayaba," Alicia Gaspar de Alba, "Malinchista, A Myth Revised," *Infinite Divisions: An Anthology of Chicano Literature,* eds. Tey Diana Rebolledo & Eliana S. Rivero (Tucson: University of Arizona Press, 1993).

61. Frances Karttunen, *Between Worlds: Interpreters, Guides, and Survivors* (New Brunswick: Rutgers UP, 1994) 1-22; Hernández-Ávila, "Open letter to Chicanas."

62. Karttunen, *Between Worlds.*

63. See notes 1-3.

64. For recent coverage of the unsolved murders of Mexican women of the US-Mexico border, see Ginger Thompson, "Wave of Women's Killings Confounds Juárez," *The New York Times,* 10 December 2002: A1 and A14.

65. For a discussion of sexual violence in eighteenth- and nineteenth-century California, see: Castañeda, "Sexual Violence and the Politics of Conquest: Amerindian Women and the Spanish Conquest of Alta California"; Bouvier, *Women and the Conquest of California;* Albert Hurtado, *Intimate Frontiers: Sex, Gender, and Culture in Old California* (Albuquerque: University of New Mexico Press, 1999); Clifford E. Trafzer and Joel R. Hyer, eds. *Exterminate Them!: Written Accounts of the Murder,*

Rape, and Enslavement of Native Americans during the California Gold Rush (East Lansing: Michigan State UP, 1999).

EL CUERPO Y EL BAILE

THE BODY AS SITE OF KNOWLEDGE
WITH DRS. ANTONIA CASTAÑEDA
AND LUZ MARÍA GORDILLO

When the hop harvest was over, we'd lived seven months there, the boys had gotten sick, I'd gotten pneumonia and had to go to the doctor. Well— with the fright we'd had on the road, we didn't feel like returning [to Texas] and we decided to stay in Washington. The work ended in Brownstown and we came to Toppenish. Then we went to live at the Golding hop farm— this was made up of rows of shacks—without doors and all falling apart— there was only a wall between the next unit where another person lived. The houses weren't insulated—they didn't have floors, and we worked in the hop. They paid us women $.75 per hour and $.85 for the men.[1]

Irene Castañeda, "Personal Chronicle of Crystal City."[2]

Figure 1. Drs. Antonia Castañeda and Luz María Gordillo, San Antonio, TX 2011.

Courtesy of Luz María Gordillo

Out in the empty fields near Crystal City and in front of recording devices, Castañeda recreated movements that as a young woman she repeatedly performed while picking potatoes. Dr. Castañeda's anachronistic "danza del jale," her rhythmically graceful though punishing movements, represented a sense of dignity and accomplishment of the body as well as a sense of sensuality and sexuality—the miracle of a gendered social, cultural and political resistance.

When I conducted the interview "El Cuerpo y El Baile," Dr. Castañeda and I had already engaged in discussions about the body and its movement while working in the fields and living at the camps. Neither one of us knew exactly how the conversation and interview would develop, but we knew it was important. Castañeda had been working with different concepts regarding the body and knowledge for some time while I was working with transnational sexualities that included experiences of working class Mexicanas in the United States.

Both of us felt it was important that we did not exoticize the fields and diminish or minimize the intensity and exploitative impacts of the labor; but on the other hand we needed to recognize the influence that field labor camp life had on the body itself and on the experience of growing up. Castañeda was able to articulate and theorize experiences of the body and labor; throughout the interview we were able to break this down and analyze it together. Such crossroads—of body, theory and knowledge— make historians of color hesitate as they negotiate with archival work, memories, facts and experiential images in order to write history that is fair to the subjects of that history but also theoretically clear for those who have been biased, and rendered Chicanas/os' experiences invisible in U.S. mainstream narratives. This is an interview at those crossroads.

Abject living conditions, unfair wage practices, gender and racial discrimination, health problems and no health care, lack of access to formal education, and constant physically punishing work however, were everyday components of a larger context of Tejanas/os lives. These threatening terrains and spaces also represented home and family, community and history. Resistance and personal struggles recreated tales of strength, community formation, and love; resistance and personal struggles also brought respect and love for the land where all of these bodies converged to work and to share in the construction of migrant worker communities.

LMG: Let's talk about how, on the one hand, working in the fields was terribly punishing. And on the other, you experienced a sense of fluidness in the body—a sense of freedom, a sense of touching the earth with your hands, a sense of connection.

AC: The fields... I was going to say particularly the row crops, but actually all of the crops, whether they were row crops; hops, which are on vines; or orchards, although we didn't work a lot on orchards, in the early years. Farm labor is very hard punishing work, like all things in this society, it is also hierarchical with respect to Mexicans and Anglos. So when we got to Eastern Washington, the orchard [workers] were, at that point, principally Anglos—Euro-Americans, at least where we were. In other parts of Washington, like the Okanagan, Native Americans were the earliest orchard workers. The issue is that orchard work does not require one to stoop; it is not stoop labor.

When I think about the fields, I think about, on the one hand, very hard work, punishing work, if you will. But the fields were also an incredible universe: a universe of learning, a universe of understanding, a universe of exploration and imagination. Those contradictory realities were ever-present for us. Sometimes we were able to think about it and to focus on it, and sometimes we just lived it. It took me a while to understand, but eventually I did and came to appreciate my body and what it did, how it functioned, how it moved, and how it worked.

The fields and that punishing hard work also made us very conscious and very aware of our bodies, of our physical beings because that was what we used, that was our tool—that was our instrument: our legs and our hands and our knees, our spine, our neck, our head. So it was a whole universe, not only of learning, but a universe of being. So yes, the fields were a physically taxing space. We came out of those fields dragging, sometimes crawling, and sometimes the work involved literally crawling—or if not crawling on your hands and knees then moving on your knees, kind of walking on your knees and moving from plant to plant, depending on what crop you're working .

As a woman, as a young woman, as a teenager, I realized—I don't know as I was really thinking about it per se, but I came to a realization that working in the fields, or what I did in that physical labor, also became the basis for appreciating my body and its ability to work very hard. That hard work also taught me how to push my body; we learned how far it would go and its strength and its endurance and its power. That knowledge, or understanding, became the basis for moving through space— for moving through space in the fields, in the camp where we lived, but also on the dance floor.

And so, we danced with a kind of freedom of movement and ease, we were at ease with our bodies and later, as I thought about it, that was not only a basis for an appreciation of your physical being, but also of your sexual being. I think of that movement, and although I didn't think about it at the time, there was a freedom with one's body that was not acceptable and was not accepted by Euro-American society.... I'm working on an essay about the body in that regard. Not just as a body that labors, but as a body—your laboring body—as a basis of learning about your body and learning about movement and moving through space— it's an energy. Not just a field of energy, but it becomes energy itself.

I comment that there are elements of sensuality and sexuality in labor —at least there were for me. It was in the fields that I first became aware of my sexual self. A confession that I've certainly never made publicly or ever told anybody: I was just working, in the hops, and from one moment to the next, there was an orgasm, and I didn't know what was happening. I must have been thirteen. It was a particular movement of legs and hips, maybe dragging myself along to the next plant. Though I did not know what it was, I somehow understood I was not to talk about it.

So one learns, it's a universe of learning—and how could we not learn? We experienced and daily saw life and death in the fields. It wasn't just life and death of the plants, the crops we were working—certainly it was that because there is a seasonal cycle; you plant the crop, whatever it is, whether tomatoes, potatoes, hops, or anything else. They grow, ripen, and die as you perform the work cycle of planting, irrigating, weeding, pruning, and harvesting.We not only saw the plants, we also saw animals: birds, rodents, spiders, bugs, insects, bees and so we were aware of all kinds of life in the fields—not just our lives, and the lives of plants, but we also saw the lives of other entities that were present. That universe was very important to my formation and to who I am;

I believe it was important to the formation of all of us who worked in the fields, who did farm labor.

At the same time, it was punishing work and it was exploitative work in many respects. And Mexican workers, field workers, were needed but not wanted. I've written about how, when we came in flatbed trucks from the camps into town to buy groceries or to go to the park, Euro-Americans in town looked at us with fearful eyes, sometimes with disdain —actually a lot with disdain.[3] So it was complex. I don't romanticize it. There was nothing romantic about it. But it was certainly a place of learning, a universe, a university, if you will, that provided what I've come to understand is a world of depth. I am only now having the time to go back and examine and explore that. But I'm particularly interested in how work also became the basis for our understanding, or at least the basis for our moving through space and occupying space. And I didn't know it at the time, but that —not so much understanding —that being, just that sense of being and that sense of movement and that sense of freedom of movement [was part of the understanding].

Working in the fields, as I've said, gave me, at least, and the women in the community that raised me, a flexibility and a freedom of movement, and an ease. I was at ease with my body. I liked my body. I still do. Those are all elements that I'm now beginning to not only think about but to talk about and to begin to write about. There is much there and I'm very grateful for that experience. I can now appreciate it. At the same time, it was punishing work and we were very aware that we worked the land, and that the land was not ours. And I was also equally aware that the owners needed our labor but did not want our presence in their world; one could not help but be aware, and it also became the basis, for what I subsequently studied and wrote.

LMG: You said that when you danced, you danced with freedom. Take me back to you getting ready for one of these dances. I want to hear the conversation again.

AC: So we're out in the fields and it's late afternoon and we're sweating like crazy. We're dripping. We covered our head with a bandana, and a hat on top to protect the face and head from the sun because we didn't want to get sunstroke. So we're dripping wet, if it's the middle of June, as it can get very very warm—up to 110 degrees in the middle of overgrown fields. And so we're hurrying like crazy and probably cutting the plants as well as weeds, if we're weeding, in order to get to the dance because we all want to go to the dance.

We're living in the camp and there are communal showers just like there are outdoor toilets. There is a communal water faucet that's a bit of a distance from the particular cabin, or long house, that we live in. So everybody—the women in particular (the men, I'm sure are having their own conversations) but our conversations as teenagers, was about who we were going to dance with con aquel o "no voy a bailar con él porque andaba con ella," y "que te vas a poner." "y no tienes hair spray." So these were the conversations as we were getting ready to go and then we would tease each other about being in such a hurry that we didn't even want to take the time to shower. We were just going to put "Tabu" on ourselves and go. Tabu was this very stinky kind of perfume, real cheap in a blue bottle, I think in a heart-shaped bottle. We were just very happy to have a dance to go to.

We are getting ready and going to the shower ... and the communal shower is also the communal lavandería (laundry room) because, in addition to the shower, there are sinks. The sinks are ridged in the front, where you bend into the sink, so that you can scrub clothes—and big faucets. And then we go and presumably by the time we've showered we have ironed our dresses and all of those crinolines that are starched beyond belief and they pouf-out the skirt. And we go to the dance. I'm allowed mainly to go to wedding dances. It is rare that my parents, specifically my father, allow me to go to the other dances, which are the dances where people pay to get in, like a cover charge.

This is the 50s, so ... la música ... more than the boleros, it is usually the polkas, the polquitas that we dance. Dancing, obviously is another kind of movement. The unspoken protocol of the arena is that everybody dances in the same direction. But sometimes, if you get a little charge with music, sometimes going the opposite direction you bump into people. So the dances are a joy and a release, where we are able to move in ways different from how we move in the field. They are related but also different movements. And so it's all my friends and their mothers and sometimes their fathers, but the girls usually go with their mothers. And there's lots of talking and lots of looking at the dancing partners. And sometimes, if there are no male partners, and even if there are, we dance with each other. The point is to dance. The point is to move. The point is to be in sync and on rhythm with the music that is being played. And the source of that music is Tejas, and Tejas is home. So the dance is about our movements. It's about enjoyment. It's about geography. It's about flirting. It's about engaging with other people—with other girls and their mothers, in particular. It's about learning to be sociable. Portarse bien o mal—in a family in a communal setting.

But it is also about moving out of spaces of oppression and exploitation and difficulties. So the dances create those spaces for us. Or we create those spaces for ourselves in the dancing. So, for me, the memories of that period and of dancing are very, very important precisely because it was a realm in which we could be who we were and move in the way that pleased us and that mattered to us. And it is interesting to think about it now because actually the reality is that the dances were usually held at the roller rink that was no longer in use so the cement was all cracked and the walls were—re-thinking it, it was probably a shabby place or would have been considered a shabby place. But for us it was as elegant as any elegant ballroom. It could be because it was ours and because we were dancing. So it's a whole other universe. And it's a rhythm. Some of the rhythms were transported from where we were working—from our work, but we also developed other movements of body.

Figure 2. Dr. Castañeda in Crystal City at the Mexican Cemetery, 2011.

Photograph courtesy of Luz María Gordillo

NOTES

1. In his essay "Braceros in the Pacific Northwest: Laborers on the Domestic Front, 1942-1947," Erasmo Gamboa narrates how workers were systematically exploited by growers who provided inhumane working conditions with deplorable wages so much so that some workers went on strike in 1947 "because [in Walla Walla, Washington] over a twelve-day period they had grossed between $4.16 and $8.33." Cutting asparagus on a piece rate basis and received $.75 for digging ditches ten hours a day. Erasmo Gamboa "Braceros in the Pacific Northwest: Laborers on the Domestic Front, 1942-1947," *Pacific Historical Review* 56, no. 3 (August 1987): 397.

2. Antonia Castañeda, Tomás Ybarra-Frausto, Joseph Sommers, *Literatura Chicana: texto y contexto* (Englewood Cliffs, NJ: Prentice-Hall, 1972), 248.

3. In *Impossible Subjects: Illegal Alien and the Making of Modern America*, Mae M. Ngai attests to the rampant racism against Mexicans (and consequently people of Mexican descent since many Euro-Americans chose not to distinguish between them). According to Ngai, in the first half of the twentieth century, "Throughout the Southwest, and especially in Texas, all Mexicans suffered from a system of segregation that mimicked the Jim Crow practices of the South. Mexican Americans and immigrants alike lived in segregated colonias, were denied service in restaurants and drug stores that were patronized by whites, and were seated in separate sections in movie theaters. In Texas, poll taxes and, in some south Texas counties, all-white primaries effectively kept Mexican Americans outside the polity" (132). Ngae further explains how Mexican Americans were systematically ostracized from US main society among many reasons because "Mexican workers in the Southwest and California [and the Pacific Northwest] were racialized as a foreign people, an 'alien race' not legitimately present or intended for inclusion in the polity" (138). See Mae M. Ngai, *Impossible Subjects: Illegal Aliens and the Making of Modern America* (Princeton and Oxford: Princeton University Press, 2004).

PART TWO

REMAPPING A TRADITION: CRITICAL HISTORIOGRAPHIES

I have suggested here that violence toward women is part of the politics of domination. Likewise, pejorative stereotypes and the deracination of mestiza women reveal the intersection of ideologies of gender, sexuality, and race in the politics of conquest.

"Gender, Race and Culture"

"Women of Color and the Rewriting of Western History: The Discourse, Politics and Decolonization of History" (1992)[1]

"Gender, Race and Culture: Spanish Mexican Women in the Historiography of Frontier California" (1990)

Dr. Castañeda's historiographies have survived over the years, passing from hand to hand and generation to generation, in part because we have yet to accomplish that which they called us to do: to reject colonial categories of analysis, re-envision the past, center the experience of women of color in our community and national histories. Central to this section's articles is the connection between the writing of history and

social realities. We, who write about the past, play a role in either reproducing colonial projects, or in challenging them. Castañeda challenges us
to reject colonial models, develop new questions and new frameworks,
create a decolonial present and postcolonial future.

One of the first historiographies to challenge the politics of accomo-
dationist multiculturalism, "Women of Color and the Rewriting of the
Western History," called for a new history, one where the old categories
and frames were set aside so that new frames could develop and flourish.
Taking *The Gentle Tamers* as a watershed, the article mapped both the
successes and weaknesses of the text. Where the *Gentle Tamers* was able
to move Western women's history into a multicultural model, it did not
shift colonial categories, nor did it analyze structural inequalities based
on class, culture and race. Yet race and class and the socio-economic
relationships of subaltern communities to the dominant culture are critical to understanding the nation's past. Such work, Castañeda points out,
emerges with the writings of women historians of color in the 1990s, with
Deena González, Sucheng Chan, Judy Young, Shirley Ann Moore, Devon
Mihesuah, and others who shifted the categories of analysis, allowing for
a reconceptualizing of the history of women, the West and the nation. It
is this historiography, Castañeda argues, on which we all need to build.

As part of a new generation of scholarship that challenged the historiography of the "West," "Gender, Race and Culture" mapped the ways
in which the field of history played a critical role in constructing racist
stereotypes of mestiza women. Beginning with the nationalist and white
supremacist historians of the post-Civil War era and then turning to
the Turner thesis and Bolton school, Castañeda demonstrates that the
watersheds in western history did not challenge racist stereotypes, but
instead reproduced them and reshaped them, all the while normalizing
the violence of conquest. She carefully maps the structural shift that
took place in the field when Chicano historians such as Albert Camarillo,
Richard Griswold del Castillo, and Ricardo Romo centered Chicano lives
and communities in their work. The article remains unique in its time

for its critical mapping of the field, for the lacunae to which it pointed, especially the function of gender and of women of the conquering group, in this case, of Euro-American women in the U.S. imperialist project, and for the way in which it signaled the larger Chicana feminist project.

NOTES

1. "Women of Color and the Rewriting of Western History" won both the Louis Knott Koonz Award (*Pacific Historical Review*) and the Joan Jensen/Darlis Miller Award (Coalition for Western Women's History) in 1993.

CHAPTER 3

WOMEN OF COLOR AND THE
REWRITING OF WESTERN HISTORY

THE DISCOURSE, POLITICS, AND
DECOLONIZATION OF HISTORY

Historians have long struggled with the need to rewrite western history and to articulate a new, inclusive synthesis that fully incorporates the history of women of color.[1] In her concluding remarks at the Women's West Conference in Sun Valley, Idaho, in 1983, Suzan Shown Harjo (identifying herself culturally as Cheyenne and Creek and politically as Cheyenne and Arapaho) charged that women of the West

> are still possessed of inaccurate information about who we are collectively, who we are individually, and who we have been. We view each other through layers of racial, ethnic, and class biases, perpetuated by the white, male ruling institutions, such as the educational system that teaches in the early years and controls later research in the history of women in the West.[2]

This critique of the reigning historiography has changed little since then or since Joan Jensen and Darlis Miller first called for a multicultural, or intercultural, approach in their essay, "The Gentle Tamers Revisited:

New Approaches to the History of Women in the American West."[3] A decade of "multicultural" historiography has still not come to terms with the historical, theoretical, political, and ideological issues raised by Harjo at Sun Valley.

This essay discusses the historiography that was written during the 1980s about women in the nineteenth-century West. It examines the issues, politics, concepts, methodologies; and language of the "multicultural" or intercultural approach first articulated by Jensen and Miller and the ways in which the intersection of gender, race, sexuality, ethnicity, class, and culture are described, theorized, and interpreted in the recent historical literature. The first section places in context the historiography of women of color in the decade before "The Gentle Tamers Revisited" was published, while the second places in context "The Gentle Tamers Revisited" itself.

THE HISTORIOGRAPHY OF WOMEN OF COLOR AND THE POLITICS OF HISTORY

The academic discourse on the historiography of women in the West still does not accept that studying and writing the history of racial ethnic people as well as of women in the United States are avowedly political acts.[4] Yet the political and intellectual roots of the contemporary historical study of women in the West were sown in the political struggles of the late 1960s and 1970s—in the case of white women, in the women's liberation movements; in the case of women of color, in the national third-world liberation movements.[5] These movements were at times related, but their political and intellectual origins, commitments, and ideologies were markedly different.

The women's liberation movement in the United States focused specifically on gender oppression. Never of one mind or one ideology, the women's movement was nevertheless fundamentally rooted in a middle-class political liberalism that subscribed to including the excluded as long as they fit within the existing norms. Its origins, identification, and praxis sprang from the suffragist movement of the mid-nineteenth century—a movement that never reconciled its origins in abolitionism with an abiding belief in white racial superiority.

The study of women began with the political struggles of the women's movements of the 1960s and 1970s and with the feminist theories and scholarship that grew from them. The women's movement was a middle-class, white women's movement, and until very recently, the historians who have researched and written the history of women in the West have been principally white women. Many of them participated in the women's movement or are members of the generation of scholars who struggled to found women's studies programs and departments in western colleges and universities. Most feminist scholars write the history not of women, but of white women in the West.

In contrast, most women scholars of color who research and write the history of women of color look not to the women's liberation movement, but to third-world liberation movements. These movements focused on the race and class oppression of African Americans, Chicanos, Native Americans, Puerto Ricans, and Asian Americans in the U.S. and identified with global struggles of third-world peoples for economic and political freedom.[6] They found their historical and cultural origins in indigenous, native worlds that antedated European imperialism, and they began to reclaim those origins, which had been devalued and suppressed in Euro-American institutions and society.[7] These national movements interpreted the exploitation and oppression of third-world peoples in the United States as an extension of the historical, global colonial, and neocolonial relationships that tied Europe and subsequently the United States to third-world countries.[8] Drawing upon theories of dependency and, in some cases, interpreting their reality in the United States as internal colonialism, these movements had a transnational identification and praxis. Although different ideologies, including cultural nationalism, prevailed, most national liberation movements supported a Marxist or neo-Marxist perspective that focused on class and racial oppression but ignored issues of patriarchy and gender oppression, gay and lesbian oppression, and the intersection of gender, race, sexuality, and class.

Women scholars of color, however, also struggled against the internal gender oppression of their own families, organizations, and communities and against a historical sexual exploitation rooted in the intersection of their gender with their race and class. This consciousness distinguished their gender oppression markedly from that of white women and distinguished their racial and class oppression markedly from that of men of color. It also differentiated the feminist ideologies of women of color from those of white women.

Individually and collectively, in conferences, presentations, and published works, feminists of color challenged male-dominated ethnic studies departments that ignored gender and sexuality and women's studies departments that ignored race and class.[9] In the case of the latter, they were highly critical of the assumptions, the universalizing tendencies, and the lack of consciousness about the dynamics of power and privilege rooted in race and class that informed white feminist scholarship. Drawing upon contemporary writers and political activists, including Angela Davis, Dolores Huerta, Janice Mirikitani, and Janet McCloud, as well as upon their own experiences, these writers and scholars initiated a new body of creative as well as academic literature.[10] Although few in number, they began to recover the voices, histories, cultures, literatures, and experiences of women of color in the United States and to teach courses on women of color. In the decade of the 1980s they published several collections of creative and critical writings by women of color.[11] These collections, however, did not include historical studies on women of color in the nineteenth-century West. This was due to the abysmally small numbers of professionally trained women scholars of color who might have produced these studies. Statistics reveal that between 1975 and 1988 there were 192 doctoral degrees in history awarded to women of color: 8 to Native Americans, 42 to "Asians," 101 to African Americans, and 41 to "Hispanics."[12]

MULTICULTURALISM AND ITS DISCONTENTS

With the publication of "The Gentle Tamers Revisited" in 1980, Jensen and Miller launched a new era in the field of women's history. Their essay provided Euro-American feminist and nonfeminist historians with a critical base from which to challenge the historiography in two subfields of U.S. history: the history of the American West and the history of women. For this group of scholars, Jensen and Miller's essay became the foundation on which to build a historiography of women in the West. It offered then a "new, multicultural" framework from which to contest both the East Coast focus of U.S. women's history and the biases of the male-centered frontier thesis.

Jensen and Miller called for a newer, ethnically broader, and more varied image of women in the West based on a multicultural approach that recognized and included the experiences of women from different races, ethnicities, cultures, and classes. They also stated that "a multicultural approach need not eliminate class or politics from western women's history" and that "women of the West were divided not only by culture but also by the conflicts among cultures."[13] Jensen and Miller's multicultural approach appeared to be the perfect base from which to include the excluded and thereby move women in the West from the periphery to the center of the history of both women and the American West. They did not, however, examine, analyze, discuss, or theorize about the conflicts and differences among cultures. Neither did they examine the applicability of the existing categories, concepts, and paradigms or redefine culture(s), politics, the parameters of cultural conflict, or sex-gender issues and women's roles within that cultural conflict. They also failed to analyze relations of power among women of different races, classes, and cultures.

Jensen and Miller's vague outlines for multicultural approaches to the history of women in the West have been uncritically appropriated, adopted, and applied, and in some cases extended or expanded, without question or analysis by feminist and nonfeminist historians alike. These scholars have begun to apply methods from numerous disciplines to research, write, discuss, anthologize, and publish a variety of works on gender, race, and class in the West.[14] Using a multicultural, intercultural, or, to a much lesser degree, comparative perspective, they have produced two principal types of work: descriptive studies and studies of the contact between white men or women and women of color.

The first type, principally journal articles and conference papers collected in anthologies, describes the experience of Euro-American, Spanish-Mexican, Indian, and, to a much lesser extent, African American women.[15] Asian and Asian American women—whether Chinese, Japanese, Korean, Filipino, South Asian, or Southeast Asian—appear in only one anthology, a multicultural reader published in 1990.[16] Although the early studies tend to focus on the nineteenth century—beginning with Euro-American westward expansion in the 1830s and ending with Frederick Jackson Turner's "closing of the frontier"—the study of women of color has of necessity pushed the time span back to the sixteenth and seventeenth centuries for Spanish-Mexican women and much earlier for Native American women.[17] Recent studies of workers from Asia and the Pacific Islands have also pushed it forward to the twentieth century and extended the geographic region to include Hawaii and Alaska.[18] Moreover, interest in particular themes, such as widowhood and women in prisons, is beginning to result in thematic works, including the important anthology *On Their Own: Widows and Widowhood in the American Southwest, 1848–1939.* These works offer significant possibilities for the development of comparative studies across race, class, cultures, and region.[19]

The second type, which includes books as well as journal articles, focuses on Anglo perceptions of racial ethnic women or on the contact and relationships between Anglos and racial ethnic women, usually Native

American and Mexican women.[20] Generally, studies on interracial contact in the nineteenth century do not examine interculturalism, interracial unions, or mestizaje (racial and cultural mixing) in Mexico's northern territories prior to the arrival of Euro-Americans in the 1820s and thus do not recognize these as core elements in the history of the West.[21] Research on intercultural contact has recently begun to focus on prostitution, a form of labor in which women of all races and cultures participated in the postwar nineteenth-century West; interracial marriage; and the moral reform movements of Euro-American women.[22] The study of interracial marriage and Anglo reform movements now embraces the twentieth century and has begun to examine relations between Anglos and Asian and Asian American women.[23] Despite the exceptions, few studies analyze the historical gender, "racial," political, economic, and cultural issues and conflicts inherent in interracial marriage, assimilation, and acculturation.

DIVERSITY

The issue of diversity was, moreover, a reality for indigenous peoples in the Americas long before the arrival of Europeans. Although racial diversity in the West may be a relatively recent phenomenon (some two and four hundred years old in California and New Mexico, respectively), cultural diversity is not. Before the Spanish arrived in 1769, California was one of the most densely populated and culturally and linguistically diverse areas of the continent north of Mexico.[24] Precontact indigenous societies throughout the Americas included a broad spectrum of social structures ranging from the matrilineal and matrilocal societies of the Navajo and Western Apache to egalitarian, foraging bands in California to highly stratified, hierarchically organized social orders in central Mexico and Peru.[25]

Recognizing and according significance to cultural diversity are important for two reasons. First, the recent emphasis placed on the nineteenth- and twentieth-century West as, according to Peggy Pascoe the "most racially and culturally diverse region of the nation" merely reconfigures and perpetuates, in another guise, the earlier myth of western America's uniqueness. Indigenous cultural diversity was not unique to the West, and its decline in other regions of the country, the South and Southeast for example, was due precisely to the impact of European and Euro-American expansion and colonization. Moreover, although the diversity among indigenous groups declined, the importation of Africans from different parts of the continent added new elements of cultural, as well as racial, diversity to nonwestern regions. Diversity in the American West, then, merely reflects a pattern in place long before the arrival of Europeans, and the change in the composition of diverse groups across time—the decline of some groups and the addition of others—is a function of the political and economic developments occurring in a particular region.

Second, women's gender experiences and definitions were as diverse as the cultures from which they came. Women apprehended knowledge and acted within their universe according to their culture and its particular economic and socio-politico-religious organization.[26] Understanding the nature of gender systems and experiences before contact is critical to understanding how those experiences changed with conquest and colonialism and why women responded and acted the way they did in intercultural settings and relationships. It is also critical to understanding how they maintained, adapted, and transformed their own cultural forms while resisting, adopting, adapting, and affecting those of other groups.

The Ideology of Race

Jensen and Miller should not be faulted for being merely suggestive or for how their call is applied by others. They should, however, be criticized for organizing their essay and discussion around concepts, issues, categories, and language that belong to the history of middle-class white women and for not addressing how these may differ for women of color. Although ostensibly centering *all* women as historical subjects, "The Gentle Tamers Revisited" fundamentally centered only

Euro-American women. Jensen and Miller's brand of multiculturalism kept middle-class white women as the subject and the normative group for description, analysis, interpretation, and comparison. They neither challenged nor altered the standard Eurocentric focus, methodologies, or paradigms of women's history. The multicultural approach to the history of women in the West reflects the critical problem in American historiography, which, to quote Ann DuCille's recent review, "is the continued marginalization of those historically constituted as 'other.'"[27]

Jensen and Miller encoded their discussion and analysis with a range of images and stereotypes applied to and reserved exclusively for white women in the West, beginning with the term "gentle tamers."[28] None of the historical literature neither the documents of the Euro-American conquest nor studies by historians or other writers—refers to any women of color as gentle tamers, meaning bearers of culture and "civilization."

Thus Euro-American individuals or groups, both male and female, remain the true subject of multicultural studies.[29] Based principally on Euro-American, English-language sources, these studies explore Anglo perceptions of women of color and the Anglo side of the cultural equation. While some of these works, particularly the most recent ones, recognize the poststructuralist debate about the meaning and definition of culture and seen to disavow the earlier paradigm of culture adopted by social historians, theoretical approaches that incorporate the historical realities of people of color, and their own interpretation of their realities, are still wanting.[30]

While feminist scholars are beginning to examine race and miscegenation within a multicultural framework, most continue to ignore the complexities of multiple racial and cultural mixtures in the United States and to avoid examining how the prevailing construction of race has been applied differently to different racial ethnic peoples across time and space.[31] Mexicans (both native and foreign born), for example, were included in the 1920 U.S. federal manuscript census as part of the white population. In 1930, however, the U.S. Bureau of the Census classified them as nonwhite and set up "Mexican" as a race unto itself. Since Mexicans have been officially classified both as white and nonwhite, anti-miscegenation laws sometimes applied to them and sometimes did not.[32] Nevertheless, as one early study of the Mexican American community concluded, irrespective of the official racial classification, intermarriage with Mexicans was disparaged, and "the Anglo member of an intermarrying couple... is classified as a 'Mexican' by the American community."[33]

Theories about the social construction of race do not yet examine or account for these kinds of complexities. Nor does the significance of interracial marriage and mixing among peoples of color, or the mestizaje of the Mexican population, form part of how the social construction of race and studies of miscegenation are conceptualized for nineteenth- or twentieth-century North American society. Acutely aware that the new theories remain constructed and defined by the same "hegemonic voices," scholars of color have vigorously critiqued the "rush to theory" that ignores, excludes, or does not comprehend the realities of people of color and, in this case, women of color.[34]

Jensen and Miller examined the ideology of gender, but not the ideology and politics of race, culture, class, and expansionism that produced and maintained stereotypic images of white women and women of color. They acknowledged the existence of racial stereotypes and cultural conflicts without placing racial contact and cultural conflict in their historical or political or ideological context. They assumed that concepts, categories, terminology, methodology, and language are universally applicable. By doing so they remained squarely within both the Turnerian tradition of frontier history and the tradition established early in the field of women's history. White women remain, as Chandra Mohanty states, the authorial subject, "the yardstick by which to encode and represent cultural others."[35] Jensen and Miller merely substituted the experience of white males with that of white women and thus reproduced the same relationships of power and authority that male historians used when writing the canon of history. The discussions and analysis of multicultural contact and relations remain skewed, centered on, and interpreted from the Euro-American side of the relationship.

Generalizations about women of color perpetuate pernicious stereotypes. Native American, Chicana, African American, and Asian American scholars have identified two dichotomous images of women of color in the literature—"good" and "bad." These images vary among racial ethnic groups but are in all cases totally unrelated to the notion of "gentle tamers."[36] Within this dichotomy, "good" women of color are light-skinned, civilized (Christian), and virgins. They are "good" because they give aid, or sacrifice themselves, so that white men may live; white men marry them. "Bad" women are dark-skinned, savage (non-Christian), and whores; white men do not marry them.

In the case of Native American and Mexican/Mexican American women, these dichotomies translate into contradictory images of the "noble princess/savage squaw" and the "Spanish señorita/Mexican prostitute," respectively. The "noble princess" and the "Spanish señorita" are deracinated and converted into acceptable images of marriageable women. These "good" women are the "Indian princess" and the "Spanish" grandmother whom many white pioneer families proudly claim as ancestors. According to the mythology within which these stereotypes are steeped, such women reject their own kind, native men, in favor of their white saviors. Marriage to the blue-eyed strangers saves them from the oppression of their own men and thus from the savagery of their race, culture, group, and nation.

The negative stereotypes were applied to all Native American and Mexican women except those few belonging to what Euro-Americans considered the native ruling class, with whom they could form beneficial alliances, including marriage. They sexualize Indian and Mexican women, devaluing and dehumanizing them as women who give away or sell sexual intercourse. Within this stereotype, Indian women relate to "idle, shiftless, thieving, drunken" Indian men, while Mexican women are "fandango-dancing, *monte*-dealing consorts of Mexican bandits."

The historical literature presents stereotypic images of women that center on sexuality and the relationship that the particular women and their racial or national group, or both, have to the political economy. Moreover, the relation to the political economy informs the history of women of color and distinguishes the daughters of the country—Native American or Mexican women—from African American and Asian women.

During the first stages of contact and conquest, marriage to a Native American or a Mexican woman of a particular family or class had significant economic and political value. These marriages were often the vehicle by which Euro-American men gained access to land or other economic resources as well as to political and military alliances.[37] This was not the case with African American or Asian women in the nineteenth-century West. As enslaved or contract workers, African American and Asian women had neither economic nor political value as marriage partners. The miscegenation laws, which criminalized marriage to people of African descent, were later extended to Asians.[38]

Consequently, stereotypes of African and Asian women center almost exclusively on the pejorative "bad/whore." This image simultaneously sexualizes women and impugns their sexuality. The implicit sociopolitical message is clear: women of color are immoral because their peoples, races, and nations are immoral.[39] Whereas the pejorative stereotype of African American and Asian women is rooted in sexuality, the positive stereotype, when it appears at all, is rooted in work and servitude. "Good" African American and Asian women serve their owners, or former owners, well. They do not run away, join or lead revolts, learn to read or write, or cause trouble.

THE POLITICS OF RACE AND POWER

Jensen and Miller did not analyze the relations of power among women of different races, classes, or cultures in the West. The devaluation of the sexuality of women of color, and by extension the devaluation of their people, was an important element in the rationale for war, conquest, exploitation, and subsequently exclusion.[40] It was—and remains—a central part of the racist argument that served the political and economic interests of an expansionist United States.

Anne Butler, for example, in her recent study of prostitution in the American West, paints Chinese and Mexican cultures as undifferentiated, static, and monolithic. She presents Mexican and Chinese women as unthinking, passive victims—entities with no agency. In this work, Mexican women come from a society and history of

> an unending cycle of victory and defeat, oppression and submission that comprise the history of the Southwest.... Oriental women carried with them to North America the societal hierarchy that they had lived within China.... The emigrants... came from a life of control and rigidity, similar to the structure the Chinese merchants established.... These women simply moved from one controlling hierarchy to another without transformation in their own societal roles. Brought from a pre-industrial society and closeted in a minority subculture, Oriental prostitutes had little opportunity to develop changed self-concepts in their new environment.[41]

Butler judges Mexican and Chinese women and their cultures by traditional Euro-American norms of "progress" and ignores both the political economy of prostitution for women of color in the West and women's agency under extreme conditions of oppression and exploitation. Nor does she recognize, for example, that the "Chinese merchants who had a status in the U.S. they did not have in Chinese" society created the so-called minority subculture within a context of exclusion, racism, and inequality.[42]

Multicultural works about women written during the decade of the 1980s tend to emphasize harmonious, cooperative, mutually supportive relations between women of color and Anglo women in the American West.[43] Although they do not ignore the reality of racist attitudes among white women, their accounts are remarkably free of intercultural conflict in a land bloodied by three centuries of war and conquest.[44] Yet white women are "gentle tamers" because they are the female counterparts of white men who "tame the wild West." "Taming the West," gently in the case of white women and violently in the case of white men, is a metaphor for expansionism. Within their gender spheres and based upon the power and privilege of their race and class, Euro-American men and women expanded the geo-political-economic area of the United States and established Euro-American hegemony in the region. They did so by waging war, by displacing and removing the occupants, and by appropriating the land. By skirting the issue of conflict in expansionism, these studies perpetuate the myth of the "bloodless conquest" of California, the West, and the Southwest, one of the central tenants of the expansionist ideology that rationalized and justified war and conquest.

The multicultural approach also ignores the myriad roles—which sometimes include cultural, ideological, social, and physical violence— that women of the conquering group(s) assume in establishing hegemony over another group. It also ignores the economic and other privileges that women of the conquering group derive from the oppression of women and men of the group being oppressed. Ironically, by emphasizing the benign, conflict-free relationships between white women and women of color in the American West, multicultural studies reaffirm the notion that white women are the "gentle tamers." This harmonic view contrasts sharply with the reality. Rosalía Vallejo's reminiscences of the Bear Flag Revolt in California, court records of cases in which Mexican women were plaintiffs as well as defendants against Anglos, including women, accounts of the wholesale sexual violence against Indian women, the efforts of African-American women to free themselves from bondage, and the sexual exploitation of Asian women reveal the truth of those relations.[45]

The brutally violent conflicts engendered by expansionism and the establishment of Euro-American hegemony—including conflicts between white women and women of color—remain part of our daily lives and are expressed in the contemporary writing of women of color. According to Paula Gunn Allen, "like our sisters who resist in other ways, we Indian women who write have articulated and rendered the experience of being in a state of war for five hundred years."[46] Histories of the West in which women of color are the subject, have agency, and are located within their own culture are only now being researched, written, and published.

THE EMPIRE WRITES BACK: THE DECOLONIZATION OF WESTERN HISTORY[47]

The literature by contemporary women writers of color in the United States vividly depicts the conflicts, tensions, violence, and warfare— physical, ideological, psychological, and cultural—that affect their own lives and form part of the collective memories and lives of their female kin and communities. This new, immensely rich, powerful, and growing body of literature—such as the autobiographical, biographical, and fictionalized writings of Louise Erdrich, Gloria Anzaldúa, Amy Tan, and Toni Morrison —helps to offset the dearth of historical studies about women of color, at least for the twentieth century.[48] Women of color are at the center of these works, describing, analyzing, and expressing their own historical and cultural subjectivities. Rooted in what theorist Chela Sandoval terms oppositional consciousness, this literature offers a critical base for new definitions, forms, expressions, and theories of culture, that is, of what writers of color have, in their call for reimaging America, termed cultures of collectivity and struggle.[49] These cultures are rooted in knowledge and experience that both antedate and supersede—just as much as they are shaped by, adapted to, resistant to, and coexistent with—European and Euro-American cultures of colonial domination. Collected in a wealth of new anthologies by and about women of color, this oppositional literature blurs academic disciplines and literary genres and crosses national boundaries. It expresses the complex, multiple subjectivities that women of color have lived, which Shirley Geok-Lin Lim describes as "the plural singularity" of Asian American women.[50]

This plural singularity refers to both the commonalities and the differences of gender, race, culture, class, and sexuality among women. It is present in the new historiography that examines women's history within the concepts and theories that frame the discourse of colonialism in historical studies, and discursive colonization in literary and cultural studies. Initially derived from the Marxist and neo-Marxist studies of Latin America, Africa, and India, this interdisciplinary approach draws upon methodologies and theories from cultural anthropology, ethnohistory, sociology, literature, and feminism to examine the conquest and colonization of the Americas. This approach, states Ramón Gutiérrez, views history as a "dialogue between cultures, each of which had many voices that often spoke in unison, but just as often were diverse and divisive."[51] Conceptualizing the historical process "as a story of contestation, mediation, and negotiation between cultures and between social groups," this approach clarifies the power dynamics of the European conquests and the contest of cultures that began in 1492 and remains very much with us.[52]

Especially important to historical scholarship on women of color in the United States, including the west, is the work of third-world feminists and other third-world scholars and writers who employ critical theory, postmodern anthropology, and poststructuralist literary criticism to analyze how the colonizer represented African, Native American, mestiza, and Asian women.[53] Analyzing woman and the female body as a metaphor for conquest, these scholars interpret the white colonizers' appropriation of the native woman—by representing her as sexually available to the colonizer and as oppressed within her own culture—to be pivotal to the ideology and the political agenda of colonialism. In analyzing colonialism, Malek Alloula, for example, interprets the colonizer's possession of the native woman by constructing false images of her and her society as "less of a conquest than a deformation of the social order."[54]

These scholars not only examine the centrality of sex-gender to the politics of colonialism but also focus on the relations of power both among cultures and within cultures. They view scholarship and the production of knowledge as a political and discursive practice—it has a purpose and is ideological. Within this broad framework, third-world feminists reexamine, reconstruct, and re-present native women within their own cultures as well as responding to colonialism. In doing so, they interrogate their own traditions from within. They call into question traditions, conventions, and contemporary relations of power and offer searching critiques of their own societies and historical conditioning.

This analysis, which examines both the historical and the contemporary writing on native African, Asian, and American women produced by Westerners, criticizes feminist writing on third-world women. Placing Western feminist writing within the context of a first/third world balance of power, Chandra Mohanty, for example, characterizes much of this work as rooted in "assumptions of privilege and ethnocentric universality, on the one hand, and inadequate self-consciousness about the effect of western scholarship on the 'third world' in the context of a world system dominated by the West, on the other."[55]

REWRITING THE NINETEENTH-CENTURY WEST

For the nineteenth-century West, historical studies on comparative frontiers that begin to examine frontier expansion within a global context of European colonization and capitalist development employ the dialogic framework.[56] These historians define the frontier as a territory or zone of encounter, interchange, and conflict between distinct societies—one indigenous and one intrusive. Taking a macrotheoretical approach, they argue that the "history of frontier expansion in the Americas is the history of the expansion of European capitalism into non-European areas."[57] Americanist Patricia Limerick interprets the history of the American West as one chapter in the global and bloody story of Europe's expansion and centuries-long contest for property, profit, and cultural dominance.[58] Similarly, historian Rosalinda Méndez González argues that if we are to understand the experience of all women we must study "the larger, more fundamental political-economic forces in the development of the West."[59] Scholars who study Native Americans and Mexicans include the resistance to domination, and those who examine the pattern of global frontier expansion concentrate on the differences specific to each nation, region, and frontier.[60]

Work in ethnic and women's history has added gender, race, sexuality, and culture to class as categories of historical analysis in studies of global capitalist development. Placing these at the center of historical examination—that is, using them as organizing principles—provides the basis for reconceptualizing and reanalyzing all aspects of history and the historical process. Chicana/Latina historians who study Spanish-Mexican women in eighteenth-century California and nineteenth-century New Mexico reveal, for example, that sex-gender, race, and culture are central to the politics and policies of conquest and colonization and to the sociopolitical and economic development of these regions as they changed from Spanish to Mexican to Euro-American rule.[61] Gender, race, culture, and class are political designations as much as they are social constructions.

This approach enables us to examine the specific realities in which women of different races, cultures, and classes live in any society at any given time. It also allows us to examine gender systems and women's experiences within the sociopolitical and economic context of local, national, and international developments at any given historical moment and to compare similarities and differences among women within one society and across societies. Most particularly, doing so allows us to study gender experiences, which are rooted in and intersect with race, culture, and class, within distinct economies and societies—both precapitalist and capitalist. In brief, it allows us to be historically specific, to recognize women's agency, and to understand, in Mohanty's words, "the contradictions inherent in women's location within various structures."[62]

Anthropological studies, for example, examine women's relations of production in precontact societies and refute earlier interpretations of Native American women.[63] They reject principal tenets of Western feminism that had been applied to women worldwide, including the universality of male dominance and the dichotomy between public and private acts. These studies conclude that within egalitarian foraging band societies, women exercised control over their own lives and activities and operated formally and publicly in their own interest. Social and sexual relations were reciprocal and complementary. Human sexuality, but most particularly women's sexuality, was not controlled by males, and a broad spectrum of sociosexual relations existed. Moreover, each society had its own customs for marriage, divorce, polygamy, polyandry, the berdache, and cross-gender dressing.

Historians are also reexamining various dimensions of the issue of sexuality within the context of colonization. Focusing on the response of native women to sexual and other violence, Albert Hurtado, among others, is detailing the historical resistance of Native American women.[64] Similarly, anthropologist Patricia Albers concludes that despite the structural and other changes wrought by capitalism, Dakota women and their communities did not dramatically change their basic values of reciprocity, collectivity, and complementarity.[65] These and other values were central to their resistance to and survival of colonialism and its attendant oppressions.

Moreover, while earlier studies dealt with Native American sexuality principally in terms of the "unspeakable things" done to white women captives, historical documents reveal that different practices of war prevailed in the Americas and that female captives fared according to the practices of the victorious group. Some of the native Californian groups, for example, practiced ritual but not physical warfare; some warred not at all; and some practiced warfare and captured women and children but never sexually molested female captives. Such was the case with the Yuma, who believed that intimate contact with enemy women caused sickness.[66]

Focusing on women of color changes the discourse and enables historians to examine how those women responded to changes in the economic and social order—including the changes wrought by violence—based on their own values, norms, and circumstances. Deena González, for example, examines interracial marriages as part of Spanish-Mexican patterns of racial and cultural contact. She focuses on the culture-specific gender strategies that Spanish-Mexican women in Santa Fe, New Mexico, used to resist and subvert structures of Euro-American colonialism in the nineteenth century.[67] Using Spanish-language sources, González weaves her analysis with the women's own language, imagery, and consciousness, which reveal the subjectivities, complexities, tensions, strategies, conflicts, and contradictions of their lives, as well as their sense of honor, propriety, justice, and right. Placing Chicana history in time, space, and social relationships prior to the arrival of Euro-Americans, González's work provides a critical new point of departure for studies of nineteenth- and twentieth-century Chicana/Latina history.

Likewise, Asian American historians, Sucheng Chan and Judy Yung, among others, use Chinese and other Asian-language sources to recover, reconstruct, and reinterpret the complex realities of Chinese, Japanese, Korean, Filipino, South Asian, and Southeast Asian women in the American West from the mid-nineteenth century to the present.[68] In addition to cultural and class differences, Asian-language sources, including oral history interviews, reveal that Chinese and Japanese women who consented to come to the United States as workers and subsequently as picture brides had their own individual motives for doing so. Some sought to contribute to the family economy; others wanted to be educated and to see the world.[69] Once in the United States, Asian women resisted marital and other conditions they did not like despite the difficulties and lack of recourse.

In her recent work on the Chinese in California, historian Chan studies gender issues imbedded in the Chinese Exclusion Laws of 1881-1882 and adds a vital new chapter to immigration history in general and to Asian

American women's history in particular.[70] Shifting the focus of earlier studies on migration from "Chinese patriarchal culture and the sojourner mentality thesis" and centering on gender issues and U.S. immigration policy, Chan chronicles how different groups of Chinese women were targeted for exclusion and denied entry to the United States. Examining the legislation from the 1870s to 1943, Chan finds the sexuality of Chinese women to be a pivotal issue in legislative hearings, committee meetings, and statutes as well as in municipal ordinances. She concludes that

> contrary to the common belief that laborers were the target of the first exclusion act, the effort to bar another group of Chinese— prostitutes—preceded the prohibition against laborers. Given the widely held view that all Chinese females were prostitutes, laws against the latter affected other groups of Chinese women who sought admission into the country as well.[71]

The stereotype that all Chinese women were prostitutes whose presence would corrupt the morals of the nation's youth can be traced to the 1850s and prevailed well into the twentieth century. The Page law, passed in 1875, was designed to end the threat of cheap Chinese labor and to prevent "immoral Chinese women" from landing in the United States. New laws passed in 1903, 1907, and 1917 were designed to deport alleged prostitutes, which included all Chinese women. According to Chan, "no Chinese woman, regardless of her social standing, was safe from harassment."[72]

Similarly, George Peffer argues that the government's targeted exclusion of Chinese women effectively prevented Chinese families from forming and thus kept a full-fledged Chinese/Chinese American society (or societies) from establishing itself in the United States during the nineteenth century.[73] Although Peffer's brief essay does not fully develop the relationship between sex-gender and economic issues, the links are certainly there to be examined and explored. That is, in Chinese contract labor, the expanding, postwar boom economy of the mid-nineteenth-century West found what it most needed: a large, mobile, exploitable, expendable source of cheap manual labor. Chinese laborers—

both women and men—were brought in to do particular kinds of work in a segmented labor force that kept them mobile, transient, exploitable, and expendable.[74] Unlike men, Chinese women were also brought to perform sexual intercourse, and their sexuality could be and was impugned.

Moreover, the "sexuality/immorality" of Chinese prostitutes became the rationale for excluding not only all Chinese women, as Chan and Peffer demonstrate, but, with the beginning of the economic downturn of the 1870s, all Chinese.

The Chinese experience was not singular. Similar issues of sex-gender, contract labor, immigration policy, and exclusion prevail in the history of Japanese immigration to Hawaii and the mainland.[75] Hawaiian sugar planters began contracting Japanese laborers, both male and female, and importing Japanese women to Hawaii for purposes of prostitution beginning in the late 1860s. Agricultural interests in the West subsequently followed suit. In a pattern established earlier with the Chinese, the "sexuality/immorality" of Japanese women was a key element in the rationale for excluding the Japanese in the first decade of the twentieth century.[76]

The intersection of gender, race, and labor is also central in new studies of African-American women in the West. Historian Shirley Ann Moore examines these issues in her study reconstructing the experience of African-American women workers in Richmond, California, from 1910 to 1950.[77] Using extensive oral history interviews, family memoirs, documents, music, memorabilia, and other archival material, Moore explores the "development of strategies of economic empowerment of women who labored under the tripartite yoke of oppression and were compelled to develop resourceful, self-affirming strategies to carve out some measure of economic autonomy for themselves and their families."[78] This is the first study to examine the experience of the generation of African-American women who took part in the "great migration" in the prewar years of the early 1900s and who built and shaped African-American communities in the West.

Earlier studies of women and of African-Americans in the West discussed African-American women in general or focused on individual women such as Mary Ellen Pleasant and Biddy Mason; they did not use gender as a category of historical analysis or examine gender issues and women's experiences of slavery, freedom, or the boom-bust economy in the nineteenth-century West.[79] With the exception of Jack Forbes's work on Africans and Native Americans, no historians have focused on the nature of interracial marriage or other socio-sexual and political relationships among people of color. The recovery of factual information and the interpretation of African-American women's lives in the nineteenth- and early twentieth-century West, like that of Native American and Asian American women and Chicanas, is only now being undertaken.

***

In focusing on women of color as historical subjects in the nineteenth-century Euro-American West, and employing gender, race, class, culture, and sexuality as categories of analysis within the context of colonization, newer studies, principally by women historians of color, are reexamining old sources, discovering new sources, using new methodologies, and challenging earlier interpretations of women in general. They are also refuting previous interpretations of women of color in particular. These scholars, states historian Deena González, have found it necessary first to "deconstruct the racialized and sexualized history of women of color in order to reconstruct it."[80]

Their examinations reveal important commonalities and differences based on historical presence and on gender and its intersection with race, sexuality, culture, and class. These new findings form a critical new basis for reconceptualizing and reinterpreting not only women's and racial ethnic history, but the labor, economic, political, immigration, cultural, and social history of the West as well.

They have sketched some of the broad themes that are of importance to women of color, including sexual and other physical, as well as psychological, violence within the context of the politics of expansionism;

devaluation of their sexuality by Euro-American society; discrimination based on race, culture, and class; resistance to oppression; use as labor (enslaved, contract, and wage); the *mestizaje* within Mexican communities as well as intermarriage and racial-cultural mixing among people of color; settlement; family; religion; and community building. Other themes, such as accommodation and adaptation to the Euro-American presence in their homeland; intermarriage with Euro-Americans; immigration; deportation; and the experience of slavery and freedom from bondage in the West, are more specific to one group or another.

Drawing upon new, interdisciplinary methodologies and frameworks defined in the scholarly studies of third-world women, these studies examine and analyze women of color within their own cultures; in particular, they examine how these women responded to the alien, hostile, often violent society of the nineteenth-century American West. These studies focus on women's agency and on how women of color use their own culture and knowledge to sustain them, how they subvert and/ or change the environment, and how they adopt or create new cultural forms. Further, these studies explore the multiple contradictions of women's lives in colonialism. They explore both the hegemonic and counterhegemonic strategies, roles, and activities that women, depending on their position in society, developed and employed in both the historical and contemporary period. Women of all races, classes, and cultures are active subjects, not passive objects or victims of the historical process.

Validating and drawing upon knowledge rooted in the experience of colonialism (but still manifest in their daily lives), and drawing as well upon knowledge antedating colonialism, these historians are examining both the historical and the contemporary writing on African American, Asian American, Chicana, and Native American women and their communities on the land base we now call the American West. They are deconstructing, reconceptualizing, and reconstructing the histories of women and communities of color in this region. Thus they are equally critical of the early historical literature and of the recent historical studies, including those employing the multicultural approach to the history of women in the West and feminist writings on women of color.

Historians, including feminist historians and other feminist scholars, must examine their assumptions as well as their racial, class, and gender positions as they redefine historical and other categories of analysis. The structures of colonialism are the historical legacy of the United States and, as such, inform the profession of history and the production of historical scholarship as much as they do any other human relationship and endeavor. If western history is to be decolonized, historians must be conscious of their power and ideology within the structures of colonialism, and conscious as well of the ways in which historical scholarship has helped to sustain and reproduce those structures. The study of women of color requires us to reexamine, challenge, and change those structures. Only then will we decolonize western history.

NOTES

1. I use the term "women of color" to refer collectively to African American, Asian American, Mexican American/Chicana, and Native American women in the United States. I use the terms third world, third world woman/women, and third world movements with knowledge of the problems associated with the terms as discussed in Chandra Talpade Mohanty, Ann Russo, and Lourdes Torres, eds., *Third World Women and the Politics of Feminism* (Bloomington, Ind., 1991), ix-x. I use the terms raced ethnic and racial ethnic interchangeably with the term people of color to refer to the larger community that includes both men and women. For the term raced ethnic, see Norma Alarcón, "Chicana Feminism: In the Tracks of 'the' Native Woman," *Cultural Studies*, 4 (1990), 248-256; for the term racial ethnic, see Evelyn Nakano Glenn, "Racial Ethnic Women's Labor: The Intersection of Race, Gender, and Class oppression," *Review of Radical Political Economics*, 17 (Fall 1985), 86-108. For a brief synthesis of some of the central issues in the recent historical literature on women in the West, see "Historical Commentary: The Contributions and Challenges of Western Women's History—Four Essays by Sarah Deutsch, Virginia Scharff, Glenda Riley, and John Mack Faragher," *Montana, the Magazine of Western History*, 41 (Spring 1991), 57-73. For scholarly discussion of the debates and the historiography of frontier history/history of the West, generally exclusive of the issue of gender, see Patricia Limerick, *The Legacy of Conquest: The Unbroken Past of the American West* (New York, 1987); Roger L. Nichols, ed., *American Frontier and Western Issues: A Historiographical Review* (Westport, CT, 1986); Michael P. Malone, *Historians and the American West* (Lincoln, NE, 1983); "Historical Commentary: Western History, Why the Past May be Changing—Four Essays by Patricia Nelson Limerick, Michael P. Malone, Gerald Thompson, and Elliot West," *Montana, the Magazine of Western History*, 40 (Summer 1990), 60-77; Brian Dippie, "The Winning of the West Reconsidered," *Wilson Quarterly*, 14 (Summer 1990) 70-85; Sandra Myres, "What Kind of Animal Be This?" *Western Historical Quarterly*, 20 (1989), 5-17; Charles S. Peterson, "The Look of the Elephant: On Seeing Western History," *Montana, the Magazine of Western History*, 39 (Spring 1989), 69-73; Arnoldo De León, "Whither Borderlands History? A Review Essay," *New Mexico Historical Review*, 64

(1989), 349-360; William G. Robbins, "Western History: A Dialectic on the Modern Condition," *Western Historical Quarterly*, 20 (1989), 429-449; Martin Ridge, "The American West: From Frontier to Region," *New Mexico Historical Review*, 64 (1989), 125-142; Gerald E. Poyo and Gilberto M. Hinojosa, "Spanish Texas and Borderlands Historiography in Transition: Implications for United States History," *Journal of American History*, 75 (1988) 393-416; Donald Worster, "New West, True West: Interpreting the Region's History," *Western Historical Quarterly*, 18 (1987), 141-156; David J. Weber, "John Francis Bannon and the Historiography of the Spanish Borderlands: Retrospect and Prospect," *Journal of the Southwest*, 29 (1987), 331-363; Gerald D. Nash, "Where's the West?" *Historian*, 49 (1986), 1-9; Richard White, "Race Relations in the American West," *American Quarterly*, 38 (1986), 396-416; Gene M. Gressley, "The West: Past, Present, and Future," *Western Historical Quarterly*, 17 (1986), 5-23; Walter Nugent, "Western History: Stocktaking and New Crops," *Reviews in American History*, 13 (1985), 319-329; Rodman W. Paul and Michael P. Malone, "Tradition and Challenge in Western Historiography," *Western Historical Quarterly*, 16 (1985), 26-53; David Weber, "Turner, the Boltonians, and the Borderlands," *American Historical Review*, 91 (1986), 66-81; Gene M. Gressley, "Whither Western American History? Speculations on a Direction," *Pacific Historical Review*, 53 (1984), 493-501; John W Caughey, "The Insignificance of the Frontier in American History," *Western Historical Quarterly*, 5 (1974), 6-15; W. N. Davis, Jr., "Will the West Survive as a Field in American History?," *Mississippi Valley Historical Review*, 50 (1964), 672-685; Jack Forbes, "Frontiers in American History," *Journal of the West*, 1 (1962), 63-73.

2. Suzan Shown Harjo, "Western Women's History: A Challenge for the Future," in *The Women's West*, eds. Susan Armitage and Elizabeth Jameson (Norman, OK, 1987), 307. After the first conference at Sun Valley in 1983, three additional conferences were held during the 1980s and one, entitled "Suspect Terrain: Surveying the Women's West," is being planned for 1992 at Lincoln, Nebraska. Issues of race and class bias surfaced at each of the conferences both in discussions of the new historiography of women in the West as well as in the conceptualization and organization of the conferences themselves. These same issues will inform the 1992 conference.The conferences of the 1980s were "Western Women: Their Land, Their Lives," Tucson, AZ, 12-15 January 1984; 'The Women's West, 1984," Park City, UT, 11-14 July 1984; "The Women's West: Race, Class, and Social Change," San Francisco, CA, 13-15 August

1987. Two edited anthologies of works presented at the first two conferences have been published: Armitage and Jameson, eds., *Women's West*,
and Lillian Schlissel, Vicki Ruiz, and Janice Monk, eds., *Western Women:
Their Land, Their Lives* (Albuquerque, 1988).

3. Joan M. Jensen and Darlis A. Miller, "The Gentle Tamers Revisited: New
Approaches to the History of Women in the American West," *Pacific
Historical Review*, 40 (1980), 173-214.

4. Rodolfo Acuña, *Occupied America: A History of Chicanos* (3d ed., New
York, 1988), 307-362; Joan Wallach Scott, *Gender and the Politics of His-
tory* (New York, 1988); Gary T. Okihiro, ed., *In Resistance: Studies in
African, Caribbean and Afro-American History* (Amherst, MA, 1986);
Gary T. Okihiro, "Education for Hegemony, Education for Liberation,"
in *Ethnic Studies*, ed. Gary Y. Okihiro, 2 vols. (New York, 1989), 1:3-10.

5. Adela de la Torre and Beatriz Pesquera, "Introduction," in *Building with
Our Hands: New Directions in Chicana Scholarship*, eds. Adela de la Torre
and Beatriz Pesquera (Berkeley, 1993); Cheryl Johnson-Odim, "Common
Themes, Different Contexts: Third World Women and Feminism," in
Third World Women and the Politics of Feminism, eds. Mohanty, Russo,
and Torres, 314-327; Alarcón, "Chicana Feminism," 248-256; Alma Gar-
cía, "The Development of Chicana Feminist Discourse, 1970-1980," in
Unequal Sisters: A Multicultural Reader in US. Women's History, eds. Ellen
Carol DuBois and Vicki L. Ruiz (New York, 1990), 418-431; Esther Ngan-
Ling Chow, "The Feminist Movement: Where Are All the Asian Ameri-
can Women?" in *Making Waves: An Anthology of Writings by and about
Asian Women*, ed. Asian Women United of California (Boston, 1989),
362-376; Nancy Diao, "From Homemaker to Housing Advocate: An Inter-
view with Mrs. Chang Jok Lee," ibid., 377-387; Teresa de Lauretis, "Fem-
inist Studies/Critical Studies: Issues, Terms, and Contexts," in *Feminist
Studies/Critical Studies*, ed. Teresa de Lauretis (Bloomington, 1986), 1-19;
Linda Gordon, "What's New in Women's History," ibid., 20-30; Marilyn
J. Boxer, "For and about Women: The Theory and Practice of Women's
Studies in the United States," in *Feminist Theory: A Critique of Ideol-
ogy*, eds. Nannerl O. Keohane, Michelle Z. Rosaldo, and Barbara C.
Gelpi (Chicago, 1982), 237-372; Patricia Hernández, "Lives of Chicana
Activists: The Chicano Student Movement (A Case Study)," in *Mexican
Women in the United States: Struggles Past and Present*, eds. Magdalena
Mora and Adelaida R. Del Castillo (Los Angeles, 1980), 7-16; Roxanne
Dunbar Ortiz,"Toward a Democratic Women's Movement in the United
States," ibid., 29-36.

6. For representative descriptions and discussions of the various national liberation movements, see *The Struggle for Chicano Liberation* (New York, 1972); Armando B. Rendón, *Chicano Manifesto* (New York, 1971); Alvin M. Josephy, Jr., ed., *Red Power: The American Indians' Fight for Freedom* (New York, 1971); Vine Deloria, *Custer Died for Your Sins: An Indian Manifesto* (New York, 1969); Julius Lester, *Revolutionary Notes* (New York, 1969); Stokley Carmichael, *Black Power: The Politics of Liberation in America* (New York, 1967).

7. I use the terms native and indigenous to mean belonging to a particular place by birth. For an examination of the problems associated with the use of these terms, see Trinh T. Minh-ha, *Woman, Native, Other* (Bloomington, 1989).

8. Daniel Offiong, *Imperialism and Dependency: Obstacles to African Development* (Washington, DC, 1982); Ronald H. Chilcote and Joel C. Edelstein, eds., *Latin America: The Struggle with Dependency and Beyond* (New York, 1974); Ronald H. Chilcote, *Dependency and Marxism: Towards a Resolution of the Debate* (Boulder, CO, 1982).

9. For early critiques by women of color of the biases of feminist theories and the politics of what Chandra Talpade Mohanty has termed "imperial feminism," as well as for unexamined philosophical positions in feminist and other scholarship, see Chandra Mohanty, "Under Western Eyes: Feminist Scholarship and Colonial Discourses," *Boundary 2: A Journal of Lost-Modern Literature and Culture* (Spring/ Fall 1984) 333-358; Adaljiza Sosa Riddell, "Chicanas en el Movimiento," *Aztlán*, 5 (1974), 155-165; Cherríe Moraga and Gloria Anzaldúa, eds., *This Bridge Called My Back: Writings by Radical Women of Color* (Watertown, MA, 1981), xxii-xxvi; Barbara Smith, "Racism in Women's Studies," in *All the Women are White, All the Men are Black, But Some of Us Are Brave*, eds. Gloria T. Hull, Patricia Bell Scott, and Barbara Smith (New York, 1982), 48-56; Hazel V. Carby, "White Woman Listen: Black Feminism and the Boundaries of Sisterhood," in *The Empire Strikes Back: Race and Racism in Seventies Britain*, ed. Center for Contemporary Cultural Studies (London, 1982), 212-235; Bonnie Thorton Dill, "Race, Class and Gender: Perspectives for an All-Inclusive Sisterhood," *Feminist Studies,* 9 (1983) 131-150; Mujeres en Marcha, *Chicanos in the 80s: Unsettled Issues* (Berkeley, 1983), 130-150; Bell Hooks, *Feminist Theory: From Margin to Center* (Boston, 1984); Alice Y. Chai, "Toward a Holistic Paradigm for Asian American Women's Studies: A Synthesis of Feminist Scholarship and Women of Color's Feminist Politics," *Women's Studies International Forum,* 8 (1985), 59-66; Cyn-

thia Orozco, "Sexism in Chicano Studies and the Community," in *Chicana Voices: Intersections of Class, Race, and Gender,* eds. Teresa Córdova, Norma Cantú, Gilberto Cárdenas, Juan García, and Christine M. Sierra (Austin, 1986), 11-18; Alma García, "Studying Chicanas: Bringing Women into the Frame of Chicano Studies," ibid., 19-29; Barbara Christian, "The Race for Theory," *Feminist Studies,* 14 (1988), 67-70; Jonella Butler, "Difficult Dialogues," *Women's Review of Books,* 6 (February 1989), 16; Bell Hooks, *Talking Back: Thinking Feminist, Thinking Black* (Boston, 1989). For the critiques of the 1990s, see "Editor's Note," and "Speaking for Ourselves: From the Women of Color Association," *Women's Review of Books,* 8 (February 1990), 27-29; Gloria Anzaldúa, "Introduction" and "Section 7: 'Doing' Theory in Other Modes of Consciousness," in *Making Face, Making Soul: Haciendo Caras,* ed. Gloria Anzaldúa (San Francisco, 1990), xv-xxviii and 335-402; Emma Pérez, "Sexuality and Discourse: Notes from a Chicana Survivor," in *Chicana Lesbians: The Girls our Mothers Warned Us About,* ed. Carla Trujillo (Berkeley, 1991), 159-184.

10. For a discussion of gender in the historiography of colonial and nineteenth-century California, including early studies in Chicano history, see Antonia I. Castañeda, "Gender, Race, and Culture: Spanish-Mexican Women in the Historiography of Frontier California," *Frontiers: A Journal of Women's Studies* [a special issue on Chicanas] 11 (1990), 8-20. For feminist activist-scholar-philosopher Angela Davis, see Angela Davis, *With My Mind on Freedom: An Autobiography* (New York, 1974); for Dolores Huerta, vice-president of the United Farm Workers Union, see the UFW newspaper *El Malcriado* (published at Delano and Keene, California, from the mid-1960s to the 1970s); for Janet McCloud, a Tulalip woman who was one of the founders and leaders of the Survival of American Indians Association, Inc., and a leader in the struggle for Native American fishing rights in Washington State, see Laura McCloud, "Is the Trend Changing," in *Red Power: The American Indians' Fight for Freedom,* ed. Alvin M. Josephy, Jr. (New York, 1971), 99-104; for activist-poet Janice Mirikitani, see Janice Mirikitani, *Awake in the River* (San Francisco, 1978) and Mirikitani, *Shedding Silence* (Berkeley, 1987).

11. Moraga and Anzaldúa, eds., *This Bridge Called My Back*; Hull, Scott, and Smith, eds., *But Some of Us Are Brave*; Gretchen M. Bataille and Kathleen Mullen Sands, eds., *American Indian Women: Telling Their Lives* (Lincoln, NE, 1984); Shirley Geok-lin Lim, Mayumi Tsutakawa, Margarita Donnelly, eds., *The Forbidden Stitch: An Asian American Women's Anthol-*

ogy (Corvallis, OR, 1989); Asian Women United, ed., *Making Waves*; Anzaldúa, ed., *Making Face, Making Soul.*

12. American Historical Association, *Guidelines on Hiring Women Historians in Academia* (3d ed., Washington, DC, 1990). The guidelines homogenize distinct populations into broad "Asian" and "Hispanic" categories. See also, Joan M. Jensen, "Committee on Women Historians, 1970-1990: A Twenty-Year Report," *Perspectives: American Historical Association Newsletter,* 29 (March 1991), 8-9; Deena J. González, "Commentary: The Rose Report, the Twenty-Year Report of the Committee on Women Historians, and National Ethnic Minority Women in the Professions" (Comments prepared for the American Historical Association Roundtable, Washington, DC, December 1990).

13. Jensen and Miller, "The Gentle Tamers Revisited," 212-213.

14. Peggy Pascoe, "At the Crossroads of Culture," *Women's Review of Books,* 7 (February 1990), 22-23, raises critical questions about feminist theory, ideology, and politics. Although Pascoe argues for multiculturalism and inclusion of women of color in the women's history curriculum, she neither questions nor analyzes the concepts and assumptions of multiculturalism. Pascoe, in "Gender, Race, and Intercultural Relations: The Case of Interracial Marriage," *Frontiers: A Journal of Women's Studies,* 12 (1991), 5-18, argues for the social construction of race and raises critical questions about historical scholarship and paradigms of culture but accepts uncritically Euro-centered notions of multiculturalism. Elizabeth Jameson, in "Toward a Multicultural History of Women in the Western United States," *Signs: Journal of Women in Culture and Society,* 13 (1988), 761-791, expands and updates the categories of a multicultural approach but does not analyze the concepts or theories and thus reaffirms Euro-centered definitions of multiculturalism. Sarah Deutsch, in "Women and Intercultural Relations: The Case of Hispanic New Mexico and Colorado," ibid., 12 (1987), 719-739, and in her subsequent book (cited below) conceptualizes "intercultural" and issues of assimilation, acculturation, and resistance for Nuevo Mexicanas as originating with the arrival of Euro-Americans and ignores the historical reality of Mexican/Native American interculturalism as well as the significance of this history in the subsequent relations with Euro-Americans. For troublesome generalizations about women of color rooted in unexamined concepts and assumptions about culture and people of color, see Deutsch, *No Separate Refuge: Culture, Class, and Gender on an Anglo-Hispanic Frontier in the American Southwest, 1880-1940* (New York, 1987); and Anne

M. Butler, *Daughters of Joy, Sisters of Misery: Prostitutes in the American West, 1865-90* (Urbana, 1987). For a similar critique of Deutsch's *No Separate Refuge*, see Rodolfo Acuña, "The Struggles of Class and Gender: Current Research in Chicano Studies," *Journal of American Ethnic History* 8 (Spring 1989), 134-135. Marion Goldman, *Gold Diggers and Silver Miners: Prostitution and Social Life on the Comstock Lode* (Ann Arbor, 1981), examines prostitution within the boom-bust economy of the Comstock Lode and discusses racial and class hierarchies in prostitution within an economic, not a cultural or multicultural, framework.

15. Schlissel, Ruiz, and Monk, eds., *Western Women: Their Land, Their Lives*; Armitage and Jameson, eds., *Women's West,* Joan M. Jensen and Darlis A. Miller, eds., *New Mexico Women:.Intercultural Perspectives* (Albuquerque, 1986); Cathy Luchetti in collaboration with Carol Olwell, *Women of the West* (St. George, UT, 1982), a pictorial history with a section on "Minority Women" and photographs of African-American, Chinese, and Native American women—but no Mexican women; Janet Lecompte, "The Independent Women of Hispanic New Mexico, 1821-1846," *Western Historical Quarterly*, 12 (1981), 17-35.

16. DuBois and Ruiz, eds., *Unequal Sisters*. Much of the periodical literature on Asian women has been collected in anthologies by and about Asian American women that are not conceptualized within the framework of the multicultural approach examined here.

17. Rosalind Z. Rock, "'Pido y Suplico': Women and the Law in Spanish New Mexico," *New Mexico Historical Review*, 65 (1991), 145-160; Jameson, "Toward a Multicultural History"; Cheryl J. Foote and Sandra K. Schackel, "Indian Women of New Mexico, 1535-1680," *New Mexico Historical Review*, 65 (1991), 1-16; Salomé Hernández, "Nueva Mexicanas as Refugees and Reconquest Settlers, 1680-1696," ibid., 17-40; Sylvia Van Kirk, *Many Tender Ties: Women in Fur-Trade Society, 1670-1870* (Norman, OK, 1980).

18. Mary Paik Lee, *Quiet Odyssey: A Pioneer Korean Woman in America*, ed. Sucheng Chan (Seattle, 1990); Ronald Takaki, *Strangers from a Different Shore: A History of Asian Americans* (New York, 1989); Yuji Ichioka, *The Issei: The World of the First Generation Japanese Immigrants, 1885-1924* (New York, 1988); Evelyn Nakano Glenn, *Issei, Nisei, War Bride: Three Generations of Japanese American Women in Domestic Service* (Philadelphia, 1986); Akeme Kikumura, *Through Harsh Winters: The Life of a Japanese Immigrant Woman* (Novato, CA, 1981); Judy Yung, "The Social Awakening of Chinese American Women as Reported in Chung Sai

Yat Po, 1900-191," DuBois and Ruiz, eds., 195-207. See the following essays, all of which are contained in Asian Women United of California, ed., *Making Waves*. Dorothy Córdova, "Voices from the Past: Why They Came," 42-49; Sun Bin Yum, "Korean Immigrant Women in Early Twentieth-Century America," 50-61; Marcelle Williams, "Ladies on the Line: Punjabi Cannery Workers in Central California," 148-158; Barbara Posadas, "Mestiza Girlhood: Interracial Families in Chicago's Filipino Community since 1925," 273-282. See also David Beesley, "From Chinese to Chinese American: Chinese Women and Families in a Sierra Nevada Town," *California History*, 67 (1988), 168-179; Joan Hori, "Japanese Prostitution in Hawaii during the Immigration Period," Nobuya Tsuchida et al., ed., *Asian and Pacific American Experiences: Women's Perspectives* (Minneapolis, 1982), 75-87; Alice Y. Chai, "Korean Women in Hawaii, 1903-1945," ibid., 56-65; Yuji Ichioka, "Amerika Nadeshiko: Japanese Immigrant Women in the United States, 1900-1924," *Pacific Historical Review*, 40 (1980), 339-357.

19. Arlene Scadron, ed., *On Their Own: Widows and Widowhood in the American Southwest, 1848-1939* (Chicago, 1988); Anne M. Butler, "Still in Chains: Black Women in Western Prisons, 1865-1910," *Western Historical Quarterly*, 20 (1989), 19-36.

20. Sherry L. Smith, "A Window on Themselves: Perceptions of Indians by Military Officers and Their Wives," *New Mexico Historical Review*, 64 (1989), 447-462; Sherry L. Smith, "Beyond Princess and Squaw: Army Officers' Perceptions of Indian Women," in *Women's West*, eds. Armitage and Jameson, 68-75; Lisa Emmerich, "Civilization and Transculturation: Field Matrons and Native American Women, 1891-1938" (Paper presented at the conference, "The Women's West: Race, Class, and Social Change," San Francisco, CA, 13-15 August 1987); Glenda Riley, *Women and Indians on the Frontier, 1825-1915* (Albuquerque, 1984); Annette Kolodny, *The Land before Her: Fantasy and Experience of the American Frontiers, 1630-1860* (Chapel Hill, NC, 1984); Darlis A. Miller, "Cross-Cultural Marriages in the Southwest: The New Mexico Experience, 1846-1900," *New Mexico Historical Review*, 57 (1982), 335-359; Sandra L. Myres, "Mexican Americans and Westering Anglos: A Feminine Perspective," ibid., 414-430; Rebecca McDowell Craver, *The Impact of Intimacy: Mexican-Anglo Intermarriage in New Mexico, 1821-1846* (El Paso, 1982).

21. Susan L. Johnson's "Sharing Bed and Board: Cohabitation and Cultural Difference in Central Arizona Mining Towns, 1863-1873," in *Women's West*, eds. Armitage and Jameson, 77-92, addresses the specific Mexican

history of informal unions in its discussion of cohabitation among Mexican women and Anglo men as well as their conflicting values concerning informal unions. Johnson, however, generalizes about Mexican culture, Mexican women, and Mexican communities in Arizona mining towns without any gender-centered primary research on the issue of informal unions in Mexican culture and without any substantive evidence upon which to base her generalizations.

22. Butler, *Daughters of Joy*; Goldman, *Gold Diggers and Silver Miners*; Darlis A. Miller, "Foragers, Army Women, and Prostitutes," *New Mexico Historical Review*, 65 (1991), 141-168.

23. Peggy Pascoe, *Relations of Rescue: The Search for Female Moral Authority in the American West, 1874-1939* (New York, 1990); Pascoe, "Gender, Race, and Intercultural Relations"; Posadas, "Mestiza Girlhood," 273-282.

24. Joseph L. Chartkoff and Kerry Kona Chartkoff, *Archaeology of California* (Stanford, 1984); Robert E Heizer and Albert B. Elsasser, *The Natural World of the California Indian* (Berkeley, 1980); Sherburne F. Cook and Woodrow Borah, *Essays in Population History: Mexico and the Caribbean*, 3 vols. (Berkeley, 1971-1979); Sherburne F. Cook, *The Population of the California Indians, 1769-1970* (Berkeley, 1976).

25. Irene Silverblatt, *Moon, Sun, and Witches: Gender Ideologies and Class in Inca and Colonial Peru* (Princeton, N.J., 1987); June Nash, "Aztec Women: The Transition from Status to Class in Empire and Colony," Mona Etienne and Eleanor Leacock, eds., *Women and Colonization: Anthropological Perspectives* (New York, 1980).

26. Ramon A. Gutiérrez, *When Jesus Came, the Corn Mothers Went Away: Marriage, Sexuality, and Power in New Mexico, 1500-1846* (Stanford, 1991), xvii-36; Sarah M. Nelson, "Widowhood and Autonomy in the Native American Southwest," in *On Their Own*, ed. Scadron, 22-41; Alice Schlegel, "Hopi Family Structure and the Experience of Widowhood," ibid., 42-64; see the following essays in Eleanor Leacock and Richard Lee, eds., *Politics and History in Band Societies* (Cambridge, MA, 1982): Eleanor Leacock and Richard Lee, "Introduction," 1-20; Lee, "Politics, Sexual and Non-Sexual, in an Egalitarian Society," 23-36; and Leacock, "Relations of Production in Band Society," 159-170. See also June Nash, "A Decade of Research on Women in Latin America," in *Women and Change in Latin America*, eds. June Nash and Helen I. Safa (South Hadley, MA, 1986), 3-21; Etienne and Leacock, eds., *Women and Colonization*, 1-24; Eleanor Burke Leacock, *Myths of Male Dominance: Collected Articles on Women Cross-Culturally* (New York, 1981); Eleanor Leacock, "Women, Develop-

ment, and Anthropological Facts and Fictions," *Latin American Perspectives*, 4 (Winter-Spring 1977), 8-17; Eleanor Leacock, "Women in Egalitarian Societies," in *Becoming Visible: Women in European History*, eds. Renate Bridenthal and Claudia Koonz (Boston, 1977), 11-35.

27. Anne Ducille, "Othered Matters: Reconceptualizing Dominance and Difference in the History of Sexuality in America," *Journal of the History of Sexuality*, 1 (1990), 102-127 (quote is from page 103).

28. Dee Brown, *The Gentle Tamers: Women of the Old Wild West* (New York: Bantam Books, 1974). Although Brown may have coined and been the first to use the term "gentle tamers," the concept of Euro-American women as the gentle, genteel bearers of "civilization" across successive frontiers is standard fare in the historical literature.

29. For an earlier, succinct critique of this approach, see Deena González, "Commentary [on a paper by John Mack Faragher, 'The Custom of the Country: Cross-Cultural Marriage in the Far Western Fur Trade']" *Western Women*, 217-222.

30. Rayna Green, ed., *Native American Women: A Contextual Bibliography* (Bloomington, 1983), 1-19; Green, "Native American Women," *Signs: Journal of Women in Culture and Society*, 6 (1980), 248-267; and Green, "The Pocahontas Perplex: The Image of Indian Women in American Culture," *Massachusetts Review*, 16 (1975), 698-714; Antonia I. Castañeda, "The Political Economy of Nineteenth-Century Stereotypes of Californianas," in *Between Borders: Essays in Mexicana/Chicana History*, ed. Adelaida del Castillo (Los Angeles, 1990), 213-236; Castañeda, "Gender, Race, and Culture: Spanish-Mexican Women in the Historiography of Frontier California."

31. For a discussion of the new approaches to culture in literature and history, see Lynn Hunt, ed., *The New Cultural History* (Berkeley, 1989). For a discussion of the issues in anthropology, see James Clifford, *The Predicament of Cultures* (Cambridge, 1988); for the earlier approaches in social history, see Peter N. Stearns, "Social History and History: A Progress Report," *Journal of Social History*, 19 (1985), 319-334.

32. Richard Griswold del Castillo, *The Los Angeles Barrio, 1850-1890: A Social History* (Berkeley, 1979), App. A, 180-181; Leo Grebler, Joan W. Moore, and Ralph C. Guzmán, *The Mexican American People: The Nation's Second Minority* (New York, 1970); José Hernández, Leo Estrada, and David Alvírez, "Census Data and the Problem of Conceptually Defining the Mexican American Population," *Social Science Quarterly*, 53 (1973), 671-687. See also Ricardo Romo, "Southern California and the Origins of

Latino Civil-Rights Activism, "Western Legal History, 3 (1990), 379-406; Ramón A. Gutiérrez, "Ethnic and Class Boundaries in America's Hispanic Past, in *Social and Gender Boundaries in the United States*, ed. Sucheng Chan (Lewiston, NY, 1989), 37-53; Gloria A. Miranda, "Racial and Cultural Dimensions of Gente de Razón Status in Spanish and Mexican California," *Southern California Quarterly*, 70 (1988), 265-278.

33. Grebler, Moore, and Guzmán, *Mexican-American People*, 322.

34. Alarcón, "Chicana Feminism"; Christian, "The Race for Theory"; Henry Louis Gates, Jr., ed., *Race, Writing, and Difference* (Chicago, 1986); Mohanty, "Under Western Eyes"; Cornel West, "Minority Discourse and the Pitfalls of Canon Formation," *Yale Journal of Criticism*, 1 (Fall 1987), 173-200.

35. Mohanty, "Under Western Eyes," 336.

36. Deena J. González, "La Tules Image and Reality: Euro-American Attitudes and Legend Formation on a Spanish Mexican Frontier" in De la Torre and Pesquera, eds., *Building with Our Hands;* Patricia Albers and William James, "Illusion and Illumination: Visual Images of American Indian Women in the West," in *Women's West*, eds. Armitage and Jameson, 35-50, examine the unrealistic images of American Indian produced for postcards for the tourist trade; Green, ed., *Native American Women,* 1-19; Green, "Native American Women," 248-267; Green, "Pocahontas Perplex," 698-714; Maryann Oshana, "Native American Women in Westerns: Reality and Myth," *Frontiers: A Journal of Women Studies,* 6 (Fall 1981), 46-50; Castañeda, "Political Economy of Nineteenth Century Stereotypes," 213-236; Castañeda, "Gender, Race, and Culture"; Renee E. Tajima, "Lotus Blossoms Don't Bleed: Images of Asian Women," *Making Waves,* ed. Asian Women of California; Paula Giddings, *When and Where I Enter: The Impact of Black Women on Race and Sex in America* (Toronto, 1984), 31.

37. Castañeda, "The Political Economy of Stereotypes"; Green, "The Pocahontas Perplex."

38. Megumi Dick Osumi, "Asians and California's Anti-Miscegenation Laws," in *Asian and Pacific American Experiences*, ed. Tsuchida, 1-37; Akemi Kikumura and Harry H. L. Kitano, "Interracial Marriage: A Picture of the Japanese Americans," ibid., 193-205. The Kikumura and Kitano essay was first published in 1973. Although California was a "free" state, slave owners still brought slaves to it and other western territories, and Euro-Americans still tried to enslave Indians. The fact that enslaved black people were able to win their freedom in California if they could

get their case heard does not obviate the reality of enslavement in the West nor the need to examine it.

39. Castañeda, "The Political Economy of Stereotypes."

40. For a discussion of the devaluation of the sexuality of women of color as central to imperialism, with a specific focus on Native American women in California, see Antonia I. Castañeda, "Sexual Violence in the Politics and Policies of Conquest," in *Building with Our Hands*, eds. De la Torre and Pesquera.

41. Butler, *Daughters of Joy*, 11-12.

42. Ibid.,12

43. Armitage, "Through Women's Eyes," in Armitage and Jameson, eds., *Women's West*, 9-19; Kolodny, *The Land before Her*; Riley, *Women and Indians on the Frontier*; Myres, "Mexican Americans and Westering Anglos."

44. For discussion of sexual and other violence toward women of color in frontier California, see Albert Hurtado, *Indian Survival on the California Frontier* (New Haven: 1990), 169-192; Castañeda, "Sexual Violence in the Politics and Policies of Conquest" and "The Political Economy of Nineteenth-Century Stereotypes"; Giddings, *When and Where I Enter*, Lucie Cheng Hirata, "Chinese Immigrant Women in Nineteenth-Century California, in Tsuchida, ed., *Asian and Pacific American Experiences*, 38-55; and Lucie Cheng Hirata, "Free, Indentured, Enslaved: Chinese Prostitutes in Nineteenth-Century America," *Signs: Journal of Women in Culture and Society*, V (1979), 3-29.

45. Rosalia Vallejo de Leese, "History of the Bear Flag Party," Manuscript Collection, Bancroft Library, University of California, Berkeley; Hurtado, *Indian Survival in California*; Giddings, *When and Where I Enter*, Hirata, "Chinese Immigrant Women," 1.

46. Paula Gunn Allen, ed., *Spider Woman's Granddaughters* (New York, 1989), 2.

47. The first part of this subtitle is derived from Bill Ashcroft, Gareth Griffiths, and Helen Tiffin, eds., *The Empire Writes Back: Theory and Practice in Post-Colonial Literatures* (New York, 1989).

48. For representative works, see Gloria Anzaldúa, *Borderlands-La Frontera: The New Mestiza* (San Francisco, 1987); Amy Tan, *The Joy Luck Club* (New York, 1989); Toni Morrison, *Beloved* (New York, 1987); Louise Erdrich, *Love Medicine* (New York, 1984).

49. Chela Sandoval, "U.S. Third World Feminism: The Theory and Method of Oppositional Consciousness in the Postmodern World," *Genders*, X

(Spring 1991), 1-24; Bernice Johnson Reagan, "Forward: Nurturing Resistance," in Mark O'Brien and Craig Little, eds., *Reimaging America: The Arts of Social Change* (Philadelphia, 1990), 1-8.

50. Shirley Geok-Lin Lim, "Introduction: A Dazzling Quilt," in Lim, Tsutskawa, Donnelly, eds., *Forbidden Stitch,* 12; Alarcón, "Chicana Feminism."

51. Gutiérrez, *When Jesus Came,* xvii-xviii.

52. Ibid.

53. See the excellent collection of essays in Mohanty, Russo, and Torres, eds., *Third World Women;* Kumkum Sangari Sudesh Vaid, eds., *Recasting Women: Essays in Indian Colonial History* (New Brunswick N.J., 1990); Minh-ha, *Woman, Native, Other;* Malek Alloula, *The Colonial Harem,* translated by Myrna Godzich and Wlad Godzich (Minneapolis, 1986).

54. Alloula, *Colonial Harem,* xiv

55. Mohanty, "Under Western Eyes," 335.

56. Howard Lamar and Leonard Thompson, eds., *The Frontier in History: North America and Southern Africa Compared* (New Haven, 1981).

57. Ibid., 7.

58. Limerick, *Legacy of Conquest,* 26-27.

59. Rosalinda Méndez González, "Distinctions in Western Women's Experience: Ethnicity, Class, and Social Change," in *Women's West,* eds. Armitage and Jameson, 237-252.

60. Deena J. González, *Refusing the Favor: The Spanish-Mexican Women of Santa Fé, 1820-1880* (New York, 1999); Hurtado, *Indian Survival;* Victoria Brady, Sarah Crome, and Lyn Reese, "Resist! Survival Tactics of Indian Women," *California History,* 63 (1984), 140-149; Lamar and Thompson, *Comparative Frontier History;* George Harwood Phillips, *Chiefs and Challengers: Indian Resistance and Cooperation in Southern California* (Berkeley, 1975); Jack Forbes, *Apache, Navaho, and Spaniard* (Norman, 1960).

61. Helen Lara-Cea, "Notes on the Use of Parish Registers in the Reconstruction of Chicana History in California Prior to 1850," in *Between Borders,* ed. Del Castillo, 131-160; González, *Refusing the Favor;* Angelina Veyna, "A View of the Past: Women in Colonial New Mexico, 1744-1767," in *Building with Our Hands,* eds. De la Torre and Pesquera; Antonia I. Castañeda, "Presidarias y Pobladoras: Spanish Mexican Women in Frontier Monterey, California, 1770-1821" (PhD diss., Stanford University, 1990).

62. Mohanty, "Under Western Eyes," 346; Chandra P. Mohanty and Saya P. Mohanty, "Review: Contradictions of Colonialism," *Women's Review of Books,* 8 (March 1990), 19-21.

63. Etienne and Leacock, *Women and Colonization*; Leacock and Lee, *Politics and History in Band Societies*; Evelyn Blackwood,"Sexuality and Gender in Certain Native American Tribes: The Case of Cross-Gender Females," *Signs: Journal of Women in Society and Culture*, 10 (1984), 27-42.
64. Hurtado, *Indian Survival in California;* Brady, Crome, and Reese, "Resist!"
65. Lois Risling, "Native Women in California" (Paper presented at the Huntington Library Seminar in Women's Studies, San Marino, CA, 20 January 1991); Patricia Albers, "Autonomy and Dependency in the Lives of Dakota Women: A Study in Historical Change," *Review of Radical Political Economics*, 17 (Fall 1985), 109-134; Patricia Albers and Beatrice Medicine, eds., *The Hidden Hay: Studies of Plains Indian Women* (New York, 1983); see Gutiérrez, *When Jesus Came*, for a discussion of socio-sexual reciprocity among the Pueblos of New Mexico.
66. On the Yuma, see Hugo Reid, "Letters on the Los Angeles County Indians," in *A Scotch Paisano: Hugo Reid's Life in California, 1832-1852*, ed. Susana Dakin (Berkeley, 1939), App. B, 215-216, 240; see also Castañeda, "Presidarias y Pobladoras," 63-113.
67. González, *Refusing the Favor*. For a discussion of Nuevo Mexicanas and widowhood in the postwar period, see Deena J. González, "The Widowed Women of Santa Fe: Assessments on the Lives of an Unmarried Population, 1850-80," in *On Their Own*, ed. Scadron, 65-90.
68. Sucheng Chan, "The Exclusion of Chinese Women, 1870-1943," in *Entry Denied: Exclusion and the Chinese Community in America, 1882-1943*, ed. McCalin (Philadelphia, 1991), 94-146; Ichioka, *The Issei*; Marlon K. Horn, *Songs of Gold Mountain: Cantonese Rhymes from San Francisco Chinatown* (Berkeley, 1987); Judy Yung, *Chinese Women of America: A Pictorial History* (Seattle, 1986); Judy Yung, "The Social Awakening of Chinese American Women," in *Unequal Sisters*, eds. DuBois and Ruiz, 195-207. The following articles appear in Tsuchida, ed., *Asian and Pacific American Experiences*. Hirata, "Chinese Immigrant Women in Nineteenth-Century California," 53-55; Hirata, "Free, Indentured, Enslaved," 3-29; Hori, "Japanese Prostitution in Hawaii," 56-65; and Emma Gee, "Issei Women," 66-74.
69. Gail M. Nomura, "Issei Working Women in Hawaii," in *Making Waves*, ed. Asian Women United of California, 135-147; Ichioka, *Issei*, 164-175; Glenn, *Issei, Nisei, War Bride*, 42-66.
70. Chan, "Exclusion of Chinese women," 94-146.
71. Ibid., 95
72. Ibid., 132.

73. George Anthony Peffer, "Forbidden Families: Emigration Experiences of Chinese Women under the Page Law, 1875-1882," *Journal of American Ethnic History*, 6 (Fall 1986), 28-46.

74. Lucie Cheng and Edna Bonacich, eds., *Labor Immigration under Capitalism: Asian Workers in the United States before World War II* (Berkeley: University of California, 1984); Mario Barrera, *Race and Class in the Southwest* (Notre Dame, IN: University of Notre Dame Press, 1979).

75. Nomura, "Issei Working Women in Hawaii," 135-147; Ichioka, *Issei*, 28-90; Ichioka, "Amerika Nadeshiko," 339-357; Ichioka, "Ameyuki-san: Japanese Prostitutes in Nineteenth-Century America," *Amerasia Journal*, 4 (1977), 1-21; Glenn, *Issei, Nisei, War Bride*, 3-20; Hori, "Japanese Prostitution in Hawaii," 56-65.

76. Ichioka, *Issei*, 20-39.

77. Shirley Ann Moore, "Not in Somebody's Kitchen: African-American Women Workers in Richmond, California, 1910-1950" (Paper presented at the Huntington Library Seminar in Women's Studies, San Marino, CA, 19 January 1991); Shirley Ann Moore, *To Place Our Deeds: The African American Community in Richmond, California, 1910-1963* (California, 2000).

78. Moore, "Not in Somebody's Kitchen."

79. Joan Jensen and Gloria Ricci Lothrop, *California Women: A History* (San Francisco: Boyd and Fraser, 1987), 32, 37; Rudolph M. Lapp, *Afro-Americans in California*, 2d ed. (San Francisco: Materials for Today's Learning, 1987); William Loren Katz, *The Black West: A Documentary Pictorial History*, 3d ed. (Seattle, 1987); Lawrence B. de Graaf, "Race, Sex, and Region: Black Women in the American West, 1850-1920," *Pacific Historical Review*, 40 (1980), 285-313; Delilah L. Beasley, *The Negro Trail Blazers of California* (1919; New York, 1969).

80. Deena J. González, "The Spanish-Mexican Women of Santa Fe: Mocking the Conquerors" (Paper presented at the Writing on the Border Conference, Claremont Colleges, Claremont, CA, 27 October 1989).

CHAPTER 4

GENDER, RACE, AND CULTURE

SPANISH-MEXICAN WOMEN IN THE
HISTORIOGRAPHY OF FRONTIER CALIFORNIA

Historians, whether writing for a popular or a scholarly audience, reflect contemporary ideology with respect to sex, race, and culture. Until the mid-1970s, when significant revisionist work in social, women's, and Chicano history began to appear, the writing of California history reflected an ideology that ascribed racial and cultural inferiority to Mexicans and sexual inferiority to women.[1] Not only do ideas about women form an integral part of the ideological universe of all societies, but the position of women in society is one measure by which civilizations have historically been judged.[2] Accordingly, California historians applied Anglo, middle-class norms of women's proper behavior to Mexican women's comportment and judged them according to their own perceptions of Mexican culture and of women's positions within that culture.

This essay pays a good deal of attention to the popular histories of frontier California because of the inordinate influence they have had on the more scholarly studies. In particular, the factual errors and stereotypes in the work of Hubert Howe Bancroft, Theodore H. Hittell, and Zoeth Skinner Eldredge have been propagated not only by other nineteenth- and twentieth-century popularizers but also by scholars—in the few instances where they include women at all. Although historians of the Teutonic, frontier hypothesis, and Spanish borderlands schools barely mention women, an implicit gender ideology influences their discussions of race, national character, and culture. The more recent literature in social, women's, and Chicano history breaks sharply with the earlier ideology and corollary interpretations with respect to race and culture or gender and culture, but it has yet to construct an integrative interpretation that incorporates sexgender, race, and culture.

THE POPULAR HISTORIES OF THE LATE NINETEETH CENTURY

> Women were not treated with the greatest respect: in Latin and in savage countries they seldom are; hence, as these were half Latin and half savage, we are not surprised to learn that the men too often idled away their time, leaving the women to do all the work and rear the family.[3]

Written by lawyers, bankers, and other prominent men who came to California in the aftermath of the Mexican War and the gold rush, the multivolume popular histories of the late nineteenth century provide the first composite description and interpretation of Spanish-Mexican California.[4] These histories fundamentally reflect the political and socioracial ideology that informed both the war with Mexico and the subsequent sociopolitical and economic marginalization of Mexicans in California.[5] With respect to women, they reaffirm the contradictory but stereotypic images found in the travel journals and other documents written by entrepreneurs, merchants, adventurers, and other members of the advance guard of Euro-American expansion between the 1820s and 1840s.[6]

In the tradition of the patrician historians whose romantic literary style set the standards and popular patterns from the end of the nineteenth century until well into the twentieth, Bancroft, Hittell, and other popularizers intersperse their voluminous histories of California with

musings about race, religion, national character, savagery, and civilization.[7] Riddled with the nationalistic fervor of the post-Civil War decades
and with an unquestioning belief in Nordic racial superiority, these
historians predictably conclude that the Anglo-Saxon race and civilization are far superior to the Latin race and Spanish Mexican civilization
that had produced in California, according to Bancroft, "a race halfway
between the proud Castillian and the lowly root digger," existing "halfway
between savagery and civilization."[8] Only Amerindians ranked lower
than the minions of Spain.

In the works on early colonial development, the discussion of women
is only incidental to the larger consideration of specific institutions—the
mission, presidio, and pueblo—or of great men—the governors. Thus, for
example, a brief discussion of the maltreatment of Amerindian women
in the mission system has no importance beyond its illustration of
institutional development and Spanish brutality, which, in the tradition
of the "Black Legend" spared not even women.[9] Similarly, Bancroft treats
sexual and other violence against native women primarily in relation
to the bitter conflict between the institutions of church and state, and
attributes it to the moral degeneration of the racially mixed soldier-
settler population.

Bancroft and his colleagues also introduce individual elite women
to their readers. The portraits of two in particular set the tone for the
consistent romanticization of "Spanish" as opposed to "Mexican" women.
A prototype of the tempestuous Spanish woman, Eulalia Callis, high-born
Catalán wife of the doughty Governor Fages, was dubbed the "infamous
governadora" (governor's wife) for refusing Fages her bed upon his
refusal to relinquish the governorship and return the family to Mexico.[10]

Even more important in the development of the "Spanish" stereotype
was Concepción Arguello, the young daughter of Don José Arguello,
Commandant at the Presidio of San Francisco. Prototype of the tragic
maiden, Doña Concepción became betrothed to the Russian ambassador
and chamberlain, Nickolai Petrovich Resanov, in 1806.[11] Resanov had

sailed to California from Alaska aboard the brig *Juno*, seeking to trade the ship's entire cargo for foodstuffs desperately needed to stave off starvation and mass desertions in Sitka. But Governor Arillaga, bound by Spain's policy of prohibiting trade with foreigners, refused to negotiate. Undaunted, Resanov wooed the young Concepción and, upon her acceptance of his proposal of marriage persuaded her father to intercede with the governor, who finally agreed to the trade.

Resanov left for Alaska and thereafter for Russia, promising to return as soon as he had the Czar's permission to marry, but he died while in Russia. Doña Concepción continued to await his return, for she did not learn of his death until many years later. After a life spent in nursing and charitable work, she became, in 1851, the first novice in the newly established Dominican convent in Monterey. She took her vows as Sister María Dominica in 1852 and died five years later at age sixty-six.[12]

Bancroft's commentary addresses not only the diplomatic and political strategy evident in Resanov's courtship and proposal of marriage but also the character of the Californians, both male and female: "What wonder that court life at St. Petersburg was fascinating, or that this child, weary of the sunbasking indolence of those about her, allowed her heart to follow her ambitions."[13] This aura of exotic drama and romance informs all later descriptions of "Spanish" women, in popular and scholarly works alike.

Bancroft also briefly discusses women in the context of colonial settlement and the family. He records the arrival of the first group of Spanish-Mexican women and families in 1774 and the overland journeys of the Anza and Rivera soldier-settler families in 1775-1776 and 1781 respectively. He also comments on Governor Borica's efforts to attract single women to the distant frontier and on the arrival of the *niñas de cuna*, the ten orphan girls brought to Alta California in 1800 as future marriage partners for single presidial soldiers.[14]

In general, the popular historical accounts of the Spanish period (1769–1821) are notable for their absence of pejorative gender-specific sexual stereotypes. Instead, pejorative stereotypes are generalized to the entire group and focus on race. In accounts of Mexican California (1822–1846), the popular historians divide women into two classes: "Spanish" and "Mexican." Although the vast majority of Californians, including the elite, were mestizo or mulato and Mexican, not Spanish, in nationality, women from long-time Californian elite, land-owning families, some of whom married Europeans or Euro-Americans, were called "Spanish." Women from more recently arrived or non-elite families were called "Mexican." "Spanish" women were morally, sexually, and racially pure; "Mexican" women were immoral and sexually and racially impure. These sexual stereotypes not only reveal the convergence of contemporary political and social ideological currents but also underscore the centrality of the politics of sex to the ideological justification of expansion, war, and conquest. The dominant social Darwinism of the late nineteenth century, which used scientific theory to rationalize Nordic racial superiority and male sexual supremacy, also held that a society's degree of civilization could be judged by the status and character of its women. The Victorian True Woman, like her predecessor the Republican Mother, represented the most advanced stage of civilized society.[15] Physically and mentally inferior to men but possessed of the cardinal female virtues—piety, purity, submissiveness, and domesticity—she was confined to the home, where she could neither threaten nor challenge the existing order. She was the norm by which historians judged Mexican women, individually and collectively, and thus one of the norms by which they judged Mexican society. Like other reductionist representations of Mexicans in the literature that treats the Mexican period as a "backdrop to the coming of Old Glory," pejorative stereotypes of Mexicanas thus served a political purpose.[16] The worst stereotypes of women appeared in the histories of the Mexican rather than the Spanish period not just because the primary sources were written largely by white men who visited and/or lived in Mexican, not Spanish, California, but because the war was fought with Mexico.

The most extensive treatment of Mexican women appears in Bancroft's interpretative social history, *California Pastoral,* in which he devotes an entire chapter to "Woman and Her Sphere."[17] By virtue of publishing the earliest work of this genre, Bancroft became the main source for the stereotypes of women in Mexican California in subsequent histories.

In the work of Bancroft, Hittell, and their modern successors, the portrayals of Mexican men, the wartime foes, are uniformly stereotypic and pejorative, focusing both on their racial origins and on a national character formed by Spanish tyranny, absolutism, and fanaticism. Bancroft describes Mexicans as "droves of mongrels" deriving from a "turgid racial stream" and concludes that they were "not a strong community either physically, morally, or politically." He depicts life in Mexican California as a long, happy holiday in a lotus land where "to eat, to drink, to make love, to smoke, to dance, to ride, to sleep seemed the whole duty of man."[18]

His stereotypes of women, however, are contradictory and reveal greater gradation. Women's position in Mexican society, especially, is treated contradictorily. "The Californians, violent exercise and lack of education makes them rough and almost brutal. They have little regard for their women, and are of a jealous disposition ... they are indifferent husbands, faithless and exacting and very hard taskmasters," Bancroft says at one point. Yet several pages later he comments, "there was strong affection and never a happier family than when a ranchero, dwelling in pastoral simplicity saw his sons and his sons' sons bringing to the paternal roof their wives and seating them at the ever-lengthening table."[19]

Bancroft's Mexican women are dunces and drudges. They work laboriously and continuously; bear twelve, fifteen, and twenty children; and are subject to being prostituted by their husbands, who "wink at the familiarity of a wealthy neighbor who pays handsomely for his entertainment." Women have no recourse to laws, which men make and women obey. At the same time, however, Bancroft quotes earlier writers to the effect that "the women are pretty, but vain, frivolous, bad managers, and extravagant. They are passionately fond of fine, showy dresses and jewelry... their morality is none of the purest; and the coarse and lascivious dances show the degraded tone of manners that exist."

Nevertheless, infidelity is rare because Californianas fear the swift and deadly revenge exacted by jealous husbands.[20]

Bancroft based his negative images of Mexican women on the accounts of Richard Henry Dana and others who visited California in the 1840s, on the eve of the war with Mexico. But he also recorded a positive image derived from the writings of Alfred Robinson and other Euro-Americans who traveled to California in the 1820s and 1830s to ply the hide and tallow trade and who married elite Californianas and settled there.[21]

Robinson's accounts expressed similar negative stereotypes of men but presented positive portrayals of "Spanish" or "Californio" women. Robinson, who married María Teresa de la Guerra y Noriega, wrote that "the men are generally indolent and addicted to many vices ... yet ... in few places of the world ... can be found more chastity, industrious habits and correct deportment than among the women."[22] Similar images appeared in literary pieces written on the eve of the Mexican War by individuals who had no firsthand experience of California. In this literature, Spanish-speaking women invited the advances of Euro-American men whom they anxiously awaited as their saviors from Mexican men. For example, "They Wait for Us" published in Boston at the time that John C. Frémont's outlaw band was raising the Bear Flag at Sonoma in June 1846, treats Mexican women as the symbol for the country about to be conquered:

They Wait for Us

> The Spanish maid, with eyes of fire
> At balmy evening turns her lyre,
> And, looking to the Eastern sky,
> Awaits our Yankee Chivalry
> Whose purer blood and valiant arms,
> Are fit to clasp her budding charms.
>
> The man, her mate, is sunk in sloth—
> To love, his senseless heart is loth:
> The pipe and glass and tinkling lute,
> A sofa, and a dish of fruit;

A nap, some dozen times by day;
Sombre and sad, and never gay.[23]

The meaning is clear—Mexicans cannot appreciate, love, direct, or control their women/country.

Forty years later, Bancroft and Hittell underscored this theme in the primary sources. "It was a happy day," writes Bancroft "for the California bride whose husband was an American." According to Hittell, Californian señoritas eagerly sought American husbands, who "might not touch the guitar as lightly" but "made better husbands than those of Mexican blood."[24] The chaste, industrious Spanish beauty who forsook her inferior man and nation in favor of the superior Euro-American became embedded in the literature. The negative image that Bancroft et al. picked up from the English-language primary sources was reserved for Mexican women: fandango-dancing, monte-dealing prostitutes, the consorts of Mexican bandits.[25] These dual stereotypes became the prototypic images of Spanish-speaking women in California. They were the grist of popular fiction and contemporary newspapers throughout the latter part of the nineteenth and early twentieth centuries, and they resurfaced in the popular historical literature of the twentieth century, including the few works that focused specifically on women of Spanish California.

THE MAKERS OF MODERN HISTORIOGRAPHY: THE TEUTONIC HISTORIANS

While Bancroft, Hittell, and other popularizers stereotyped women in their sweeping general histories of California, their scholarly contemporaries, the Teutonic historians, barely mentioned women at all. As professional historical scholarship took root in the post-Civil War era, the question of gender became a nonissue.[26]

Rather, the new scientific historians, reflecting the period's conservative, organic nationalism, were concerned principally with explaining the origin, nature, and Old World antecedents of Euro-American institutions in the United States. Their studies focused on political institutions, the pivotal structures perceived both as the sources of a nation's order and coherence and as the hallmarks that distinguished one civilization from another. They dichotomized such institutions into free and nonfree, defining democratic institutions based on representative government as free and superior, and institutions based on monarchies as unfree and inferior.[27] The Teutonics divided contemporary New World civilizations deriving from European origins accordingly.

For these historians, deification of the national state was closely linked to glorification of Anglo-Saxon people and institutions. Euro-American civilization in the United States, according to the Teutonic germ theory of history, was characterized by superior, free institutions transplanted from medieval England and Germany by Anglo-Saxons, the superior Caucasian race, and destined to expand to the entire North American continent. The Teutonics did not question the earlier romantic historians' interpretation of continental expansion as God-ordained manifest destiny; instead, they recast the same view in terms of evolutionary theory.[28] In the inexorable sweep of Anglo-Saxons across the continent, inferior races and civilizations were to be swept aside.

The Teutonic historians' emphasis on Old World antecedents focused their attention on the eastern region of the United States rather than on the Far West, which had but recently been incorporated into the Union. The few early scholarly studies of colonial California and the Southwest focused on Spanish institutional development.[29] For post-Civil War historians concerned with nationalism and national unification, the important question was how to explain the Spanish-Mexican institutions rooted in California and the Southwest. A corollary question was how to incorporate the new region intellectually and ideologically into the history of the United States.[30]

While imbued with the more objective scientific approach to historical research being taught at Johns Hopkins and other graduate schools, scholarly studies were nevertheless informed by the racist attitudes that saturated the primary sources and popular histories, particularly those of the Mexican War era, and by the colonial legacy of the Black Legend. In explaining the Spanish presence and institutions in the region ceded to the United States, the Teutonic historians concluded that Spain had failed to implant permanent institutions in this area, for two reasons. First, Spanish political institutions were not free. Second, Spanish cohabitation with inferior Amerindian and Negroid races in the Americas had produced an even more inferior, mongrelized population incapable of self-government.[31] The low level of population across New Spain's vast northern region, its inability to pacify Amerindian groups fully, and its lack of strong agricultural, commercial, or industrial development were offered as proof positive that Spanish institutions had been a dismal failure. Spain's colonizing institutions, the missions, presidios, and pueblos, were not adequate to develop the region, nor did they leave a lasting influence on the people or landscape.

While the Teutonics' major documentary sources were Euro-American, they also cited French, English, and Russian travel accounts to California and the writings of Franciscan missionaries.[32] The anti-Spanish sentiments of French, English, and Euro-American expeditionary forces, as well as these countries' continued interest in acquiring California, are obvious in the logs, journals, and reports of Jean Francois Galaup de La Perouse, George Vancouver, William Shaler, and other foreigners who visited Spanish California.[33] The reports, petitions, and correspondence of the mission priests, most of whom were peninsular Spaniards, cast aspersions on the racially mixed soldiers and settlers sent to this remote outpost of the empire. Historian Manuel Servín suggests that in California, prejudice and discrimination against persons of mixed blood can be traced to the pejorative racial attitudes of peninsular Franciscans and other españoles during the Spanish colonial era.[34]

Since women were not a formal part of institutional life, the Teutonic historians did not discuss them.[35] Frank W. Blackmar, for example, who relies heavily on Bancroft for his description of colonial California, makes only passing reference to women in his discussion of the institution of the mission and the social and political life of the Spanish colonies.[36] But popular and amateur historians of the time continued to include women in their works, stereotyping Mexican women on the basis of both sex and race, as we have seen. These stereotypes take on additional significance when we recognize that, as Rodman Paul recently stated, the West, particularly California, that most romanticized, mythologized, and distorted of western states, "is a primary meeting ground of professional historiography, popular interests, and popular writers."[37]

Throughout the late nineteenth and early twentieth centuries, then, even as Frederick Jackson Turner successfully challenged the germ theory of Euro-American history, the history of California remained the province of popular historians, journalists, and writers. Professional historians, now writing within the developing frontier hypothesis school of historiography, continued the Teutonics' neglect of women.

Nonetheless, ideas about gender and race formed a part of their intellectual subsoil. As the United States moved from expansionism to imperialism by going to war against Spain and by preparing to absorb former Spanish colonies, race and culture became pivotal political issues for imperialists and anti-imperialists alike. In addition, increased immigration from southern and eastern Europe occasioned considerable discussion about the assimilability of certain races and ethnic groups as well as alarm over the high birth rate among the new immigrants. At the same time, social and political theorists were alarmed by the decline in the birth rate among the white middle class; the potential threat that women's greater economic independence posed to the existing social order; and the women's rights movement. The survival and destiny of the Anglo-Saxon race, they determined, rested with women. In particular, eugenicist theorists like Karl Pearson and Havelock Ellis glorified an ideal of motherhood that required women's self-sacrifice for the good of the race. Though it rested on social function rather than on biological constraint, the eugenicist ideal denied women's individuality, removed them as potential economic competitors, and silenced their potential political voices.[38]

TURNER'S FRONTIER HYPOTHESIS AND THE FANTASY SPANISH HERITAGE

As the mission revival movement and the rediscovery of California's "Spanish" past gained force toward the end of the nineteenth century, Frederick Jackson Turner's presidential address to the American Historical Association in 1893 redefined Euro-American history and civilization. By the early twentieth century, Turner's concept, the "frontier hypothesis," had supplanted the Teutonic germ theory of history and American institutions.[39]

Instead of looking to Old World antecedents to explain the development of representative government and EuroAmerican civilization, Turner focused on the New World itself, whose environment alone explained the differences between the civilizations of Europe and America. In his view, expansion into new areas recreated the conditions of primitive social organization as successive waves of trappers, traders, miners, farmers, and cattlemen adapted to and molded the environment on continuous frontiers -"the meeting point between savagery and civilization." The men engaged in this continuous process were imbued with a "rugged individualism" that, combined with frontier conditions, promoted democracy and representative government. From the very beginning, then, the frontier was a democratizing agent. Departing from the Teutonic emphasis on Anglo-Saxon racial origins, Turner argued that "in the crucible of the frontier [redemptioners of non-English stock] were Americanized, liberated and fused into a mixed race, English in neither nationality nor characteristic."[40] American development represented a severance, a discontinuity with European origins, patterns, and institutions.

While on the one hand Turner conceived of Euro-American history as discontinuous from European origins, on the other hand his reinterpretation merely shifted the emphasis on institutional origins from the Old to the New World—from the German forest to the American wilderness—and stressed the impact of the new environment on diverse groups of Caucasian males. It left intact the Teutonics' basic assumptions about representative government, democratic institutions, race, culture, gender, and economics. In both interpretations, neither women nor non-Caucasian men were active participants in the creation of democratic institutions. That both were legally prohibited from direct participation in such institutions was not an issue; rather, their exclusion was consistent with theories of biological and social evolution.

Joan Jensen and Darlis Miller have identified four major stereotypes of Euro-American women in the Turnerian literature of the western frontier: gentle tamers, sunbonneted help-meets, hell raisers, and bad women.[41] The first two types were extolled as bastions of the pioneer family; the second two were condemned as libertines, created by the same frontier influence that liberated men. But in the Turnerian studies that extol and stereotype Euro-American women, Spanish-Mexican women were entirely absent—a fact hardly surprising in view of the school's racist attitudes toward non-Caucasian peoples and its ignoring of what Richard Hofstadter called "the shameful aspects of Western development, including the arrogance of American expansion, the pathetic tale of the Indians, anti-Mexican [and] anti-Chinese nativism."[42]

With respect to Mexicans, the revisionist frontier historians, if they addressed the pre-American period at all, retained the Teutonic interpretation of Spanish institutional failure while dismissing the Mexican period as an unimportant interlude between the Spanish and North American eras. Maintaining the stereotype of indolent Mexicans, Frederic L. Paxson argued that in losing California, Mexico had "paid the penalty under that organic law of politics which forbids a nation to sit still when others are moving," and thus "determined the inevitability of the United States War with Mexico and the Conquest of California and the South West."[43]

Having thus easily dismissed the obstacles that Indians and Mexicans, as prior occupants, represented to acquisition of the land base, the frontier historians focused their white, malecentered studies on the "Westward Movement" of Anglo-American pioneers into Oregon, Utah, the Pacific Northwest, and, most particularly, gold-rush California. Most recently, historians reexamining the literature of the frontier and the West have concluded that the initial success of Turner's thesis was due largely to the fact that he told an emerging industrial nation rising to world power what it wanted to hear. "Turner," states Michael Malone, "told a maturing nation... that it was not an appendage of a decadent Europe, but rather was a unique and great country in its own right."[44]

Meanwhile, Anglo-Westerners were searching for roots in the land they now occupied. To collect, exhibit, and publish their past the new westerners organized local county and state historical societies, museums, and journals during the late nineteenth and early twentieth centuries. And, in the tradition of the earlier historical literature, the histories published by these institutions were romantic, provincial, nationalistic, and rife with filial piety.[45]

But in California, the search for roots that fit into national history ran into hardpan—the Indians and Mexicans on the land. While the United States Army and the federal government had largely removed the Indians from their midst, historically minded Californians still had to deal with Mexicans and with the fact of Spanish-Mexican colonization and institutions on the slopes that they now called home.[46] Whereas their scholarly Teutonic forebears had dismissed Spain and its institutions, the new westerners now took an interest in the region's "Spanish" past. In Spain's Caucasian racial origins and former imperial grandeur they found an acceptable European past for one particular class of the former Mexican citizens in their midst, whose blood flowed in some of their own veins. In the now decaying Spanish missions and their "laudable" effort to Christianize the native population they found one institution worthy of preserving—at least structurally—for posterity.

The mission revival movement, which initiated a Spanish Mediter-
ranean architectural style for public and private buildings, dates from
this period. Historical societies and journals published histories of the
missions and pueblos, along with reminiscences of the halcyon days in
the former Spanish colony.[47] Preservationists targeted first the missions,
then the adobes. Leading Anglo denizens in towns up and down the state
organized "fiesta days" that included parades, music, food, rodeos, and a
fandango (dance) or two. In Santa Barbara, Helen Hunt Jackson's novel
Ramona was converted into a play that was performed year after year.
Some of the descendants of California's "best Spanish families," who
aided and abetted both the creation and the perpetuation of the Spanish
myth, joined these celebrations.[48]

The majority of Anglo Californians seeking to understand their past
probably did not read the scholarly studies of the frontier historians.
The newspapers, novels, and nonprofessional histories that they did
read continued the romanticized "Spanish" stereotypes first applied to
mestizas in the primary sources and in Bancroft. In these works, women
were featured prominently, and even males were now romanticized.[49]

The gratuitous determination that Mexican California's landowning
class, some of whom still had kinship and/or economic ties to the new
westerners, were pure-blooded Spaniards was a principal feature of the
newly fabricated "fantasy Spanish heritage," to use Carey McWilliams's
term.[50] Taking some of their cues from contemporary newspaper stories
that "the best families were of Castillian stock, many of them pure in
blood and extremely fair of skin," the new popularizers created a new
racial and social history for the landowning class that the Euro-American
conquest had displaced and now appropriated. In these fabulous histories,
"the men went to Old Spain or Mexico for their wives and there was
but little mixture of the high-bred Spanish families with the Mexicans
and Indians." In *Spanish Arcadia*, which focuses on the Mexican period,
Nellie Van de Grift Sánchez wrote that the Californios "kept their white

blood purer than did the Mexicans or South Americans," and thus, "as a race, are greatly superior to the Mexicans."[51]

Dispossessed of their lands and politically disenfranchised, the former rancheros represented no threat to Euro-American supremacy and thus could be safely romanticized. The new popular histories converted Mexican rancheros into "the California Dons," dashing, silver-saddled caballeros who roamed baronial estates from dawn to dusk in a remote Spanish past. The new Dons, however, continued to be inept; incapable of hard work, they lacked the genius or moral strength to develop California's lush, fertile land. (Gertrude Atherton, who published short stories, novels, and popular histories in the late nineteenth and early twentieth centuries, entitled one collection of short stories about Mexican California *The Splendid Idle Forties.*)[52]

The women of Spanish California, however, according to these novels and histories, surpassed the men. Like the primary sources of the 1840s, the new popularizers concluded that women were men's superiors in "modesty, moral character, and sound common sense."[53] California's "Spanish" (read Caucasian) daughters were industrious, chaste, and morally as well as racially pure. In short, they could be claimed as the pure-blooded "Spanish" grandmothers of many a Euro-American frontier family. But Mexican women fared less well. While the literature seldom specifically discusses Mexican women, a designation that included non-elite Californianas and Mexicanas who came during the gold rush, it implies that they were licentious women—common prostitutes who, like their male counterparts, deserved to be wiped out. Thus popular historical interpretations of California's Spanish-Mexican past essentially dichotomized Calfornianas the same way the scholarly frontier historians dichotomized and stereotyped Anglo-American women—as good and bad women. For Californianas, however, the values of good and bad were explicitly related to their race and culture or class.

Meanwhile, among professional historians, Spain's presence in the American Southwest resurfaced as a historiographical issue. In the early decades of the twentieth century a reexamination of the history of colonial institutions in the old Spanish borderlands by a young scholar named Herbert Eugene Bolton led to a reinterpretation of those institutions and to a "new" school of historiography.

THE SPANISH BORDERLANDS SCHOOL

In the 1930s Turner's frontier thesis came under increasing scrutiny and attack. A new generation of revisionist historians argued that national development resulted not from a single cause but from many, from economic and class forces as well as from ideas rooted in East Coast intellectualism rather than western individualism.

The Great Depression, too, provoked a reexamination of the social unanimity implicit in Turner's interpretation of United States history. The climate of national questioning, internationalism, and a Good Neighbor Policy toward Mexico and Latin America prompted scholars to tackle once more the history of California, the Southwest, and the Far West. At the University of California at Berkeley, Herbert Eugene Bolton and his students developed a new revisionist school, the Spanish borderlands school of historiography. The new school revised the Teutonics' original theory of Spanish institutional failures by turning it on its head. Basing their arguments on a concept of "a Greater America" and on archival research in unmined Spanish language collections, Bolton and his students argued that, contrary to prevalent scholarly wisdom, which they characterized as nationalistic, chauvinistic, and distorted, Spanish institutions had not failed.[54]

Examining the Spanish borderlands in the broad context of European exploration, exploitation, and colonization of the American continents from the sixteenth to the nineteenth centuries, Bolton conceptualized Spain's far northern frontiers as integral parts of Euro-American history. He concluded that, with the exception of New Mexico, Spain's movement into its far northern frontier was defensive in nature. He argued further that Spain's frontier institutions—the mission, presidio, and pueblo—not only were admirably suited to frontier conditions and defensive needs but also had exerted a lasting impact on the landscape and had paved the way for subsequent Euro-American colonizers. Missions and ranchos had broken ground for subsequent Anglo-American agricultural and pastoral development. Spanish pueblos had been the nucleus of major urban centers throughout the West. Spanish laws had influenced western mining, water, and community property rights, and Spanish terminology continued in use throughout the western states.[55]

Rejecting both the Hispanophobia of the Teutonics and the strident nationalism of the Turnerians, the borderlands school effectively refuted the allegation of Spain's institutional failure. Nevertheless, Bolton and his students retained their predecessors' definitions of the makers and nature of history. Caucasian males engaged in exploration and in the development of religious, political, military, and economic institutions make history. But the Spaniards whom the Teutonics had disparaged as a cruel, greedy, bigoted nonwhite lot of miscreants the Boltonians lauded as valiant, daring, heroic Europeans.[56] Where the Teutonics had seen institutional failure, the Boltonians saw a seedbed for Spanish civilization.

In either view, however, women and nonwhite males do not contribute to history. While the Boltonians did address the exploitation of the Indians, their discussion revolved around the mission's efficacy as a frontier institution, not around the lot of the Indian.[57] The early Spanish borderlands studies rarely mention racially mixed soldiers and settlers. When Bolton does briefly discuss California's mestizo and mulato colonists, he reaffirms Bancroft's views of their idle but kindly, hospitable, and happy character; and, like the contemporary popular historians, he makes a racial distinction between Californians and Mexicans: "Californians were superior to other Spanish colonists in America, including Mexicans," a superiority that he attributes to "the greater degree of independence, social at least if not political," caused by their isolation from Mexico and to their "good Castillian blood."[58] Women, who (to the historians) were neither intrepid explorers, barefooted black-robed missionaries, nor valiant lancers for the king, do not figure in Spanish borderlands studies. Until very recently, mention of women was limited to scattered references to intermarriage in the Americas, to women's relationship to the men who founded Spanish institutions, or, in the case of Amerindian women, to the institution of the mission itself.

Though Bolton touches briefly on the cultural significance of marriage between Spanish conquistadores and Amerindian women in the early conquest of the Americas, borderlands discussions of California native women center on their relation to the mission. Borderlands descriptions of rapacious attacks on Amerindian women by soldiers focus not on the women but on the conflict over authority that these attacks exacerbated between officials of church and state.[59] Until recently borderlands historians, like the Teutonics, attributed the problems of Spanish institutional development to the despicable behavior of the common soldiers, which was in turn blamed on their socioracial origins. In the 1970s, however, borderlands historians began to examine the experiences and contributions of the racially mixed *soldado de cuera* (leather-jacket soldier) and poblador (settler), who derived largely from the lower social classes of colonial Spanish society. Although this new generation of historians has dealt more equitably with the issue of race, it has still focused exclusively on soldiers and male settlers.[60]

Just as the early Boltonians dismissed the common soldier, so they dismissed the racially mixed wives of the artisans, soldiers, settlers, and convicts—women who endured difficult ocean voyages or who trekked over desert wastelands to settle Alta California. The only women systematically included are the wives of the governors, principally Eulalia Callis, with her marital strife, her "scandalous behavior;" and the problems that she caused the missionaries.[61]

Although the borderlands school studies end with the close of the Spanish colonial era, Bolton makes brief reference to Mexican women in connection with EuroAmerican expansion into the old Spanish borderlands in the 1820s and 1830s. Though he shows an awareness of the importance of intermarriage and miscegenation to frontier development, and of the significance of Mexican women's economic roles as property owners and consumers on the borderlands, he joins the popular historians in his uncritical acceptance of Euro-American males' claims that Mexican women preferred them to Mexican males.[62] While noting that James Ohio Pattie was a notorious braggart, Bolton nevertheless paraphrases Pattie's report that "at a fandango in Taos, the gateway to New Mexico, the American beaux captured not only all the señoritas, but the señoras as well. The jealous caballeros drew their knives." And "in California, long before the Mexican War," wrote Bolton, "it was a customary boast of a señorita that she would marry a blue-eyed man."[63] Thus Bolton accepts the distorted view that equated California women with the land that promised "freedom-loving, adventure-loving, land-hungry Americans" romance, exoticism, and adventure.[64]

PRESIDARIAS, POBLADORAS, CALIFORNIANAS, CHICANAS: REINTERPRETING SPANISH-MEXICAN WOMEN IN FRONTIER CALIFORNIA

Within the last two decades, social historians and feminist historians have illuminated nineteenth-century U.S. social, women's, Chicano, borderlands, and family history; and recent studies on colonial women in Mexico and Latin America have yielded information and analysis pertinent to women in Spanish-Mexican California.[65] Yet even this new body of literature fails to deal directly with Spanish-Mexican women on the remote outposts of empire. There are no published book-length scholarly studies of Mexicanas on nineteenth-century frontiers, and the periodical literature is sketchy and impressionistic rather than grounded in substantive primary research.

Recent studies of women in the Far West reflect a historiography in the initial stages of development. Current works include edited and annotated compilations of primary materials, most specifically of "westering" Anglo women's diaries and journals; descriptive works with varying degrees of analysis within the context of social, economic, and family history; and edited anthologies.[66]

Descriptive studies, including those of Sandra L. Myres and Julie Roy Jeffrey, have emphasized the perspective of Euro-American women and, in a neo-Turnerian version of the frontier as place (environment) and process, have viewed Amerindian and Mexican women as part of the new environment to which Yankee, midwestern, and southern white women pioneers must adapt.[67] Glenda Riley and Annette Kolodny have probed Euro-American women's images of Amerindians; and Sandra Myres has described Anglo women's response to Mexicans.[68] These works find that Anglo women generally shared Anglo men's racial antipathy to Amerindians and Mexicans, though they tended to be more sympathetic to women of other racial and cultural groups.[69] Proximity sometimes served to break down barriers, and in some instances Anglo women struck up friendships with Amerindian and Mexican women based on "mutual respect and trust."[70] Three anthologies, *New Mexico Women: Intercultural Perspectives* (1986), *The Women's West* (1987), and *Western Women: Their Land, Their Lives* (1988), address the critical, albeit thorny, issues of race, sex, class, and cultural interaction in the frontier West and Southwest.[71]

In many respects, however, these initial efforts continue to mirror the larger problems of the earlier historiography. That is, the new scholarship lacks a clear framework to examine the historical experience of women whose race and culture are not Anglo North American. Moreover, it often reflects the underlying assumptions and race and class biases of the earlier historiography. Historians of women in the frontier West, for example, have not yet grappled with defining the term "frontier" from a non-Anglo perspective, nor have they yet tackled the roles of English-speaking women in the imposition of Anglo hegemony. The new scholarship has indeed focused on gender, but its concept of gender ignores nonwhite, non-middle-class experiences on the frontier. And the lack of an integrative conceptual framework particularly hampers attempts to address the question of race and the nature of interracial contact, including interracial marriage.

Thus, Myres, Riley, and Susan Armitage find a "more peaceful version of Indian-white contact" in the diaries and journals of literate Anglo women, but they fail to reconcile this version with the brutality and violence that Amerindian and Mexican women experienced during the Anglo North-American conquest of the western frontier.[72] Although the underlying assumption that westering Anglo women were less violent than Anglo men may in fact be true, it is also true that Anglo women benefited directly from male violence that occurred before their own arrival in a particular region: frontier wars, army massacres, and the violence during the California gold rush.[73] Anglo women may have neither committed nor witnessed this violence, but they reaped its fruits: removal of Amerindians and Mexicans from the land base. And in addition to general violence rife in a society under conquest, Amerindian and Mexican women also suffered sexual violence.[74] Gerda Lerner and other feminist scholars have concluded that under conditions of military and/or political conquest, rape, abduction, and other acts of sexual violence against women of the conquered group are acts of domination.[75] Although Albert Hurtado and other scholars studying the history of Amerindian people in California have begun to address sexual violence, historians of women in the frontier West have not examined this subject, which is pivotal to the history of Amerindian and Mexican women.[76] While certainly women of all races and classes in the West experienced domestic violence, conquest and racism intensified sexual assault. Because racial inferiority was equated with sexual impurity—even prostitution—nonwhite women could be raped with impunity, just as they could be enslaved, killed, or worked to death like beasts of burden.

Anglo attitudes toward Mexican women have been the subject only of brief essays. In "Californio Women and the Image of Virtue," David Langum concludes that the pejorative stereotypes of Mexican women were class based, derived from the perceptions of lower-class Mexican women by upper-class Yankees like Richard Henry Dana.[77] But Dana did have the opportunity to observe elite Californianas, and Langum does not address Dana's underlying gender ideology. Furthermore, Langum's class explanation is merely an extension to women of Cecil Robinson's earlier interpretation of pejorative stereotypes of Mexicanos, an interpretation that has already been refuted.[78] In "The Independent Women of New Mexico," Janet Lecompte attributes Anglos' negative views of Nuevo Mexicanas' morality to sexist Anglo behavioral norms conditioned by the relatively constricted position of women in North American society and culture, and by the corollary view of womanhood as the upholder and symbol of American morality.[79] Unfortunately Lecompte does not develop the gender-based argument, nor does she fully address the issue of race.

Jane Dysart, Darlis Miller, and Rebecca Craver have published the only studies to date on the subject of interracial marriage.[80] These works describe but do not analyze significant historical, political, economic, and cultural issues inherent in interracial marriage and assimilation; and despite their recognition that intermarriage existed before the Anglo North American conquest, their point of departure is generally North American culture and society. Yet intercultural contact, interracial marriage, and mestizo children were part of Mexican women's historical reality long before the arrival of Anglo Americans on the landscape; this subject, especially, requires examination within a broader context.[81] Moreover, in the early periods of contact, when whites sought to establish trapping, trading, and other commercial relations with Indians and Mexicans, intermarriage and consensual unions were as much economic as they were sexual or romantic alliances. White men who married or lived with nonwhite women were assimilated into the women's culture. This pattern was conditioned by sex ratio, itself a manifestation of the particular stage of contact, which we must take into account before we can generalize about intermarriage and assimilation. In her exemplary study of the Spanish-Mexican women of Santa Fe, 1820–1880, Deena González grounds her examination of interracial marriage in Spanish-

Mexican patterns of racial and cultural contact, while also charting the economic changes that her subjects experienced with the change of legal and political institutions from Mexican to Anglo-American patterns.[82]

Earlier studies of nineteenth-century Chicano history include general discussions of Chicanas, particularly in relation to labor and the family, but they do not incorporate gender as a category of analysis. Those of Albert Camarillo, Richard Griswold del Castillo, and Ricardo Romo begin on the eve of the Mexican-American War and center on the development of Chicano communities in California's urban centers during the latter half of the nineteenth and early twentieth centuries.[83] Griswold del Castillo's more recent study on the Chicano family also begins after the US war with Mexico, as does the earliest social history of the Californios; and Roberto Alvarez's anthropological examination of family migration in Baja and Alta California focuses mainly on the period after 1880.[84] Recent social and frontier histories of Spanish and Mexican California and the Southwest, whether they derive from the Spanish borderlands school or from Mexican historical studies, either ignore women entirely or discuss them in very general terms.[85] For colonial California, one unpublished dissertation and three brief articles on marriage and childrearing patterns and on race, all by Gloria Miranda, constitute the totality of recent scholarly studies.[86]

But there is new scholarship in colonial Mexican and Latin American women's and family history that is invaluable to the study of Spanish-speaking women in eighteenth- and nineteenth-century California. Ramón Gutiérrez's *When Jesus Came the Corn Mothers Went Away* offers a singularly important point of departure for an examination of gender and marriage in colonial New Mexico.[87] Although Gutiérrez's is the only recent study that focuses on New Spain's northern frontier, Patricia Seed's *To Love Honor and Obey in Colonial Mexico* examines the changing laws and conflicts over marriage choice.[88] Sylvia Arrom's *The Women of Mexico City, 1790–1857* and Asunción Lavrin's work on nuns and women's wills address the status of colonial women in law, in the patriarchal family, in religious orders, and in social, economic, and political life.[89] The new scholarship revises earlier interpretations of Mexicanas as passive, male-dominated, and powerless. While most of these studies do not focus on frontier women, they provide a well-defined sociocultural and political context for such discussion by illuminating gender-specific Spanish colonial and Mexican laws and policies.

And there are rich sources for the study of frontier Spanish-Mexican women.[90] Though the standard archival sources for the Spanish colonial period are official reports, correspondence, diaries, and journals written by male missionaries and military authorities, they yield factual information about women's work and life in the missions and presidios, as well as insights into the gender ideology of the era. And although few Spanish-speaking women were literate, they did have petitions and letters penned for them.[91] There are also quantifiable sources: censuses, court records, and mission registers of baptisms, marriages, and deaths. The marriage registers reveal the extent of interracial marriage between Amerindian women and Spanish-mesitizo men. Both ecclesiastical and military records document the violence that soldiers committed against Amerindian women.[92]

For the Mexican period, civil, criminal, and ecclesiastical court records reveal that women sued and were sued for divorce (legal separation), for land, and for custody of children and godchildren, as well as for numerous social transgressions.[93] Court records document a significant increase in domestic violence against women; they also document violence by women. Court records, official reports, and correspondence yield information about race relations. Libros de solares (books of lots) record women's ownership of town lots, and there are also documents proving women's receipt and ownership of Mexican land grants. Before secularization in 1836, interracial marriages—now of Mexican women with European and Euro-American men—may be traced through mission registers.

For the era just before and after the American conquest, there are further quantifiable sources, in addition to the journals and correspondence of Anglo men and women, contemporary newspapers, and the literature of the gold rush. The records of the Land Grant Commission detail Mexican women's loss and retention of land grants. Extant Ayuntamiento (later City Council) records and Sole Trader records permit examination of Mexican women's economic life, as do the federal manuscript censuses. Women's wills and probate court records reveal the nature and disposition of women's property. Justice of the peace and parish records document interracial marriage. Justice of the peace and superior court records document crimes with which women were charged, crimes of which women were the victims, and indentures of children. Hubert Howe Bancroft's collection includes narratives from eleven Mexican women that provide significant information and insight into women's lives, work, family, race relations, and politics up to the 1870s, when the women were interviewed. Finally, family collections and papers in various repositories throughout the state contain women's correspondence, diaries, and journals of elite, literate Californianas and, in some cases, middle-class Mexican women who came to California in the latter half of the nineteenth century.[94]

The threads of Spanish-Mexican women's history run throughout these sources. What is missing is an approach to the history of the frontier that integrates gender, race, and culture or class as categories of historical analysis. An integrative ethnohistorical approach would enable us to examine women's roles and lives in their societies of origin, as well as to describe and interpret how conquest changed their lives and restructured economic and social relationships not only between the sexes but also among persons of the same sex. For example, although we know that Spanish-Mexican and Anglo-American societies were stratified along gender, as well as racial and class lines, research is wanting on the nature or extent of male domination and the subordination of women in Amerindian societies before 1769. Feminist anthropologists have suggested that male domination was not universal in the Americas, and that foraging societies—such as those that existed in California— were essentially egalitarian, but this hypothesis has not been tested. Nor have historians compared gender stratification and patriarchy in Spanish-Mexican and Euro-American frontier California. I have suggested here that violence toward women is part of the politics of domination. Likewise, pejorative stereotypes and the deracination of mestiza women reveal the intersection of ideologies of gender, sexuality, and race in the politics of conquest. But it is premature to generalize about women and race relations, intermarriage, and assimilation on the frontiers of expansion. We have not yet done the research.

For three centuries, American frontiers were bloody battlegrounds of European and Euro-American expansion and conquest and of Amerindian resistance. Impoverished Spanish-speaking mestiza, mulata, and other casta women who migrated to Alta California in the eighteenth century came as part of soldier-settler families recruited and subsidized to popu- late the military forts in imperial Spain's most remote outpost. These women began the process of reproducing Hispanic culture and society on this frontier. Their daughters and granddaughters continued it as the region changed from Spanish to Mexican political control. A developing agropastoral economy built on trade and Amerindian labor gave rise to greater social stratification and the beginning of class distinctions. By the mid 1840s the great-granddaughters of the first generation of women, then in the midst of their own childbearing years, themselves experienced war, conquest, and displacement. Many of them became part of the menial wage labor force of a new, expanding, capitalist economy and society that bought their labor as cheaply as possible while it devalued their persons racially, culturally, and sexually. It is time to reexamine the history of these women within a conceptual framework that acknowl- edges the sexgender, race, and culture or class issues that inhered in the politics and policies of frontier expansion, and to reinterpret the terms that define our changing reality on this frontier—presidarias, pobladoras, Californianas, Chicanas.

El ensayo se dedica a las mujeres que trabajan en los files del valle de Yakima. Ellas me lo elaboraron con su sudor, sus lágrimas y su risa. C/S

NOTES

1. For comprehensive bibliographies on the Spanish-Mexican frontier see John Francis Bannon, *The Spanish Borderlands Frontier, 1531–1821* (New York: Holt, Rinehart, and Winston, 1970), 257–87; Oakah L. Jones, Jr., *Los Paisanos: Spanish Settlers on the Northern Frontiers of New Spain* (Norman: University of Oklahoma Press, 1979), 309–32; David J. Weber, *The Mexican Frontier: 1821–1846* (Albuquerque: University of New Mexico Press, 1982), 377–407; Weber, "Mexico's Far Northern Frontier, 1821–1846: A Critical Bibliography," *Arizona and the West* 19 (Autumn 1977): 225–66; Weber, "Mexico's Far Northern Frontier: Historiography Askew," *Western Historical Quarterly* 7 (July 1976): 279–93. The following (not exhaustive) list includes titles discussing Spanish-Mexican women in early biographies, family histories, and histories of ranchos: Susanna Bryant Dakin, *A Scotch Paisano: Hugo Reid's Life in California, 1832–1852* (Berkeley: University of California Press, 1939); Bess Adams Garner, *Windows in an Old Adobe* (1939; reprint Claremont, CA: Bronson Press, 1970); Henry D. Hubbard, *Vallejo* (Boston: Meador Publishing Company, 1941); Tory E. Stephenson, "Tomas Yorba, His Wife Vicenta, and His Account Book," *The Quarterly Historical Society of Southern California* 23 (March 1944): 126–55; Myrtle McKittrick, *Vallejo: Son of California* (Portland, OR: Bindfords and Mort Publishers, 1944); Susanna Bryant Dakin, *The Lives of William Hartnell* (Stanford, CA: Stanford University Press, 1949); Angustias de la Guerra Ord, *Occurrences in Hispanic California*, trans. Francis Price and William Ellison (Washington, DC: Academy of Franciscan History, 1956); Edna Deu Pree Nelson, *The California Dons* (New York: Appleton-Century-Crofts, 1962); *The 1846 Overland Trail Memoir of Margaret M. Hecox*, ed. Richard Dillon (San Jose, CA: Harlan-Young Press, 1966); Madie Brown Emparan, *The Vallejos of California* (San Francisco: Gleeson Library Association, 1968); Virginia L. Carpenter, *The Ranchos of Don Pacifico Ontiveros* (Santa Ana, CA: Friis Pioneer Press, 1982). For a discussion of race as a central theme in the history of the West and a review of the most recent historical literature, see Richard White, "Race Relations in the American West," *American Quarterly* 38 (1986): 396–416. Herbert Eugene Bolton criticized American historiography for its nationalistic chauvinism in "The Epic of Greater America," *American Historical Review* 38 (April 1933): 448–74. See also Weber,

"Mexico's Far Northern Frontier: Historiography Askew." For a review of pervasive ideas about female inferiority, see Rosemary Agonito, *History of Ideas on Women: A Sourcebook* (New York: Perigee Brooks, 1977).

2.   Eileen Power, *Medieval Women*, ed. by M. M. Postan (London, New York, Melbourne: Cambridge University Press, 1975), 9.

3.   Hubert Howe Bancroft, *California Pastoral, 1769–1848* (San Francisco: The History Company, 1888), 305; Theodore S. Hittell, *History of California*, 4 vols. (San Francisco: The History Company, 1897), 2:469–511; see especially Hubert Howe Bancroft, *History of California*, 7 vols. (San Francisco: The History Company, 1886–1890); Zoeth Skinner Eldredge, *History of California*, 5 vols. (New York: The Century Company, 1915).

4.   Franklin Tuthill, *The History of California* (San Francisco: H. H. Bancroft and Co., 1866); Lucia Norman, *A Popular History of California from the Earliest Period of Its Discovery to the Present Time* (1867; reprint San Francisco: A. Roman, AGT, Publisher, 1883); J. M. Guinn, *A History of California and an Extended History of Los Angeles and Environs Also Containing Biographies of Well Known Citizens of the Past and Present*, 3 vols. (Los Angeles: Historic Record Company, 1915).

5.   Thomas R. Hietala, *Manifest Design: Anxious Aggrandizement in Late Jacksonian America* (Ithaca, N.Y., and London: Cornell University Press, 1985); Reginald Horsman, *Race and Manifest Destiny: The Origins of Racial Anglo-Saxonism* (Cambridge and London, 1981); Frederick Merk, *A Reinterpretation of Manifest Destiny and Mission in American History* (New York: Alfred Knopf, 1963); *The Mexican War: Was It Manifest Destiny?* edited by Ramon Eduardo Ruiz (New York: Holt, Rinehart and Winston, 1963).

6.   For a discussion of the contradictory but stereotypic images of women in Euro-American travel literature, see Antonia I. Castañeda, "The Political Economy of Stereotypes of Californianas," in *Between Borders: Essay on Mexicana/Chicana History*, edited by Adelaida del Castillo (Los Angeles: Floricanto Press, 1990).

7.   For a discussion of the early traditions of United States historical writing, see Michael Kraus and Davis D. Joyce, *The Writing of American History*, rev. ed. (Norman: University of Oklahoma Press, 1985): 92–135; John Higham, *History: Professional Scholarship in America* (New York, Evanston, San Francisco, London: Harper and Row, 1965): 3–25, 68–74, 148–49; David Levin, *History as Romantic Art: Bancroft, Prescott, Motley and Parkman* (Stanford, Calif.: Stanford University Press, 1959).

8. Bancroft, *California Pastoral*, 180; see also Edward N. Saveth, "The Conceptualization of American History, " in *American History and the Social Sciences*, ed. Edward N. Saveth (London: The Free Press of Glencoe, 1964), 10–11.

9. The Black Legend refers to an anti-Spanish policy perpetrated by Spain's European enemies accusing the Spanish monarch of brutal tyranny more extreme than that of their own absolutist regimes. See James J. Rawls, *Indians of California: The Changing Image* (Norman and London: University of Oklahoma Press, 1984), 42–43, 55, 64; Charles Gibson, ed., *The Black Legend: Anti-Spanish Attitudes in the Old World and the New* (New York: Alfred A. Knopf, 1971); Phillip Wayne Powell, *Tree of Hate: Propaganda and Prejudice Affecting United States Relations with the Hispanic World* (New York and London: Basic Books, 1971).

10. For discussion of Eulalia Callis, see Bancroft, *History of California*, 1:389–93; and Eldredge, *History of California* 1:5–8.

11. Bancroft, *History of California*, 2:64–78, footnote 23, 78; Bancroft, *California Pastoral*, 331–32; Richard A. Pierce, *Resanov Reconnoiters California: A New Translation of Resanov's Letters, Parts of Lieutenant Khvostov's Log of the Ship Juno, and Dr. Georg von Langsdorff's Observations* (San Francisco: The Book Club of San Francisco, 1972), 15–23, 69–72.

12. Bancroft, *History of California*, 2: 77–78, footnote 23, 78; and Susanna Bryant Dakin, *Rose, or Rose Thorn? Three Women of Spanish California* (Berkeley: The Friends of the Bancroft Library, 1963), 25–56.

13. Bancroft, *History of California*, 2:72.

14. Bancroft, *History of California*, 1:224, 257–69, 341–45, 603, footnote 6, 603, and footnote 13, 606.

15. For discussion of Nordic superiority in North American history, see Kraus and Joyce, *The Writing of American History*, 136, 145, 165; Bert James Lowenberg, *American History in American Thought* (New York: Simon and Schuster, 1972), 347–49, 371–75, 380–98; 458–65; Levin, *History as Romantic Art*, 85–87; and Edward Saveth, *American Historians and European Immigrants, 1875–1925* (New York: Russell and Russell, 1965), 90–92.For discussion of male supremacy, see Mary P. Ryan, *The Empire of the Mother: American Writing about Domesticity, 1830–1860* (New York and London: Harrington Park Press, 1985); Carroll Smith-Rosenberg, *Disorderly Conduct: Visions of Gender in Victorian America* (New York and Oxford: Oxford University Press, 1985); Mary Beth Norton, "The Evolution of White Women's Experience in Early America," *The American Historical Review* 89 (June 1984): 593–619; Lorna Duffin,

"Prisoners of Progress: Women and Evolution," in *The Nineteenth Century Woman: Her Cultural and Physical World*, eds. Sara Delamont and Lorna Duffin (New York: Barnes and Noble Books, 1978), 57–91; Agonito, *History of Ideas on Women*, 251–63; Susan Phinney Conrad, *Perish the Thought: Intellectual Women in Romantic America, 1830–1860* (New York: Oxford University Press, 1976), 15–41; Linda K. Kerber, *Women of the Republic: Intellect and Ideology in Revolutionary America* (1980; reprint New York and London: W. W. Norton & Company, 1986).

16. Weber, *The Mexican Frontier, 1821–1846*, 17.

17. Bancroft, *California Pastoral*, 305–34; Bancroft, *History of California*, vols. 2, 3, and 4.

18. Bancroft, *California Pastoral*, 76–79, 292–93; Bancroft, *History of California*, 2:69.

19. Bancroft, *California Pastoral*, 279–80, 305.

20. Bancroft, *California Pastoral*, 279–80, 322; Hittell, *History of California*, 2:491.

21. With few exceptions, Euro-Americans who left published accounts of Mexican California in their memoirs, journals, and correspondence described Mexican men in racist terms and consistently expressed expansionist sentiments toward US acquisition of California. Bancroft draws heavily upon these published sources, and he also had access to numerous unpublished manuscripts of similar sentiment. See Castañeda, "The Political Economy of Stereotypes of Californianas"; see also notes 78 and 79, below.

22. Alfred Robinson, *Life in California* (1846; reprint Santa Barbara: Peregrine Press, 1970), 51, and as quoted in Bancroft, *California Pastoral*, 326.

23. "They Wait for Us," as quoted in Horsman, *Race and Manifest Destiny*, 233.

24. Bancroft, *California Pastoral*, 312; Hittell, *History of California*, 2:179.

25. In Spanish-Mexican California, el fandango was a specific dance, while un fandango referred to an informal dancing party. Euro-Americans used the term loosely and applied it to all dances and any dancing occasion. Monte is a card game. See Lucille K. Czarnowski, *Dances of Early California Days* (Palo Alto: Pacific Books, 1950), 16, 22.

26. For early critiques of sexism in the historical scholarship, see "Part I: On the Historiography of Women," in *Liberating Women's History: Theoretical and Critical Essays*, ed. Berenice A. Carroll (Urbana: University of Illinois Press, 1976), 1–75; Gerda Lerner, *The Majority Finds Its Past: Placing Women in History* (New York and Oxford: Oxford University Press, 1979).

27. Discussion of the Teutonic hypothesis is based primarily on Kraus and Joyce, *The Writing of American History;* Lowenberg, *American History in American Thought;* George Callcots, *History in the United States, 1800–1860: Its Practices and Purpose* (Baltimore and London: The John Hopkins Press, 1970); John Higham, *Writing American History: Essays on Modern Scholarship* (Bloomington and London: Indiana University Press, 1970); Holt W. Stull, *Historical Scholarship in the United States and Other Essays* (Seattle: University of Washington Press, 1967); Saveth, *American Historians and European Immigrants.*

28. Kraus and Joyce, *The Writing of American History,* 165; Callcott, *History in the United States, 1800–1860,* 154, 162, 165–72; Lerin, *History as Romantic Art,* 78, 82–85, 121–37.

29. Frank W. Blackmar, *Spanish Institutions in the Southwest* (1891; reprint Glorieta, NM: Rio Grande Press, 1976).

30. Kraus and Joyce, *The Writing of American History,* 92–135, 164–209; Higham, *History,* 151–52, 167; Lowenberg, *American History in American Thought,* 131–32, 200–20, 328, 424.

31. Blackmar, *Spanish Institutions in the Southwest;* Lewis Hanke, ed., *Do the Americas Have a Common History? A Critique of the Bolton Theory* (New York: Alfred A. Knopf, 1964).

32. Rawls, *Indians of California,* 32–43.

33. Jean Francois Galaup de La Perouse, *A Voyage Round the World in the Years 1785, 1786, 1787 and 1788,* edited by M. L. A. Milet-Mureau, 3 vols. (London: J. Johnson, 1798), 2:202–4, passim; George Vancouver, *Vancouver in California, 1792–1794: The Original Account of George Vancouver,* Early California Travel Series, nos. 9, 10, and 22, ed. Marguerite Eyer Wilbur (Los Angeles: Glen Dawson, 1953–54), 19, 243–48; William Shaler, *Journal of a Voyage between China and the Northwestern Coast of America Made in 1804 by William Shaler* (Claremont, CA: Saunders Studio Press, 1935).

34. Manuel Patricio Servín, "California's Hispanic Heritage," *The Journal of San Diego History* 19 (1973): 1–9.

35. Trained in the Teutonic school, Henry Adams sometimes rebelled against its canons; see "The Primitive Rights of Women," in his *Historical Essays* (New York: Charles Scribner's Sons, 1891), 1–41.

36. Blackmar, *Spanish Institutions in the Southwest,* 112–51, 255–79.

37. Rodman W. Paul and Michael P. Malone, "Tradition and Challenge in Western Historiography," *The Western Historical Quarterly* 16 (January 1985): 27.

38. Saveth, *American Historians and European Immigrants*, 32–65; Richard Hofstadter, *Social Darwinism in American Thought* (1944; reprint New York: George Braziller, Inc., 1959), 170–200; Duffin, "Prisoners of Progress: Women and Evolution," 57–91.

39. Frederick Jackson Turner, *The Frontier in American History* (1920, reprint New York: Robert E. Krieger Publishing Company, 1976), 1-38. Turner's "The Significance of the Frontier in American History" first appeared in the *American Historical Association, Annual Report of the Year 1893* (Washington, DC, 1894), 199–227. Discussion of Turner and the frontier hypothesis of American history is based on the following: Ray Allen Billington, *America's Frontier Heritage* (New York, Chicago, and San Francisco: Holt, Rinehart, and Winston, 1966); *The Frontier Thesis: Valid Interpretation of American History?* ed. Ray Allen Billington (1966, reprint New York: Robert E. Krieger Publishing Company, 1977); *The Turner Thesis: Concerning the Role of the Frontier in American History*, ed. George Rogers Taylor (Lexington: DC Heath and Company, 1956); Richard Hofstadter, *The Progressive Historians: Turner, Beard, Parrington* (New York: Alfred A. Knopf, 1968); Earl Pomeroy "The Changing West," in *The Reconstruction of American History*, ed. John Higham (London: Hutchinson & Co., 1962), 64–81.

40. Turner, *The Frontier in American History*, 3, 23.

41. Joan M. Jensen and Darlis A. Miller, "The Gentle Tamers Revisited: New Approaches to Women in the American West," *Pacific Historical Review* 49 (May 1980): 173–213.

42. Hofstadter, *The Progressive Historians*, 104.

43. Frederick Logan Paxson, *The Last American Frontier* (New York: The Macmillan Company, 1910), 107.

44. Michael P. Malone, ed., *Historians and the American West* (Lincoln and London: University of Nebraska Press, 1983), 5.

45. See, for example, "California Historical Society, 1852–1922," *California Historical Society Quarterly* 1 (July–October 1922): 9–22.

46. Rawls, *Indians of California*, 137–70; Patricia Nelson Limerick, *The Legacy of Conquest: The Unbroken Past of the American West* (New York and London: Norton, 1987), 44–45, 82.

47. See, for example, "Society of Southern California: Fifteen Years of Local History Work," *Historical Society of Southern California Publications* (hereafter cited as HSSCP) 4 (1898): 105–10; Walter Bacon, "Value of a Historical Society," HSSCP 4 (1899): 237–42; Marion Parks, "In Pursuit of Vanished Days: Visits to the Extant Historic Adobe Houses of Los

Angeles County," Part 1, *Historical Society of Southern California Annual Publications* (hereafter cited as HSSCAP) 14 (1928): 7–63; Part 2, HSSCAP 14 (1929): 135–207.

48. Helen Hunt Jackson, *Ramona* (1884; reprint Boston: Little, Brown and Company, 1922); Richard Griswold del Castillo, "The del Valle Family and the Fantasy Heritage," *California History* 59 (Spring 1980): 2–15.

49. Tirey L. Ford, *Dawn and the Dons: The Romance of Monterey* (San Francisco: A. M. Robertson, 1926); Nellie Van de Grift Sánchez, *Spanish Arcadia* (San Francisco, Los Angeles, Chicago: Powell Publishing Company, 1929); Sydney A. Clark, *Golden Tapestry of California* (New York: Robert M. McBride and Company, 1937).

50. Carey McWilliams, *North from Mexico: The Spanish-Speaking People of the United States* (1948; reprint New York: Greenwood Press, 1968), 35–47.

51. Mabel Clare Craft, "California Womanhood in 1848," *San Francisco Chronicle*, 23 January 1898, 12–13. Van de Grift Sánchez, *Spanish Arcadia*, 237.

52. Charlotte S. McClure, *Gertrude Atherton* (Boston: Twayne Publishers, 1979); Lawrence Clark Powell, *California Classics: The Creative Literature of the Golden State* (Los Angeles: Word Ritchie Press, 1971), 103–14. For discussion of Anglo images and stereotypes of Californios that mention but do not focus on women, see James D. Hart, *American Images of Spanish California* (Berkeley: Friends of the Bancroft Library, 1960); Harry Clark, "Their Pride, Their Manners, and Their Voices: Sources of the Traditional Portrait of Early Californians," *California Historical Society* 52 (Spring 1974): 71–82; David J. Langum, "Californios and the Image of Indolence," *The Western Historical Quarterly* 9 (April 1978): 181–96; David I. Weber, "Here Rests Juan Espinosa: Toward a Clearer Look at the Image of the 'Indolent' Californios," *The Western Historical Quarterly* 10 (January 1979), 61–68.

53. Van de Grift Sánchez, *Spanish Arcadia*, 375.

54. Bolton, "The Epic of Greater America"; Bolton, *Wider Horizons of American History* (1930; reprint New York and London: D. Appleton-Century Company, 1939), 55–106. For a critique of the Bolton theory, see Hanke, *Do the Americas Have a Common History?*

55. Bolton, "The Mission as a Frontier Institution in the Spanish American Colonies," in his *Wider Horizons of American History*, 107–48; Bolton, *The Spanish Borderlands: A Chronicle of Old Florida and the Southwest* (New Haven, CT: Yale University Press, 1921), 7–10; Bolton, "Defensive

Spanish Expansion and the Significance of the Spanish Borderlands," in *Bolton and the Spanish Borderlands*, ed. John Francis Bannon (Norman: University of Oklahoma Press, 1964), 32–66.

56. John W. Caughey, "Herbert Eugene Bolton," in *Turner/Bolton/Webb: Three Historians of the American Frontier*, ed. Wilbur Jacobs, John W Caughey, and Joe B. Frantz (Seattle and London: University of Washington Press, 1965), 49; David J. Weber, "Turner, the Boltonians, and the Borderlands," *American Historical Review* 91 (February 1986): 68.

57. Bolton, "The Mission as a Frontier Institution"; Bolton, *The Spanish Borderlands*, 188–91; 192–202, 215–17, 279–87; Charles E. Chapman, *A History of California: The Spanish Period* (New York: The Macmillan Company, 1930), 352–96.

58. Bolton, *The Spanish Borderlands*, 294. The reciprocal influence between popular and scholarly history is worth noting in the case of Bolton and Van de Grift Sánchez, professional and popular historians who worked together: See John Francis Bannon, *Herbert Eugene Bolton: The Historian and the Man* (Tucson: University of Arizona Press, 1978), 171, 173.

59. Bolton, "Defensive Spanish Expansion and the Significance of the Borderlands," 61, 63; Bolton, "The Epic of Greater America," 452.

60. Jones, *Los Paisanos*; Max L. Moorhead, "The Soldado de Cuera: Stalwart of the Spanish Borderlands"; and Leon G. Campbell, "The First Californios: Presidial Society in Spanish California, 1769–1822," in *The Spanish Borderlands: A First Reader*, ed. Oakah L. Jones, Jr. (Los Angeles: Lorrin L. Morrison, 1974), 85–105 and 106–18.

61. Donald A. Nuttall, "The Gobernantes of Upper California: A Profile," *California Historical Quarterly* 51 (Fall 1972): 253–80.

62. Bolton, "Epic of Greater America," 452; Bolton, "Significance of the Borderlands," 56–58. Bolton, "Spanish Resistance to Carolina Traders," in *Bolton and the Spanish Borderlands*, ed. John Francis Bannon (Norman: University of Oklahoma Press, 1964), 148.

63. Bolton, "Significance of the Borderlands," 56, 58.

64. Ibid., 54.

65. For theories of gender and discussion of gender as a category of social and historical analysis in women's history, see Linda J. Nicholson, *Gender and History: The Limits of Social Theory in the Age of the Family* (New York: Columbia University Press, 1986); Smith-Rosenberg, *Disorderly Conduct*, 11-52; Linda Gordon, "What's New in Women's History"; and Carroll Smith-Rosenberg, "Writing History: Language, Class, and Gender," in *Feminist Studies-Critical Studies*, ed. Teresa de Lauretis (Bloom-

ington: Indiana University Press, 1986), 20–30 and 31–54; Joan Kelly-Gadol, "The Social Relation of the Sexes: Methodological Implications of Women's History," in *Sex and Class in Women's History*, ed. Judith L. Norton, Mary P. Ryan, and Judith Walkowitz (London: Routledge and Kegan Paul, 1983), 1–15; Catharine A. MacKinnon, "Feminism, Marxism, Method, and the State: An Agenda for Theory," in *Feminist Theory: A Critique of Ideology*, eds. Nannerl O. Keohane, Michelle Z. Rosaldo, and Barbara C. Gelpi (Chicago: The University of Chicago Press, 1982), 1–30. For early discussion of Chicana history see Rosaura Sánchez, "The History of Chicanas: Proposal for a Materialist Perspective," in *Between Borders: Essays on Mexicana/Chicana History*, ed. Adelaida del Castillo (Los Angeles: Floricanto Press, 1990); Mario García, "The Chicana in American History: The Mexican Women of El Paso, 1880–1920—A Case Study," *Pacific Historical Review* 49 (May 1980): 315–37; María Linda Apodaca, "The Chicana Woman: An Historical Materialist Perspective," in *Women in Latin America: An Anthology from Latin American Perspectives*, ed. Eleanor Burke Leacock (Riverside, CA: Latin American Perspectives, 1979), 81–100. For studies that use gender as a category of historical analysis with respect to Spanish-speaking women in the present West and Southwest, see Ramón Gutiérrez, *When Jesus Came the Corn Mothers Went Away: Marriage, Sexuality and Power in New Mexico, 1500-1846* (Stanford, CA: Stanford University Press, 1991); Sarah Deutsch, *No Separate Refuge: Culture, Class and Gender on an Anglo–Hispanic Frontier in the American Southwest, 1880–1940* (New York: Oxford University Press, 1987); Salomé Hernández, "Nuevo Mexicanas as Refugees and Reconquest Settlers," in *New Mexico Women: Intercultural Perspectives*, eds. Joan M. Jensen and Darlis Miller (Albuquerque: University of New Mexico Press, 1986), 41–70; Deena Gonzáles, "The Spanish-Mexican Women of Santa Fe: Patterns of Their Resistance and Accommodation, 1820–1880" (PhD diss., University of California, Berkeley, 1985); Antonia I. Castañeda, "Presidarias y Pobladoras: Spanish-Speaking Women in Monterey, California, 1770–1821" (PhD diss., Stanford University, 1990).

66. For a review of the historical literature and citations relative to new approaches to the history of women in the frontier West, see Glenda Riley "Frontier Women," in *American Frontier and Western Issues: A Historiographical Review*, ed. Roger L. Nichols (New York: Greenwood Press, 1986), 179–98; Sandra L. Myres, "Women in the West," in *Historians and the American West*, ed. Michael Malone (Lincoln: University of Nebraska Press, 1983), 369–86; Jensen and Miller, "The Gentle

Tamers Revisited"; Glenda Riley, "Images of the Frontierswoman: Iowa as a Case Study," *Western Historical Quarterly* 8 (1977): 189–202. For a discussion of literary stereotypes in historical portraits of frontier women, see Sandra L. Myres, *Westering Women and the Frontier Experience, 1800-1915* (Albuquerque: University of New Mexico Press, 1982), 1–11; see also William Cronon, Howard Lamar, Katherine G. Morrissey, and Jay Gitlin, "Women and the West: Rethinking the Western History Survey Course," *The Western Historical Quarterly* 17 (July 1986): 269–90; and Susan Armitage, "Women and Men in Western History: A Stereotypical Vision," *The Western Historical Quarterly* 16 (October 1985): 381–95. For studies taking more inclusive, multicultural approaches to women in the West, see del Castillo, ed., *Between Borders*; *Western Women: Their Land, Their Lives*, eds. Lillian Schlissel, Vicki Ruiz, and Janice Monk (Albuquerque: University of New Mexico Press, 1988); *The Women's West*, eds. Susan Armitage and Elizabeth Jameson (Norman and London: University of Oklahoma Press, 1987); Joan M. Jensen and Gloria Ricci Lothrop, *California Women: A History* (San Francisco: Boyd and Fraser Publishing Company, 1987); and Jensen and Miller, eds., *New Mexico Women*. For examples of edited and annotated source material on women in the West, see Sandra L. Myres, ed., *Ho for California: Women's Overland Diaries from the Huntington Library* (San Marino: Henry E. Huntington Library and Art Gallery, 1980); Rodman W. Paul, ed., *A Victorian Gentlewoman in the Far West: The Reminiscences of Mary Hallock Foote* (San Marino: The Huntington Library, 1980); Christine Fischer, ed., *Let Them Speak for Themselves: Women in the American West, 1849–1900* (New York: E. P. Dutton, 1977); Dame Shirley (Louise A. K. S. Clappe), *The Shirley Letters* (1854–1855; reprint Santa Barbara and Salt Lake City: Peregrine Smith, Inc., 1970).

67. For generally descriptive studies see Myres, *Westering Women*; Lillian Schlissel, *Women's Diaries of the Westward Journey* (New York: Schocken Books, 1982); Julie Roy Jeffrey, *Frontier Women: The Trans-Mississippi West, 1840–1900* (New York: Hill and Wang, 1979). For women and the family in California and the Far West, see Richard Griswold del Castillo, *La Familia: Chicano Families in the Urban Southwest, 1848 to the Present* (Notre Dame, IN: University of Notre Dame Press, 1984); Robert L. Griswold, *Family and Divorce in California, 1850–1890* (Albany: State University of New York Press, 1982); John Mack Faragher, *Women and Men on the Overland Trail* (Yale University Press, 1979).

68. Annette Kolodny, *The Land before Her: Fantasy and Experience of the American Frontiers, 1630–1860* (Chapel Hill and London: University of North Carolina Press, 1984); Glenda Riley, *Women and Indians on the Frontier, 1825–1915* (Albuquerque: University of New Mexico Press, 1984); Sandra L. Myres,"Mexican Americans and Westering Anglos: A Feminine Perspective," *New Mexico Historical Review* 57 (1982): 414–30.

69. Ibid.

70. Riley, *Women and Indians on the Frontier*, 224.

71. Jensen and Miller, eds., *New Mexico Women*; Armitage and Jameson, eds., *The Women's West*; Schlissel, Ruiz, and Monk, eds., *Western Women: Their Land, Their Lives.*

72. Susan Armitage, "Through Women's Eyes: A New View of the West," in *The Women's West*, eds. Susan Armitage and Elizabeth Jameson (Norman and London: University of Oklahoma Press, 1987), 17.

73. Limerick, *The Legacy of Conquest.*

74. Albert L. Hurtado, *Indian Survival on the California Frontier* (New York and London: Yale University Press, 1989), 169–92; Antonia I. Castañeda, "Sexual Violence in the Politics and Policies of Conquest: Amerindian Women and the Spanish Conquest of Alta California," in *Building with Our Hands: New Directions in Chicana Studies*, eds. Adela de la Torre and Beatrice M. Pesquera (Berkeley: University of California: 1993); Castañeda, "The Political Economy of Nineteenth-Century Stereotypes."

75. Gerda Lerner, *The Creation of Patriarchy* (New York and Oxford: Oxford University Press, 1986); see also Susan Brownmiller, *Against Our Will: Men, Women, and Rape* (1975; reprint Toronto, New York, London, Sydney, Aukland: Bantam Books, 1976); Christine Ward Gailey, "Evolutionary Perspectives on Gender Hierarchy," in *Analyzing Gender: A Handbook of Social Science Research*, eds. Beth B. Hess and Myra Marx Ferree (Newbury Park, Beverly Hills, London, New Delhi: Sage Publications, 1987), 32–67; Carole J. Sheffield, "Sexual Terrorism: The Social Control of Women," in *Analyzing Gender*, eds. Hess and Ferree, 171–89; Jalna Hanmer and Mary Maynard, "Introduction: Violence and Gender Stratification," in *Women, Violence and Social Control*, eds. Jalna Hanmer and Mary Maynard (Atlantic Highlands, New Jersey: Humanities Press International, Inc., 1987), 1–12; see also Anne Edwards, "Male Violence in Feminist Theory: An Analysis of the Changing Conceptions of Sex/Gender Violence and Male Dominance"; and David H. J. Morgan, "Masculinity and Violence," in *Women, Violence and Social Control*, eds. Hanmer and Maynard, 13–29 and 180–92.

76. See note 74.

77. David Langum, "Californio Women and the Image of Virtue," *Southern California Quarterly* 59 (Fall 1977): 245–50.

78. Cecil Robinson, *With the Ears of Strangers: The Mexican in American Travel Literature* (Tucson: University of Arizona Press, 1963); Ramond A. Parades, "The Mexican Image in American Travel Literature, 1831–1869," *New Mexico Historical Review* 52 (January 1977): 5–29; Paredes, "The Origins of Anti-Mexican Sentiment in the United States," *New Scholar* 6 (1977): 139–65; Doris L. Meyer, "Early Mexican American Responses to Negative Stereotyping," *New Mexico Historical Review* 53 (January 1978): 75–91; David J. Weber, "Scarce More than Apes: Historical Roots of Anglo-American Stereotypes of Mexicans in the Border Region," in *New Spain's Far Northern Frontier: Essay on Spain in the American West, 1540–1821*, ed. David J. Weber (Albuquerque: University of New Mexico Press, 1979), 295–307.

79. Janet Lecompte, "The Independent Women of Hispanic New Mexico, 1821–1846," *The Western Historical Quarterly* 12 (January 1981): 17–35; see also James H. Lacy, "New Mexico Women in Early American Writings," *New Mexico Historical Review* 34 (January 1959): 41–51; Beverly Trulio, "Anglo American Attitudes toward New Mexican Women," *Journal of the West* 12 (April 1973): 229–39.

80. Jane Dysart, "Mexican Women in San Antonio, 1830–1860: The Assimilation Process," *The Western Historical Quarterly* 7 (October 1976): 365–75; Darlis A. Miller, "Cross-Cultural Marriages in the Southwest: The New Mexico Experience, 1846–1900," *New Mexico Historical Review* 57 (October 1982): 335–59; Rebecca McDowell Craver, *The Impact of Intimacy: Mexican-Anglo Intermarriage in New Mexico, 1821–1846* (Southwestern Studies, Monograph No. 66, El Paso: Texas-Western Press, 1982); see also Kathleen Crawford, "María Amparo Ruiz de Burton: The General's Lady," *Journal of San Diego History* 30 (Summer 1984): 198–211.

81. González, "The Spanish-Mexican Women of Santa Fe," 111–53; Antonia I. Castañeda, "Presidarias y Pobladoras," Chapter 5.

82. González, "The Spanish-Mexican Women of Santa Fe"; for comparative purposes and studies of differing quality, see Sylvia Van Kirk, *Many Tender Ties: Women in Fur Trade Societies, 1670–1870* (Norman: University of Oklahoma Press, 1980); Walter O'Meara, *Daughters of the Country: The Women of the Fur Traders* (New York: Harcourt, Brace, and World, 1968); William R. Swagerty, "Marriage and Settlement Patterns of Rocky Moun-

tain Trappers and Traders," *The Western Historical Quarterly* 49 (1980): 159–80.

83. Albert Camarillo, *Chicanos in California: A History of Mexican Americans in California* (San Francisco: Boyd and Fraser Publishing Company, 1984); Ricardo Romo, *East Las Angeles: History of a Barrio* (Austin: University of Texas Press, 1983); Camarillo, *Chicanos in a Changing Society: From Mexican Pueblos to American Barrios in Santa Barbara and Southern California, 1848–1930* (Cambridge, MA, and London: Harvard University Press, 1979); Richard Griswold del Castillo, *The Los Angeles Barrio, 1850–1890: A Social History* (Berkeley and Los Angeles: University of California Press, 1979); see also Leonard Pitt, *The Decline of the Californios: A Social History of the Spanish-Speaking Californians, 1846–1890* (Berkeley and Los Angeles: University of California Press, 1971); Gloria H. Miranda, "Racial and Cultural Dimensions in Gente de Razón Status in Spanish and Mexican California," *Southern California Quarterly* 70 (Fall 1988): 235–64; Miranda, "Hispano-Mexicano Childrearing Practices in Pre-American Santa Barbara," *Southern California Historical Quarterly* 65 (1983): 307–20; Miranda,"Gente de Razón Marriage Patterns in Spanish and Mexican California: A Case Study of Santa Barbara and Los Angeles," *Southern California Historical Quarterly* 63 (1981): 1–21. For Chicano histories that treat pre-twentieth-century New Mexico, Texas, or the entire Southwest and include discussion of women, see David Montejano, *Anglos and Mexicans in the Making of Texas, 1836–1986* (Austin: University of Texas Press, 1987); Arnoldo De León, *They Called Them Greasers: Anglo Attitudes toward Mexicans in Texas, 1821–1900* (Austin: University of Texas Press, 1983); Gilberto Miguel Hinojosa, *A Borderlands Town in Transition: Laredo, 1755-1870* (College Station: Texas A&M University Press, 1983); Mario T. García, *Desert Immigrants: The Mexicans of El Paso, 1880–1920* (New Haven, CT, and London: Yale University Press, 1981); Alicia V. Tjarks, "Comparative Demographic Analysis of Texas, 1777–1793," *Southwestern Historical Quarterly* 77 (January 1974): 291–338.

84. Griswold del Castillo, *La Familia*; Pitt, *The Decline of the Californios*; Roberto Alvarez, Jr., *Familia: Migration and Adaption in Baja and Alto California, 1800-1975* (Berkeley, Los Angeles, London: University of California Press, 1987).

85. See note 60.

86. Gloria Elizarraras Miranda, "Family Patterns and the Social Order in Hispanic Santa Barbara, 1784–1848" (PhD diss., University of Southern Cal-

ifornia, Los Angeles, 1978); Miranda, "Racial and Cultural Dimensions in Gente de Razón Status"; Miranda, "Hispano-Mexicano Childrearing Practices"; Miranda, "Gente de Razón Marriage Patterns."

87. Gutiérrez, *When Jesus Came the Corn Mothers Went Away*, see also Ramón Gutiérrez, "Honor Ideology, Marriage Negotiation, and Class-Gender Domination in New Mexico, 1690-1846," *Latin American Perspectives* 44 (Winter 1985): 81–104.

88. Patricia Seed, *To Love, Honor, and Obey in Colonial Mexico: Conflicts over Marriage Choice, 1574–1821* (Stanford: Stanford University Press, 1988).

89. Sylvia M. Arrom, *The Women of Mexico City, 1790–1857* (Stanford: Stanford University Press, 1985); Asunción Lavrin, "Women in Convents: Their Economic and Social Roles in Colonial Mexico," in *Liberating Women's History: Theoretical and Critical Essays*, ed. Berenice A. Carroll (Urbana: University of Illinois Press, 1976), 250–77; Asunción Lavrin and Edith Couturier, "Dowries and Wills: A View of Women's Socioeconomic Role in Colonial Guadalajara and Puebla, 1640–1790," *Hispanic American Historical Review* 59 (May 1979): 280–304; *Latin American Women: Historical Perspectives*, edited by Asunción Lavrin (Westport, CT: Greenwood Press, 1978).

90. The sources identified in the following discussion are selective and representative. Each archival repository, including city and county libraries, museums, and historical societies, must be examined and/or reexamined for materials pertinent to women and must be approached with gender-specific questions.

91. The standard archival sources for Spanish-Mexican California history that contain transcripts and/or abstracts of government reports and correspondence, censuses, transcripts of hearings, petitions letters, testimonies, etc. include the bound volumes of *The Archives of California*, 63 vols., and the microfilm copy of the multivolume *Archivo de la Nación*, Bancroft Library, University of California, Berkeley, California; see also *The Writings of Junipero Serra*, 4 vols., ed. Antonine Tiebesar (Washington, DC: Academy of Franciscan History); *Writings of Francisco de Lasuen*, 2 vols., ed. (Washington, DC: Academy of American Franciscan History, 1965).

92. The Mission Archives at Mission Santa Barbara, Santa Barbara, CA, include, among numerous other sources, the extant *Book of Marriage, Books of Baptism, and Book of Death* for each mission, marriage testimonies, petitions for dispensation of consanguinity, mission censuses,

sermons, official reports, and correspondence. Also, individual missions may have additional archival material.

93. For the Mexican period, see *Archives of California*, as well as the "Vallejo Collection" and the reminiscences of individual women in the manuscript collection, including Catarina Avila de Rios, Angustias de la Guerra Ord, Apolinaria Lorenzana, Felipa Osuna de Marrón, Juana Machado de Ridington, Eulalia Pérez, María Inocenta Pico, Mariana Tortes, Dorotea Valdez, Rosalía Vallejo de Leese, Bancroft Library, Berkeley, CA. For the civil and criminal court records for the northern district of Mexican California, and the Libros de Solares for Monterey, see *The Monterey Archives*, 16 vols., Office of the County Recorder and Clerk, Salinas, CA; see also the Monterey Collection, San Marino, CA.

94. María Ignacia Soberanes de Bale, Papers and Correspondence, Bale Family Papers, Manuscript Collection, Bancroft Library, Berkeley, CA; *Records of the Land Grant Commission*, Archives of the State of California, Sacramento, CA.

"Pero No Somos Princesas ni Príncipes" (But We're Neither Princesses nor Princes)

With Dr. Antonia and Dr. Tomás Ybarra Frausto

We heard the tale of Washington—that there was lots of money, that they paid real well, and we thought about coming to Washington. We didn't have a car to travel in and this man, Eduardo Salinas used to contract people and we came with him. We didn't have much money we paid him $25 for us and $15 for each of the children. This was the first time we had traveled. This man said that he had housing and everything for the people, but it wasn't true.[1]

Irene Castañeda, "Crónica Personal de Cristal"[2]

Figure 3. Antonia Castañeda in Puebla, Mexico, 2011.

Courtesy of Luz María Gordillo

The interview between Drs. Tomás Ybarra-Frausto and Antonia Castañeda took place in the home of Dr. Ybarra-Frausto and his partner Dudley Brooks. Inside their downtown loft, white walls displayed a collection of Mexican masks and large bookcases with works on Chicana/o and Latin American art and literature surrounded the welcoming living room where we conducted the interview. Dr. Ybarra-Frausto is another founder of the inter-disciplinary academic field of Chicana/o Studies; he along with Dr. Joseph Summers, and Antonia Castañeda co-edited and published *Literatura Chicana: Texto y Contexto/Chicano Literature: Text and Context* (1972), a pivotal book in which they placed Chicano literature within historical antecedents in the Americas, and within a hemispheric context. The singular plurality of this text included among others: Mayan poetry, early literature by Latin American writers, an installment by Sor Juana Inés de la Cruz, and a letter by Irene R. Castañeda to her daugher, Antonia Castañeda. Family and community formation was at the core of

Chicana/o communities in the Pacific Northwest and other areas of the United States where Chicanas/os, while demanding their social space, nurtured a political identity that propelled a historiography of Chicana/o resistance in the US.

Drs. Ybarra-Frausto and Castañeda began to reminisce in the cozy living room where we all sat surrounded by Chicana/o creative work. While conversing and laughing, they narrated their story along with the story of thousands of Tejanos who were forced to migrate West in hope of not only better economic futures for their families, but perhaps most importantly of building legacies of resistance, hope, and dignity.

TY: When I was in San Antonio, my best buddy, who lived across the street, once every year... it was very strange... I would wake up to see the family start nailing their windows shut. And then their door shut. And the lady had a little garden and she wouldn't come to water it because they were packing to leave. And then a great big truck would come and he would go away—every year. And I would ask my mom, "a dónde se va?" He was my favorite buddy. "Al Norte" and I always wondered where the Norte was. And so, when I came to the Northwest, I realized this is the Norte. This is where a lot of migrants from Texas used to come to work in the hops and the apples and so on in Washington State. So it was very strange that I finally got to the place I wanted to go—but *you* were there.

AC: We were part of those families, Tomás. We migrated from Eagle Pass. I was born in Crystal City but when I was two we moved to Eagle Pass and then we migrated, when I was four, from Eagle Pass. But there were a lot of families from San Antonio in the labor camps in eastern Washington. In the labor camp where I lived there were mainly people from the lower valley, that is McAllen, Donna, Mercedes, Edinburg. But it was all part of that larger migration. And some families, beginning in the 1920s, went to the Midwest—to Ohio, Michigan, Minnesota, Illinois, and then especially after the Second World War, the migrations began from Texas, South Texas and San Antonio, to the Pacific Northwest.

We were in eastern Washington since 1946 and were among those families who settled out early and stayed precisely for the reason that you didn't have to migrate—because your father had a full time job, full time, not seasonal work. My father was semi-skilled as a carpenter, he had a year-round job in the labor camp. So, unlike most everybody else in the camp, who worked as seasonal migratory labor—we had steady income year-round. And that was all the difference in the world. That meant we didn't have to, like your friend, leave school in the middle of the year; we could go to school year-round.We were able to go from elementary through junior high through high school.

TY: I was teaching a television program for children. This was the time of NDEA, the National Defense Education Act, when the US government realized that America was falling behind. We were very insular. This was the era of Sputnik. So they put a lot of money into teaching languages to children. And I was working with Tug Anderson at the University of Texas. He was an expert on teaching languages to children and so that's how I got to the Northwest; because they had an NDEA summer institute at the University of Washington. And since I was going to be a language teacher for kids, that's how I ended up in the Northwest. But the real meeting with you and the meaning of the Northwest was when I went from Seattle to Eastern Washington because that's where the Chicana raza is.

AC: Yes.

TY: And I always will remember—I keep saying, Antonia, that I became a Chicano in the Northwest, not in San Antonio. Not in Tejas. Or I never considered myself a minority, but when I got to Washington, one weekend I decided to take the Greyhound bus and go across the Cascade Mountains to the Yakima Valley. I was working at the University of Washington; then I got a job in a little town called Bellevue, Washington. And so ... it was quite an adventure to go across the mountains. It was a Saturday evening, and I got off the Greyhound bus. It was dusk. And I saw the guys—those jovencitos. They had just taken a shower. Their hair was wet and curly. They had their camisas bien planchaditas. They were looking at the girls.

AC: It was a *paseo.*

TY: You know, they were eyeing each other and there was this electricity. And so I followed them and they went to a restaurantito, and they had Mexican food and it was like a homecoming because it was a kind of people that I had seen and had grown up with in Tejas. Working class people with a kind of a beauty, you know, they were quite beautiful. And then that weekend I went to church and found out, you know, the church was—I would call it segregated.

AC: It was segregated.

TY: The people, the growers sat downstairs and the Mexicanos sat in a little balcony in the church. And I thought, well, that was strange.

AC: My family was in eastern Washington since 1946 and the language of minority wasn't present when I was growing up, but we knew we were Mexican. We knew we were workers. We were made to feel that we didn't belong, even though most of us who were in those camps migrated from Tejas, were not from anywhere else but from Tejas. We didn't come from Mexico. We didn't come from Germany. We didn't come from any other place. In many of our cases, our grandparents and great-grandparents and tatarabuelos were in Tejas since the eighteenth century. In other cases, as in my mother's, they came during the Mexican Revolution. But this is almost two generations later. So this is a migration of "American citizens." But still that disdain, and I didn't think about it at the time in quite this way, but certainly it's clear that this disdain in which we were held in the Yakima Valley was because we were Mexican or Mexican-Americans, but also because we were workers. So it was both a question of race and class. And then, for those of us who were women, it was also a question of gender.

And so [the farm workers movement] was the realm, the venue, the vehicle, for which all of those issues that were present, and that were part of our lives and that were so deep and so profound, were finally able to be expressed. So this was the UFW, the United Farm Workers, which at that point was still the organizing committee, the United Farm Workers Organizing Committee (later it became the UFW). For us in the Pacific Northwest, because particularly there in the Yakima Valley we were all farm workers or related to farm labor, the movement crystallized our resistance. There were no Chicano/Chicana lawyers or doctors or engineers or professionals at the time. We were all workers. And even though the "American dream" at the time was "finish high school and you'll go far," my brothers all finished high school, as had I, as had other people, and they weren't able to get jobs in anything but agricultural work as manual laborers.[3] So the issue of opportunity, even as it is extolled as American virtues and dreams, was not present, was not available to us. Así es que cuando estalló el movimiento, when the movement hit, we all were hungry for a means by which we could come together and express the issues we had grown up with. The UFW in the Pacific Northwest, and particularly in Eastern Washington, precisely because it was a farm workers movement, was especially central to us. That's where that originates. Speaking for myself, the farm workers movement was critically important because it was a basis for public expression and action.

TY: Expression—even culturally. Maybe we should talk, Antonia, a little bit about Calmecac, because that was also a very key moment for me in the Pacific Northwest.

AC: Let's do, but let's talk about Calmecac in relation to you and me winding up at the University of Washington, studying with Joe [Sommers]. We are in his classes, as well as in the classes of other professors. There are very few of us at the University of Washington— You, me, Roberto Maestas, and Lupe Gamboa, who was about to start law school. On the basis of very few graduate students and a few undergraduates, we began to organize. We formed a consortium and pushed the university to fund us to recruit students in the Yakima Valley. Four undergraduates and I spent the next summer touring the valley, going to dances, going to churches, going to community halls, going to the camps, going everywhere we could to recruit undergraduate students. On the basis of that work we recruited ninety students and began to develop a critical mass at the University of Washington. It was the following summer that you and Dudley and the rest of us began to develop Calmecac—you and Dudley were central to that. It comes out of your idea of the need for a school. Why don't you talk about it.

TY: Well, Calmecac... thirty or somewhat years later we can critique a lot of the things. One of the critiques, of course, was that the movimiento sort of made everybody into a pre-Columbian prince or princess. The Calmecac, as you know, is a school de los nobles, in pre-hispanic times, where they instructed los hijos de los nobles, los príncipes, las princesas.

AC: Well, we weren't príncipes y princesas.

TY: [They taught them] the culture of their society. But our Calmecac was a people-centered Calmecac.

AC: Yes it was.

TY: It was a little Catholic church in Granger, Washington, that had been deconsecrated; it was right across from the town's elementary school. By this time I had met several of the people in the community. To me, it was like una revelación because there was so much culture. People could play the guitar. They could sing corridos. They could recite poetry. They could cook wonderfully. They could embroider. So we decided that they were going to be the teachers. The women were going to cook and show how to make tortillas, how to make frijoles, you know, our culture in an ordinary sense.

I had collected Mexican art. I remember I had a collection of pottery. I had gone to every state in Mexico and had bought one pot that I carried on the Greyhound bus until I came to Tejas and then I had the twenty-eight pots from each region in México, and so I gave them and we decided to have a little museum. It was a Calmecac museum. And I remember, this was a time when everything we had, we used. Maybe that's where I developed this notion that we all know how to, hacer de tripas corazón, to make what you can with what you have. So we decided to have this little museum. ... And I wanted to create a theater group and so I created, with the people in the community, El Teatro del Piojo. And of course this was the moment when black is beautiful—whatever has been negative in your culture, turn it upside down and make it positive. I guess we would say now, instead of a deficiency model, we were working on an asset model. What are the assets that the communities have? Well they have music, they have literature, they have orality, they have story telling. They are people who go to a movie and they would tell the story.

AC: They would re-tell the story.

TY: This is a kind of indomitable spirit. And so this is what, I think, flowed through the people. For example, in the teatro group we had people who were workers who left their job to go on tour because we thought it was important. We all knew that culture was significant and important. Not like in the larger society, where culture is away from the people. You have to pay to go to a museum. No. It was the food they ate. I remember always: It's our food—our values are what make us terrific. Anyway, this is for me the greatest treasure of the Northwest, and you, I think, exemplify all these qualities. You know, you're one of these treasures of the Northwest. De mucho corazón, Antonia. It was so wonderful to meet you and to meet your community, which took me in, in Eastern Washington.

AC: Indeed, Tomás. But you'll recall that that community was the community that you came from. We were Tejanos. We were Tejanas. We were from Tejas. And so you were an urban Chicano in San Antonio, which was always that mecca that we wanted to go to. But I think that that indomitable spirit, I think perhaps every people in their own time and their own place certainly have it. But what we're talking about is a particular espiritu Tejana. And I think that it came, in part, also because ... the Alamo is here in San Antonio. And so it's that spirit of energy and resistance to not being erased. Even though we weren't in the books and we weren't in the "official institutions." But we knew that we were there and we knew that we had not only survived but thrived within the realm that we created.I've talked at different times about the fact that one of the greatest lessons for me, growing up the way we did, was that no matter what the circumstances, and they were dire, there was always a sense of joy and a sense of beauty and a sense of creativity just from being alive.

NOTES

1. The national migration of migrant workers from Texas to the Pacific Northwest has largely evaded academic production. Historian Erasmo Gamboa was one of the few academics to turn his attention to the study and analysis of labor history of Mexicans in the Pacific Northwest. Though he provides a thorough analysis of Braceros between 1942 and 1947, in this article, he largely disregards Chicanas/os presence in the migratory process. Braceros, Chicanas/os, and Mexican American agricultural workers, however experienced similar living and working conditions while working in the fields. Gamboa states, "During the summer, the men were often driven from the tents by 100 degree temperatures, and in fall and winter, the fabric structures offered little protection from the inclement Northwest weather. Stoves, if provided, were virtually ineffective because the loose sides of the tent allowed heat to escape quite easily. Moreover, the frequent lack of adequate supplies of kerosene, coal, or dry wood meant that the stove heaters were often useless." See Erasmo Gamboa, "Braceros in the Pacific Northwest: Laborers on the Domestic Front, 1942-1947," *Pacific Historical Review* 56, no. 3 (August 1987): 378-398.

2. Antonia Castañeda, Tomás Ybarra-Frausto, and Joseph Sommers, eds., *Literatura Chicana, Texto y Contexto/Chicano Literature, Text and Context* (Englewood Cliffs, NJ: Prentice-Hall, Inc., 1972), 248.

3. Until the liberation movements of the 1960s and 1970s, most Chicanas and Chicanos were restricted to the secondary labor sector regardless of educational achievment. See Denise Segura, "Chicanas and Triple Oppression in the Labor Force," in *Chicana Voices: Intersections of Race, Class, Gender*, eds. Teresa Córdova et al. (Albuquerque: University of New Mexico, 1990); Mario Barrera, *Race and Class in the Southwest: A Theory of Racial Inequality* (Notre Dame: University of Notre Dame, 1979).

PART THREE

WRITING MESTIZA
AND INDIGENOUS
WOMEN INTO HISTORY

Engendering the history of Alta California, moving gender and the body to the center of historical inquiry, challenges us to rethink our conceptual, empirical, analytic and interpretive categories. It challenges us to question and reevaluate extant sources and our own assumptions as we approach them, and further summons us to expand the sources we use to study nonwritten text and other constructs of history.

"Engendering History"

"Sexual Violence in the Politics and Policies of Conquest: Amerindian Women and the Spanish Conquest of Alta California" (1993)

"Engendering the History of Alta California, 1769-1848: Gender, Sexuality and the Family" (1997)

Answering her own call, as well as that of other Chicana historians, to shift the frames and categories in which we study history, in both "Sexual

Violence in the Politics and Policies of Conquest," and "Engendering the History of Alta California," Castañeda moves the body, sex and gender to the center of historical analysis. Thus, in the following essays, sexual violence and the patriarchal family structure women's lives, evoke resistance, and frame the world in which they live.

The 1990s saw a growth and diversification in Chicana feminist scholarship, with Carla Trujillo's *Chicana Lesbians: The Girls Our Mothers Warned Us About*, Tey Diana Rebolledo's *Women Singing in the Snow*, and Aída Hurtado's *The Color of Privilege* as the tip of the iceberg. Chicana feminist scholars and theorists, throughout the disciplines, called for a centering of the body in critical analysis. Adela de la Torre and Beatriz M. Pesquera's co-edited anthology, *Building with Our Hands: New Directions in Chicana Studies* was part of this shift, and helped to fuel it. It was in this collection that Castañeda published "Sexual Violence and the Politics and Policies of Conquest," noting the marked absence of the body, especially women's bodies, as sites of knowledge in the historical scholarship on colonial California. In centering the body as a site of knowledge, Castañeda mapped the violent cultural shift that took place when the Spanish introduced sexual violence into the cultural landscape of eighteenth- and nineteenth-century California. Whereas sexual violence was not part of the culture of California indigenous communities, it was a central tool in colonial processes. Only with this basic understanding of the role of sexual "sociopolitical terrorism" in colonial California, she argues, can we begin to comprehend the persistence of sexual violence on the part of soldiers, priests, and settlers.

Likewise, in "Engendering the History of California," Castañeda names gender, sexuality and the family, as colonial tools in building, creating and bringing forth the colonial project on Spain and Mexico's northern frontier. Thus, the women's revolts that populate written and nonwritten texts of history, stand as bridges, where the Tongva leader Toypurina, among other indigenous women, drew on pre-colonial political and religious traditions to wage resistance against the colonial violence of their times. Extending her analysis to settler families, Castañeda demonstrates how Californio women were constrained by, participated in, and at times challenged, the patriarchal family structures that shaped colonial society. In utilizing social constructions of sex and social institutions, such as the family, as central axis of historical analysis, Castañeda sets a new level of inquiry for feminist historians to reach as we look to engender a new era of critical history.

CHAPTER 5

SEXUAL VIOLENCE IN THE POLITICS AND POLICIES OF CONQUEST

AMERINDIAN WOMEN AND THE SPANISH CONQUEST OF ALTA CALIFORNIA

In the morning, six or seven soldiers would set out together . . . and go to the distant rancherias [villages] even many leagues away. When both men and women at the sight of them would take off running . . . the soldiers, adept as they are at lassoing cows and mules, would lasso Indian women—who then became prey to their unbridled lust. Several Indian men who tried to defend the women were shot to death.

Junipero Serra, 1773

In words reminiscent of sixteenth-century chroniclers Bernal Díaz del Castillo and Bartolomé de las Casas, the father president of the California missions, Junipero Serra, described the depredations of the soldiers against Indian women in his reports and letters to Viceroy Antonio María Bucareli and the father guardian of the College of San Fernando, Rafael

Verger. Sexual assaults against native women began shortly after the founding of the presidio and mission at Monterey in June 1770, wrote Serra, and continued throughout the length of California. The founding of each new mission and presidio brought new reports of sexual violence.

The despicable actions of the soldiers, Serra told Bucareli in 1773, were severely retarding the spiritual and material conquest of California. The native people were resisting missionization. Some were becoming warlike and hostile because of the soldiers' repeated outrages against the women. The assaults resulted in Amerindian attacks, which the soldiers countered with unauthorized reprisals, thereby further straining the capacity of the small military force to staff the presidios and guard the missions. Instead of pacification and order, the soldiers provoked greater conflict and thus jeopardized the position of the church in this region.[1]

Serra was particularly alarmed about occurrences at Mission San Gabriel. "Since the district is the most promising of all the missions," he wrote to Father Verger, "this mission gives me the greatest cause for anxiety; the secular arm down there was guilty of the most heinous crimes, killing the men to take their wives."[2] Father Serra related that on October 10, 1771, within a month of its having been founded, a large group of Indians suddenly attacked two soldiers who were on horseback and tried to kill the one who had outraged a woman. The soldiers retaliated. "A few days later," Serra continued, "as he went out to gather the herd of cattle . . . and [it] seems more likely to get himself a woman, a soldier, along with some others, killed the principal Chief of the gentiles; they cut off his head and brought it in triumph back to the mission."[3]

The incident prompted the Amerindians of the coast and the sierra, mortal enemies until that time, to convene a council to make peace with each other and join forces to eliminate the Spaniards. The council planned to attack the mission on October 16 but changed the plan after a new contingent of troops arrived at the mission.[4] Despite this narrowly averted disaster, the soldiers assigned to Mission San Gabriel continued their outrages.

The soldiers' behavior not only generated violence on the part of the native people as well as resistance to missionization, argued Serra; it also took its toll on the missionaries, some of whom refused to remain at their mission sites. In his 1773 memorial to Bucareli, Serra lamented the loss of one of the missionaries, who could not cope with the soldiers' disorders at San Gabriel. The priest was sick at heart, Serra stated: "He took to his bed, when he saw with his own eyes a soldier actually committing deeds of shame with an Indian who had come to the mission, and even the children who came to the mission were not safe from their baseness."[5]

Conditions at other missions were no better. Mission San Luis Obispo also lost a priest because of the assaults on Indian women. After spending two years as the sole missionary at San Luis, Father Domingo Juncosa asked for and received permission to return to Mexico because he was "shocked at the scandalous conduct of the soldiers" and could not work under such abominable conditions.[6] Even before San Luis Obispo was founded in the early fall of 1772, Tichos women had cause to fear. The most notorious molesters of non-Christian women were among the thirteen soldiers sent on a bear hunt to this area during the previous winter of starvation at Monterey.[7]

The establishment of new missions subjected the women of each new area to sexual assaults. Referring to the founding of the mission at San Juan Capistrano, Serra wrote that "it seems all the sad experiences that we went through at the beginning have come to life again. The soldiers, without any restraint or shame, have behaved like brutes toward the Indian women."[8] From this mission also, the priests reported to Serra that the soldier-guards went at night to the nearby villages to assault the women and that hiding the women did not restrain the brutes, who beat the men to force them to reveal where the women were hidden. Non-Christian Indians in the vicinity of the missions were simply not safe. They were at the mercy of soldiers with horses and guns.[9]

In 1773, a case of rape was reported at San Luis Rey, one at San Diego, and two cases at Monterey the following year.[10] Serra expressed his fears and concern to Governor Felipe de Neve, who was considering establishing a new presidio in the channel of Santa Barbara. Serra told Neve that he took it for granted that the insulting and scandalous conduct of the soldiers "would be the same as we had experienced in other places which were connected with presidios. Perhaps this one would be worse."[11]

Native women and their communities were profoundly affected by the sexual attacks and attendant violence. California Amerindians were peaceable, non-aggressive people who highly valued harmonious relationships. Physical violence and the infliction of bodily harm on one another were virtually unknown. Women did not fear men. Rape rarely, if ever, occurred. If someone stole from another or caused another's death, societal norms required that the offending party make reparations to the individual and/or the family. Appropriate channels to rectify a wrong without resorting to violence existed.[12]

Animosity, when it did surface, was often worked out ritualistically— for example, through verbal battles in the form of war songs, or song fights that lasted eight days, or encounters in which the adversaries threw stones across a river at each other with no intent actually to hit or physically injure the other party. Even among farming groups such as the Colorado River people, who practiced warfare and took women and children captive, female captives were never sexually molested. The Yumas believed that intimate contact with enemy women caused sickness.[13]

Thus, neither the women nor their people were prepared for the onslaught of aggression and violence the soldiers unleashed against them. They were horrified and terrified. One source reported that women of the San Gabriel and other southern missions raped by the soldiers were considered contaminated and obliged to undergo an extensive purification, which included a long course of sweating, the drinking of herbs, and other forms of purging. This practice was consistent with the people's belief that sickness was caused by enemies. "But their disgust and abhorrence," states the same source, "never left them till many years after."[14] Moreover, any child born as a result of these rapes, and apparently every child with white blood born among them for a very long time, was strangled and buried.[15]

Father Pedro Font, traveling overland from Tubac to Monterey with the Anza expedition between September 1775 and May 1776, recorded the impact of the violence on the native people he encountered. Font's diary verifies the terror in which native Californians, especially the women, now lived. Everybody scattered and fled at the sight of Spaniards. The women hid. They no longer moved about with freedom and ease. The people were suspicious and hostile. The priests were no longer welcome in the living quarters.

The Quabajay people of the Santa Barbara Channel, Font wrote, "appear to us to be gentle and friendly, not war-like. But it will not be easy to reduce them for they are displeased with the Spaniards for what they have done to them, now taking their fish and their food . . . now stealing their women and abusing them."[16] Upon encountering several unarmed Indians on Friday, February 23, Font commented that "the women were very cautious and hardly one left their huts, because the soldiers of Monterey . . . had offended them with various excesses."[17]

At one village, Font noted, he was unable to see the women close at hand because as soon as the Indians saw his party, "they all hastily hid in their huts, especially the girls, the men remaining outside blocking the door and taking care that nobody should go inside."[18] Font attempted to become acquainted with the people of another village on the channel. He went to the door, but "they shut the inner door on me ... this is the result of the extortions and outrages which the soldiers have perpetrated when in their journeys they have passed along the Channel, especially at the beginning."[19] Font echoed Serra's concern that the sexual assaults and other outrages had severely retarded missionization in California.

Serra and his co-religionists had great cause for concern, because the missions were not meeting their principal objective of converting Amerindians into loyal Catholic subjects who would repel invading

European forces from these shores. By the end of 1773, in the fifth year of the occupation of Alta California, fewer than five hundred baptisms and only sixty-two marriages had been performed in the five missions then existing.[20] Since the marriages probably represented the total adult converts, that meant that the remaining four hundred converts were children. These dismal statistics fueled arguments for abandoning the California missions. While various reasons may be cited for the failure to attract adult converts, certainly the sexual attacks and the impact of that violence on women and their communities were primary among them.

Few historians have recognized that the sexual extortion and abuse of native women gravely affected the political, military, religious, and social developments on this frontier. In 1943, Sherburne F. Cook commented that "the entire problem of sexual relations between whites and the natives, although one which was regarded as very serious by the founders of the province, has apparently escaped detailed consideration by later historians."[21] Cook tackled the issue in demographic terms and wrote about the catastrophic decline in the Indian population as a result of alien diseases, including venereal diseases, brought in by Europeans, as well as other maladies of the conquest.[22]

Almost thirty years later, Edwin A. Beilharz wrote that "the major causes of friction between Spaniard and Indian were the abuse of Indian women and the forced labor of Indian men. . . . Of the two, the problem of restraining the soldiers from assaulting Indian women was the more serious."[23] In his study of the administration of Governor Felipe de Neve, Beilharz notes that Neve recognized the seriousness of the problem and tried to curb the abuses.

Since the 1970s, the decade that saw both the reprinting of Cook's work and the publication of the Beilharz study, the development of gender as a category of analysis has enabled us to reexamine Spanish expansion to Alta California with new questions about sex and gender. Cook, Beilharz, and other scholars initiated but did not develop the discussion about the centrality of sex/gender issues to the politics and policies of conquest.

It is clear that the sexual exploitation of native women and related violence seriously threatened the political and military objectives of the colonial enterprise in California. Repeated attacks against women and summary reprisals against men who dared to interfere undermined the efforts of the priests to attract Amerindians to the missions and to Christianity. They also thwarted whatever attempts the military authorities might make to elicit political or military allegiance from the native peoples.[24]

From the missionaries' point of view, the attacks had more immediate, deleterious consequences for the spiritual conquest of California, because such actions belied significant principles of the Catholic moral theology they were trying to inculcate. As the primary agents of Christianization/Hispanicization, the missionaries argued that they could not teach and Amerindians could not learn and obey the moral strictures against rape, abduction, fornication, adultery, and all forms of sexual impurity while the soldiers persisted in their licentiousness and immorality. Their actions repudiated the very morality the friars were to inculcate.[25]

Early conflict between ecclesiastical and civil-military officials over deployment and discipline of the mission escort soon gave rise to constant bitter disputes centering on the question of authority and jurisdiction over the Indians in California. The conflict over control of the Indians revolved around the issue of their segregation from the non-Indian population. Rooted in the early conquest and consequent development of colonial Indian policy, the issue has been extensively discussed by other historians. The concern here is to examine it specifically from the point of view of sex/gender and to define a context for explaining why, despite strenuous efforts by church and state alike, there was little success in arresting the attacks on Indian women.[26]

Serra, for his part, blamed the military commanders and, once appointed, the governor. They were, he said, lax in enforcing military discipline and unconcerned about the moral fiber of their troops. They failed to punish immoral soldiers who assaulted native women, were flagrantly incontinent, or took Amerindian women as concubines. In California, he stated, secular authorities not only condoned the soldiers' assaults on Indian women but interfered with the missionaries' efforts to counter the abuse, and thereby exceeded their authority with respect to Amerindians.[27]

To argue his case against Lieutenant Pedro Fages, the military commander, and to muster political and economic support for the California establishments, Serra made the arduous trip to Mexico City for an audience with Viceroy Bucareli. He left California in September of 1772 and arrived in Mexico the following February. At the viceroy's request, Serra submitted a lengthy work entitled "Report on the General Conditions and Needs of the Missions and Thirty-Two Suggestions for Improving the Government of the Missions."[28] Serra addressed sex/gender issues as part of several grievances against Fages's command. His recommendations for curtailing the sexual violence and general malfeasance of the soldiers were that Fages should be removed and that Spaniards who married Indian women should be rewarded.

Once the viceroy had removed the lieutenant, Serra continued, he should give strict orders to Fages's successor that, upon the request of any missionary, "he should remove the soldier or soldiers who give bad example, especially in the matter of incontinence . . . and send, in their place, another or others who are not known as immoral or scandalous."[29]

Drawing on colonial tradition established much earlier in New Spain, wherein colonial officials encouraged intermarriage with Amerindian noblewomen in order to advance particular political, military, religious, or social interests, Serra suggested that men who married newly Christianized "daughters of the land" be rewarded.[30] In the second to last of his thirty-two suggestions, Serra asked Bucareli to "allow a bounty for those, be they soldiers or not, who enter into the state of marriage with girls of that faraway country, new Christian converts."[31]

Serra specified the three kinds of bounty to be given the individual: an animal for his own use immediately upon being married; two cows and a mule from the royal herd after he had worked the mission farms for a year or more; and, finally, allotment of a piece of land. Since soldiers were subject to being transferred from one mission or presidio to another, Serra further recommended that he who married a native woman should be allowed to remain permanently attached to his wife's mission.[32]

With this recommendation, which he discussed in more detail in a subsequent letter to the viceroy, Serra hoped to solve several related problems.[33] He sought to curb the sexual attacks on Indian women as well as to induce soldiers to remain and become permanent settlers in Alta California. Theoretically, soldiers would thereby remain on the frontier, and formal and permanent unions with Indian women would allay the natives' mistrust and help to forge a bond between them and the soldiers. These marriages would thus help to ease Indian-military tensions while also cementing Catholic family life in the region.[34]

It was equally important to remove temptation and opportunity for licentious behavior. Thus, in a second memorial to the viceroy, written in April of 1773, a little over a month after his report, Serra forcefully argued against the proposal that the annual supply ships from San Blas be replaced with mule trains coming overland. In addition to the greater expense of an overland supply line, he reasoned, the presence of one hundred guards and muleteers crossing the country would add to "the plague of immorality" running rampant in California.[35]

The document that resulted from the official review of Serra's memorial, the *Reglamento Provisional*—generally known as the *Echeveste Regulations*—was the first regulatory code drawn up for California. The *Echeveste Regulations* acted favorably on twenty-one of Serra's thirty-two original recommendations, including the removal of Fages as military commander.[36]

Implementation of the new regulations, however, did not stop the abuse of women or the immorality of the soldiers. Serra continued to blame the civil-military authorities. He charged Captain Fernando de Rivera y Moncada, who replaced Fages, with currying the soldiers' favor;

and he subsequently accused the newly appointed governor, Felipe de Neve, of antireligiosity and anticlericalism. Thus, in the summary of Franciscan complaints against Neve, which Francisco Panagua, guardian of the College of San Fernando, sent Viceroy Mayorga in 1781, Father Panagua wrote that "another consequence . . . of the aversion which the said Governor [Neve] has for the religious, is that the subordinates . . . live very libidinously in unrestrained and scandalous incontinence as they use at will Indian women of every class and strata."[37] Serra further charged that Neve allowed fornication among the soldiers, "because, so I have heard him say, . . . it is winked at in Rome and tolerated in Madrid."[38]

Serra's charges against Fages, Rivera, and Neve were not well founded. As head of the California establishments, each was fully cognizant that the soldiers' excesses not only undermined military discipline, and thus their own command, but also seriously jeopardized the survival of the missions and the presidios. Fundamentally, the assaults against women were unwarranted, unprovoked, hostile acts that established conditions of war on this frontier. Although the native peoples by and large did not practice warfare, they were neither docile nor passive in the face of repeated assaults. The people of the South were especially aggressive. The country between San Diego and San Gabriel remained under Indian control for a long time.[39] It was in this region that the Indians marshaled their strongest forces and retaliated against the Spaniards. Some of the engagements, such as the one at San Gabriel in 1771, were minor skirmishes. Others were full-fledged attacks. In 1775 at Mission San Diego, for example, a force of eight hundred razed the mission, killed one priest and two artisans, and seriously wounded two soldiers. Women participated and sometimes even planned and/or led the attacks. In October 1785, Amerindians from eight *rancherías* united under the leadership of one woman and three men and launched an attack on Mission San Gabriel for the purpose of killing all the Spaniards. Toypurina, the twenty four-year-old medicine woman of the Japchivit *ranchería,* used her considerable influence as a medicine woman to persuade six of the eight villages to join the rebellion.

The attack was thwarted. Toypurina was captured and punished along with the other three leaders.[40]

Throughout their terms, Fages, Rivera, and Neve were keenly aware that Amerindians greatly outnumbered Spain's military force in the fledgling settlement and that, ultimately, the soldiers could not have staved off a prolonged Indian attack. Neve's greatest fear, expressed in his request to Bucareli for more commissioned officers, was that "if an affair of this kind [disorders caused by soldiers] ever results in a defeat of our troops, it will be irreparable if they [the Indians] come to know their power. We must prevent this with vigor."[41]

Therefore, during their respective administrations, the military authorities enforced Spain's legal codes, as well as imperial policy regarding segregation of Amerindians from non-Indians as a protective measure for the former. They prosecuted soldiers for major and minor crimes, and they issued their own edicts to curb the soldiers' abuse of Amerindians in general and women in particular. Their authority, however, was circumscribed by Spain's highly centralized form of government.[42]

While the governor of the Californias was authorized to try major criminal cases such as those involving homicide and rape, judgment and sentence were decided at the viceregal level in Mexico City. With the separation of the Interior Provinces from the kingdom of New Spain in 1776, the commandant-general, who combined in his office civil, judicial, and military powers, became the final arbiter.[43]

A 1773 case illustrates the complexity of legal procedures. This case —in which a corporal, Mateo de Soto, and two soldiers, Francisco Avila and Sebastian Alvitre, were accused of raping two young Amerindian girls and killing one of them near the mission of San Diego—dragged on for five years. Fages, Rivera, and Neve all dealt with the case, which occurred while Fages was military commander. Fages received the official complaint from Mariano Carrillo, sergeant at the San Diego presidio, who had interviewed the young survivor at that presidio in the presence of four soldiers acting as witnesses. The girl was accompanied to the presidio by two mission priests and an interpreter, who was also present at the interview.[44]

Fages forwarded the documents to Viceroy Bucareli in Mexico City and, on Bucareli's order, subsequently sent a copy to Felipe Barri, then governor of the Californias, at Loreto. When Rivera replaced Fages, he complied with the viceroy's order to bind the men for trial and to send them to Loreto, the capital of the Californias, in Baja California. By 1775, when Rivera sent Avila and Alvitre to Loreto (Soto had deserted and was never apprehended), Neve had replaced Barri as governor of the Californias. It fell to Neve to hear testimony and conduct the trial, which he opened on October 19, 1775.

The trial, including testimony from six soldiers and comments from the accused after Carrillo's charges were read to them, produced voluminous documents. Neve concluded the trial on November 22 and sent a copy of the entire proceedings to the viceroy for final disposition, along with a statement noting certain discrepancies from proscribed judicial procedure. Upon receipt of the proceedings, Bucareli turned the file over to Teodoro de Croix, recently appointed commandant-general of the Interior Provinces, which included the Californias.[45]

Almost three years elapsed before Croix called in the case.[46] On August 26, 1778, his legal adviser, Pedro Galindo Navarro, submitted his opinion to Croix. In Navarro's opinion, the accusation of rape and homicide was not proven. The dead child's body, he argued, was not examined or even seen; the identification of the soldiers accused was unsatisfactory, since it appeared to have been prompted by the interpreter; the entire charge rested on the testimony of a child, "poorly explained by an interpreter." Finally, the accused denied the charge.[47]

Navarro recommended that the penalty for Avila and Alvitre, who had been detained during the five years of the trial, be commuted to time served and that they should be sentenced to remain and become citizens of California. Croix accepted these recommendations. He issued the order, and the two discharged soldiers were enrolled in the list of settlers at the new pueblo of San José de Guadalupe.[48]

Whether local officials would have convicted the soldiers of rape and homicide must remain a matter of conjecture. In any event, despite laws and prosecutions, the sexual exploitation of Indian women did not cease. The missionaries continuously reported that soldiers "go by night to nearby villages for the purpose of raping Indian women."[49] And while some cases were recorded, many more must surely have gone unreported. Nevertheless, it is clear that the commandants and the governors did prosecute and take disciplinary action when charges were filed against individual soldiers. Contrary to Serra's charges of laxity and complicity, Fages, Rivera, and Neve did exert the full measure of their authority in this and other reported cases of sexual violence or abuse. Abundant evidence details the dual policy of prevention and punishment implemented by the three seasoned frontier administrators in their ongoing effort to check the soldiers' excesses.[50]

Ever concerned that Amerindians would discover the real weakness of the Spanish position in California, Neve sought to prevent the sexual attacks, and thereby to defuse the military and political conflicts they gave rise to, by forbidding all troops, including sergeants and corporals, from entering Indian villages. Only soldiers escorting the priests on sick calls were exempt from this order, and then the soldier was not to leave the missionary's side. Escort guards were strictly admonished against misconduct and were severely punished if they disobeyed.[51]

In the same vein, he prohibited soldiers of the mission guard from spending the night away from the mission—even if the priests demanded it. Neve emphatically repeated this same order in the instructions he left to Pedro Fages, who succeeded him as governor in September of 1782. "It is advisable," Neve further instructed Fages, "that we muzzle ourselves and not exasperate the numerous heathendom which surround us, conducting ourselves with politeness and respect. . . . It is highly useful to the service of the King and the public welfare that the heathen of these establishments do not learn to kill soldiers."[52]

Governor Fages was equally emphatic when he issued the following order in 1785: "Observing that the officers and men of these presidios are comporting and behaving themselves in the missions with a vicious license which is very prejudicial because of the scandalous disorders which they incite among the gentile and Christian women, I command you, in order to prevent the continuation of such abuses, that you circulate a prohibitory edict imposing severe penalties upon those who commit them."[53]

A decade later, Viceroy Branciforte followed up Neve's earlier order with his own decree prohibiting troops from remaining overnight away from the presidios, because among other reasons this practice was "prejudicial to good discipline and Christian morals."[54] Governor Diego de Borica, who succeeded Fages in 1794, issued a similar order the following year. These edicts had little effect.

Soldiers and civilian settlers alike disregarded the civil laws against rape as well as military orders against contact with Amerindian women outside of narrowly proscribed channels. The records verify that sexual attacks continued in areas adjacent to missions, presidios, and pueblos throughout the colonial period. Amerindian women were never free from the threat of rapacious assaults.

Why, despite strenuous efforts by officials of both church and state, did the sexual attacks persist unabated? Why, despite the obviously serious political and military conflicts the assaults ignited, did they continue? In view of extensive legislation, royal decrees, and moral prohibitions against sexual and other violence, what, in the experience of the men who came here, permitted them to objectify and dehumanize Indian women to the degree that chasing and lassoing them from mounted horses and then raping them reveals?

Until recently, scholars attributed sexual violence and other concurrent social disorders in early California to the race and culture of the mixed-blood soldier-settler population recruited or banished to this frontier. Institutional historians concluded, with Bancroft, that the "original settlers, most of them half-breeds of the least energetic classes . . . , were of a worthless character."[55] Institutional studies generally concurred with Serra's view that the soldiers were recruited from the scum of the society. Serra had repeatedly beseeched Bucareli to send "sturdy, industrious Spanish families" and asked him to advise the governor of the Californias "not to use exile to these missions as punishment for the soldier whom he may detest as insolent or perverse."[56]

In the last two decades, the conditions that shaped institutional development on this frontier have been reexamined. In addition, studies of the social history of the people recruited to Alta California have been undertaken. As a result, the earlier interpretations have been rejected. Scholars now conclude that the slow development of colonial institutions in California was attributable to limited resources, lack of uniform military codes, and other structural problems—and not to the racial or social-class origins of the soldier-settler population.[57]

Instead, the mixed-blood recruits—who themselves derived from other frontier settlements—were admirably able to survive the harsh privations and onerous conditions. In so doing, they established lasting foundations of Spanish civilization in California and the Southwest. Although the cuera (leather-jacket) soldiers were indeed unruly and undisciplined, their behavior reflected a particular informality and a "peculiar attitude of both officers and men."[58] According to revisionist studies, the isolation and distance from the central government, a shared life of hardship and risk, and the fact that blood and marriage ties existed among officers and common soldiers—all contributed to this attitude of informality and independence. Oakah Jones, Jr., makes essentially the same argument for contentious frontier settlers and extends the analysis. In his view, the racially mixed settlers responded to the often brutal conditions on the far northern and Pacific frontiers by creating a distinct frontier culture, characterized by self-reliance, individualism, regionalism, village orientation, resistance to outside control, innovativeness, family cohesiveness, and the preservation of Roman Catholicism as a unifying force.[59]

But these revisionists do not address sex/gender issues. The informality of disciplinary codes does not explain the origins or the continuation of sexual violence against native women. Moreover, as the documents for Alta California clearly reveal, Spanish officials enforced colonial criminal statutes and punished sexual crimes to the extent of their authority. However, neither the highly regulatory Laws of the Indies (the extensive legislation enacted to protect the rights of Amerindians), which mandated nonexploitive relations with Amerindians, nor punishment for breaking the laws arrested the violence.[60]

To begin to understand the soldier-settler violence toward native women, we must examine the stratified, patriarchal colonial society that conditioned relationships between the sexes and races in New Spain; the contemporary ideologies of sex/gender and race; and the relations and structures of conquest imposed on this frontier. While rape and other acts of sexual brutality did not represent official policy on this or any other Spanish frontier, these acts were nevertheless firmly fixed in the history and politics of expansion, war, and conquest. In the history of Western civilization writ large, rape is an act of domination, an act of power.[61] As such, it is a violent political act committed through sexual aggression against women.

"The practice of raping the women of a conquered group," writes historian Gerda Lerner, "has remained a feature of war and conquest from the second millennium to the present."[62] Under conditions of war or conquest, rape is a form of national terrorism, subjugation, and humiliation, wherein the sexual violation of women represents both the physical domination of women and the symbolic castration of the men of the conquered group. These concepts and symbolic meanings of rape, as discussed by Lerner, Susan Brownmiller, Anne Edwards, and others, are rooted in patriarchal Western society—in the ideology that devalues women in relation to men while it privatizes and reifies women as the symbolic capital (property) of men.[63] In this ideology, rape has historically been defined as a crime against property and thus against "territory." Therefore, in the context of war and conquest, rape has been considered a legitimate form of aggression against the opposing army a legitimate expression of superiority that carries with it no civil penalty. In nonmilitary situations, punishment for rape and other crimes of sexual violence against women in Western civilization has, until very recently, generally been determined by the social condition or status of the women violated and by the status of the violator.[64]

In eighteenth-century California, the status of Amerindian women—as members of non-Christian, indigenous groups under military conquest on Spain's northernmost outpost of empire—made them twice subject to assault with impunity: they were the spoils of conquest, and they were Indian. In the mentality of the age, these two conditions firmly established the inferiority of the Amerindian woman and became the basis for devaluing her person beyond the devaluation based on sex that accrued to all women irrespective of their sociopolitical (race, class) status. The ferocity and longevity of the sexual assaults against the Amerindian woman are rooted in the devaluation of her person conditioned by the weaving together of the strands of the same ideological thread that demeaned her on interrelated counts: her sociopolitical status, her sex, and her gender.

From their earliest contact with Amerindian peoples, Europeans estab-lished categories of opposition, or otherness, within which they defined themselves as superior and Amerindians as inferior.[65] These categories were derived from the Aristotelian theory that some beings are inferior by nature, and therefore should be dominated by their superiors for their own welfare, and from the medieval Spanish concept of "purity of blood," which was based on religion and which informed the sense of national unity forged during the reconquest.[66] These ideas—which were fundamentally political concepts that separated human beings into opposing, hierarchical subject-object categories—prevailed during the era of first contact with Amerindians and the early conquests of the Americas.

By the late eighteenth century, a different political concept—racial origin defined place and social value in the stratified social order of colonial New Spain. Race was inextricably linked to social origin and had long been a symbol for significant cleavages in society; it was one primary basis for valuation—and devaluation—of human beings.[67] In the contemporary ideology and society, Amerindian women were thus devalued on the basis of their social and racial origins, which placed them at the bottom of the social scale, and as members of a conquered group.

Two aspects of the devaluation of Amerindian women are especially noteworthy. First and foremost, it is a political devaluation. That is, it is rooted in and driven by political considerations and acts: by war, conquest, and the imposition of alien sociopolitical and economic structures of one group over another. Second, the devaluation rationalized by conquest cuts across sex. At this level, women and men of the conquered group are equally devalued and objectified by the conquering group. Amerindian women and men were both regarded as inferior social beings, whose inferiority justified the original conquest and continued to make them justifiably exploitable and expendable in the eyes of the conqueror. The obverse, of course, also holds in this equation: women and men of the conquering group share the characterization and privileges of their group. In this instance, the primary opposition is defined by sociopolitical status, not sex.

Although the ideological symbols of sociopolitical devaluation changed over time—from religion to socioracial origins to social class—the changing symbols intersected with a sex/gender ideology that has remained remarkably constant from the fifteenth to the twentieth century.[68] As the term implies, the sex/gender ideology defines two categories of opposition—sex and gender—within which women are characterized as superior or inferior in relation to others.

With respect to sex stratification, women are placed in opposition and in an inferior position to men, on the assumption that in the divine order of nature the male sex of the species is superior to the female. In this conception, the ascribed inferiority of females to males is biologically constructed.

The opposition centering on gender revolves around sexual morality and sexual conduct. This opposition creates a level of superior-inferior or good-bad stratification based on social and political value-centered concepts of women's sexuality. This dichotomization provides a very specific, socially constructed, "sexual morality" category for valuing or devaluing women.

Rooted in the corollary patriarchal concepts of woman as the possession of man and of woman's productive capacity as the most important source of her value, this ideology makes woman a pivotal element in the property structure and institutionalizes her importance to the society in the provisions of partible and bilateral inheritance. It also places woman's value, also termed her "honor," in her sexual accessibility—in her virginity while single and, once wed, in the fidelity of her sexual services to the husband to ensure a legitimate heir.[69]

Within this construct, women are placed in opposition to one another at two extremes of a social and moral spectrum defined by sexuality and accessibility. The good woman embodies all the sexual virtues or attributes essential to the maintenance of the patriarchal social structure: sexual purity, virginity, chastity, and fidelity. Historically, the norms of sexual morality and sexual conduct that patriarchal society established for women of the ruling class have been the norms against which all other women have been judged. These norms are fundamentally rooted in questions of the acquisition and transference of economic and political power, and of women's relationship to that power base.

Since the linchpins of these ideological constructs are property, legitimacy, and inheritance, a woman excluded from this property/inheritance structure for sociopolitical reasons (religion, conquest, slavery, race, class), or for reasons based on sexual immorality (any form of sexual misconduct), is consequently excluded from the corresponding concepts and structures of social legitimacy. A woman so excluded cannot produce legitimate heirs because she is not a legitimate social or sexual being.

The woman who is defined out of social legitimacy because of the abrogation of her primary value to patriarchal society, that of producing heirs, is therefore without value, without honor. She becomes the other, the bad woman, the embodiment of a corrupted, inferior, unusable sex: immoral, without virtue, loose. She is common property, sexually available to any man that comes along. A woman (women) thus devalued may not lay claim to the rights and protections the society affords to the woman who does have sociopolitical and sexual value.[70] In colonial New Spain, as in most Western societies until the very recent period, the woman so demeaned, so objectified, could be raped, beaten, worked like a beast of burden, or otherwise abused with impunity.

The soldiers, priests, and settlers who effected the conquest and colonization of Alta California in the last third of the eighteenth century perceived and acted toward Amerindians in a manner consistent with the ideology and history of conquest regarding them as inferior, devalued, disposable beings against whom violence was not only permissible but often necessary. For, despite the Laws of the Indies, the contradictions in the ideology and corresponding historical relations of conquest were great from the very beginning. These contradictions were generally exacerbated, rather than resolved, across time, space, and expansion to new frontiers.

From the very beginning, the papal bulls and scholarly (ideological) debates that affirmed the essential humanity of Amerindians and initiated the legislation to effect their conversion and protection sanctioned violence and exploitation under certain conditions. Loopholes in the royal statutes that were technically intended to protect Amerindians and guarantee their rights, but more specifically protected the crown's interest in Indian land and labor, had permitted virulent exploitation of Indians since the laws were first passed.[71]

More contemporary military and civil laws, such as those enacted by Neve, Fages, and Borica, carried severe penalties for illegal contact with or maltreatment of Indians; but these laws were especially contradictory because they were intended to curb certain kinds of violence by soldiers who were trained to kill Indians and who were sent to California to effect the temporal (military) conquest of this region.[72] Thus, violence against Amerindians was permissible when it advanced the particular interests of the Spanish Conquest, but punishable when it did not. Since the sexual violence that occurred in this region was but the most contemporary manifestation of a national history that included the violation of enemy women as a legitimate expression of aggression during conquest, it would seem that sexual violence became a punishable offense only when it was the source of military or political problems.[73]

Finally, perhaps the greatest contradictions were those of the greatest champion of Amerindian rights—the Catholic Church. On the one hand, Catholic clergy sought to remove Amerindians from contact with Spaniards, in order to protect them from the exploitation and violence of conquistadores, soldiers, and colonists; on the other hand, Jesuits, Franciscans, and other religious orders relied heavily on corporal punishment in their programs to Christianize and Hispanicize native people. While proclaiming the humanity of Amerindians, missionaries on the frontier daily acted upon a fundamental belief in the inferiority of the Indian. Their actions belied their words.

Accordingly, in his lengthy memorial of June 19, 1801, refuting the charges of excessive cruelty to Amerindians leveled against the Franciscans by one of their own, Father President Fermín Francisco de Lasuén disputed the use of extreme cruelty in the missions of the New California. Force was used only when absolutely necessary, stated Lasuén; and it was at times necessary because the native peoples of California were "untamed savages . . . people of vicious and ferocious habits who know no law but force, no superior but their own free will, and no reason but their own caprice."[74] Of the use of force against neophyte women, Lasuén wrote that women in the mission were flogged, placed in the stocks, or shackled only because they deserved it. But, he quickly added, their right to privacy was always respected—they were flogged inside the women's dormitory, called the monjero (nunnery). Flogging the women in private, he further argued, was part of the civilizing process because it "instilled into them the modesty, delicacy, and virtue belonging to their sex.[75]

A key element in the missionaries' program of conversion to Christianity included the restructuring of relations between the sexes to reflect gender stratification and the corollary values and structures of the patriarchal family: subservience of women to men, monogamy, marriage without divorce, and a severely repressive code of sexual norms.

In view of the fact that the ideologies, structures, and institutions of conquest imposed here were rooted in two and a half centuries of colonial rule, the sexual and other violence toward Amerindian women in California can best be understood as ideologically justified violence institutionalized in the structures and relations of conquest initiated in the fifteenth century.[76] In California as elsewhere, sexual violence functioned as an institutionalized mechanism for ensuring subordination and compliance. It was one instrument of sociopolitical terrorism and control first of women and then of the group under conquest.

NOTES

1. Fray Junípero Serra to Antonio María de Bucareli y Ursua, Mexico City, 21 May 1773, in *Writings of Junípero Serra,* ed. Antonine Tibesar, O.F.M., 4 vols. (Washington, DC: Academy of Franciscan History, 1955), 1:363.
2. Serra to Father Rafael Verger, Monterey, 8 August 1772, in *Writings,* 1:257.
3. Serra to Bucareli, Mexico City, 21 May 1773, in *Writings,* 1:361.
4. George Harwood Phillips, *Chiefs and Challengers: Indian Resistance and Cooperation in Southern California* (Berkeley: University of California Press, 1975), 22.
5. Serra to Bucareli, Mexico City, 21 May 1773, in *Writings,* 1:363.
6. Serra to Father Guardian [Francisco Pangua], Monterey, 19 July 1774, in *Writings,* 2:121.
7. Serra to Verger, Monterey, 8 August 1772, in *Writings,* 1:259, 261.
8. Serra to Father Francisco Pangua or his Successor, Monterey, 6 June 1777, in *Writings,* 3:159.
9. José Francisco Ortega, Diligencias Practicadas por Sargento Francisco de Aguiar, 1777, Julio 11, San Diego, *Archives of California,* 55:279, Bancroft Library, University of California, Berkeley.
10. Sherburne F. Cook, *Conflict between the California Indian and White Civilization* (Berkeley: University of California Press, 1976), 24. (Originally published 1943.)
11. Serra to Father Juan Figuer, Monterey, 30 March 1779, in *Writings,* 3:305.
12. Robert F. Heizer and Albert B. Elsasser, *The Natural World of the California Indians* (Berkeley: University of California Press, 1980), 25.
13. Hugo Reid, "Letters on the Los Angeles County Indians," in *A Scotch Paisano: Hugo Reid's Life in California, 1832-1852,* ed. Susana Dakin (Berkeley: University of California Press, 1939), App. B, 215-216, 240; Heizer and Elsasser, *Natural World of the California Indians,* 52-53.
14. Reid, "Letters on the Los Angeles County Indians," 262.
15. Ibid.; see also Herbert Howe Bancroft, *History of California,* 7 vols. (San Francisco: A. L. Bancroft, 1984-1985), 1:180 and n. 29 (same page).
16. Herbert Eugene Bolton, trans. and ed., *Font's Complete Diary: A Chronicle of the Founding of San Francisco* (Berkeley: University of California Press, 1931), p. 256.
17. Ibid., 247.

18. Ibid.

19. Ibid., 251-252.

20. Charles E. Chapman, *A History of California: The Spanish Period* (New York: Macmillan, 1930), 246-247.

21. Cook, *Conflict*, 24.

22. Ibid. 25-30, 101-134.

23. Edwin A. Beilharz, *Felipe de Neve: First Governor of California* (San Francisco: California Historical Society, 1971), 72-73.

24. This argument is based on my analysis of the documents.

25. Reverend Heribert Jone, *Moral Theology, Englished and Adapted to the Laws and Customs of the United States of America by Reverend Urban Adelman* (Westminster, MD: Newman Press, 1960), 145-161.

26. The conflict between church and state in California, which Irving Richman calls the conflict between State Secular and State Sacerdotal, is extensively discussed in general histories of Spanish California. See Bancroft, *History of California,* vol. 1; Irving Berdine Richman, *California under Spain and Mexico, 1535-1847* (Boston: Houghton Mifflin, 1911), 142-158.

27. Serra to Father Fermín Francisco de Lasuén, Monterey, 8 January 1781, in *Writings,* 4:63; Beilharz, *Felipe de Neve,* 77; Richman, *California under Spain and Mexico,* 116-337.

28. Serra to Bucareli, Mexico City, 13 March 1773, in *Writings,* 1:295-329; see also Bernard E. Bobb, *The Viceregency of Antonio María Bucareli in New Spain, 1771-1779* (Austin: University of Texas Press, 1962), 163.

29. Serra to Bucareli, Mexico City, 13 March 1773, in *Writings,* 1:299, 301, 305, 307; Serra to Teodoro de Croix, Santa Barbara, 28 April 1782, in *Writings,* 4:129.

30. Magnus Morner *(Race Mixture in the History of Latin America* [Boston: Little, Brown, 1967], 35-37) discusses interracial marriage in the early colonial period as part of the early social experiments of the sixteenth century. I discuss the promotion of intermarriage more specifically as an instrument of conquest in chapter 5 of "Presidarias y Pobladoras: Spanish-Mexican Women in Frontier Monterey, California, 1770-1821," (PhD diss., Stanford University, 1990).

31. Serra to Bucareli, Mexico City, 13 March 1773, in *Writings,* 1:325.

32. Ibid.

33. Serra to Bucareli, Monterey, 24 August 1775, in *Writings,* 2:149, 151, 153.

34. This is my interpretation of the documents.

35. Serra to Bucareli, Mexico City, 22 April 1773, in *Writings,* 1:341.

36. Bancroft, *History of California*, 1:206-219; Bobb, *Viceregency of Bucareli*, 162-163; Chapman, *History of California: The Spanish Period*, 289-291.

37. As quoted in Beilharz, *Felipe de Neve*, 77.

38. Serra to Lasuén, Monterey, 8 January 1781, in *Writings*, 4:63.

39. Bancroft, *History of California*, 1:546-549; Phillips, *Chiefs and Challengers*, 23.

40. Fages al Comandante General, 7 de noviembre de 1785, Monterey; 30 de deciembre de 1785, San Gabriel; 5 de enero de 1786, San Gabriel—all in *Archives of California*, 22:348-349. For the interrogation of Toypurina and her coleaders of the rebellion at Mission San Gabriel, see Diligencias que del órden del Gobernador practicó el Sargento Joseph Francisco Olivera, *Archivos general de la nación: Provincias Internas*, vol. 120, microfilm, Bancroft Library, University of California, Berkeley. For a popular account of Toypurina's leadership role in the rebellion, see Thomas Workman Temple II, "Toypurina the Witch and the Indian Uprising at San Gabriel," *Masterkey* 32 (September–October 1958): 136-152. For a discussion of Amerindian rebellions in California, see Bancroft, *History of California*, 1:249-256; Cook, *Conflict*, 65-90; Phillips, *Chiefs and Challengers*.

41. As quoted in Beilharz, *Felipe de Neve*, 83.

42. Bobb, *Viceregency of Bucareli*; Alfred Barnaby Thomas, *Teodoro de Croix and the Northern Frontier of New Spain, 1776-1783* (Norman: University of Oklahoma Press, 1941).

43. Thomas, *Teodoro de Croix*, 16-57, 230-246; Max L. Moorhead, *The Presidio: Bastion of the Spanish Borderlands* (Norman: University of Oklahoma Press, 1975), 27-160; Sidney B. Brinckerhoff and Odie B. Faulk, *Lancers for the King: A Study of the Frontier Military System of Northern New Spain, with a Translation of the Royal Regulations of 1772* (Phoenix: Arizona Historical Foundation, 1965), 7.

44. Representación de Don Pedro Fages sobre el estupro violento que cometerión los tres soldados que espresa, año de 1774, Californias, *Archivos general de la nación: Californias*, vol. 2, Part 1, microfilm. The five-year chronology of this case is from Beilharz, *Felipe de Neve*, 27-30.

45. Beilharz, *Felipe de Neve*, 29.

46. Bobb, *Viceregency of Bucareli*, 128-171; Thomas, *Teodoro de Croix*, 17-57, 230-246; Beilharz, *Felipe de Neve*, 29.

47. Beilharz, *Felipe de Neve*, 29-30.

48. Ibid.

49. Ortega, Diligencias, 1777, Julio 11, San Diego, *Archives of California*, 55:258-279; Cook, *Conflict*, 106-107.
50. Beilharz, *Felipe de Neve*, 67-84, 160-162.
51. Pedro Fages to Diego Gonzales, Monterey, 1 July 1785, *Archives of California*, 54:175; Cook, *Conflict*, 106.
52. As quoted in Beilharz, *Felipe de Neve*, 73; see also Neve's instructions to Fages, his successor, in Appendices, same source, 161-162.
53. Fages to Gonzales, 1 July 1785, *Archives of California*, 54:175.
54. Branciforte al Gobernador de California, "Sobre escoltas a los religiosos ... ," 5 de octubre de 1795, Mexico, *Archives of California,* 7:256; Gobernador a Comandantes de Presidios, "Excesos de la tropa con las indias, su corrección ... ," 11 de abril de 1796, Monterey, *Archives of California,* 23:421-422.
55. Bancroft, *History of California*, 1:601.
56. Serra to Bucareli, Mexico City, 11 June 11, 1773; Serra to Pangua, Monterey, 6 June1777, in *Writings*, 1:383, 3:159.
57. Oakah L. Jones, Jr., *Los Paisanos: Spanish Settlers on the Northern Frontier of New Spain* (Norman: University of Oklahoma Press, 1979); Brinckerhoff and Faulk, *Lancers for the King;* Max L. Moorhead, "The Soldado de Cuera: Stalwart of the Spanish Borderlands"; and Leon G. Campbell, "The First Californios: Presidial Society in Spanish California, 1760-1822," in *The Spanish Borderlands: A First Reader*, ed. Oakah L. Jones, Jr. (Los Angeles: Lorrin L. Morrison, 1974), 87-105 and 106-118, respectively. Moorhead's essay was originally published in the *Journal of the West* in January 1969, and Campbell's first appeared in the *Journal of the West* in October 1972.
58. Moorhead, "The Soldado de Cuera," 91.
59. Jones, *Los Paisanos*, 252-253.
60. Juan de Solórzano y Pereyra, *Politica indiana*, 5 vols. (Buenos Aires: Compañía Ibero-Americana de Publicaciones, 1972); José María Ots y Capdequi, *Instituciones* (Barcelona: Salvat Editores, S.A., 1959), and *Historia del derecho español en America y del derecho indiano* (Madrid: Ediciones S. A. de Aguilar, 1967).
61. The discussion about rape and other forms of sexual violence against women is based on the following sources: Gerda Lerner, *The Creation of Patriarchy* (New York: Oxford University Press, 1986); Susan Brownmiller, *Against Our Will: Men, Women and Rape* (New York: Bantam Books, 1976); Christine Ward Gailey, "Evolutionary Perspectives on Gender Hierarchy," in *Analyzing Gender: A Handbook of Social Science*

Research, ed. Beth B. Hess and Myra Marx Ferree (Newbury Park, CA: Sage, 1987), 32-67; Carole J. Sheffield, "Sexual Terrorism: The Social Control of Women," in *Analyzing Gender*, 171-189; Jalna Hanmer and Mary Maynard, "Introduction: Violence and Gender Stratification," in *Women, Violence and Social Control*, ed. Jalna Hanmer and Mary Maynard (Atlantic Highlands, NJ.: Humanities Press International, 1987), 1-12; Anne Edwards, "Male Violence in Feminist Theory: An Analysis of the Changing Conceptions of Sex/Gender Violence and Male Dominance," and David H. J. Morgan, "Masculinity and Violence," in *Women, Violence and Social Control*, 13-29 and 180-192, respectively.

62. Lerner, *Patriarchy*, 80.

63. Lerner, *Patriarchy*, 80; Brownmiller, *Against Our Will*, 23-24; Edwards, "Male Violence in Feminist Theory," 19; Ramón Arturo Gutiérrez, "Marriage, Sex, and the Family: Social Change in Colonial New Mexico, 1690-1846" (PhD diss., University of Wisconsin–Madison, 1980), 15.

64. Lerner, *Patriarchy*, 96; Brownmiller, *Against Our Will*, 18-20; Sheffield, "Sexual Terrorism," 173-174.

65. Tzvetan Todorov, *The Conquest of America: The Question of the Other*, trans. Richard Howard (New York: Harper and Row, 1982).

66. Lewis Hanke, *The Spanish Struggle for Justice in the Conquest of America* (Philadelphia: University of Pennsylvania Press, 1949), 111-132; Verena Martínez-Alier, *Marriage, Class, and Color in Nineteenth-Century Cuba: A Study of Racial Attitudes and Sexual Values in a Slave Society* (Cambridge, England: Cambridge University Press, 1974), 76; Morner, *Race Mixture*, 3-5, 36; Health Dillard, "Women in Reconquest Castile: The Fueros of Sepulveda and Cuenca," in *Women in Medieval Society*, ed. Susan Mosher Stuard (Philadelphia: University of Pennsylvania Press, 1976), 86

67. Martínez-Alier, *Marriage, Class, and Color in Nineteenth-Century Cuba*, 76.

68. Edwards, "Male Violence in Feminist Theory," 28, n. 4. Although some feminist scholars prefer not to make an analytical distinction between sex (biological) and gender (sociocultural) categories, I believe that the distinction is important because of the distinct oppositions within which each category places women. The biological distinction of sex places women in opposition and in a subordinate position relative to men; the sociocultural distinction of gender places women in opposition and in an inferior position to other women. This sociocultural distinction is based on concepts of sexual morality and conduct that are informed by political and economic values. With few exceptions, however, the sociocultural

construction of gender has not accounted for the political and economic dimensions that historically related (if not defined) a woman's sexual morality and gender value to her sociopolitical (religion, race, class) status—and vice versa.

69. Lerner, *Patriarchy*, 80-88; Sylvia Marina Arrom, *The Women of Mexico City, 1790-1850* (Stanford, CA: Stanford University Press, 1985), 71; Health Dillard, *Daughters of the Reconquest: Women in Castilian Town Society, 1100-1300* (Cambridge, England: Cambridge University Press, 1984), 12-35, see especially 30-32, and "Women in Reconquest Castile," 86, 91.

70. For a discussion of the concept of women's honor and dishonor drawn from codes of sexual conduct and used as a basis for devaluation of women in medieval Spain, see Dillard, *Daughters of the Reconquest*, 168-212; for a discussion of the concept of family honor and the political issues inherent in the devaluation of women on the basis of class and race, see Martínez-Alier, *Marriage, Class, and Color in .Nineteenth-Century Cuba*, 11-41, 71-81; for a discussion of these issues in the northern frontier of colonial New Spain, see Ramón A. Gutiérrez, "From Honor to Love: Transformations of the Meaning of Sexuality in Colonial New Mexico," in *Kinship Ideology and Practice in Latin America,* ed. Raymond T. Smith (Chapel Hill: University of North Carolina Press, 1984), 237-263; see also Gutiérrez, "Marriage, Sex, and the Family."

71. Hanke, *The Spanish Struggle for Justice*, 133-146.

72. Moorhead, "The Soldado de Cuera," 102.

73. For discussions of sexual violence in the national history of Spain, first during the reconquest and then during the conquest of Mexico, see Dillard, *Daughters of the Reconquest*, 206-207, and "Women in Reconquest Castile," 85-89; Todorov, *Conquest of America*, 48-49, 59, 139, 175.

74. Refutation of Charges, Mission of San Carlos of Monterey, 19 June 1801, in *Writings of Fermín Francisco de Lasuén*, 2 vols., trans. and ed. Finbar Kenneally, O.F.M. (Washington, D.C.: Academy of American Franciscan History, 1965), 2:194-234; quotes are from 2:220.

75. Ibid., 2:217.

76. Sheffield, "Sexual Terrorism," 171-189.

CHAPTER 6

ENGENDERING THE HISTORY OF ALTA CALIFORNIA, 1769–1848

GENDER, SEXUALITY, AND THE FAMILY

The frontier is a liminal zone . . . its subjects, interstitial beings. . . . For more than two centuries the North was a society organized for warfare.

Ana María Alonso[1]

From 1769, when the first *entrada* (incursion) of soldiers and priests arrived in California to extend Spanish colonial hegemony to the farthest reaches of the northern frontier, women and girls were the target of sexual violence and brutal attacks. In the San Gabriel region, for example, soldiers on horseback swooped into villages, chased, lassoed, raped, beat, and sometimes killed women.[2] As had occurred in successive incursions into new territory since the fifteenth century, sexual aggression against native women was among the first recorded acts of Spanish colonial domination in Alta California. This political violence effected on the bodies of women made colonial California a land of endemic warfare.

This essay examines the gendered and sexualized construction of the colonial order and relations of power in Alta California from 1769 to

1848 as this land passed from Spanish to Mexican to Euro-American rule. Using gender and sexuality as categories of analysis, it explores how women articulated their power, subjectivity, and identity in the militarized colonial order reigning on this remote outpost. In this study, gender denotes the social construction of masculinity, as well as of femininity and thus the social construction of distinctions between male and female. Gender is also a principal realm for the production of more general effects of power and meaning. Thus, gender is here interpreted as a relational dimension of colonialism and as one aspect of an imperial power matrix within which gender, sexuality, race, class, and culture operate. This matrix is brought to bear in recent studies on gender and colonialism on the northern frontiers of New Spain by historian Ramón Gutiérrez and anthropologist Ana María Alonso, who examine the ideology of honor in order to theorize and interpret constructions of masculinity and femininity within the power relations of colonialism.[3]

This chapter examines how indigenous and mestiza women (Indo-mestiza and Afro-mestiza) became subjects of colonial domination in California. It draws on studies that view gender and sexuality as dimensions of subjectivity that are both an "effect of power and a technology of rule," and that analyze colonial domination in relation to the construction of subjectivities—meaning forms of personhood, power, and social positioning. It also focuses on female agency, that is, the ways in which women manipulated circumstances and used cultural, spiritual, religious, and legal actions to resist patriarchal domination.[4]

Figure 4. Young Huchnom woman with the characteristic facial tattooing of their people.

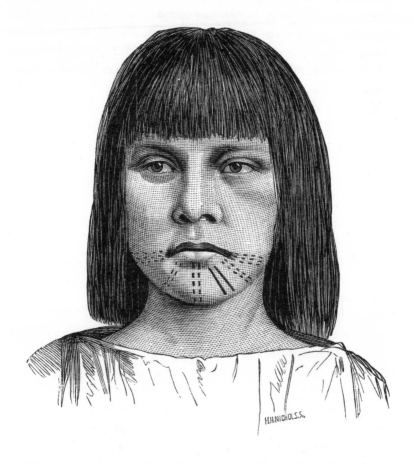

Although knowledge of pre-Hispanic Indian gender and sexuality systems is slender, it is generally thought that, despite male dominance in most spheres, a more open and flexible relation existed between the sexes than obtained in European society. Among the Huchnom, whose lands lay along the South Fork of the Eel River, it was the custom for newly married couples to settle with the bride's relations, one of several exceptions to the otherwise patrilocal practice of California Indians. From Stephen Powers, *Tribes of California.* Courtesy of Lars Krutak

Recent interdisciplinary works center women and other subordinated (subaltern) groups as subjects of history and use gender and sexuality as categories of analysis to examine broad historical processes. This scholarship seeks to find and analyze the subalterns' voices, agency, and identities in the fissures and spaces, the interstices, the hidden, masked meanings of events and documents.[5] Using gender and sexuality to analyze resistance strategies within larger structures and processes, these studies explore women's power to reshape and refabricate their social identity—to fashion their own response, their own experience, and their own histories.

GENDER, SEXUALITY, AND OPPOSING IDEOLOGIES

Little is known about native systems of gender and sexuality in California at the time of the Spanish invasion.[6] Nevertheless, it is clear that indigenous practices were antithetical to a patriarchal ideology in which gender hierarchy, male domination, and heterosexuality were the exclusive organizing principles of desire, sexuality, marriage, and the family. In the European order, until passage of the Bourbon Reforms in the late eighteenth century, Roman Catholic ideology and canon law, which conceptualized the body as base and vile, imposed a regime of sexual repression that tied sexuality to morality.[7] While canon law regulated marriage and the sociosexual life, of the physical body, civil law regulated the body politic and controlled family law, reinforcing inheritance and property rights and strengthening the patriarchal family. In this ideology, woman was conceptualized in opposition to, and as the possession of, man. Woman's reproductive capacity, as the vehicle for the production of legitimate heirs and the transference of private property, was defined as the single-most important source of her value. Spanish law defined women as sexual beings and delineated their sexual lives through the institution of indissoluble, monogamous marriage. And although canon law upheld the principle that marriage required the consent of both parties, that principle was not always adhered to.

Sexual intercourse, in theory, was confined to marriage, a sacrament intended for the procreation of children, for companionship, and for the containment of lust. Woman's sexuality had to be controlled through virginity before monogamous marriage and fidelity after in order to ensure legitimate transference of the patrimony. By regularizing inheritance of status and property, marriage institutionalized the legal exchange of women's bodies. The family, the sociopolitical organization within which these transactions occurred, reproduced the hierarchical, male-dominated social order. The Spanish cultural idiom of honor—the ideology of personal subordination to familial concerns—held the larger patriarchal edifice together at the fundamental unit of the family and family relationships.

Gender was a key dimension of honor, which defined the value accorded to both the individual person (personhood) and the family. Thus, ideal social conduct was defined by gender and differed according to appropriate male and female qualities and roles. Women's honor centered on their sexuality, and on their own and their family's control of it. Men's honor and ideal conduct centered on their conquest and domination of others, including women, as well as on protection, which included protecting the honor (sexual reputation) of females in the family. These gendered qualities of honor maintained the patrimony and perpetuated an honored image of the self and family across time. The result was extreme sexual oppression of women and a double standard of sexual behavior. Individuals possessed individual honor, and families possessed collective honor.

Figure 5. A page dated April 1781 from the San Carlos Borromeo "First Book of Matrimony."

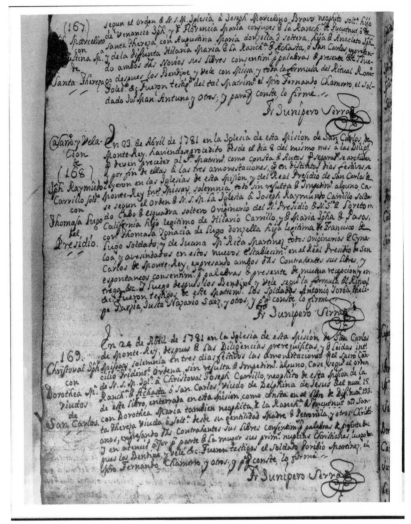

This document was where Fray Junípero Serra recorded marriages of neophytes, as well as of Spanish soldiers, performed in the mission church. The ceremony of Christian marriage, with its attendant imperatives of appropriate social and sexual relations between men and women, was part of the complex pattern of Hispanic life that the Franciscans imposed on the California Indians, thereby radically reshaping traditional native society. Courtesy, California Historical Society at the University of Southern California, Title Insurance and Trust, and C.C. Pierce Photography Collection, University of Southern California, CHS-9994.

Systems of gender and sexuality among indigenous peoples, in contrast, generally conceptualized females and males as complementary, not opposed, principles.[8] Woman was not a derivative of man, sexuality was not repressed, and both gender and sexual systems were relatively fluid. With variations, native systems included gender parallelism, matriarchal sociopolitical organization, and matrilineal forms of reckoning and descent. Within these diverse cultures, women's power and authority could derive from one or more elements: the culture's basic principle of individual autonomy that structured political relationships, including those between men and women; women's important productive or reproductive role in the economy; and the authority accorded women by their bearing and raising of children.[9] Further, women's power and authority were integral to, and also derived from, the tribe's core religious and spiritual beliefs, values, and traditions, which generally accorded women and men equivalent value, power, and range of practices.

As part of the natural world, sexuality, for many indigenous people, was related to the sacred and, as such, was central to their religious and cosmic order. Sexuality was celebrated by women and men in song, dance, and other ritual observances to awaken the earth's fertility and ensure that they were blessed with fecundity. Accepted practices extended to premarital sexual activity, polygamy, polyandry, homosexuality, transvestitism, same-sex marriage, and ritual sexual practices. Divorce was easily attainable, and, under particular conditions, abortion and infanticide were practiced.

Woman—the female principle—was a pivotal force in American cosmologies and worldviews. Woman, whether in the form of Grand-mother, Thought Woman, or another female being, was at the center of the originating principle that brought the people into being and sustained them. On arriving in California in 1769, Europeans confronted the reality of Amerindian societies in which women not only controlled their own resources, sexuality, and reproductive processes, but also held, religious, political, economic, and sometimes, military power.[10] The colonial church and state sought to eradicate native traditions that were centered on and controlled by women. In California, the Franciscan mission system was the principal vehicle for efforts to extirpate native systems of gender and sexuality and hence of women's resistance to them.

In the confessional, priests queried both women and men about their sexual lives and activities and meted out punishments. While prohibitions against fornication, adultery, masturbation, sodomy, incest, bestiality, and coitus interruptus applied to all, abortion and infanticide—violations of the Fifth Commandment, which condemned killing—applied specifically to women and were punished harshly.[11] Hugo Reid writes that the priests at Mission San Gabriel attributed all miscarriages to infanticide and that Gabrielino women were punished by "shaving the head, flogging for fifteen subsequent days, [wearing] iron on the feet for three months, and having to appear every Sunday in church, on the steps leading up the altar, with a hideous painted wooden child [a *monigote*] in her arms" representing the dead infant.[12]

The imperative to control and remake native sexuality, in particular to control women's procreation, was driven as much by material interest as by doctrinal issues. California needed a growing Hispanicized Indian population as both a source of labor and as a defense against foreign invasion, and thus missionaries sometimes took extraordinary measures to assure reproduction. Father Olbes at Mission Santa Cruz ordered an infertile couple to have sexual intercourse in his presence because he did not believe they could not have children. The couple refused, but Olbes forcibly inspected the man's penis to learn "whether or not it was in good order" and tried to inspect the woman's genitalia.[13] She refused, fought with him, and tried to bite him. Olbes ordered that she be tied by the hands, and given fifty lashes, shackled, and locked up in the *monjero* (women's dormitory). He then had a *monigote* made and commanded that she "treat the doll as though it were a child and carry it in the presence of everyone for nine days." While the woman was beaten and her sexuality demeaned, the husband, who had been intimate with another woman, was ridiculed and humiliated. A set of cow horns was tied to his head with leather thongs, thereby converting him into a cuckold, and he was herded to daily Mass in cow horns and fetters.

Franciscan priests also prohibited initiation ceremonies, dances, and songs in the mission system. They sought to destroy the ideological, moral, and ethical systems that defined native life. They demonized noncomplying women, especially those who resisted openly, as witches. Indeed, Ramón Gutiérrez argues that, in the northern borderlands of New Spain, "One can interpret the whole history of the persecution of Indian women as witches . . . as a struggle over [these] competing ways of defining the body and of regulating procreation as the church endeavored to constrain the expression of desire within boundaries that clerics defined proper and acceptable."[14]

NATIVE WOMEN, POWER, AND RESISTANCE

No trayaba armas . . . vino para animarlos a que tubieran corazón para pelear. (She was unarmed . . . she came to animate their will to fight.)

—Toypurina, "Ynterrogatorio de la india gentil" (1785)

Some indigenous women countered the everyday violence inflicted upon them with gender-centered strategies that authorized them to speak, to act, to lead, and to empower others. They fought the ideological power of the colonial church and state with powerful ideologies that vested women with power and authority over their own sexuality.

Toypurina, the medicine woman of the Japchavit *ranchería*, in the vicinity of Mission San Gabriel, used her power as a wise woman in an attempt to rid her people of the priests and soldiers. On October 25, 1785, Toypurina and three Gabrielino men led eight villages in an attack against the priests and soldiers of the mission. Toypurina, who had been about ten years old when the villages from the coast and the nearby mountains had attacked the mission some thirteen years earlier, used her influence as a medicine woman to recruit six of the eight villages that joined the 1785 battle.

At San Gabriel, the soldiers got wind of the attack and, lying in wait, captured Toypurina, her three companions, and twenty other warriors. Governor Pedro Fages convicted the four leaders and sentenced them to *prisión segura* in the missions. After a three-year imprisonment at San Gabriel, Toypurina was exiled north to Mission San Carlos Borromeo in 1788. The twenty warriors captured with her were sentenced to between twenty and twenty-five lashes plus time already served. This punishment was levied as much for following the leadership of a woman as for rebelling against Spanish domination. On sentencing them, Fages stated that their public whippings were "to serve as a warning to all," for he would "admonish them about their ingratitude, underscoring their perversity, and unmasking the deceit and tricks by which *they allowed themselves to be dominated by the aforesaid woman*" (emphasis added).[15]

Toypurina's power and influence derived from a non-Western religious-political ideological system of power in which women were central to the ritual and spiritual life of the tribe. Neither the source of Toypurina's religious-political power nor the threat she posed to the colonialist project in Alta California was lost on Fages, who, refusing to acknowledge her political power, constructed her instead as a sorceress. In his account, Fages sought to erase Toypurina's actual identity and to fabricate an identity consistent with colonialist gender values and ideologies.

Archival records show that native women continued to resist colonial domination with a range of actions and activities, including religious-political movements that vested power in a female deity and placed the health and well-being of the community in the hands of a female visionary.[16] In 1801, at the height of an epidemic ravaging the Chumash in the missions and the *rancherías,* a woman at Mission Santa Barbara launched a clandestine, large-scale revitalization movement. Drawing her authority from visions and revelations from Chupu, the Chumash earth goddess, this neophyte woman—who remains unnamed in the documents—called for a return to the worship of Chupu, who told her that "The pagan Indians were to die if they were baptized and that the same fate would befall the Christian Indians who would not give alms to [her] and who refused to wash their heads with a certain water."[17] Her revelation "spread immediately through all the houses of the mission. Almost all the neophytes, the *alcaldes* included, went to the house of the visionary to present beads and seeds and to go through the rite of renouncing Christianity."

Precisely because historical documents portray both Toypurina and the Chumash visionary of 1801 as "witches and sorceresses," we need to understand witchcraft within gendered relations of power in the Spanish/European world in general and within gendered relations of power and subordination under conditions of colonialism in particular. Ostensibly, all women in colonial Mexico and Latin America, like their counterparts throughout the Christian world, were suspected of being witches on the basis of gender, but women of colonized groups were suspect on multiple grounds.[18] Indian women, African-origin women, and racially mixed women—whether Indo-mestiza or Afro-mestiza—were suspect by virtue of being female, by virtue of deriving from non-Christian, or "diabolic," religions and cultures, and by virtue of being colonized or enslaved peoples who might rebel and use their alleged magical power at any moment. Thus, in the Christian imperialist gaze, non-Christian women and their mestiza daughters were sexualized, racialized, and demonized for the ostensibly religious crime of witchcraft, although they were often tried in secular courts, where witchcraft was treated as a political crime.

Yet, while ecclesiastical and civil officials dismissed, discredited, exiled, or sometimes put to death nonwhite women charged with witchcraft, women themselves used witchcraft as a means of subverting the socio-sexual order sanctioned by religion and enshrined in the colonial honor code as an ethical system.[19] Ruth Behar argues that women used sexual-ized magic to control men and subvert the male order by symbolically using their own bodies and bodily fluids as a source of power over men.

Accordingly, sexual witchcraft included the use of menstrual blood, wash water, pubic hair, and ensorcelled food to attract, tame, or tie men into submission or, sometimes, to harm or kill a physically abusive or unfaithful husband or lover. In the realm of sexualized magic, women developed a rich symbolic language and actions that were as violent as men's beating of wives. Women's actions within this spiritual domain represented a form of power.

If colonizing males thought of Indian women's bodies, both symbolically and materially, as a means to territorial and political conquest, women constructed and used their bodies, both symbolically and materially, as instruments of resistance and subversion of colonial domination. Toypurina and the Chumash visionary placed their bodies in the line of fire and organized and led others to do likewise. Other women resisted in less visible, day-to-day practices: they poisoned the priests' food, practiced fugitivism, worshipped their own deities, had visions that others believed and followed, performed prohibited dances and rituals, refused to abide by patriarchal sexual norms, and continued to participate in armed revolts and rebellions against the missions, soldiers, and ranchos. Participants cited the priests' cruelty and repression of traditional ceremonies and sexual practices among primary reasons for the attacks on the missions, for the assassination of the friar Andrés Quintana at Mission Santa Cruz in 1812, and for the great Chumash *levantamiento* of 1824.[20]

Secularization of the missions after 1834 ended the systematic, day-to-day institutional assault on native peoples' sexuality. It did not, however, end the sexual violence against indigenous women in the ensuing eras of Mexican and Euro-American rule. Although Albert Hurtado examines the violence toward native women in the second half of the nineteenth century and initiates an important discussion of Indian survival, the nature of Amerindian women's resistance and strategies of survival in the post-mission era remains largely uncharted terrain.[21]

That colonialism for all its brutal technologies and distorted narratives, could not completely destroy native women's historical autonomy is something native peoples have always known, but scholarly researchers are just beginning to learn.[22] Native oral traditions have preserved the histories, telling and retelling women's identities and remembering across time, space, and generations. Through oral and visual traditions, and other means of communicating counter-histories, native women's power, authority, and knowledge have remained part of their peoples' collective memory, historical reality, and daily struggles of "being in a state of war for five hundred years."[23]

Certainly ideologies of resistance and social memory, as the recent wealth of Native American literature reveals, center women as pivotal figures in historical and contemporary resistance in their peoples' collective memory. Thus, Vera Rocha, the contemporary hereditary chief of the Gabrielinos, received the story of Toypurina and the Gabrielinos as a very young girl from her great-grandmother, who received it from her mother.[24] Rocha, in turn, transmitted the story to her children and grandchildren and, more recently, to the world in general in the form of a public monument—a prayer mound dedicated to Toypurina developed in conjunction with Chicana artist Judith F. Baca. Such histories remain archived in tribal, family, and individual memory, as well as in other texts—some written, most not.

The effort to reconstruct the historical agency of Amerindian women is inseparable from the effort to reconstruct the autonomy of the racially and culturally mixed women who, with their families, were recruited by the colonial state to colonize Alta California five years after the initial arrival of soldiers and missionaries in 1769. The second part of this chapter examines mestiza women's agency, and the record they left of it, within the contradictory roles they occupied as both dominated and dominating native subjects.

Reproducing the Colony: Gender, Sexuality, and the Family in Alta California

Settlers must be men of the soil, tillers of the field, accompanied by their families . . . of upright character . . . likely to set a good example to the heathen.

> —Teodoro de Croix, 1781, quoted in *Southern California Quarterly* 15, 1931

In Spain's New World empire, the central role of the conjugal family in consolidating the conquest of new territory was rooted in methods initially developed during the wars of the reconquest of the Iberian peninsula from the Muslims.[25] First formulated in the charters of medieval Spanish towns, the role of the family in imposing Spanish hegemony was transplanted to the Americas in the form of social legislation and colonization policies such as the policy of domestic unity, or unity of residence.[26] Backed by royal decrees and a system of economic and political rewards and punishments, this policy was designed to solidify the development of the institution of Christian marriage and the patriarchal family and to reproduce Spanish-Catholic civilization in the colonies.

The arrival of single soldiers and priests in California in 1769 reproduced sociosexual conditions similar to those of Spain's earlier sixteenth-century conquests elsewhere. By 1772, fearing that the California settlements were on the verge of collapse and acknowledging the slow rate of local Amerindian conversions, Junipero Serra argued that the survival of the colony required the presence of "Spanish," meaning Hispanicized, women and families.[27] Thus, racially mixed soldier and settler families were recruited, outfitted, subsidized, and transported by the colonial state to populate Alta California and to reproduce Christian family life and society. Attracting families to the remote military outpost, however, was no easy matter. Serra first promoted intermarriage between soldiers and newly Christianized native women in California as a way to establish Catholic family life, to foster alliances between the soldiers and the

Indians, and to curb the soldiers' sexual attacks against native women. To promote these families, Serra recommended that soldiers who married indigenous "daughters of the land" be rewarded with three kinds of bounty: a horse, farm animals, and land.[28]

In 1773, five newly converted Rumsien women married Catalán and mestizo soldiers at the Mission San Carlos de Borromeo, three married at San Luis Obispo, and three married at San Antonio de Padua. California's first mestizo families derived from these and similar unions at the presidios and missions. However, the intermarriage of soldiers with native women could neither meet the immediate need for families to populate the colony nor fulfill the civilizing mission assigned to sturdy Spanish families. To that end, between 1774 and 1781, colonial officials sent captains Fernando Rivera y Moncada and Juan Bautista de Anza on three modestly successful expeditions to recruit and bring to Alta California soldier, settler, and artisan *gente de razón* (Hispanicized) families from the northern provinces of Sonora-Sinaloa and Guadalajara. Subsequent attempts to recruit more families were decidedly unsuccessful, however. The Yuma rebellion of 1781, which closed the land route from Sonora, effectively arrested overland migration, and travel by sea was always perilous. During the decades of the 1780s and 1790s, colonial efforts to sentence convicts to California in lieu of other punishment and to bring settlers from Guadalajara also met with little success. Although a handful of families came with supply ships, most other new settlers were men.

Figure 6. The Wife of a Monterey Soldier.

Drawn in 1791 by the Spanish expeditionary artist José Cardero, this is the earliest known image of a Hispanic woman in California. Efforts to recruit single women from Mexico met with little success throughout the colonial period, and most soldiers who married on the California frontier wed indigenous women converts from one of the Missions. Courtesy Museo de América, Madrid. Photograph courtesy Iris Engstrand.

Governor Diego de Borica repeatedly sought to recruit single women as marriage, and thus sexual, partners for these men. However, viceregal authorities were unable to meet Borica's call in 1794 or his requests in 1798, first for "young healthy maids" *(doncellas)* and then simply for 100 women.[29] Instead, in 1800, with the help of the church, colonial officials shipped nineteen *niñas y niños de cuna* (foundlings)—ten girls and nine boys—to Alta California, where, according to Apolinaria Lorenzana, who arrived as a seven-year-old, they were "distributed like puppies" to various families.[30] With the exception of Apolinaria Lorenzana, all of the young women eventually married, though not without resistance.

The foundlings of 1800 were part of the last government-sponsored effort to recruit or promote colonizing families until the era of Mexican rule, when new invaders—Europeans and Euro-Americans—began arriving in California. Mexico responded by sending the Hijar-Padres expedition of 1834, which arrived with forty-two families, including fifty children, plus fifty-five single men and thirteen single women.[31] Instead of soldiers, this expedition was comprised of teachers, artisans, farmers, and their families. By this time, "Anglos" from the United States had begun to intermarry with Californio "daughters of the land," descendants of California's first soldier-settler families.

Despite the scarcity of *hispanas* despite the church's promotion of intermarriage between soldiers and Christianized Indian women, despite the colonists' own racially mixed backgrounds, and despite the blurring of racial and ethnic distinctions, rates of intermarriage between the soldier-settler population and Amerindians in the Monterey area, where I have completed the research, were high only in the initial period.[32] Between 1773 and 1778, 37 percent of the soldier-settler marriages were with Christianized Amerindian women. For the entire colonial period, however, only 15 percent of all marriages in Monterey were interracial. As elsewhere in the Spanish colonial world, conquering and colonizing men in California seldom formalized their sexual relations with Amerindian women after the early stages of conquest, when there were fewer alternative mates and intermarriage held particular economic, political, and military dividends. To reproduce the colony in Alta California, women's race and ethnicity mattered as much as their procreative capacities.

The betrothal and marriage of María Antonia Isabela de Lugo to Ygnacio Vicente Ferrer Vallejo illustrate the interrelation between race and contractual marriage.[33] Lugo was betrothed to Vallejo, a soldier serving escort duty at Mission San Luis, on the day of her birth. The contract between Vallejo and Lugo's parents bound her to marry him when she reached menarche. On February 18, 1791, at the age of fourteen and a half, Lugo married Vallejo, by then forty years old and retired from military service. Vallejo had entered into a marriage contract with a family who, like himself, was classified as "Spanish" rather than as mestizo, mulato, coyote, pardo, or any other mixed-blood designation. Once married, he applied for an official decree of *legitimidad y limpieza de sangre* (legitimacy and purity of blood) for the Vallejo name. In 1806, after fifteen years of marriage, the family received the decree, which certified that the Vallejo bloodline was untainted by Jewish, African, or any other non-Christian blood.[34] Henceforth, the Lugo-Vallejo family, two of whose daughters married Euro-Americans while a third married a Frenchman, rested their prominence and high social standing, in good part, on their officially certified purity of blood. Thus, though historically, racially, and culturally related to indigenous and African peoples, the *gente de razón* soldiers and families articulated their own identity as "Californios."[35]

During the Mexican era, after 1821, an expansionist North American neighbor sent a new group of single, foreign males—Europeans and Euro-Americans—to California's shores.[36] Some came as individual wanderers, some as part of exploring expeditions, merchant capitalist ventures, or reconnaissance missions. Spain's earlier economic and political reforms and Mexico's independence from Spain in 1821 established the basis for an expanding economy and related developments that affected marriage and family life in California. The rise of private property in the form of large rancho grants, liberalization of colonization, and trade policies, the secularization of the missions, the development of an agropastoral economy, and the increasing demand for imported goods established economic ties between Euro-American merchants and entrepreneurs and the landowning Californio families.

The intermarriage of daughters of the Californios to Euro-Americans and other foreigners who converted to Roman Catholicism and became naturalized Mexican citizens was, in many cases, the basis of these economic relationships.[37] From the early 1820s to the end of Mexican rule in 1846, intermarriages were celebrated between the daughters of families who controlled the economic and political power in California and the Euro-Americans, who would join in the overthrow of Mexican rule. These unions, which generally gave the Anglo husbands landed wealth (sometimes in the form of women's dowries, sometimes not) created still another group of mixed parentage. They also became the basis for the "old Spanish Californio family ancestry" claimed by Euro-American pioneers in narratives, memoirs, and histories of "Spanish California" published in the latter part of the nineteenth century, though often written in the wake of the US-Mexican War and subsequent dispossession of the Californios.[38]

These narratives, many of which were commissioned and collected in the 1870s and 1880s by Hubert Howe Bancroft for his multivolume *History of California,* became the primary source for the interpretations of gender and gender relations, women's sexual and moral conduct, their racial characteristics, and the nature of the family that dominate subsequent histories of early California.[39] Descriptions of the patriarchal Spanish-Mexican family, reproductive patterns, and family size abound in these nineteenth-century narratives of Euro-Americans and elite Californios, produced within the conflicting ideologies of the prewar and postwar eras. Becoming the authoritative social and cultural histories, the texts described California women as "remarkably fecund" and frequently commented that families were exceptionally large, with women bearing twelve, fifteen, and twenty children.[40] Women in California did, indeed, marry young, but the story is more complex. The study of marriage and the family in late eighteenth and early nineteenth-century California is far from complete.

Figure 7. A California Wedding Party of 1845

One of a series of pen-and-ink drawings produced by Emanuel Wyttenbach under the supervision of William Heath Davis. Courtesy California State History Room, California State Library, Sacramento, California. Call no. 2000-0100.

Examining lists of colonizing expeditions, marriage investigations (*diligencias*), marriage records, baptismal records, and population censuses for 1790 and 1834 for Santa Barbara and Los Angeles, historian Gloria Miranda has charted differences between and changes in the traditional, essentially military community of the presidio and the less economically stable, more flexible community of the pueblo.[41] Numerous factors, including the stage of colonization, the paucity of eligible women, and the young age and frequent turnover of military personnel, contributed to the young age of first marriages in the presidios. They also contributed to the very low numbers of single women and to the continuation of arranged marriages among the *hispano* population. Widowhood was generally short-lived, and multiple serial marriages were common for women. By custom, as well as because of frontier conditions, both sexes attained adulthood at a chronically tender age, and marriage registers document girls marrying between the ages of thirteen and sixteen and boys marrying between sixteen and seventeen. Across the span of the colonial period, however, the average marriage age in presidial society was sixteen to seventeen years for women and twenty-seven years for men. And although the population of the pueblo was more stable and permanent than in the presidio, the greater diversity of the population and economic instability of Los Angeles delayed the age of marriage there. The average age of marriage for women in Los Angeles was twenty years, while men married in their early thirties.

Similarly, Katharine Meyer Lockhart concluded that a steady increase in wealth, particularly among the *pobladores* whose occupation was ranching, was a distinctive, positive feature that affected the demographic pattern at the pueblo of San José.[42] San José registered a steady two-year increase in women's average age at marriage and a small decrease for men across three generations.

During the Mexican period, the rising social and economic complexity of town life, the marked emergence of an increasingly diversified population of foreigners, and the decline in the prestige of the military establishment as the presidio brought California closer to the marriage patterns that had emerged much earlier in Spain's older frontiers. Thus, in the era after Mexican independence, marriage age increased slightly for women, the age gap between spouses decreased, and, with the immigration of foreigners, racial exogamy increased. Interestingly, the rate of intermarriage between Californio women and Euro-American and European men during the Mexican period in Monterey was 15 percent—the same rate of intermarriage recorded for Amerindian women and mestizo men during the colonial period.[43]

Despite the young age at marriage, families in California were considerably smaller than commonly thought, although there were regional variations. While Miranda found a provincial average of slightly more than three children per family in 1790 and a homogeneous pattern of three to four children across the forty-four-year span between the 1790 and 1834 censuses, Lockhart found an average of seven children per family in San José.[44] Although "for some Californians, having large families was considered a mark of status" and some members of affluent clans, including the De la Guerras, the Ortegas, and the Vallejos, had as many as thirteen and even nineteen children, this was not the norm in the province.[45] Similarly, demographic studies of colonial New Mexico and Texas have shown that, contrary to common belief, large families were not the norm in either of these two colonies.[46] Miranda and other scholars attribute small family size among married *gente de razón* couples to various factors, including high infant mortality rates, miscarriages, infertility, marital discord, the extended absence of husbands, and personal choice.

Miranda's and Lockhart's studies, and my own research in progress, reveal that age at marriage and family size of the mestizo population in colonial California are consistent with patterns identified for the borderlands region writ large and for parts of colonial Mexico and Latin America.[47] This was generally true for other patterns, including high incidence of female-headed households, concubinage, illegitimacy, adultery, and premarital sex. Across time, sexual patterns in California increasingly resembled the broader nineteenth-century postcolonial Mexican and Latin American world.[48]

The meaning of these patterns, which challenge conventional notions of marriage and the patriarchal extended family, as well as standard analytic categories, has yet to be fully interpreted. Analytic and interpretive categories that explain the larger differences between colonials and European patterns as well as internal differentiation remain elusive, and, at this juncture, questions more than answers are at the forefront of scholarly discussion. Certainly part of the problem besetting the development of interpretive models remains rooted in the difficulty of reconstructing the lives of subaltern subjects from written sources that often ignore or distort their existence. The evidence historians have

developed thus far, however, illustrates that the patriarchal family—
ostensibly the norm in colonial California—was always a highly contested
realm.

Contesting Families: Women's Power, Resistance, and Contradictions

I am a woman and helpless . . . [but] they will not close the doors
of my own honor and birth, which swing open in natural defense and
protection of itself.

—Eulalia Callis, 1786

Though few women and men who colonized Alta California in the
latter third of the eighteenth century were literate, their voices and actions
are inscribed in official and unofficial sources detailing the colonization
of this remote outpost. Women's actions, if not often their words, appear
in documents written largely by men, though sometimes penned in
women's own hand and at other times written at their behest. These
documents expose internal hierarchies, tensions, and contradictions
in power relations among women and men as well as among women
themselves. The following discussion of mestiza resistance is framed by
the acknowledgement that, in the words of historian Florencia Mallon,
"No subaltern identity can be pure and transparent; most subalterns are
both dominated and dominating subjects, depending on the circumstances
or location in which we encounter them."[49]

These sources reveal that women frequently contested Hispanic patriarchal norms and acted outside the cultural constructions of femininity
that required of women not merely chastity, if single, and fidelity, if
married, but also demanded submissiveness, modesty, and timidity in
order to affirm their sexual purity. During the period under study, some
women in Alta California—from the high-born Eulalia Callis to the
impoverished widow María Feliciana Arballo—consistently resisted and
defied patriarchal control of their social and sexual bodies. In some cases,

they openly defied the norms that were supposed to control them; in others, they strategically used the idiom of honor to defend themselves, even as their actions violated the honor codes of femininity.

We can only speculate what words and language the twenty-three-year-old, recently widowed Feliciana Arballo spoke to convince Juan Bautista de Anza, over Father Pedro Font's strenuous objections, to let her, a woman alone with two young daughters and no male guidance or protection, accompany his overland expedition from Sinaloa to Alta California in 1775–1776.[50] Arballo's husband had died after the family signed up with the expedition to establish settlements on San Francisco Bay, but before they had left Horcasitas. Throughout the journey, Font publicly castigated and rebuked the widow Arballo and remonstrated De Anza for her presence. On the freezing night of December 17, when the weary but jubilant colonists held a dance to celebrate their safe crossing of the treacherous Colorado Desert, Font, who was already angry because people were partying instead of praying, became incensed when the young widow joined the party and began singing. "Cheered and applauded by all the crowd," he wrote, "a very bold widow sang some verses that were not very nice."[51] For these *poblador* families, whose subsidy upon becoming colonists allowed them rations for five years, the wages of sailors for two years, and free transportation to the new colony, joining the expedition to Alta California signified a release from the grip of poverty and misery in which the depressed economy of Sinaloa-Sonora submerged them.[52] Arballo, however, did more than defy the priest. She subverted his effort to shame her and control her behavior by inverting the positions, appropriating the public space, and performing within it.

Figure 8. The Anza Expedition, 1775-1776.

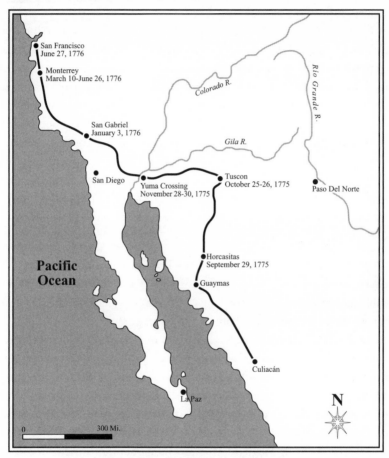

The Anza expedition, 1775-1776

Courtesy of Alexander Mendoza

At the other end of the social and economic spectrum, Eulalia Callis, La Gobernadora, also refused to abide the dictum of feminine submissiveness, timidity, and enclosure in the home.[53] Like Arballo, Callis made private matters public and "created a scandal" in February of 1785 by publicly accusing her husband, Governor Pedro Fages, of infidelity and refusing to sleep with him. Fages denied her accusations, saying she fabricated his infidelity as a ploy to force him to relinquish his governorship and return with her and their two children to Mexico. In her petition for legal separation, Callis stated that when she refused the advice of her priest and other men to be *recogida* or *depositada* (sheltered or deposited in another's home) and continued to accuse her husband publicly, she was arrested and, although ill, taken to Mission San Carlos Borromeo, where she was kept incommunicado in a locked and guarded room for several months. During her incarceration, Father de Noriega excoriated her from the pulpit and repeatedly threatened her with shackles, flogging, and excommunication. Callis, a wealthy woman from an influential family, was manipulating the idiom of gender-honor and notions of women's helplessness to defend her actions.

Historians of early California have dubbed Eulalia Callis the "notorious *gobernadora,*" writing with tongue-in-cheek about Fages's domestic problems and alternately portraying Callis as a fiery, tempestuous Catalán woman or as a hysterical woman suffering postpartum depression.[54] Today, Callis's actions seem to have been more a strategy for survival. Callis, who was pregnant four times in six years, was all too familiar with the precariousness of life on the frontier. She gave birth to Pedrito in 1781, had a miscarriage at Arispe in 1782, traveled to California while pregnant with and was ill after the birth of María del Carmen in 1784, and buried an eight-day-old daughter in 1786. Thus her demand that the family return to Mexico City, her public denouncement of Fages, and her suit for ecclesiastical divorce can be reasonably interpreted as part of an overall strategy to ensure her own survival and that of her two remaining children.

Figure 9. Doña Mariana Coronel grinds corn on a *metate*.

Painting by Alexander Harmer, an American artist who in 1893 married the daughter of an old California family in Santa Barbara. Antonio F. Coronel Collection, GPF 1000. Courtesy Seaver Center for Western History Research, Los Angeles County Museum of Natural History.

Though from different ends of the social spectrum, and with attendant differences of power, Arballo and Callis refused to obey male authority and subverted gender-honor requirements that they be subservient, meek, and powerless. Both made private matters public and refused their respective priest's mandate of conduct. Both not only subverted the gender-honor code for women, they also undermined the Christianizing and "civilizing" mission by which *gente de razón* women were to be exemplar models of Spanish-Catholic womanhood's subservience to male authority. In Callis's case, her behavior further subverted the sociopolitical order that Spanish officials were attempting to impose on a racially and culturally mixed population of colonists, whom they already judged to be unruly, undisciplined, and disrespectful of authority.[55] Callis's actions, which carried the weight of her family's wealth and influence in Spain as well as her position as La Gobernadora, posed a particularly grave threat to the imposition of Spanish hegemony in the newly conquered territory. If the scarcity of *gente de razón* women and their importance to survival of frontier colonies liberalized some aspects of gender inequality, patriarchal structures nevertheless remained fundamentally unaltered and the technologies of rule enforced. Thus women's strategies of resistance, how they manipulated their circumstances, had to be carefully and subtly laid.

In view of the political and military imperative to populate Alta California with Christian families, officials of the colonial church and state consistently pressured women to marry, or, in the case of widows, remarry.[56] Despite the pressures, some women resisted entering the institution that gave them status in the community. Although the foundling girls of 1800 were brought explicitly as marriage partners for California soldiers, five of the ten girls informed the paymaster at Monterey in 1801 that they "did not want to receive suitors because they did not want to be burdened with marriage."[57] Apolinaria Lorenzana, the one *niña de cuna* who never married, tells us in her *testimonio* that although she had received a proposal of marriage as a young girl, "I refused his offer ... because I was not particularly inclined toward that state [of matrimony] even though I knew the merits of that sacred institution."[58]

Instead, Lorenzana, who became known as *La Beata* (the pious one), entered a life of work and service in the missions as a *llavera, enfermera, cocinera,* and *maestra* (keeper of the keys/matron, nurse, cook, teacher). She maintained her independence, earned her livelihood by working for the Catholic Church, devoted her life to the "civilizing mission" the state assigned to mestiza colonists, and taught herself and others to write. A resourceful and intelligent woman, Lorenzana was respected and well-loved for her good works and selfless devotion to the health and well-being of Indians and mestizos alike. Lorenzana escaped the bonds of matrimony and control of her sexuality. As the *llavera* at Mission San Diego, however, her duties included policing the sexuality of the young neophyte women living in the mission compound by locking them in the *monjero* at nightfall and releasing them in the morning. She both resisted and enforced the control of women's sexuality and the sexual norms that Spanish colonial hegemony imposed in California.

Other women—both single and married mestiza women—contested patriarchal control of their sexuality by engaging in "scandalous" and illicit sexual activity.[59] During the period of conquest and settlement, women's sexual "transgressions" appear, in the records at least, to have been confined to adultery and *deshonra* (premarital sex). As California during the Mexican era evolved from a subsidized, military society to a more complex agropastoral, ranching, and market economy with more pronounced racial and social stratifications, cases of concubinage and prostitution were added to the list of mestiza women's illicit sexuality. Sexual violence, in the form of rape and incest, and sexually related violence—beating women to correct their sexual behavior—were present throughout.

Figure 10. The famed southern California ranchero Juan Bandini and his daughter.

JUAN BANDINI AND HIS DAUGHTER YSIDORA

(From the Historical Collection of Title Insurance and Trust Company)

Courtesy, California Historical Society at the University of Southern California, Title Insurance and Trust, and C. C. Pierce Photography Collection, University of Southern California, CHS-7130.

Female and male sexuality in the Spanish colonial world was strictly regulated by the civil code, to say nothing of the moral code. Fornication, adultery, concubinage, prostitution, rape, incest, sodomy, bigamy, bestiality, and scandalous behavior were civil crimes for which perpetrators were prosecuted, and women were prosecuted more vigorously than men.[60] Moreover, since civil and canon law vested authority over a woman's sexuality in the male members of her family, the sexuality of a mother with a grown son, such as forty-year-old Josefa Bernal, was subject to her son's authority as well as to that of all other male relatives, whether living in the household or not. Bernal barely escaped being beaten by her twenty-five-year-old son Francisco when he found her in an adulterous relationship with Marcelo Pinto.[61]

It is clear that women's sexuality was also at risk within and without the family. An instance each of rape and incest appears in the colonial records, though a few more cases of rape, and a case of a teacher accused of molesting female students, were recorded during the Mexican period.[62] In this era, too, cases of concubinage, prostitution, and a significant increase in family violence, most specifically directed at women, appear in the records. Whether the low incidence of sexual violence toward mestiza women in colonial California was due to its nonexistence, to underreporting, or to the fact that most of the sexual violence was directed at Amerindian women has not yet been researched. What is clear is that across the eighty years of Spanish-Mexican rule, sexual violence and sexually related violence toward women became generalized throughout society. Some women responded with equal violence. Most, however, filed formal criminal charges against violent spouses in court.[63] Women had frequent recourse to the judicial system, and the records of Mexican tribunals contain cases that women filed in civil as well as criminal court, where they appear as both plaintiffs and defendants.

One approach to analysis of women's resistance during the Mexican period centers on the nineteenth-century narratives. Thus, Genaro Padilla finds that while Californio men's narratives remained embedded in patriarchal constructs, Californio women's narratives "voiced resistance to patriarchal domination that characterized social relations...and assertively figured themselves as agents in the social world they inhabited."[64] Women's narratives offered gendered perspectives that were critical of patriarchal constraints, affirmed women's presence in the public realm, and refuted the common assumption that Californio women welcomed the Euro-American conquest.

CONCLUSIONS

The construction of Amerindian and mestiza women's subjectivities in Alta California, as this essay has demonstrated, has historically been contested terrain. Most specifically, women's sexual and social bodies, their sexuality, their procreation, and the control of it have been the province of the patriarchal family, church, and state. Some women resisted, defied, and subverted patriarchal control of their sexuality within the family and without. From differing positions of power, as well as from contradictory locations, they carved out spaces, took actions, and fashioned responses within the family, which was at once a primary place of resistance, power, authority, and conflict.

The family was, and is, the most basic unit of sociopolitical organization and relations of power internally as well as externally. It was the primary place where women in eighteenth- and nineteenth-century Alta California constructed identity and subjectivity within the historical process of successive waves of conquest and colonialism, wherein mestizas were alternately part of the colonizing forces and part of the colonized peoples. In the Spanish colonial world, and particularly in new territories under conquest, the "Western" family, in its Spanish-Catholic incarnation was deployed as a pivotal technology of rule. We are only now beginning to grapple with the complexities and contradictions of what that meant in the construction of "native" women's identities and subjectivities on the California homeland that was then, as it is now, contested space.

Engendering the history of Alta California, moving gender and the body to the center of historical inquiry, challenges us to rethink our conceptual, empirical, analytic, and interpretive categories.[65] It challenges us to question and reevaluate extant sources and our own assumptions as we approach them, and further summons us to expand the sources we use to study nonwritten text and other constructs of history. This chapter forms a small part of the larger feminist effort to engender and rethink history.

NOTES

1. Ana María Alonso, *Thread of Blood: Colonialism, Revolution, and Gender on Mexico's Northern Frontier* (Tucson: University of Arizona Press, 1955), 21.
2. Fray Junípero Serra to Antonio María de Bucareli y Ursúa, 21 May 1773, in *Writings of Junípero Serra*, 4 vols., ed. Antonine Tibesar (Washington, D.C.: Academy of Franciscan History, 1955), 1: 363; Antonia I. Castañeda, "Sexual Violence in the Politics and Policies of Conquest: Amerindian Women and the Spanish Conquest of Alta California," in *Building with Our Hands: New Directions in Chicana Studies*, eds. Adela de la Torre and Beatriz M. Pesquera (Berkeley: University of California Press, 1993), 15-33; Antonia I. Castañeda, "Presidarias y Pobladoras: The Journey North and Life in Frontier California," in *Renato Rosaldo Lecture Series Monograph* 8 (1990-91): 25-54; Richard C. Trexler, *Sex and Conquest; Gendered Violence, Political Order, and the European Conquest of the Americas* (Ithaca: Cornell University Press, 1995); Albert L. Hurtado, "Sexuality in California's Franciscan Missions: Cultural Perceptions and Sad Realities," *California History* 71 (Fall 1992): 370-85; Albert L. Hurtado, *Indian Survival on the California Frontier* (New Haven: Yale University Press, 1988); Antonia I. Castañeda, "Amazonas, Brujas, and Fandango Dancers: Women's Sexuality and the Politics of Representation on the Borderlands," paper presented at the American Historical Association Annual Conference (January 1995); Virginia María Bouvier, "Women, Conquest, and the Production of History: Hispanic California, 1542-1840" (PhD diss., University of California, Berkeley, 1995); Antonia I. Castañeda, "Presidarias y Pobladoras: Spanish-Mexican Women in Frontier Monterey, Alta California, I770-1821" (PhD diss., Stanford University, 1990).
3. See works by Ramón A. Gutiérrez: "Family Structures: The Spanish Borderlands" and "Sexual Mores and Behavior: The Spanish Borderlands," in *Encyclopedia of the North American Colonies*, 3 vols., eds. Jacob Ernest Cooke et al. (New York: Charles Scribner's Sons, 1993), 2: 672-82 and 700-710; *When Jesus Came, the Cornmothers Went Away: Marriage, Sexuality, and Power in New Mexico, 1500-1846* (Stanford, Calif.: Stanford University Press, 1991); "Marriage and Seduction in Colonial New Mexico," in *Between Borders: Essays on Mexicana/Chicana History*, ed. Ade-

laida R. del Castillo (Los Angeles: Floricanto Press, 1990), 447-57; and "From Honor to Love: Transformation of the Meaning of Sexuality in Colonial New Mexico," in *Kinship Ideology and Practice in Latin America,* ed. Raymond T. Smith (Chapel Hill: University of North Carolina Press, 1984), 81-104.

4. See the following works by Deena J. González: *Refusing the Favor: The Spanish-Mexican Women of Santa Fe, 1820-1880* (New York: Oxford University Press, 1999); "La Tules of Image and Reality," in *Building with Our Hands,* eds. de la Torre and Pesquera , 75-90; "Gender Relations: The Spanish Borderlands," and "Old Age and Death: The Spanish Borderlands," in *Encyclopedia of the North American Colonies,* eds. Cooke, et al., 2: 406-412 and 780-82; and "The Widowed Women of Santa Fe: Assessments on the Lives of an Unmarried Population, 1850-1889," in *On Their Own: Widowhood and Aging in the American Southwest,* ed. Arlene Scandron (Chicago: University of Illinois Press, 1988), 45-64. See also the work of Asunción Lavrín: "Lo Feminino: Women in Colonial Historical Sources," in *Coded Encounters: Writing, Gender, and Ethnicity in Colonial Latin America,* eds. Francisco Javier Cevallos-Candau, et al. (Amherst: University of Massachusetts Press, 1994), 153-76; "In Search of the Colonial Woman in Mexico: The Seventeenth and Eighteenth Centuries," in *Latin American Women: Historical Perspectives, Asunción Lavrín* (Westport, CT: Greenwood Press, 1978), 23-59; and "La vida feminina como experiencia religiosa: Biografía hagiografía en Hispanoamérica colonial," *Colonial Latin American Review* 2 (1993): 27-52; as well as Asunción Lavrín and Edith Couturier, "Las mujeres tienen la palabra: Otras voces en la historia colonial de México," *Historia Mexicana* 31 (1981): 278-313.

5. Rosaura Sánchez, *Telling Identities: The California Testimonios* (Minneapolis: University of Minnesota Press, 1995); Gyan Prakash, "Subaltern Studies as Postcolonial Criticism," *American Historical Review* 99 (1994): 1475-90; Florencia E. Mallon, "The Promise and Dilemma of Subaltern Studies: Perspectives from Latin American History," *American Historical Review* 99 (1994): 1491-1515; "Founding Statement: Latin American Subaltern Studies Group," *Boundary* 2 20 (Fall 1993): 110-21; Gayatri Chakravorty Spivak, "Can the Subaltern Speak?" in *Marxism and the Interpretation of Culture,* eds. Cary Nelson and Lawrence Grossberg (Urbana: University of Illinois Press, 1988), 271-313; Gayatri Chakravorty Spivak, "The Rani of Simur: An Essay in Reading the Archives," *History and Theory* 25 (1985): 247-72.

6. See Laura F. Klein and Lillian A. Ackerman, eds., *Women and Power in Native North America* (Norman: University of Oklahoma Press, 1995); Nancy Shoemaker, ed., *Negotiators of Change: Historical Perspectives on Native American Women* (New York: Routledge, 1995); Kevin Gosner and Deborah E. Kanter, eds., *Ethnohistory*, special issue, *Women, Power, and Resistance in Colonial Mesoamerica* 42 (Fall 1995); Greg Sarris, *Mabel McKay: Weaving the Dream* (Berkeley: University of California Press, 1994); Greg Sarris, *Keeping Slug Woman Alive: A Holistic Approach to American Indian Texts* (Berkeley: University of California Press, 1993); Greg Sarris, "'What I'm Talking about When I'm Talking about My Baskets': Conversations with Mabel McKay," in *De/Colonizing the Subject: The Politics of Gender in Women's Autobiography*, eds. Sidonie Smith and Julia Watson (Minneapolis: University of Minnesota Press, 1992); Carol Devens, *Countering Colonization: Native American Women in the Great Lakes Missions, 1630–1900* (Berkeley: University of California Press,1992); Gretchen M. Bataille and Kathleen Mullen Sands, eds., *American Indian Women: Telling Their Lives* (Lincoln: University of Nebraska Press, 1984); Paula Gunn Allen, *The Sacred Hoop: Recovering the Feminine in American Indian Traditions* (Boston: Beacon Press, 1992); Paula Gunn Allen, *Grandmothers of the Light: A Medicine Woman's Sourcebook* (Boston: Beacon Press, 1992); Paula Gunn Allen, ed., *Spider Woman's Granddaughters: Traditional Tales and Contemporary Writing by Native American Women* (New York: Fawcett Columbine, 1989); Beatrice Medicine and Patricia Albers, eds., *The Hidden Half: Studies of Plains Indian Women* (Lanham, MD: University Press of America, 1983); Victoria Brady, Sarah Crome, and Lyn Reese, "Resist! Survival Tactics of Indian Women," *California History* 63 (Spring 1984): 141-51; Rayna Green, *Native American Women: A Contextual Bibliography* (Bloomington: Indiana University Press, 1983).

7. Antonia I. Castañeda, "Marriage: The Spanish Borderlands," in *Encyclopedia of North American Colonies*, eds. Cooke et al. 2:727-38; Gutiérrez, *When Jesus Came*; Francois Giraud, "Mujeres y Familia en Nueva España," in *Presencia y transparencia: La mujer en la historia de México*, ed. Carmen Ramos Escandón (Mexico City: Colegio de Mexico, 1987), 61-77; Asunción Lavrín, ed., *Sexuality and Marriage in Colonial Latin America* (Lincoln: University of Nebraska Press, 1989), see especially the essays by Asunción Lavrín, Serge Gruzinski, Ann Twinam, Ruth Behar, Richard Boyer, and Thomas Calvo; Sylvia Arrom, *The Women of Mexico City, 1790-1857* (Stanford, CA: Stanford University Press, 1985); Patricia

Seed, *To Love, Honor, and Obey in Colonial Mexico: Conflicts over Marriage Choice, 1574-1821* (Stanford, CA: Stanford University Press, 1988).

8. Klein and Ackerman, eds., *Women and Power in Native North America*, see especially Klein and Ackerman's introduction and essays by Victoria D. Patterson, Mary Shepardson, Sue-Ellen Jacobs, and Daniel Maltz and JoAllyn Archambault; Shoemaker, ed., *Negotiators of Change*, especially Shoemaker's introduction and essays by Lucy Eldersveld Murphy and Carol Douglas Sparks; Gosner and Kanter, eds., *Ethnohistory*, special issue, especially the essays by Alvis E. Dunn, Martha Few, and Irene Silverblatt.

9. Shoemaker, ed., *Negotiators of Change*, 7; Devens, *Countering Colonization*.

10. See Lucy Eldersveld Murphy, "Autonomy and the Economic Roles of Indian Women of the Fox-Wisconsin Riverway Region, 1763-1832," in *Negotiators of Change*, ed. Shoemaker, 72-89; Edward D. Castillo, "Introduction," in *Native American Perspectives on the Hispanic Colonization of Alta California, Spanish Borderlands Source-Book*, ed. Edward D. Castillo 26 (New York: Garland Publishing, Inc., 1991), xvii–xlv; Eleanor Leacock and Richard Lee, eds., *Politics and History in Band Societies* (Cambridge: Cambridge University Press and Editions de la Maison des Sciences de l'Homme, 1982), especially the introduction and articles by Leacock and Lee; Mona Etienne and Eleanor Leacock, eds., *Women and Colonization: Anthropological Perspectives* (New York: Praeger, 1980), especially the articles by June Nash, Irene Silverblatt, and Robert Steven Grumet.

11. See Harry Kelsey, ed., *The Doctrina and Confesionario of Juan Cortes* (Altadena, CA: Howling Coyote Press, 1979), 112-16 and 120-23; Madison S. Beeler, ed., *The Ventureno Confesionario of José Señán, O.F.M.*, University of California Publication in Linguistics 47 (Berkeley: University of California Press, 1967), 37-63.

12. Hugo Reid, "Letters on the Los Angeles County Indians," in *A Scotch Paisano in Old Los Angeles: Hugo Reid's Life in California, 1832-1852 Derived from His Correspondence*, ed. Susana Bryant Dakin (Berkeley: University of California Press, 1939), App. B: 275.

13. Quotes in this paragraph are from Bouvier, "Women, Conquest, and the Production of History," 363-69.

14. Gutiérrez, "Sexual Mores and Behavior," 701.

15. "Ynterrogatorio sobre la sublevación de San Gabriel, 10 octubre de 1785," Archivo General de la Nación, Provincias Internas Tomo I (Californias): 120, Microfilm Collection, Bancroft Library, Berkeley, CA.

16. Robert F. Heizer, "A Californian Messianic Movement of 1801 among the Chumash," *American Anthropologist* 43 (1941, reprint, 1962): 128-29. For discussion of the warrior woman tradition, women's councils, religion, and spirituality as a source of women's power and resistance, and of women's cultural mediation and resistance in Native American history, see Elizabeth Salas, *Soldaderas in the Mexican Military* (Austin: University of Texas Press, 1990), 1-10; Clara Sue Kidwell, "Indian Women as Cultural Mediators," *Ethnohistory* 39 (Spring 1992): 97-107; Beatrice Medicine, "'Warrior Women'—Sex Role Alternatives for Plains Indian Women," in *The Hidden Half,* Medicine and Albers, 267-80.

17. Heizer, "A Californian Messianic Movement of 1801 among the Chumash."

18. Antonia I. Castañeda, "Witchcraft on the Spanish-Mexican Borderlands," in *The Reader's Companion to U.S. Women's History,* eds. Wilma Mankiller, Gwendolyn Mink, Marysa Navarro, Barbara Smith, and Gloria Steinem (New York: Houghton Mifflin Company, 1998).

19. Ruth Behar, "Sexual Witchcraft, Colonialism, and Women's Power: Views from the Mexican Inquisition," in *Sexuality and Marriage in Colonial Latin America,* Lavrín, 178-206; Ruth Behar, "Sex and Sin, Witchcraft, and the Devil in Late Colonial Mexico," *American Ethnologist* 14 (February 1987): 34-54; Ruth Behar, "The Visions of a Guachichil Witch in 1599: A Window on the Subjugation of Mexico's Hunter-Gatherers," *Ethnohistory* 34 (Spring 1987): 115-8; see also Solange Alberro, "Herejes, brujas, y beatas: Mujeres ante el Tribunal del Santo Oficio de la Inquisición en la Nueva España," in *Presencia y transparencia,* ed. Escandón 79-94; Henry Kamen, *Inquisition and Society in Spain in the Sixteenth and Seventeenth Century* (Bloomington: Indiana University Press,1985); Henry Kamen, "Notes on Witchcraft, Sexuality, and the Inquisition," in *The Spanish Inquisition and the Inquisitorial Mind,* ed. Angel Alcalá (Boulder, CO: Social Science Monographs, 1987), 237-47; María Helena Sánchez-Ortega, "Woman as a Source of 'Evil' in Counter-Reformation Spain," in *Culture and Control in Counter-Reformation Spain,* eds. Anne J. Cruz and Mary Elizabeth Perry *Hispanic Issues* 7 (Minneapolis: University of Minnesota Press, 1992); Marc Simmons, *Witchcraft in the Southwest: Spanish and Indian Supernaturalism on the Rio Grande* (Lincoln: University of Nebraska Press, 1980).

20. Bouvier, "Women, Conquest, and the Production of History," 363-84; Edward D. Castillo, trans. and ed., "The Assassination of Padre Andrés Quintana by the Indians of Mission Santa Cruz in 1812: The Narrative

of Lorenzo Asisara," *California History* 68 (Fall 1989): 117-25; Edward D. Castillo, "Introduction" and "The Native Response to the Colonization of Alta California," in *Native American Perspectives on the Hispanic Colonization of Alta California*, ed. Castillo xvii-xlv and 423-40; Antonia I. Castañeda, "Comparative Frontiers: The Migration of Women to Alta California and New Zealand," in *Western Women: Their Land, Their Lives*, eds. Lilian Schlissel, Vicki L. Ruiz, and Janice Monk (Albuquerque: University of New Mexico Press, SR), 283-300, especially 292-94; James Sandos, "Levantamiento! The 1824 Chumash Uprising," *The Californians* 5 (January-February 1987): 8-11; Bruce Walter Barton, *The Tree at the Center of the World: A Study of the California Missions* (Santa Barbara: Ross-Erickson Publications, 1980), 185; Sherburne F. Cook, *Conflict between the California Indian and White Civilization* (Berkeley and Los Angeles: University of California Press, 1976), 56-90.

21. Hurtado, *Indian Survival on the California Frontier.*

22. Sarris, "'What I'm Talking about When I'm Talking about My Baskets.'"

23. Gunn Allen, *Spider Woman's Granddaughters*, 2.

24. Judith F. Baca, interview by the author, 8 October 1995, San Antonio, TX; Vera Rocha, interview by the author 5 July 1996, Baldwin Park, CA.

25. Heath Dillard, *Daughters of the Reconquest: Women in Castilian Town Society, 1100-1300* (New York: Cambridge University Press, 1984); Heath Dillard, "Women in Reconquest Castile: the Fueros of Sepúlveda and Cuenca," in *Women in Medieval Society*, ed. Susan Mosher Stuard (Philadelphia: University of Pennsylvania Press, 1976), 71-94; Salomé Hernández, "Nueva Mexicanas as Refugees and Reconquest Settlers, 1680-1696," in *New Mexico Women: Intercultural Perspectives*, eds. Joan M. Jensen and Darlis A. Miller (Albuquerque: University of New Mexico Press, 1986), 41-70.

26. José María Ots y Capdequi, *Instituciones sociales de la América española en el período colonial* (La Plata: Biblioteca Humanidades, 1934), 183– 206.

27. Serra to Antonio María de Bucareli y Ursúla, Monterey, 24 August 1774, *Writings*, 2: 143; Serra to Bucareli, Monterey, 8 January 1775, *Writings*, 2: 203; Serra to Bucareli, Monterey, 30 June 1778, *Writings*, 3: 199.

28. Serra to Bucareli, Mexico City, 13 March 1773, *Writings*, 1: 325; Serra to Bucareli, Mexico City, 22 April 1773, *Writings*,1: 341; Serra to Bucareli, Monterey, 24 August 1775, *Writings*, 2:149, 151, and 153.

29. Branciforte al Governador, "Sobre envío de mujeres para pobladores," Orizaba, 25 enero de 1798, Archives of California, 14: 284, Bancroft Library; Salomé Hernández, "No Settlement without Women: Three

Spanish California Settlement Schemes, 1790-1800," *Southern California Quarterly* 72 (Fall 1990): 203-33.

30. Memorias de Doña Apolinaria Lorenzana, "La Beata," marzo de 1878, Santa Barbara, Manuscript Collection, 1, Bancroft Library.

31. C. Alan Hutchinson, *Frontier Settlement in Mexican California: The Hijar-Padres Colony and Its Origins, 1769-1835* (New Haven: Yale University Press, 1969).

32. Entries 3, 49, 50,154, 180, 181, 182, 197, 290, 334, 387, 405, 528, 529, and 563, Libro de Matrimonios: Misión de San Carlos de Borromeo, vol. 1; Serra to Bucareli, "Report of the Spiritual and Material Status of the Five California Missions, 5 February 1775," *Writings*, 2: 237, 241. The findings for Monterey are consistent with those for Mexico. See Sherburne F. Cook and Woodrow Borah, *Essays in Population History: Mexico and the Caribbean*, 3 vols. (Berkeley: University of California Press, 1971-79), 1: 248-53. For early discussion of the racially and culturally mixed population that colonized California, see Jack Forbes, "Hispano Mexican Pioneers of the San Francisco Bay Region: An Analysis of Racial Origins," *Aztlán* (Spring 1983): 175-189; Jack Forbes, "Black Pioneers: The Spanish-Speaking Afroamericans of the Southwest," in *Minorities in California History*, eds. George E. Frakes and Curtis B. Solberg (New York: Random House, 1971), 20-33, first published in 1966.

33. Charles Howard Shinn, "Pioneer Spanish Families in California," *The Century Magazine*, n.s., 5, no. 19 (1891): 377-89; Gloria E. Miranda, "Racial and Cultural Dimensions of Gente de Razón Status in Spanish and Mexican California," *Southern California Quarterly* 70 (Fall 1988): 265-78.

34. Jose María Estudillo, comandante de la compañia presidial, Información sobre nobleza de sange del Sargento Ignacio Vallejo y decreto concedido lo pedido, 20 julio 1807, Monterey, California, Archives of California, 16:356; and Ynformación sobre la legitimidad y limpieza de sangre de Don Ignacio Vicente Ferrer Vallejo, padre del General Don Maríano Vallejo, 1806-1847, M. G. Vallejo Collection, Documentos para la Historia, Bancroft Library.

35. The origin and meaning of the term "Californio" remains unstudied. The earliest reference I have found to the use of this term is in the records of accounts of animals, crops, and the distribution of corn and wheat for the years 1782, 1784, and 1787 at Mission San Carlos de Borromeo. However, it is unclear whether the term refers to neophyte Indians or to the soldier/settler population. See Copias de varios documentos en la Parroquia de Monterey. Parroquia de Monterey, C-C 24:31, 34, Bancroft

Library; Lisbeth Haas, *Conquest and Historical Identities* (Berkeley: University of California Press, 1995), 43. See also Genaro Padilla, *My History, Not Yours: The Formation of Mexican American Autobiography* (Madison: University of Wisconsin Press, 1993); Ramón A. Gutiérrez, "Unraveling America's Hispanic Past: Internal Stratification and Class Boundaries," *Aztlán* 17 (1986): 79-101.

36. Douglas Monroy, *Thrown among Strangers: The Making of Mexican Culture in Frontier California* (Berkeley: University of California Press, 1990); David J. Langum, *Law and Community on the Mexican California Frontier: Anglo-American Expatriates and the Clash of Legal Traditions, 1821-1846* (Norman: University of Oklahoma Press, 1987); David J. Weber, *The Mexican Frontier, 1821-1846: The American Southwest under Mexico* (Albuquerque: University of New Mexico Press, 1982); Leonard Pitt, *The Decline of the Californios* (Berkeley: University of California Press, 1966),1-47.

37. For discussion of unions between Californio women and foreigners, see Sánchez, *Telling Identities;* Monroy, *Thrown among Strangers,* 158-61; Antonia I. Castañeda, "The Political Economy of Nineteenth-Century Stereotypes of Californianas," in *Between Borders,* ed. Del Castillo, 213-36.

38. Five of the eleven Californiana narratives from the Bancroft Collection are published in Rosaura Sánchez, Beatrice Pita, and Bárbara Reyes, eds., "Nineteenth Century Californio Testimonials," *Critica: A Journal of Critical Essays* (University of California, San Diego: Critica Monograph Series, Spring 1994). For analysis of the Euro-American narratives and the Californiano/Californiana counter-narratives, with a focus on the latter, see Genaro Padilla, "Recovering Mexican American Autobiography," and Rosaura Sánchez, "Nineteenth-Century Californio Narratives: The Hubert H. Bancroft Collection," in *Recovering the US Hispanic Literary Heritage,* eds. Ramón Gutiérrez and Genaro Padilla (Houston: Arte Público Press, 1993), 153-78 and 279-92; Genaro Padilla, "Discontinuous Continuities: Remapping the Terrain of Spanish Colonial Narrative," in *Reconstructing a Chicana/o Literary Heritage: Hispanic Colonial Literature of the Southwest,* ed. María Herrera-Sobek (Tucson: University of Arizona Press, 1993), 24-36; Genaro Padilla, "Yo Sola Aprendí: Mexican Women's Personal Narratives from Nineteenth-Century California," in *Revealing Lives: Autobiography, Biography, and Gender,* eds. Susan Groag Bell and Marilyn Yalom (New York: State University of Press of New York, 1990).

39. Antonia I. Castañeda, "Gender, Race, and Culture: Spanish-Mexican Women in the Historiography of Frontier California," *Frontiers: A Journal of Women Studies* 11 (1990): 8-20.

40. Castañeda, "Gender, Race, and Culture"; Castañeda, "Political Economy of Nineteenth-Century Stereotypes"; Hubert Howe Bancroft, *California Pastoral, 1769-1848* (San Francisco: History Company, 1888), 305-34.

41. Miranda, "Gente de Razón Marriage Patterns."

42. Katharine Meyer Lockhart, "A Demographic Profile of an Alta California Pueblo: San Jose de Guadalupe, 1777-1850" (PhD diss., University of Colorado, 1986), 114.

43. Miranda, "Hispano-Mexicano Childrearing Practices in Pre-American Santa Barbara." Twenty-six, or 15 percent, of the 170 Mexican women who married between 1822 and 1846 in Monterey married Euro-American or European men, see Castañeda, "Presidarias y Pobladoras: Spanish-Mexican Women in Frontier Monterey," 286-87, 291, n. 1.

44. Lockhart, "A Demographic Profile of an Alta California Pueblo," 60-69.

45. Miranda, "Hispano-Mexicano Childrearing Practices," 309.

46. Alicia V. Tjarks, "Demographic, Ethnic, and Occupational Structure of New Mexico, 1790," *The Americas* 35 (July 1978): 45-88; Alicia V. Tjarks, "Comparative Demographic Analysis of Texas, 1777-1793," *Southwestern Historical Quarterly* 77 (January 1974): 291-338.

47. Miranda,"Gente de Razón Marriage Patterns"; Miranda, "Hispano-Mexicano Childrearing Practices"; Lockhart, "A Demographic Profile of an Alta California Pueblo."

48. Castañeda, "Presidarias y Pobladoras: Spanish-Mexican Women in Frontier Monterey," 266-74; Lockhart also found low rates of illegitimacy in San José; see Lockhart, "A Demographic Profile of an Alta California Pueblo," 112-14. For family and household composition after 1848, which reveals rates of female-headed households consistent with the nineteenth-century pattern identified for parts of Mexico and Latin America, see Richard Griswold del Castillo, *La Familia: Chicano Families in the Urban Southwest, 1848 to the Present* (Notre Dame: University of Notre Dame Press, 1984); Barbara Laslett, "Household Structure on an American Frontier: Los Angeles, California, in '1850," *American Journal of Sociology* 81 (January 1975): 109-28.

49. Mallon, "The Promise and Dilemma of Subaltern Studies," 1511.

50. Herbert Eugene Bolton, trans. and ed., *Anza's California Expeditions*, 5 vols. (Berkeley: University of California Press, 1930), 4:138, 428.

51. Ibid., 4: 428.

52. Ibid., 1: 228.

53. Ynstancia de Doña Eulalia Callis, Muger de Don Pedro Fages, governador de California, sobre que se le oyga en justicia, y redima de la opresión que padece, 23 August 1785, Archivo General de la Nación, Provincias Internas, 120: 66-81, Collection, Bancroft Library.

54. Bancroft, *History of California,* 1: 389-93; Irving Berdine Richman, *California under Spain and Mexico, 1535-1847* (Boston: Houghton Mifflin Co., 1911), 156-58; Charles C. Chapman, *A History of California: The Spanish Period* (New York: Macmillan Company, 1921), 398-400; Castañeda, "Presidarias y Pobladoras: The Journey North," 41-43, 54, n. 103.

55. See Manuel Patricio Servín, "California's Hispanic Heritage: A View into the Spanish Myth," *Journal of San Diego History* 19 (1973):1-9; Oakah L. Jones, Jr., *Los Paisanos: Spanish Settlers on the Northern Frontier of New Spain* (Norman: University of Oklahoma Press, 1979); Sidney B. Brinckerhoff and Odie B. Faulk, *Lancers for the King: A Study of the Frontier Military System of Northern New Spain, with a Translation of the Royal Regulations of 1772* (Phoenix: Arizona Historical Foundation, 1965); Max Moorhead, "The Soldado de Cuera: Stalwart of the Spanish Borderlands," in *The Spanish Borderlands: A First Reader,* ed. Oakah L. Jones, Jr. (Los Angeles: Lorrin L. Morrison, 1974), 87-105; Leon G. Campbell, "The First Californios: Presidial. Society in Spanish California, 1760-1822," in *The Spanish Borderlands,* ed. Jones, Jr., 106-18.

56. Bancroft, *History of California,* 1: 603-606; Castañeda, "Presidarias y Pobladoras: Spanish-Mexican Women in Frontier Monterey," 168-69, 203-204.

57. Castañeda, "Presidarias y Pobladoras: Spanish-Mexican Women in Frontier Monterey," 171-73; Hernández, "No Settlement without Women."

58. Lorenzana, "Memorias de Doña Apolinaria Lorenzana, La Beata," 45-46.

59. Castañeda, "Presidarias y Pobladoras: Spanish-Mexican Women in Frontier Monterey," 266 –71.

60. Lavrín, "In Search of the Colonial Woman," in *Latin American Women,* Lavrín 35; Ots y Capdequi, *Instituciones sociales,* 250-51; Arrom, *The Women of Mexico City,* 65-70.

61. José Argüello a Fages, 26 noviembre de 1788, San Francisco, Trato ilícito entre un soldado y una muger casada, *Archives of California,* 4: 250

62. Carrillo, 28 de noviembre de 1806, Santa Barbara, Causa de incesto, *Archives of California,* 16: 342-56; Antonio María Pico, Juez constitucional de primera nominación, 7 de mayo de 1845, San José Guadalupe. Causa criminal contra el vecino Maríano Duarte, maestro de escuela por

tentativas de estupro en niñas de menor edad, *Archives of California*, 69: 139-42.

63. For Monterey, see Criminal Court Records, Mexican Archives of Monterey County, Office of the County Clerk, Salinas, CA.

64. Padilla, *My History, Not Yours*, 26; Sánchez, *Telling Identities*; Richard Griswold del Castillo, "Neither Activist Nor Victim: Mexican Women's Historical Discourse—The Case of San Diego, 1820-1850," *California History* (Fall 1995): 230-43.

65. For feminist theories of gender, sexuality, and history, see: Joan W. Scott, ed., *Feminism and History* (New York: Oxford University Press, 1996); Deena J. González, "A Resituated West: Johnson's Re-Gendered, Re-Racialized Perspective," in Clyde Milner III, ed., *A New Significance: Re-envisioning the History of the American West* (Berkeley: University of California, 1998); Ann-Louise Shapiro, ed., *Feminists ReVision History* (New Brunswick: Rutgers University Press, 1994); Kathleen M. Brown, "Brave New Worlds: Women's and Gender History," *William and Mary Quarterly* 50 (April 1993): 311-328; Susan Lee Johnson, "'A Memory Sweet to Soldiers': The Significance of Gender in the History of the 'American West'," *Western Historical Quarterly* 24 (November 1993): 495-518; Antonia I. Castañeda, "Women of Color and the Rewriting of Western History: The Discourse, Politics, and Decolonization of History," *Pacific Historical Review* 61 (November 1992): 501-533; Joan W. Scott, "Experience," and Ana María Alonso, "Gender, Power, and Historical Memory: Discourses of Serrano Resistance," in *Feminists Theorize the Political*, eds. Judith Butler and Joan W. Scott (New York and London: Routledge, 1994), 22-40 and 404-425; Emma Pérez, "Sexuality and Discourse: Notes from a Chicana Survivor," in *Chicana Lesbians: The Girls Our Mothers Warned Us About*, ed. Carla Trujillo (Berkeley: Third Woman Press, 1991), 159-84; Irene Silverblatt, "Interpreting Women in States: New Feminist Ethnohistories," in *Gender at the Crossroads of Knowledge: Feminist Anthropology in the Postmodern Era*, ed. Micaela di Leonardo (Berkeley, Los Angeles, Oxford: University of California Press, 1991), 140-74; Joan Wallach Scott, "Gender: A Useful Category of Historical Analysis," *American Historical Review* 91 (December 1986): 1053-75.

BIRTHING CHICANA HISTORY

ANTONIA CASTAÑEDA, EMMA PÉREZ, AND DEENA GONZÁLEZ

Antonia, in taking what was happening in those conferences, in those venues, and then not losing sight of the fact that people are people and that the layers of misunderstanding were human misunderstandings—that the interactions were human interactions and that no person deserved to be silenced or misconstrued or put down or hurt, but the purpose was really bigger than any of us—that's what she really has taught me. She taught me this in those years, and then in subsequent years.Because it's not as if Antonia only did that in 1990. She's doing that in 2011 as well.

Deena González[1]

Figure 11. Dr. Antonia Castañeda, San Antonio 2011.

Photograph Courtesy of Luz María Gordillo

Antonia's been instrumental in being supportive academically, emotionally, psychically. Just knowing she's there. You know? In the world. With her strength. With her courage. With her warriorship. With her psychic self. With her emotional self. With her beauty. That long black hair I remember still.... and those leather boots. And she's a lovely woman inside and out.

Emma Pérez[2]

The morning I interviewed three of the founders of Chicana History: Dr. Antonia Castañeda, Dr. Emma Pérez, and Dr. Deena González, I woke up feeling energized and excited. I had organized the shooting months before and a friend of Castañeda had kindly offered her loft to shoot the interview. We were all attending the NACCS annual conference (National Association for Chicana and Chicano Studies) in Pasadena, CA, and our schedules were busy and packed with events, meetings, lunches, etc.[3] Yet we were able to set aside one evening, and what was intended as an interview turned into an informal conversation between close friends, colleagues, and fellow social activists. Building community has been a pillar for Chicanas and other women of color, and Emma Pérez, Deena González, and Antonia Castañeda were among those constructing the social networks that are now the nexus of the Chicana scholarly community. Not without struggles these three historians began the arduous task of excavating and reinventing the way history is written. Reading against the grain, Castañeda, González and Pérez rescued women's testaments that created a new gendered history. Their generation of Chicana historians gave us a blueprint and created the field where we now have a firm foundation on which to build.

AC: It was 1980, in the spring. And I am visiting Chris Sierra in Santa Barbara. I'm ABD and working for The California Office of Historic Preservation, doing a survey of Latino and Chicano cultural sites. Actually, it might have been a little later, because I'm not working on the survey until a little later. So, Chris says a friend of mine is going to stop by if she's in town...

DG: I had already heard about Antonia at Stanford because at Berkeley we were so few Chicanas that we knew there were Chicanas at Stanford, but we hadn't necessarily all met. I mean, they had met as a group who were working in an informal organization called La Colectiva, so they all knew each other, but we didn't know each other across the disciplines, necessarily. So then I'm on my way to New Mexico and stop by Chris's and we had dinner....

AC: Yes. And that's how Deena and I met. Deena was the first, and at that time the only Chicana historian, a graduate student, in the history department, at UC Berkeley.

DG: And I go in and Chris says I want you to meet—and Chris is all beaming happy like she's just gotten two I don't know of the finest whatever people together in one room—and I said oh this is wonderful I've heard that Antonia is a history grad student at Stanford, but what exactly does that mean? What conversation are we going to have? What are we going to talk about? And we just started talking.

AC: And we're still talking twenty-some years later.

DG: There was a Chicana doing British history, but she left—Rosalinda somebody or other. I remember very clearly talking with her a lot the first weeks, but she left ... I think she stayed a year and she was a year before me, so the year that I got there was the year that she left. So then that was it.

AC: That was it. And I was the only Chicana graduate student at Stanford. Well, I was the first Chicana graduate student. At that point I wasn't the only one because Vicki Ruiz came the year after I came to Stanford. So I was excited and thrilled to meet another Chicana historian. And this one was from Nuevo Mexico. And so we established a life-long friendship and I say we grew up together in history. And so it's two years later, in 1982—

DG: March

AC: March of 1982. And there's a conference that we're all invited to.[4] And it's a conference organized by Adelaida del Castillo and Juan Gómez Quiñones—also an historic conference because Juan [is a historian] and Adelaida is an anthropologist. At that point she was a graduate student and Juan was a professor of Mexican and Chicano History at UCLA, and still is. Adelaida is an anthropologist who was beginning her graduate work and was about to study Mexican women on the border. And they organized this conference—a Chicana/Mexicana Conferencia.

DG: And it's big because they invite everyone who does work in the area so it's not just historians, it's political scientists. There were some art folks; there was a whole variety of people.

EP: But it was focused on history—for the first time. It was called the first Chicana/Mexicana History Conference.

DG: I think it's been the only Chicana/Mexicana history conference except for what Antonia organized—the Gender on the Borderlands in San Antonio in 2001.[5]

AC: But we're jumping forward. And so it's 1982. We're at this conference and we're congregating in the lobby and we're talking and then in walks this woman in a leather jacket. With zippers. And straps. And buckles.

EP: Were you checking me out, Antonia?

AC: I was checking you out.

DG: And there's Emma Pérez.

AC: There's Emma Pérez.

EP: I was a graduate student at UCLA at the time—In history. Juan was my mentor and I had met Adelaida. I went into the graduate program in history because I had been taking women's history classes and then it all opened. A whole world opened up to me. And Juan had a core of us who were all graduate students. And we all happened to be from Tejas at the time.

And I remember you when I was giving my paper, because I was doing my paper on the Partido Liberal Mexicano because that was Juan's work... I was really into being a socialist feminist communist radical Chicana lesbian. And very out, which in 1982, people were like, "the L word." Although I guess they still do that. And I remember seeing Antonia at the door and she was sexy. She had long curly hair. You had long curly hair. Leather boots that went up to here.

AC: So that's how that relationship of a lifetime began.

EP: That's how we began. The Chicana/Mexicana history conference. Because I realized there were two other Chicana historian graduate students: One at Berkeley, one at Stanford. And y'all were both brilliant. And I was like oh my God, because I wasn't clicking with anybody at my university. Nobody was really doing gender the way I wanted to. Nobody was really engaging race and class the way I wanted to and then I heard y'all and I was like, finally—finally! It was like waking up —getting slapped in the face or something.

AC: And that really was a historic conference. The three of us were there.

But what I think is important here to remember is that those four at UCLA, Al Camarillo, Richard Griswold Del Castillo, Douglas Monroy, and Ricardo Romo are that first generation of US Chicano historians—that is, whose Ph.D. is in US History. And we're the Chicanas; we followed them almost ten years later—or eight or seven years later. So Emma Pérez, Deena González, Antonia Castañeda, Vicki Ruiz; we're the first generation of Chicana historians in US history. But the point of that is that US history departments did not want us.

EP: They didn't admit us—

DG: They didn't admit us and they did not want us.

EP: And it was because we had people like Juan, who was Mexican history in US history; he was instrumental in the development of Chicano history.

DG: He was in the history department but Chicano history was in the boundaries and borderlines of US history.

AC: He was developing it.

EP: He was developing it and ... he recruited a bunch of us.

DG: And the thing that people don't remember is also that, as undergraduates, we had no Chicano or Chicana history. We had no Chicano or Chicana studies.

AC: Or women's studies.

EP: Chicanos—the guys had been looking at labor history and you know examining—

AC: Mobility studies.

EP: Right, mobility studies. Which was very male centered. Why do they do that?

DG: But the important thing, the important thing is too that Antonia—Antonia and Vicki, as those first out—and then later it would be George and David, but Antonia and Vicki had something very special, which was that they had a Chicano historian who was—

AC: —who was trained in US history; he had worked with Noris Hundley, a US California historian, a historian of the US West.

DG: And that was the other piece to it—that in mainstream history departments, we had mainstream folks. Some of them were very tolerant. Like at Berkeley, they were very tolerant. But they were tolerant in the sense that it's part of the US West. It's part of the Spanish borderlands school. So whatever you do, name everything that and you'll be fine. And then, slowly, they'd say well we don't know that you'll be able to find very much. Now, for historians to say this is really tragic because if there's one thing we know in our work is—I don't care what you need to find, there is an archive for it. And in the archives there is a wealth of discovery to be made. So the idea of discouraging.... And that's when Antonia would say to me, I remember, in those early conversations she'd say, No, no, no! I know that there is! There is this stuff on Native Americans. There is! I saw it at the Bancroft. I was at the archives in wherever it was—The Huntington or UCLA or whatever—the Mission archives and the archdiocese archives. And we would go with each other on a lot of the trips.

DG: And the worst part is if you look at Berkeley, Berkeley has never had a Chicano/a historian and it still doesn't. It still doesn't and it's the new century. UCLA still has Juan, and then Eric Avila in Chicano/a studies, even though he's jointly appointed now with history. But those are the examples in the departments in California that I think really show how even though it seems like there's so many more now, that the experience we had is probably not going to be repeated again [is a false hope]. In fact, you know, when we're gone, when we're no longer in the academy, I think people are going to be back to square one unless we manage to get new folks placed. But many of them are placed in small liberal arts colleges, in the Cal State system and there is not a cadre being trained in the UC system or the large research one universities in the far West. You look at Washington and Oregon and it's a stretch to find anybody there who can handle graduate students. San Diego, UC San Diego is producing, now, quite a few Chicana historians, Al Camarillo at Stanford has led the way, his students, Steve Pitti at Yale, for example, has also trained US Chicana/o historians... A few have come through that door.

AC: So this is the framing of the field of U.S. History and Chicana/o history and its development. It develops out of the work of Latin American historians, historians trained in Latin American history—Chicana/o historians, but trained in Latin American history. Similarly, Chicana/o literature comes out of the work of literary critics and other scholars trained in Peninsular Spanish and in Latin American literature. So we are an interdisciplinary field and, in part we're an interdisciplinary field not only because that is our orientation and proclivity, but because when we started Chicana/o studies, we had to research all fields in order to get a body of materials. And to construct ourselves as historical, literary, literate subjects.

DG: And then once that door opened, we were able to show, by the vast amount of material that there is in any archive anywhere in the Spanish borderlands, there is a history and there is a field. And now even more in places like the Midwest and other places there are Chicano and Mexicano communities who are finally getting this attention and recognition. Today it's very hard for people to say you don't have the materials to create a history or to write a book or to study. And I think that's an important shift. Now whether that translates into "we're going to hire more people because we've seen the work that you all have done or because we value Al Camarillo and that training or Juan Gómez Quiñones..." When they're gone—and they're about at retirement ... it's a really big issue and concern.

AC: Back to Deena's comments about sources—not only did we get told it doesn't exist, your field, Chicana history, I was also told there are no sources ... And so I went to the sources that had traditionally been used, but I went to those sources with other questions: Gender-centered questions, women-gender-centered questions. And nobody had looked, whether it was the Spanish borderlands or US history or Latin American history, or Mexican history or Spanish Colonial history of the area—no one had looked at those sources. Although there were historians, Bolton included, who had made reference to women, but the subject was not considered important.

DG: And "Gender, Race and Culture" is such a pivotal essay.[6] I always teach it when I teach my Chicano/a history course—The one that lays out the historiography. Because you start us out with Bancroft's work and then you take us to the Spanish Borderlands—

EP: The frontier and then Chicano and Chicana and Women's historiography and it's really brilliant, the way you track that for us, in every field, how gender was treated. "Let's look at how Bancroft referred to Mexican women." Which is incredibly racist and misogynist—and she tracks it all and you see it. And then we get to the twentieth century and unfortunately some of the Chicano history is putting women and gender in the background once again.

DG: I was race. And—

AC: I'm class, and—

EP: And I was sexuality.

EP: We just all assumed we were gender.

AC: We did. And so, it's 1982. We have met Emma. [laughter]

EP: We're back to 1982—

DG: Oh my God—the timeline. Antonia will always get us back to the timeline—

AC: Don't accuse me of being linear! OK. So it's 1982. The sparks have flown. They've gotten together.

At that point I was living in Sacramento, but I was actually teaching at UC Davis. I was teaching as an adjunct, as a lecturer in Chicana/o studies. And so Ada and I actually got together and said, OK, it's time to organize. So we sent out a call to the Berkeley women, to the women at Stanford, of course the Sacramento women and Santa Cruz. ... and we started MALCS [Mujeres Activas en Letras y Cambio Social][7] for the same reason that we started the Colectiva and that we began doing the work, the academic work that we were doing—precisely because of the neglect, the ignorance, the exclusion of Chicanas. Chicano studies did address race and class but did not address gender or sexuality. Women's studies, white women's studies, feminist studies, addressed gender and some class, but mainly gender. And they didn't start addressing sexuality, actually none of the academic programs started addressing sexuality until the lesbiana scholars started raising the issue and critiquing - whether it was Chicana studies or women's studies or feminist studies—and writing and doing the research and writing and presenting. So we started MALCS precisely because neither Chicano studies nor women's studies/feminist studies, addressed Chicanas. And that was the same argument of the African American women in terms of Black studies.

DG: The other thing that seemed to me to be very present in MALCS and I know we haven't talked about this very much, but when I go back to the original documents and things that we filled out...what always concerned me was that there was kind of a fear of being women talking together, not only as women but for women. There was reluctance. There was kind of—we don't know what this space is like. And I remember a lot of the women would raise the issue several times about why men weren't included. And we used to go "What? Why would we want an organization of our own to include men? They have all the organizations."

EP: It was homophobia. It was like this kind of sense that "Oh my God, they're going to start accusing us of lesbianism. They're going to start accusing us that we're queer" so they needed to bring their phallus into the room, right? And we weren't allowing it.

EP: And especially Deena and I and Antonia, too. We needed our space. And that's when I wrote "Sitio y Lengua" —but into the early '90s it was very much about that. There were still a lot of reactions and there were women at conference plenary sessions who stood up and said, "I'm a male-identified woman." Remember that?

AC: Oh yes!

EP: And negotiating all the different perspectives and parties was really hard, because you would see people in their different social positions and yet uninvestigated , situationally ....and we didn't have vocabulary or theory or understanding of it.

AC: We were making it.

EP: We were making it as we were doing, as we were organizing the group—

AC: The point of all of this, for me, thinking about it over the long haul, is in fact, that these are all contested spaces. And so there has never been a conflict-free development. Whether it's in Chicano/a studies or women's studies or history, US history, Latin American history, it's always a struggle—a Lucha. So NACCS and MALCS were and still are not free, but still are contested spaces. And so a couple of the very major conflicts that arose—1990 for MALCS. But I can't remember whether NACCS in Albuquerque was in the '90s ...

EP: I felt like my body and psyche had been bombed, because we had to sustain such an incredible amount of warriorship and courage and healing and it was just tough. It was tough because people came down on us hard. Well, that was when I was called, Deena and I were called "lesbian terrorists."

AC: That was in Albuquerque at MALCS.

DG: It started in Albuquerque at NACCS.

EP: And then after that whole experience, in terms of looking back at it, the other part was that it wasn't just at the moment, it was difficult and ugly and horrifying and challenging on many, many levels—through that summer and then afterwards the name-calling continued.

AC: One memorable moment of name calling was when a colleague, apparently upset with me for raising question about the absence of lesbian and mixed race (specifically Anglo-Mexican) voices at a MALCS meeting earlier in the year, aggressively asked me ". . . and who do you think you are, the patron saint of lesbians?" ("y tú que te crees, la santa patrona de las lesbianas?)"

DG: You know 1990 was that important moment because we brought the lesbian caucus to NACCS and it was a battle. It was a major battle because suddenly there was a rift and tension in the Albuquerque conference because everybody was asking "are we going to have a lesbian caucus or not?" And someone who was a well-known, respected in some circles, Chicano historian said if we're going to have a lesbian caucus we should also have the Marijuanista caucus. And that was his way of basically dismissing the significance of sexuality and the lesbian stance. So it was a battle. We did get it passed, but not without an incredible amount of hostility and homophobia.

EP: And it had to go through all these channels to have a women-only roundtable at NACCS—panels were supposed to be open to everyone, which was the same thing that MALCS faced later that summer. The panel they claimed to be open to everyone really had been submitted as a roundtable. Well, no one could find the paperwork. So, as a panel, the organizers said, it had to be open to everyone. And we said, "No. This is a closed round table." They responded, "well we don't know if we can allow that." So there were these back door discussions late into the night. Everyone wringing their hands, they don't want the men there and the men saying "we're gonna crash the panel or the workshop. We're gonna crash the doors. We're gonna force ourselves in because you should not be exclusionary."

AC: And in March of 1990 and then spring or late summer—by then we were doing the MALCS institute at UCLA —the issues reemerged. We started MALCS because we needed a place to grow and support each other intellectually, politically, culturally, linguistically, and we needed our own space, obviously. And so when we established MALCS and established bylaws, we said OK; no men and no white women as presenters. If they want to come to the plenaries, they are welcome.

AC: MALCS 1990 erupted around the same set of issues. And there's Deena and you were there too Emma, but the other dimension that was real clear was not just the issue race, of white women occupying our space and taking over like they do, but also homophobia. That too was very evident.

EP: That's when people were really calling Deena and me lesbian terrorists—because of the fact that we had gotten the lesbian caucus at NACCS.

DG: Yeah and that was going to come to pass the following year it would be officially instituted and have its first meeting. But that was the year that we laid the groundwork and it was coming to pass.

AC: Gloria Anzaldúa was at the conference también. This was the first time Gloria had come back to NACCS in years because she had gone to Ypsilanti, had presented, was subjected to severe homophobic attacks at that conference, and she just said, "I am not coming back here." Albuquerque was her putting her toes back in the water, and we were really lucky to have her back at NACCS in 1990!

LMG: ¿Cuándo empezaste a enseñar Historia Chicana? (When Did You Start Teaching Chicana History?)

AC: In both Chicana and Chicano history, but specifically in Chicana history it would be important as a way to get into our respective work and where and the state of the field is, in fact, to talk about those first classes. So it's 1970 at the University of Washington. I'm a graduate student and I'm teaching the first classes in both Chicano history and Chicana history—actually Chicano literature and Chicana history. And in Chicana history for the women's studies department or the women's studies program, and Chicano studies.

When did you first start teaching Chicana history?

EP: Well, the UTEP job—the University of Texas, in El Paso. I had other positions; I taught in Minnesota. That was probably the first time. And Deena, that's when we were together and you came and gave a guest lecture. And then Edén Torres was in my class. She was the only Chicana. It was like a group of all these gringitas and a couple of gringitos because it was Minnesota in 1982 or '83, no '85.

But Texas was my first real job, University of Texas in El Paso—living in la frontera. It was a whole other way of perceiving the world, to be in la frontera. I was teaching a class of Chicano/a history to forty, fifty, sixty students at once who were all Mexicanos, Chicanos, Chicanas, and they got my jokes.

DG: They loved your jokes.

EP: They liked my jokes and I could be bilingual and the most fun I ever had was teaching there—because a lot of them were returning students. They were older students. They were young hungry students. There were students from Juárez. There were a few of the indigenous, close by, the Yaqui. It was just an amazing space. And I still miss it. I still relish those moments in those classrooms because those students were just very present and really willing to learn everything about Chicano/a history and studies as well.

DG: I did guest teaching at Berkeley before I took my first job—and I did Chicanos in the American Southwest which was Alex Zaragosa's class. But out of that I kept thinking, you know, we need to focus on women. We really needed to focus on women. When I got to Pomona College, I was hired as a Latin Americanist. I was like, that's my second field—what the heck am I going to do? So I divided up the sections. It used to be history of Latin America part one and part two. I said that we were redefining the field. I said it's going to be called Native America and then Mexican America. And the students were great and they hung in there. But there were also a few students who were saying, we want some courses on women. So I came up with Latina feminist traditions. And I put that on the books in 1984. And then I taught it practically every year I was there. So for eighteen years I taught that class. I never taught a traditional La Chicana or La Mujer Mexicana or La Mexicana or Mexican Women's history or Chicana history course or anything like that. I always taught it in the context of something broader because that was the kind of place it was. Now at Loyola Marymount I do the Chicana/Latina feminism or Chicana/Latina studies class. And so I get to do those same sorts of things. But again, the focus is always this context of race, class, ethnicity, gender, social location now, color

AC: For me the point is that we're the generation of Chicanas with Vicki Ruiz in US history, that established Chicanas as historical subjects. We did so based on our archival research, on our analysis, and interpretation. And in doing so, we reinterpreted Chicano/a history, Women's history, US history, history of the US West. I'm an eighteenth-nineteenth century historian, that's my research and my field of study. Deena's nineteenth-early twentieth, Emma is twentieth and Vicki is twentieth.

With respect to books, *Refusing the Favor* and the *Decolonial Imaginary* just absolutely changed the field.

AC: What I mean by that is, certainly we have all relied on other historians and other theoreticians, other theoretical frameworks, but nobody understood my work in the way that Deena and Emma did while it was developing. And there was nobody else that I could rely on. I had advisors who were very supportive and very helpful as best as they could be, but they didn't know anything about Chicanas. And so even though they wanted to, they couldn't help me. And so I relied on Deena and Emma, as well as others, especially other Chicana scholars: Gloria Anzaldúa, Norma Alarcón, Norma Cantú, Aida Hurtado. And Vicki, for me, while her work is on the later periods, Vicki and I were in graduate school together, so we supported each other. But in terms of arguments, in terms of development, in terms of being able to discuss and get feedback, it was Deena and Emma. And again, not to minimize the importance of other scholars in the field in history in Chicana/o studies, but we really were breaking ground. And it was hard tack, it was hard ground. It was full of rocks and holes and stones, particularly because our advisors in various ways and faculty were telling us "you can't do that."

EP: The other obstacle we had was that the expectation in the discipline and the field was to create and write a book — or even a series of books. We never really thought that what we were going to do was what they asked as to do, or what they wanted us to do. We wanted to do what we felt needed to be done for the field so that if we had no basic information about New Mexico or its people, the numbers, the statistics, then we had to do that work while we also attended to these other big picture issues. And when we would talk about this we would tell people look, the reason why you take five years and we take ten is because we have to do this basic archival digging and create the field. You have ten books you can pull from a shelf to find any number of things you need—

AC: and that's what I find so frustrating about explaining to people the process of doing a history—of silences, basically—of people hidden and people silenced. And that's what we're up against at these institutions. It's like oh why aren't you producing more? Well, you know, researching and writing history takes a long time anyway, but I can't go into the damn archives and pick out all of these presidential documents that have been categorized for me. I remember going to the Bancroft, which I love, but you could tell what gets privileged. You know the archival work that gets privileged. And it's easy to go in, you write a book, you look through all the documents. In a year you've got your stuff. With us its years...

EP: I remember going and looking at the original documents. And we would go in and look at those and try to figure out, with each other, what it is we're going to do with them. And Antonia would say over and over again, "I want to be in the archives. I want to be in the archives. I want to look. I want to find. I'm looking for, like the first book of recipes by a woman. That's somewhere here...." And it was a search. It was a hunt to find these things, but then they led to other things.

And luckily now we're at a point where we don't have to justify the necessity of the information or the knowledge. We don't have to justify the task. We have our own book series that are selling incredibly well so we feel at least there's security in that. Others can go on and do other book series with other presses and let other presses know, if you sell out, if you have two and five and seven thousand copies sold of something in a field like Chicana studies, guess what? You have a market. So we have that record that we're able to use now, but a lot of that too is that Antonia's commitment to what we're doing here, in this field is very specific and very determined. And I think that's the part that the other Chicana historians value the most—the dedication and the commitment, Antonia, that you've had over the years—that you've sustained, no matter what.

NOTES

1. Deena González, Interview with the author, Pasadena, CA, 2010.
2. Emma Pérez, Interview with the author, Pasadena, CA, 2010.
3. *Sites of Education for Social Justice*, NACCS 38, 30 March–2 April 2011.
4. Antonia Castañeda first presented her essay "Political Economy" at the Mexicana/Chicana Women's History International Symposium in Santa Monica, CA (1982).
5. During her tenure as the O'Connor Chair in Borderlands History, Dr. Castañeda organized the Gender on the Borderlands Conference at St. Mary's University in San Antonio, Texas (2001). Castañeda co-edited selected papers from the conference published in *Frontiers: A Journal of Women Studies,* 24, nos. 2-3 (2003). In 2007 she co-edited the double issue for the University of Nebraska Press as *Gender on the Borderlands: The Frontiers Reader.*
6. González is referencing "Gender, Race and Culture: Spanish Mexican Women in the Historiography of Frontier California," first published by *Frontiers: A Journal of Women's Studies* in 1990 and reprinted as chapter four in this volume.
7. See introduction to this volume for a brief history of the organization. MALCS has grown to become the nexus of intellectual and artistic Chicana production in the US. In sharp contrast to elitist and often Eurocentric disciplinary journals, MALCS opens the door for Chicanas and Latinas to publish and for senior Chicanas to commit to mentoring and editing the younger generation's work.

PART FOUR

EMBODIED HISTORIES

To study Chicana history means to rethink regional history and to rethink the history of the United States.The lives of Tejana and other migrant worker women pose significant new questions to (en)gender that history and its meaning, introducing concepts of the body as well as dispossession, displacement and appropriation that require new ways of conceptualizing family, household economies, and the agency of working-class women.It is a question not just of inclusion, but of construction.

"Que Se Pudieran Defender"

"'Que Se Pudieran Defender': Chicanas Regional History and National Discourses" (2001)

"Language and Other Lethal Weapons: Cultural Politics and the Rites of Children as Translators of Culture" (1996)

"Lullabies y Canciones de Cuna: Embodying Chicana History" (first appearing in this volume)

"La Despedida" (2005)

Like Castañeda's earlier work, the four articles in this section highlight the need to question, critique and dismantle old categories for the writing of history. Born of nationalist and white supremacist assumptions, such categories functioned to erase Chicana histories. Thus, as Deena González notes, "add and stir" will not diversify the cannon nor will it move the field of history onto paradigms with which it can address the violence of the past in creating the inequalities of today; new models are needed. According to Castañeda, one way of reconceptualizing the past, is to make bodies visible and to listen to the bodies and the histories those bodies tell. And so "Que Se Pudieran Defender," "Language and Other Lethal Weapons," "Lullabies y Canciones de Cuna," and "La Despedida" construct their questions from the lived experience of Chicanas/os: women, children, and families. They map the lived realities of today and the yet-to-be published histories that must be told in order to understand and address how those lived realities came to be.

In "Que Se Pudieran Defender," Castañeda maps the practiced ignorance of historians who once claimed there was no field of Chicana/o history and/or no resources for building such a field; and she critiques the overtly sexist and sometimes violent nature of popular culture in its representation of Chicanas. The two are connected, with the violence of the past reproduced in the present when the paradigms of manifest destiny become ensconced and entrenched in disciplines such as history. In these times, when those with the power to shape curriculum and fund programs are working to dismantle Chicana/o Studies, Ethnic Studies and Gender Studies, this is a critical lesson to remember. Utilizing Chicana voices, including those in her own family, Castañeda demonstrates how the gaps in history, those silences of which Pérez wrote in the *Decolonial Imaginary*, are not silent, but filled with the histories that will challenge the nationalist categories of the past, creating new ways to understand the past and build new futures.

Similarly, "Language and Other Lethal Weapons," "Lullabies y Canciones de Cuna," and "La Despedida" insist that we expand our repertoire of sources. "Language and Other Lethal Weapons" holds the stories and histories of child translators up to the light of the colonial and the Chicana/o past. Today's child translators, much as the child translators at the time of conquest, live as warriors thrown into battles, sometimes empowering, sometimes traumatic, and not of their own choosing. To date, studies have failed to incorporate the experiences and stories of child translators or to place today's young translators into a larger historical and global perspective. "Lullabies y Canciones de Cuna," calls on historians to listen to women's histories through lullabies—not to neglect the filtered sources of testimonios and legal records, but to also learn to read, to listen, and to interpret women's stories "inscribed on the surface of the body," histories of conflict and survival rocked and sung into the flesh of each new generation. Finally, in "La Despedida," the author remembers a transitional event from her childhood. The history of Chicana struggles in the field is brought home as a layered and personal plain as Castañeda remembers the preparation of a farmworker woman's body for burial and for her velorio (wake). The readers are pulled into a room—a woman's space of love, labor, and loss. At the close of the preparation, the author, as young girl leaves the room "into the late afternoon sunlight." No one knows that this little girl will grow to write foundational historical texts about our communities— to become a founder of an interdiscipline. And so the young Castañeda has the last word on the work of the elder Castañeda—which she leaves with you—to build upon. The generation of Antonia Castañeda: Drs. Castañeda, González, Pérez, Ruiz, and others whose names appear in the introduction to this volume, excavated, crafted and developed a new history—a gendered and embodied history where the lives of Chicanas came to shine forth from our past. Yet Chicana studies and Chicana history are not static, abstract fields. They are fields rooted in the lives and struggles of our communities, in our bodies and the bodies of the women who came before us. They are dynamic fields which demand we take the tools of Dr. Castañeda's generation in our hands and build yet another tomorrow, beyond that afternoon sun.

In these final articles, Dr. Castañeda raises more questions than she answers, and so it is fitting that they close this collection. For if we are ever to succeed in disrupting the racist and misogynist answers of the past—those histories/answers which continue to give rise to the racist and misogynist culture of today, we will have to learn to begin in the "gaps" of the dominant narrative, find new ways to bring embodied histories and stories into public spaces where they will be heard, shift the categories from which we shape our questions and walk away from those categories which continue to shape not only the modern academy, but the national narrative itself.

CHAPTER 7

"QUE SE PUDIERAN DEFENDER (SO YOU COULD DEFEND YOURSELVES)"

CHICANAS, REGIONAL HISTORY, AND NATIONAL DISCOURSES

Chicana lives, inscribed on roadways and waterways, link people, rivers, communities, valleys, and regions in histories embedded, since long before the sixteenth century, in northward migrations from Mesoamerican valleys to Inuit shores.[1] Where and how do these lives, linked across time, space, and place, fit into regional histories that, at best, reinforce a fragmented understanding of a Chicana/o presence in the region as well as in US history? This fragmented understanding is rooted in a historiography that has excluded Chicanos, a population annexed to the United States by military conquest and international treaty in the mid-nineteenth century, from the conceptualization of both region and nation.

The power of place is in its ordering, and the ordering of space entails the operation of gender, race, and class. In this context, how does a history that recognizes the presence and continuity of Chicanas in these landscapes long before the nineteenth-century annexation reorder the regional and national space that has rendered their historical experience invisible?[2] The presence and migrations of Chicanas challenge current constructs of regional history and speak to larger epistemological, methodological, analytical, and interpretive questions and categories in the construction of US history. How do we conceptualize, tell, and write the story of the United States and its regions? Who tells the story and how? Who is authorized to tell the story? Whose story gets told? Who controls the ordering of time, space, and place?

To concretize the issues relative to Chicanas and regional history, this essay centers gendered, racialized, sexualized, and historicized working-class Chicana bodies and the transregional migration of farmworkers from Texas to Washington State during the mid-twentieth century. My examination of migration draws heavily on historian Emma Pérez's theory of Chicanas' "diasporic subjectivities" and of Chicanos as a "diasporic population."[3] I use both terms—migration and diaspora—throughout this paper. Pérez's proposition of diasporic subjectivity as the "oppositional and transformative identity that allows these women to weave through the power of cultures, to infuse, and be infused, to create and re-create newness" is critically important to the discussion.[4]

This essay argues three main points: Chicana migration within the boundaries of the United States challenges current conceptualizations and categories of analysis of US regional history. Definitions of "regions" are contingent on people's sociopolitical and geographical location; and the imposition of regional boundaries distorts the narrative of the experience of women's lives.

The article focuses on the twentieth-century "internal migration" of Chicanas from Texas to Washington. This migration, I argue, is an outgrowth of the consolidation of US military conquest, of capitalist development, and of state and national politics in the western half of the United States and must be understood within that context. It cannot be understood within a strictly regional context.

CHALLENGING REGIONAL BOUNDARIES

In the battle over history, which is fundamentally about who gets to define the stories being narrated, will the defining come from the realities of lived experiences, like those of my mother and other Tejana farmworkers, or will it come from the abstract principles that have ordered and organized US history to date? Rethinking Chicana history means rethinking regional history, and this ultimately requires rethinking the history of the United States.

Constricted by imperialist mappings of the Americas, as well as by the categories, language, and triumphalist historiography of its consequent nation-states, the act of writing Chicanas into history—to borrow historian Emma Pérez's title—requires deconstructing or rejecting existing categories of analysis, including "regional history" and the "women's West."[5] Precisely because regions, like maps, are icons of nationhood, it is necessary to deconstruct the representation and location of Chicanas within that cartography and iconography across time and space.[6] It is particularly important to explore the discursive fields and practices that have located Chicanas within the national "order of things," which in turn defines regions and thereby fixes one's place within the nation and its regions.[7]

Regional history fragments the history of Chicanas. Historians have come to focus on the historiography of Chicanas (and Chicanos) as a battle of exclusion versus inclusion. Since the 1970s, Chicana and other women historians of color have been arguing that the issue is not simply one of exclusion versus inclusion, but rather one of construction. Ours is a conceptual and historiographic struggle. We, as historians, need to do more than incorporate Chicanas into regional histories using the existing categories of analysis. We need to do more than incorporate race, gender, sexuality, and class in the historiography of a particular region. We need to look at regions within the larger fabric of national as well as global economic, social, political, and cultural issues.

When I began my graduate work at Stanford University in 1973, my eminent adviser informed me that I could not study Chicano history because "there is no such thing as Chicano history. It is not an academic discipline."[8] I could study US history and the subfield of the West, or Mexican, or Latin American history, or Modern European history with a focus on Spanish colonial history and the Spanish borderlands. Of course, nobody in the department specialized in the US West or even in the Spanish borderlands. Moreover, even if Chicano history did exist, I should not specialize in it because I would be "too emotional about it, not sufficiently objective."[9]

Subsequently, on being advanced to candidacy in US history, I discussed my dissertation topic on Chicana colonial history with another faculty adviser. He said that there is no such thing as Chicana colonial history: there are no collections, no documents, no primary sources from which to write it.[10] Moreover, such a study would contribute to Mexican history, but not to Chicano history, which began with the signing of the Treaty of Guadalupe Hidalgo in 1848. Meanwhile, at UCLA in the mid-1980s, Emma Pérez was developing her dissertation topic on Chicanas, socialist feminism, and transnational feminist history. Her adviser, a leading feminist historian, informed her that her interest in the Partido Liberal Mexicano, the Mexican Revolution, and the 1917 feminist Congress of Yucatán did not contribute to twentieth-century US women's, gender, or feminist history.[11] That was Mexican history, and Pérez, whose undergraduate degree was in political theory, was completing her doctorate in US history. Her adviser told her to develop a topic in US women's history.

Earlier, Deena González, at the University of California, Berkeley, disabused her adviser's implicit construction of her as an immigrant and of nineteenth-century Chicana/o history as immigration history at their first meeting.[12] The adviser, a preeminent colonial historian who proudly traced his ancestry back to the Puritans, asked Deena, the first Chicana graduate student in the department, "And how long has your family been in this country?" She responded, "Well, that depends on which side of the family you are asking about—since 1598 on my mother's—they came with Oñate—and for 40,000 to 50,000 years on my father's—his family is Navajo."[13] Her point was that we are native to this land, native to the Americas, native to what is now the US Southwest.

At issue in these creation stories of Chicana historiography are the challenges that women's, in this case Chicana (but also racial-ethnic, queer, and other subaltern) history poses for the conceptualization, assumptions, temporalities, and spatialities of the established historical canons, especially as these are defined by the development of the nation-state.[14] At issue, too, are the challenges it poses for canonic categories of historical analysis—for methodological approaches and strategies, for the nature of primary sources, and for the nature of evidence. It challenges the constructs and demarcations that the historical profession began establishing in the 1860s, amid the political, economic, social, and racial imperatives arising in the wake of the US-Mexican War and the US Civil War. Those imperatives revolved around gluing and regluing a white Protestant nation with large populations of Indians, Mexicans, and emancipated African-descent slaves. Operating within nineteenth-century intellectual and political imperatives, historians became Americanists (meaning one who studies the United States), Mexicanists, Latin Americanists, Europeanists (Ancient or Modern), Africanists, South East Asian specialists, and so on. Chicana/o history, we argued with advisers, professors, and graduate student peers, would not be contained within the constructs and demarcations that were the basis of our historical erasure.

Until two decades ago, US historiography constructed and normalized the nation and its regions in singularly Euro-American, male, middle-class, and heterosexual terms. Its systems of thought and categories of analysis, deriving from the European Enlightenment, defined the discursive fields that still obtain in the study of regional and national history.[15] In this discourse, Chicanas are racially and politically constructed as the "racial, alien, foreign other" and as immigrants entering this country after the US-Mexican War. We are not considered an integral part of the imagined national and regional communities.[16] Rather, this discourse delegitimizes us as subjects of national, and thereby regional, history. It constructs us as immigrants, illegal aliens, suspect citizens at best, who occupy a nether space, with no right or claim to national space, including the regions of "The West."[17]

DISLOCATION AND FORCED INTERNAL MIGRATION

The history of Mexican Americans in this country is a history of violent dispossession, dislocation, and forced internal migration. This dislocation occurred at different rates throughout California, Texas, and New Mexico beginning in 1848, when the United States annexed vast Mexican territories at the conclusion of the US-Mexico War. During the second half of the nineteenth century, land was appropriated as private property and national domain, and Mexican Americans were relegated to the status of suspect citizens in their new nation.[18]

Discriminatory state legislation in the form of the Foreign Miner's Tax of 1850, aimed at Mexican, Latin American, and Chinese miners, established economic and labor patterns of racial inequality and violence that would be mirrored throughout the industries that increasingly required vast armies of mobile, transient, disposable laborers.[19] The earliest forms of industrially organized agriculture demanding cheap, mobile, seasonal labor in the West—the wheat and beet fields and fruit orchards of California—took root on lands of the Mexican cession by the 1870s and 1880s.[20] Beginning with the gold rush, California became home to the nation's major extractive industries—mining, ranching, oil, logging, and industrial agriculture. The Land Reclamation Act of 1902 and the construction of massive dams transformed arid desertscapes into watered, cultivable fields in the first half of the twentieth century.[21] Federal subsidies, including water for irrigation and funding for seeds and equipment, made year-round agriculture and agribusiness possible, spurring the demand for seasonal workers in what Carey McWilliams calls "factories in the fields."[22]

The California gold rush, Anglo squatters, the California Land Law of 1851, racial-ethnic violence, a new language, exorbitant legal fees, lengthy court cases, second-class citizenship of Mexican Americans, and the drought of the 1860s served as the backdrop to this development, decimating the northern ranchos and dispossessing the elite Californiana/o landowners. These forces also displaced and further subjugated the rest of the population who earned their livelihood in the preindustrial pastoral economy of Mexico's California.[23] Dispossession, the denial of civil and human rights, and the ensuing political and social subjugation gave rise to the coerced internal migrations and diasporas of Mexican American families.

We need to examine the internal migration of Mexican Americans within the context of coerced displacement. The first Mexican-descent workers to migrate internally within the United States as mobile seasonal laborers were neither foreigners nor Mexican immigrants. They were Californios, Tejanos, Nuevo Mexicanos, and native-born US citizens made exiles, aliens, and foreigners in their native land.[24] This same process occurred among the Native American populations of the West. Native American nations also were annexed in the wake of wars and treaties and were coerced from their home-lands, often to far-flung reservations established by federal and state governments or, in the case of indigenous groups decimated by disease and war and deemed too few to warrant a reservation, to live without home and community, to be essentially detribalized.[25] Dispossessed, these Native American and Mexican American families and individuals became part of an internal migratory labor force. In the words of Native American scholars and activists, Indian nations were "exiled in the land of the free."[26]

Today, we would call such migrants refugees: persons who have experienced "coerced displacement ... within the borders of their own countries by armed conflicts, internal strife, and systematic violations of human rights."[27] Coerced displacement, Francis M. Deng reportedly argues, is rooted in "a crisis of national identity... The displaced, although citizens in theory, have been regarded as an alien and threatening group, usually with a different language, culture, or religion."[28] Conceptualizing nineteenth-century postwar Mexican American and Native American populations as refugees offers other categories of historical analysis within which to rethink regional histories.

Histories of coerced displacement and violent removal from ancestral homelands and of exile, landlessness, and internal migration within the boundaries of the United States thus link Native Americans and Mexican Americans within and across the regions of the American West. These histories further link western regions in a common national history in which coerced displacement and internal migration are pivotal features of the economic, political, and social development of the regions and the nation. At issue in these linkages are the politics within which Native Americans and Mexican Americans, as native-born Americans whose status as citizens is always suspect, are held outside of membership in regional and national communities.[29]

At issue is how histories of dispossession and, most specifically, histories of the internal migrations that dispossession gave rise to became part of the historical narratives of the Western regions and the nation. How, for example, did Native American and Mexican American women experience the violent dispossession of their homelands? How did they experience their removal, exile, and internal migration? The brutal sexual and other violence, including captivity, enslavement, and indenture, against Native American women in the gold rush era are documented in California newspapers and contemporary records, but these are not the accounts of Native American women themselves.[30] The records do not communicate the meaning of this holocaust, genocide, ethnocide, and violent uprooting for the women who lived it, whose world is ordered, and the meaning of life given, in the belief that they and the land are one.[31]

CENTRALITY OF GENDER, SEXUALITY, AND THE BODY: ISSUES THAT CUT ACROSS REGIONS

I have written elsewhere about the feminization and sexualization of conquest and of woman as a metaphor for land and for conquest.[32] Here I underscore the centrality of gender, sexuality, and the body to the economic and socio-political consolidation of military conquest; that is, the sexual and gendered violence against Native American and Mexican American women whose bodies had to be removed from the land in the process of conquest was as integral to the politics of dispossession as were military battles and discriminatory legislation. Feminist scholars are analyzing the ways in which "catastrophes, genocidal or otherwise, ... target women in very specific ways," as Ronit Lentin has put it.[33]

As "women," our gender further marginalizes Chicanas within the nation and its regions. Depending on our class and racial characteristics, Chicanas, like other nonwhite females, are defined out of the normalized category of "women/woman," which really means white women.[34] In other words, the "West" is not ours, the nation is not ours, and we are not women, irrespective of which region we live in.

With female sexuality as a pivotal element in the ideology and politics of national "morality," Chicana sexuality—impugned since the US-Mexican War and a critical aspect in the gender and sexual politics of the war—remains a common denominator.[35] That is, Chicana sexuality is historically, and thereby transregionally, demeaned. By way of example, I cite three contemporary instances in which groups in different regions of the country and across time reify Chicana/Mexicana sexuality in the same opprobrious terms. The groups in question are national fraternities and sororities with chapters in all, or most, regions.

At the University of Washington in the mid-1970s, fraternity brothers were invited to a BYOP, bring your own *puta* (prostitute) party.[36] The term "puta" is used in the invitational flyer. At the University of California, Los Angeles, in 1993, a fraternity sang "Lupe's Song," which celebrates the dead "hotfucking, cocksucking Mexican whore, Lupe," who can't get enough sex, even in the grave.[37] At Baylor University in Waco, Texas, in 1997, sorority sisters were invited to come to a party dressed as Mexican girls, with off-the-shoulder blouses and pillows under their billowy Mexican skirts to simulate pregnancy.[38]

Across regions, then, not only are Chicanas/Mexicanas constructed in purely sexual terms but their sexuality is also delegitimized and debased. The nineteenth-century representation of Mexican women common in the print media, in popular expressive culture, and in visual arts during the pivotal era of US territorial conquest and war is still being perpetuated. Thus the body is embedded in all historical processes, including the politics and policies of the state and the nation.[39]

In earlier work, I discuss eighteenth- and nineteenth-century colonialist representations of women on the land being contested within the gendered, sexualized, and eroticized construct of the conquest of land as feminized body.[40] Thus, "They Wait for Us," an anonymous poem published in a Boston newspaper on the eve of the US-Mexican War, deracinates mestizas and represents them as complicit in the conquest of their bodies and their homeland. They are Spanish maids "with eyes afire," eagerly awaiting their Yankee savior, "whose purer blood and valiant arms are fit to clasp her budding charms," to make her his.[41] During the California gold rush, miners sang "Pigs in the Clover": "I'll marry a rich señorita and live on a ranch in the West. Have forty young greasers to greet her and fifty if put to the test."[42]

Focusing on the late twentieth century, historian Deena González theorizes "Lupe's Song" and related cultural expressions within a collective ideology of racial hatred and misogyny that she terms "Mexican/woman-hating." She argues that national ideology sanctions the murder of Mexican-origin women, both symbolically, as in "Lupe's Song," and, literally as in gold-rush California and Civil War Texas.[43]

Farmworkers also learn early on that their bodies are workers' bodies. They know that the viejo (boss) is the person who controls the wages their labor earns and the water they need to keep working. They know what happens to the family if a body does not pull its weight, falls ill, or is injured. Bodies, according to Romana Raquel Rodríguez, midwife and healer for forty years in Crystal City, Texas, are the locus of history. When asked how she, a woman with no schooling, would know the history of the Mexican people of her South Texas community, she reportedly responded rather testily:

> Cómo no voy a saber la historia? Yo los saco de las entrañas de sus madres, les atiendo el cuerpo toda su vida, y al morir, los preparo para el entriego a las entrañas de la Santa Madre tierra. (How could I not know their history? I bring them forth from their mother's womb, attend their bodies throughout their life, and when they die, I prepare and return them to the womb of Sacred Mother earth.) [44]

According to Rodríguez, the story/history of the individual and the community is constituted by, and inscribed on, the body of the people in that community. Thinking about it much later, I recalled the midwives, healers, curanderas, sobadoras, espiritistas, rezadoras, and so-called brujas of the labor camps. As midwives and healers who attend the body from birth to death, these women are repositories of historical knowledge. The history of the community passes through their hands. These individuals, most of whom are women, are a vital source of community and regional history.

My earliest consciousness of native women's bodies as a site of history derives from the material and symbolic world of nonwhite, subaltern communities in the Pacific Northwest of the late 1950s. Most specifically, it derives from my consciousness of Tejana migrant farmworkers and Yakima Indian women and their communities living, respectively, within economically, politically, and racially designated spaces of labor camps and federal Indian reservations in Idaho, Oregon, and Washington. I observed women creating community and creating change even as they analyzed, interpreted, and strategized to affect their circumstances in varying ways. I learned from women in those circumscribed spaces that the body—its condition and ability to function under all forms of duress —matters. Recent feminist theories of embodied knowledge, and Chela Sandoval's theories of differential and oppositional consciousness now provide conceptual avenues for examining the questions that Chicana history, and particularly the questions of internal migration, pose to the construction of US regional and national history.[45]

REMAKING SELVES, REMAKING LIVES, MEJICANAS TELL THE REENGANCHE, 1900–1940

The voices of Mexican-origin women born or raised in Idaho before 1940 document the oppressive and exploitative conditions that Mexicana contract labor and their Mexican American daughters endured in Idaho and the Pacific Northwest in the first four decades of the twentieth century. In clear, plain-spoken language they narrate lives of making and remaking, of action and change in the process of moving across time and space to work, raise families, and make lives. Pérez's concept of diasporic subjectivity "as always in movement, disrupting, re-creating, and mobile in its representation, converging the past with the present for a new future" provides a theoretical framework within which to analyze and interpret the agency of Victoria Archuleta Sierra, Juanita Zazueta Huerta, Felicitas Pérez García, and Rita Pérez in a society that disparaged them as Mexicans, as workers, and as women and still denies them within constructs of regional and national histories.[46]

In California and the Southwest, Mexican reenganchados (contract laborers) came to historically Mexican-origin, Spanish-speaking communities whose history and rhythm were their own, yet different.[47] Further up, in the Far West and Pacific Northwest, they found traces of themselves in the linguistic and other markers with which eighteenth-century Spanish-Mexican exploratory and colonizing ventures inscribed their presence in this space.[48] *Corridistas* (balladeers), poets, and storytellers documented the experience of the reenganche in corridos, such as the

"Corrido de Kansas," and in family stories sung, told, and retold by women and men to succeeding generations.[49] Women's voices, rarely heard in the corridos, spoke of the Mexican Revolution, dislocations, migrations, relocations, and their strategies for survival as they refashioned the household economy and themselves in hostile northern climes. Their matter-of-fact relation of migrating across vast distances, of working in the fields, of creating and recreating households in nonexistent houses, and of recreating themselves in the exigencies of their reality speaks to Stuart Hall's concept of diasporic identities as "those which are constantly producing, and reproducing themselves anew, through transformation and difference."[50]

Felicitas Pérez García, married at age fourteen in Rincón de Romas, Mexico, relates that she and her husband came to Idaho:

> [T]o work in the sugar beet fields, to work in the harvest and thin-ning in Shelley. My husband worked for the sugar beet company for a short time, I think it was the end of 1910. The year was ending. And then he started to work in the railroads.... At Shelley, there was a sugar beet processing plant.... When we got there, we could not find a place to stay. There was a big lumber mill. We would go there and get wood and boards.... I made my bed out of boards, and I made the covers out of corn sacks. I would sew four together. Then I got some grass, or whatever there was, and put it in the middle.... My stove, well, it was a hole outside. I made an opening here and another one there. I put the firewood in this side, and the smoke came out this other way. In the middle, I would put the pots to make the food. I remember there were a lot of rabbits. I found an old discarded basket and [filled] it with grass. Then I got two sticks, and I tied them together. I raised the little basket with one stick, and that was the trap. Well shortly, the rabbits would come, they were hungry and got in. As soon as they got in, I pulled on the stick, the basket would come down, and then I had them. I grabbed those rabbits and killed and cleaned them, took out their ribs, leaving pure rabbit's meat. ... I did not go out anywhere. I made my own dresses. There was this place that sold fabric very inexpensive. It cost a dime for ten meters. I

made a large malacate [spinning wheel]. Well, I would wash my cotton, disentangle it, and spin it on the malacate. That's how I made the thread. I would sew, that was all that I did.[51]

When her husband was hired as a maintenance worker with the railroad, Pérez García got a job cooking for the large Mexican work force that had recently arrived and wanted to eat tortillas.[52] When the railroad company's cook, a Chinese man, asked her if she knew how to make tortillas, Garcia, who did not know how to make them, said that she did and went to work for a dollar a day.

Juanita Zazueta Huerta, who was born in Shelley, Idaho, in 1918, also recalls her family's migration: "My family came in a train, in a reenganche, with a lot of other Mexican families to work in agriculture. . . . They brought my parents, along with the other people, to Lincoln, near Idaho Falls. ... From there, they would send them to small agriculture towns around Idaho Falls and around Firth, Shelley, Preston, and Basalt. They planted a lot of sugar beets and potatoes in these small towns. I guess the farmers would come and take the workers they wanted." [53]

In her interview in *Voces Hispanas*, Victoria Archuleta Sierra chronicles her birth in La Junta, Colorado, in 1924 and her family's migration to Idaho by way of Chaperito, New Mexico; Grand Junction, Colorado; and Nyssa, Oregon. The family finally settled in Pocatello, Idaho, in 1942. "Many of the Mexican Americans," she recalled, "were called *manitos* [short for *hermanito*, little brother], because they were mostly from Colorado and New Mexico. They worked largely in the fields, picking peaches, topping onions, picking green beans, topping beets, thinning beets, and picking apples."[54]

Rita Pérez, in recounting her parents' migration from Jalisco, Mexico, through San Francisco and Utah to Idaho Falls, where she was born in 1930, tells of her mother's arrival and life in Idaho as a process of creation and recreation, of movement and of change.[55] Refusing the dictates of patriarchal power, Pérez's mother cut her hair, put on a pair of overalls, and pulled a cap over her ears in an effort to pass as a male. She hopped a northbound train with her husband rather than travel to the United States by herself, as he proposed. Right before they arrived in Utah, a conductor got suspicious and tried to detain them. To avoid arrest, they jumped off the train, hid under bridges, slept in the day, walked at night, and finally arrived in Idaho, where they worked in the fields.

Except for migrating to California in 1937 for one season, Pérez's family settled and worked in Idaho. They thinned beets near Idaho Falls and went on to Driggs to pick green peas, returning in mid-September for the potato harvest and, if not yet over, the beet harvest. The Pérez family, like all migrant farmworker families, was an economic unit. No matter how big or how little, everyone's labor, including that of pregnant women and nursing mothers, was necessary to the family's survival. Speaking to those realities, Pérez recalls:

> My parents would take us in the car and park it at the end of the field. My mother could come at intervals to check on the baby and nurse him. The first time I was left in charge, my younger sister was about six weeks old, and I was not quite five. The first time I worked out in the field, I was about eight years old. We worked from sunrise to sunset. Thinning beets could be from four in the morning until nine at night. Picking green peas, because the contractor set the hours, was from 6 A.M. to 6 P.M. I believe we got paid three cents per pound.[56]

Housing was always a problem. Describing the situation at Driggs, Pérez remembers, "There was a clearing in the forest where we were allowed to either pitch tents or build shelters out of bark. ... At Driggs you did not have to dig very deep to get beautiful clear, good water. So they dug a well, and we had to dip a bucket to bring the water up. My mother built a fire outside and placed stones to hold an old galvanized washtub. That was where we heated the water."[57]

In Idaho, Pérez notes:

> prejudice against Mexican Americans took many forms. Being of Mexican descent was enough to trigger deep-seated fears

and assumptions among many Whites. Speaking Spanish in the
presence of English speakers was equal cause for upbraiding. . . .
The Great Depression itself did not discriminate. Everybody was
affected by these terrible years. Federal and state relief, either
in the form of jobs or emergency assistance, was not always an
option available to persons of Mexican descent.[58]

Tejana Lives, Internal Migrations: For Work and Justice, 1940–1960

"Andale, trépate, no tengas miedo," my mother said, urging me to hop
onto the back of the flatbed truck where my brother Jorge was perched,
ready to pull three-year-old me into the troca enlonada that would take
us al norte, to los trabajos. "Andale, súbete, ya nos vamos pa'l norte,"
she repeated, as she helped me onto the splintery floorboard of the tarp-
covered truck we rode with five other families from the Rio Grande
Valley of South Tejas to the Yakima Valley of eastern Washington in
the Pacific Northwest.

Figure 12. Romana Raquel Rodríguez, Crystal City's midwife and healer, c. 1926.

Rodríguez, in the middle, stands with her daughter Irene (right) and daughter-in-law Rosa (left). They are dressed in the uniform of the Cruz Azul, the women's volunteer health service organization, of which they were members. Reprinted with permission of the Castañeda family.

Years later, working on an anthology of Chicano literature, I asked my mother, Irene Castañeda, who was born and raised in Texas and married a Tejano whose family roots in South Texas dated to the early eighteenth century, for her chronicle of our family's migration from Texas to Washington in the mid-1940s.[59] She was silent for a long while, as if she had not heard my request. She looked past me, folded and refolded the edges of her napkin, and quietly began. "*Bueno Nenita, oímos el cuento de Washington*":

> We heard the tale of Washington – that there was lots of money, that they paid real well, and we thought about coming to Washington. We didn't have a car to travel in, and this man, a *contratista*

[labor contractor] used to contract people, and we came with him. We didn't have much money; we paid him $25 for us and $15 for each of the five children. This was the first time we had traveled. This man said he had housing and everything for the people, but it wasn't true. We left on the thirteenth of March of 1946 and arrived in Toppenish on the eighteenth. On the road, the truck broke down – who knows how many times. In Utah we had to stay overnight because the road was snowed in, and we couldn't travel – we all slept sitting up with the little ones in our arms because we had no money to rent a motel. We were about twenty-five people in the truck, plus the suitcases and blankets and a mattress spread out inside, and some tires. We were packed in like sardines. Then a heavy wind came, and the tarp on the truck tore in half. They tied it as best they could. And the snow was falling. We finally got out of the storm, and then the driver lost his way. We almost turned over. But God is all-powerful, and He watched over us. We finally got to Toppenish. He didn't have housing—nothing—all lies that he told us. He finally found some old shacks, all full of knotholes, in Brownstown—about 20 miles outside of Toppenish—and he placed all the people in tents. It was bitterly cold, with wood stoves and wet wood.[60]

From the mind-numbing heat of the "man-made" Rio Grande Valley to the Winter Garden and Imperial Valleys, to the vastness of the Central Valley of California, to the undulating, verdant stretches of the Yakima, the Skagit, and the Willamette Valleys of the Northwest, Tejanas labored in fields and factories underwritten by the federal government.[61] We worked our way north, through valleys and towns with names as familiar as our family history—San Fernando, El Monte, San Jose, Benicia, Vallejo, Vacaville, Sacramento—to arrive in valley towns with strange new names—Brownstown, Toppenish, Wapato, Zillah, Sunnyside, Grandview, Mabton, Woodburn, Burley.

Figure 13. Troca enlonada (tarp-covered flatbed truck) with migrant workers leaving for beet fields in the north, taken at San Antonio, Texas, May 1946.

L-3225-B "Farm workers in truck," University of Texas at San Antonio Libraries Special Collections. Reprinted with permission UTSA Libraries Special Collections.

Under reclaimed desert skies, rows of fields, patches, orchards, vineyards, and hop yards stretched before us, waiting for our contracted bodies: cotton, spinach, potato, beet, tomato, melon, hop, cucumber, lettuce, beans, asparagus, berries, apple, grape, peach, plum, lemon, and cherry. Walking, bending, crouching, straddling, crawling, dragging, climbing, stretching, lugging sacks, pails, baskets, boxes, and crates, and wielding knives, hoes, cutting forks, and shears, we worked from March through October.

"*Jalando parejo*," working at an even pace, we ebbed and flowed—a sea of humanity moving up and down the rows chopping, hoeing, weeding, cutting, topping, twining, tying, thinning, pruning, picking, harvesting

—in keeping with the season and the crop.[62] From dawn to dusk, the tide of bent bodies was visible in fields abutting rural roadways, the self-same bodies that were hidden and invisible from dusk to dawn and that removed themselves, at day's end, to chicken coops, stables, barns, and tents given over to worker's housing in labor camps hidden from view behind groves of stately oak trees. At the work day's end, women's bodies continued working—cooking over makeshift stoves, stretching the potatoes and beans, and calculating the measurement of dry goods to tide them over in case the rains came and they could not work.

Farm labor, no less than any other work force in the United States, was hierarchical, stratified by race and gender. Mexicans, both male and female, and their children, too, were stoop labor. Anglo men were the foremen, the crew bosses, the tractor drivers, the irrigation ditch tenders. Anglo women worked inside the twine-cutting sheds, the canneries, the fruit-packing houses. Women were paid less than men, Mexicans were paid less than Anglos, and Mexican women were paid the least of all.

Despite the hardships, life was better in Washington than in Texas, but only by degrees, not in substance. The family migrated, my mother told me, because the only work my father, José Castañeda, could get in our native Texas was at "Mexican or peon wages." His last job in our hometown of Crystal City, as a day laborer on the Justice Department's Japanese-American internment camp, ended with the arrival of the internees.[63] "They didn't like the Japanese either," she whispered." In 1944, unable to find *un trabajo decente... tu papá se enganchó* [your dad contracted himself out] to a shipbuilding company recruiting laborers for their plant in Vancouver, Washington."[64] He returned to Texas in 1946 only to find the same virulent racism, dual-wage labor system, and segregated education.[65]

"*En esos tiempos* [at that time]," Doña Irene said:

> Mexicans had neither voice nor vote; many injustices were committed against them. On the one hand, they didn't understand the language, and whites didn't want them to learn it – that way

they couldn't defend themselves. In Crystal City, Mexicans were not allowed in restaurants. Those who worked in white people's homes had to eat outside or go hungry. There were no schools for Mexicans, so nobody knew how to read. Mother, who was the local *partera y curandera*, midwife and healer, also washed, starched, and ironed clothes for white people to make ends meet. She made us sit by the washtub, while she scrubbed their dirty laundry, so she could teach us our letters. That's how we learned to read in Spanish. She said, "That's why we, or rather I, had to battle, with cloak and dagger, as the saying goes, because I refused to stay in Crystal City – para que ustedes no se quedaran burros como nosotros y siquiera se pudieran defender [so that you would not stay ignorant like us and at least could defend yourselves].[66]

Wielding the authority of her motherhood—she bore six children and buried one—Doña Irene brooked the combined wrath of her husband, her mother, her older brothers, and her sisters for the family to return with him to Washington to get out of that God-forsaken *pueblo mugroso*, where Mexicans had to step off the sidewalk, or be thrown off, to let white people pass. She left behind the comfort of her family, her community, and her homeland to make sure that her children got what she did not have—an education, the weapon to defend themselves against injustice in all its forms.

She never returned to Texas. We settled our first year in Washington, living year-round in the discarded army barracks labor camp. Most of her *comadres* continued the seasonal, agricultural migrant workers' cycle —the yearly journey from Texas to California, to Washington, to Oregon or Idaho, and back again to Texas for the winter layover after the hop harvest in mid-September. She was there the next spring and for many subsequent springs to hear the cries of "*ya lluegaron las Martínez, vienen de McAllen*" that hailed the return of comadres, friends, and coworkers as the migrant labor cycle spun yet another turn to the lush valleys of the Pacific Northwest.

Born and raised in early twentieth-century Texas, Irene Castañeda understood the ideologies of racial hatred and racial misogyny all too well. They were her daily fare. "They hated Mexicans in Texas," she explained. "Well, we were Tejano and Lipan Apache too, from way back, when Texas was a Spanish colony. But that only made us Indians, as well as Mexicans. Of course, they also hated Indians. Then again, they didn't like the Japanese, or the Black people *tampoco* [either]."[67]

Like Doña Irene, her children also understood power relations at a very early age. What I understood growing up in the fields of Washington State was that nonwhite bodies were despised. The bodies of Indian and Mexican women were despised in special ways. So too were the bodies of Mexican farmworkers, both female and male, and of poor people. In that verdant valley, the bodies of Mexican farmworkers and of the poor were synonymous.

White bodies also were living in the labor camp, remnants of what I would later learn was the dust bowl migration, the "Okies." But by and large, Anglo dust bowl migrants, immortalized by novelist John Steinbeck and photographer Dorothea Lange, not Mexican American/Mexican farmworkers, got the housing set up by the Farm Labor Administration.[68] With the onset of the Great Depression and arrival of dust bowl migrants, state and federal officials began deporting or "repatriating" Mexican nationals and, in some cases, Mexican Americans to Mexico.[69]

Figure 14. Irene R. Castañeda, Crystal City, Texas.

Reprinted with permission of the Castañeda family.

Figure 15. Irene R. Castañeda, in the middle, stands with coworkers in front of a hop kiln.

This kiln was where they worked during the hop harvest at the Golding Hop Farm, Toppenish, Washington, August 1949. Reprinted with permission of the Castañeda family.

For Tejanas from the pueblos of rural South Texas and barrios of urban San Antonio, many of whose families began migrating to los trabajos in the early twentieth century, el norte could be anywhere from Michigan, Minnesota, Wisconsin, and North Dakota, to Colorado, California, Montana, Idaho, and Washington.[70] Tejanas like Emma Pérez and her family from El Campo migrated within the state. For them, los trabajos were in "el Wes," the Texas panhandle. Their "West" was in Texas.[71]

Tejano migrant families defined geographies and directions consistent with their histories, location, work, and lives. Their lived experience challenges the geophysical regional boundaries set by state or federal governments. It also contests the constructs of US historians who, except for the dust bowl migration of Anglo families during the 1930s, have rendered invisible the experience of internal migration of migrant workers in the regional and national fabric.

With clarity of purpose, Irene Castañeda migrated from her Texas homeland to the Pacific Northwest, where she remained the rest of her life. She ensured her children's claim to educational rights and lived to see them use their education to continue her struggle for human dignity and for racial and social justice. Throughout the fifteen years of her migrations, initially from Texas to Washington in the mid-1940s and then within Washington State itself working seasonal crops from eastern to western Washington until 1960, conditions of living and labor remained largely unchanged. The documentary *Harvest of Shame* that CBS produced and aired in 1960, exposed the exploitative and oppressive conditions within which migrant farmworkers lived and worked so that the nation might have fresh fruits and vegetables. *Poverty in the Valley of Plenty*, an earlier documentary about the same long-lived conditions produced in 1948 by supporters of the National Farm Labor Union's strike against the DiGiorgio Corporation in California, was banned from distribution and public viewing precisely because it made public the conditions of migrant farm labor. As part of the settlement, the farmworkers' union was required to destroy all copies of the film. The conditions were the same from one end of the United States to the other, and the differences were matters of degree, not substance.[72]

The internal migration of Chicanas and their families within the United States challenges reigning concepts and categories of regional history in this country. Their reality is best understood by listening to their own words, which speak to their agency, their dignity, their strategies for survival, their resourcefulness, and their actions. It is also best understood by looking at the ideologies and structures of dispossession, appropriation, and gendered and racial inequalities that cut across regions. Tejana migrant workers' histories are part of the national fabric of this country and must be studied in that context. To study Chicana history means to rethink regional history and to rethink the history of the United States. The lives of Tejana and other migrant worker women pose significant new questions to (en)gender that history and its meaning, introducing concepts of the body as well as dispossession, displacement, and appropriation that require new ways of conceptualizing family, household economies, and the agency of working-class women. It is a question not just of inclusion, but of construction.

Notes

1. One pivotal aspect of the Chicano Movement of the 1960s and 1970s is the affirmation of Chicanos' indigenous identity and history in the Americas, most particularly in what is now the present US Southwest and West. While some historians have addressed Chicanos' indigenous historical and cultural heritage, representation of indigenous identity is most highly developed in Chicana/o literary, artistic, and cultural expression. See Yolanda Broyles-González, ed., *Re-Emerging Native Women of the Americas: Native Chicana Latina Women's Studies* (Dubuque, IA: Kendall/Hunt Publishing Company, 2001); María Herrera Sobek, ed., *Santa Barraza, Artist of the Borderlands* (College Station: Texas A&M University Press, 2001); Victor M. Fields and Victor Zamudio Taylor, eds., *The Road to Aztlán: Art from the Mythic Homeland* (Los Angeles: Los Angeles County Museum of Art, 2001); Richard Griswold del Castillo and Arnoldo de León, *North to Aztlán: A History of Mexican Americans in the United States* (New York: Twayne Publishers, 1996), 1-12; Jack D. Forbes, *Aztecas del Norte: The Chicanos of Aztlán* (Greenwich, CT: Fawcett Publications, 1973); and Ines Hernández Avila, "An Open Letter to Chicanas: On the Power and Politics of Origin," in *Without Discovery: A Native Response to Columbus*, ed. Ray González (Seattle: Broken Moon Press, 1992), 153-66.

2. Richard White and John M. Findlay, eds., *Power and Place in the North American West* (Seattle: University of Washington Press, 1999), xix. For a cultural approach to regional history, see Barbara Allen and Thomas J. Schlereth, *Sense of Place: American Regional Cultures* (Lexington: University of Kentucky, 1990). Renewed interest and focus in regional history in the United States extends beyond academic scholarship into the public realm. During William Ferris's term as director of the National Endowment for the Humanities, the NEH initiated the establishment of regional centers across the United States for the study of regional history and cultures. See "Report of the Regional Studies Working Group," in *The National Endowment for the Humanities: Working Group Papers* (Washington DC: National Endowment for the Humanities Publications, 2001), 11-32.

3. Emma Pérez, *The Decolonial Imaginary: Writing Chicanas into History* (Bloomington: Indiana University Press, 1999), xvii-xviii, 74-98.

4. Pérez, *The Decolonial Imaginary*, 81.
5. Ibid., 3-30.
6. Edward L. Ayers et al., *All over the Map: Rethinking American Regions* (Baltimore: Johns Hopkins University Press, 1996), vii.
7. Pérez, *The Decolonial Imaginary*, xiv.
8. Stanford advising session, fall 1973, in Antonia I. Castañeda, "All I Wanted Was an Inside Job: Memories of Chicana History," unpublished manuscript.
9. Ibid.
10. Stanford advising session, spring 1979, in Castañeda, "All I Wanted Was an Inside Job."
11. Emma Pérez, interview by the author, July 1987, Riverside, CA.
12. Deena J. González, interview by the author, 1988, Pomona, CA.
13. González interview.
14. Antonia I. Castañeda, "Women of Color and the Rewriting of Western History: The Discourse, Politics, and Decolonization of History," *Pacific Historical Review* 61, no. 4 (1992): 501-33, Castañeda, "Gender, Race, and Culture: Spanish-Mexican Women in the Historiography of Frontier California," *Frontiers: A Journal of Women Studies* 11, no. 1 (1990): 8-20, and Castañeda, "The Political Economy of Nineteenth Century Stereotypes of Californianas," in *Between Borders: Essays on Mexicana/Chicana History*, ed. Adelaida R. Del Castillo (Los Angeles: Floricanto Press, 1990), 213-36.
15. Pérez, *The Decolonial Imaginary*, 3-30.
16. Benedict Anderson, *Imagined Communities: Reflections on the Origin and Spread of Nationalism* (London: Verso Press, 1983).
17. For discussion of the legal basis that defines Chicanos/Mexican Americans as US citizens, see Richard Griswold del Castillo, *The Treaty of Guadalupe Hidalgo: A Legacy of Conflict* (Norman: University of Oklahoma Press, 1990); and Griswold del Castillo, "The US Mexican War: Contemporary Implications for Mexican Americans Civil and International Rights," in *Culture y Cultura: Consequences of the US Mexican War, 1846-1848*, eds. Iris H. W. Engstrand, Richard Griswold del Castillo, and Elena Poniatowska (Los Angeles: Autry Museum of Western Heritage, 1998), 76-106.
18. Richard White, *"It's Your Misfortune and None of My Own": A New History of the American West* (New York: Norton, 1993); Rodolfo Acuña, *Occupied America: A History of Chicanos* (New York: Harper & Row, 1988); Patricia Nelson Limerick, *Legacy of Conquest: The Unbroken Past of the Amer-*

ican West (New York: Norton, 1987); David Montejano, *Anglos and Mexicans in the Making of Texas, 1836-1986* (Austin: University of Texas Press, 1987); John Chávez, *The Lost Land: The Chicano Image of the Southwest* (Albuquerque: University of New Mexico Press, 1984); David Weber, ed., *Foreigners in Their Native Land: Historical Roots of Mexican Americans* (Albuquerque: University of New Mexico Press, 1973); Leonard Pitt, *The Decline of the Californios: A Social History of the Spanish-Speaking Californians, 1846-1890* (Berkeley: University of California Press, 1971); and Carey McWilliams, *Factories in the Fields: The Story of Migratory Farm Labor in California* (Santa Barbara: Peregrine Publishers, 1971). For literary renditions of these historical themes in Texas and California, see Jovita González, *Caballero: A Historical Novel*, eds. Jose Limon and María Cotera (College Station: Texas A&M University Press, 1996); and María Amparo Ruiz de Burton, *The Squatter and the Don* (Houston: Arte Público Press, 1992).

19. McWilliams, *Factories in the Fields*; and Pitt, *The Decline of the Californios*.
20. Cletus E. Daniel, *Bitter Harvest: A History of California Farmworkers, 1870-1941* (Ithaca, NY: Cornell University Press, 1981); McWilliams, *Factories in the Fields*; and Pitt, *The Decline of the Californios*.
21. White, *"It's Your Misfortune and None of My Own"*; and Limerick, *Legacy of Conquest*.
22. McWilliams, *Factories in the Fields*, 102.
23. Douglas Monroy, *Thrown among Strangers: The Making of Mexican Culture in Frontier California* (Berkeley: University of California Press, 1990); and Albert Camarillo, *Chicanos in a Changing Society: From Mexican Pueblos to American Barrios in Santa Barbara and Southern California, 1848-1930* (Cambridge: Harvard University Press, 1979).
24. Weber, *Foreigners in Their Native Land.*
25. "Detribalization" is often considered to be a phenomenon of the twentieth century, especially of the federal Indian policy of the 1950s and 1960s. Pivotal legislation includes the Voluntary Relocation Program (1952) that relocated Indian people to urban areas, the Termination Resolution (House Concurrent Resolution 108) of 1953 that released certain tribes from federal supervision, and Public Law 280, also of 1953, which, without the consent of the tribes, gave some states civil and criminal jurisdiction over Indian reservations. See Carl Waldman, *Atlas of the North American Indian* (New York: Facts On File Publications, 1985), 194. See also William T. Hagen, "How the West Was Lost," in *Indians in American History*, ed. Frederick E . Hoxie (Arlington Heights, IL: Harlan Davidson,

Inc., 1988), 179-202; White, *"It's Your Misfortune and None of My Own"*; and Limerick, *Legacy of Conquest*.

26. Oren Lyons et al., *Exiled in the Land of the Free: Democracy, Indian Nations, and the US Constitution* (Santa Fe: Clear Light Publishers, 1992).

27. Roberta Cohen and Francis M. Deng, eds., *The Forsaken People: Case Studies of the Internally Displaced* (Washington, DC: Brookings Institution Press, 1998), vii.

28. Francis M. Deng, as paraphrased by David A. Korn, in *Exodus within Borders: An Introduction to the Crisis of Internal Displacement* (Washington DC: Brookings Institution Press, 1999), 7.

29. The stipulation in Article VIII of the Treaty of Guadalupe Hidalgo that people of Mexican descent became US citizens if they still resided within the boundaries of the territory ceded to the United States on the first anniversary of the ratification of the Treaty of Guadalupe Hidalgo varied by territory and state. See Griswold del Castillo, *The Treaty of Guadalupe Hidalgo*. For Indian people, who have struggled to retain their rights as sovereign nations, absorption into the body politic as citizens is interpreted as the effort to break up the Indian land base. Citizenship, for example, was used as an incentive to Native Americans who accepted allotment under the General Allotment Act of 1887 (Dawes Act). President Calvin Coolidge signed the Indian Citizenship Act, granting US citizenship to all Indians, on 2 June 1924. However, some states still did not grant Indians the right to vote. New Mexico, Arizona, and Maine, for example, did not grant Indians the right to vote until after World War II. See Lyons et al., *Exiled in the Land of the Free*, 318 – 36.

30. Clifford E. Trafzer and Joel R. Hyer, eds., *Exterminate Them!: Written Accounts of the Murder, Rape, and Enslavement of Native Americans during the California Gold Rush* (East Lansing: Michigan State University Press, 1999); Albert Hurtado, *Indian Survival on the California Frontier* (New Haven: Yale University Press, 1988); and James J. Rawls, *Indians of California: The Changing Image* (Norman: University of Oklahoma Press, 1984). For recent and important analyses of women and the conquest of Alta California, see Virginia Marie Bouvier, *Women and the Conquest of California, 1542-1840: Codes of Silence* (Tucson: University of Arizona Press, 2001); and Lisbeth Haas, *Conquests and Historical Identities in California, 1769 -1983* (Berkeley: University of California Press, 1995).

31. Contemporary Native American women writers and artists explore the meaning of the historical holocaust in their own lives and that of their communities from a variety of perspectives. For a select set of readings,

see Joy Harjo and Gloria Bird, eds., Valerie Martinez, contrib., *Reinventing the Enemy's Language: Contemporary Native American Women's Writings of North America* (New York: W. W. Norton, 1998); Leslie Marmon Silko, *Yellow Woman and a Beauty of the Spirit: Essays on Native American Life Today* (New York: Simon & Schuster, 1996); and Paula Gunn Allen, *The Sacred Hoop: Recovering the Feminine in American Indian Traditions* (Boston: Beacon Press, 1992).

32. Castañeda, "The Political Economy of Nineteenth Century Stereotypes of Californianas"; and Castañeda, "Malinche, Calafia, and Toypurina: Of Myths, Monsters, and Embodied History," paper presented at the Malinche Conference, University of Illinois at Champagne-Urbana, 26-28 August 1999.

33. Ronit Lentin, "Introduction: (En)gendering Geonocides," in *Gender and Catastrophe*, ed. Ronit Lentin (New York: Zed Books, 1997), 2; and Cohen and Deng, *The Forsaken People*. For discussion of the violence and brutality of the Spanish and other European conquests, see Trafzer and Hyer, eds., *Exterminate Them!*; Albert L. Hurtado, *Intimate Frontiers: Sex, Gender and Culture in Old California* (Albuquerque: University of New Mexico Press, 1999); Donna J. Guy and Thomas E. Sheridan. "On Frontiers: The Northern and Southern Edges of the Spanish Empire in the Americas," in *Contested Ground: Comparative Frontiers on the Northern and Southern Edges of the Spanish Empire*, ed. Donna J. Guy and Thomas E. Sheridan (Tucson: University of Arizona Press, 1998), 3-15; Richard C. Trexler, *Sex and Conquest: Gendered Violence, Political Order, and the European Conquest of the Americas* (Ithaca, NY: Cornell University Press, 1995); Hurtado, *Indian Survival on the California Frontier*; and Antonia I. Castañeda, "Sexual Violence in the Politics and Policies of Conquest: Amerindian Women and the Spanish Conquest of Alta California," in *Building With Our Hands: New Directions in Chicana Studies*, eds. Adela de la Torre and Beatriz Pesquera (Berkeley: University of California Press, 1993), 15-33. For new approaches to gender, sexuality, and violence see Lentin, ed., *Gender and Catastrophe*. Although the violence attendant in territorial expansion is well documented, the scholarship that specifically (en)genders and sexualizes that political violence is still very recent. I use this work in my study in two distinct ways: one, to theorize the sexual and other violence against women native to the geopolitical area we now know as the West/Southwest/Pacific Northwest across different waves of colonialism and attendant hegemonies as having fundamentally the same ends; and two, to connect native women's historical

and contemporary (past and present) reality of sexual and other violence as a form of state terrorism and to illuminate the relationship between the local, regional, national, and global in terms of gender, sex, and violence.

34. Deena J. González, "Lupe's Song: On the Origins of Mexican/ Woman-Hating in the United States," in *Race in 21st Century America*, eds. Curtis Stokes, Theresa Meléndez, and Genice Rhodes-Reed (East Lansing: Michigan State University Press, 2001), 143-58; Monica Wittig, *The Straight Mind and Other Essays* (Boston: Beacon Press, 1992); bell hooks, *Black Looks: Race and Representation* (Boston: Beacon Press, 1992); bell hooks, *Ain't I a Woman: Black Women and Feminism* (Boston: South End, 1981); Chandra Mohanty, "Under Western Eyes: Feminist Scholarship and Colonial Discourses," in *Third World Women and the Politics of Feminism*, eds. Chandra Mohanty, Ann Russo, and Lourdes Torres (Bloomington: Indiana University Press, 1991), 51-80; and Denise Riley, *Am I That Name? Feminism and the Category of "Women" in History* (Minneapolis: University of Minnesota Press, 1988).

35. Pérez, *The Decolonial Imaginary*; and Castañeda, "Gender, Race, and Culture."

36. Catalina, "Fraternity Apologizes for Offensive Poster," *The Daily of the University of Washington*, 4 May 1973, 1, 5.

37. As quoted in González, "Lupe's Song," 143.

38. Associated Press, "Baylor Sorority's Mexican Theme Party Angers Some Hispanic Students, Alumni," *Dallas Morning News*, 29 April 1998, 22A.

39. Sylvia Marcos, ed., *Gender/Bodies/Religions* (Cuernavaca, Mexico: ALER Publications, 2000); Radhika Mohanram, *Black Body: Women, Colonialism, and Space* (Minneapolis: University of Minnesota Press, 1999); Elizabeth Grosz, *Volatile Bodies: Toward a Corporeal Feminism: Theories of Representation and Difference* (Bloomington: Indiana University Press, 1994); Doreen Massey, *Space, Place and Gender* (Minneapolis: University of Minnesota Press, 1994); and Gillian Rose, *Feminism and Geography: The Limits of Geographical Knowledge* (Minneapolis: University of Minnesota Press, 1993).

40. Antonia I. Castañeda, "Engendering the History of Alta California, 1769-1848: Gender, Sexuality, and the Family," in *Contested Eden: California Before the Gold Rush*, vol. 1, California History Sesquicentennial Series, eds. Ramón Gutiérrez and Richard Orsi (Berkeley: University of California Press, 1998), 230 -59; Castañeda, "Sexual Violence in the Politics and Policies of Conquest," 15-33; and Castañeda, "Moras Encantadas,

Brujas, and Fandango Dancers: Women's Sexuality and the Politics of Representation," conference paper presented at the American Historical Association Annual Conference, Chicago, IL, 6-9 January 1995.

41. "They Wait for Us," as quoted in Reginald Horsman, *Race and Manifest Destiny: The Origins of Racial Anglo-Saxonism* (Cambridge: Harvard University Press, 1981), 233.

42. I first heard "Pigs in the Clover" in 1982 on a cassette tape recording of "Gold Rush Songs" but have been unable to find it again under that title. For the same song with a different title, see J. A. Stone, "He's the Man for Me," in *The Songs of the Gold Rush*, ed. Richard A. Dwyer and Richard E. Lingenfelter (Berkeley: University of California Press, 1964), 131-32.

43. González, "Lupe's Song," 147- 48.

44. Irene R. Castañeda, Romana Raquel Rodriguez's daughter, interview by the author, March, 1976, Union Gap, WA.

45. Chela Sandoval, *Methodology of the Oppressed* (Minneapolis: University of Minnesota Press, 2000); Marcos, *Gender/Bodies/Religions*; and Grosz, *Volatile Bodies.*

46. As quoted in Pérez, *The Decolonial Imaginary*, 79. See Erasmo Gamboa, "The Roots of Mexican American History," and "Notes toward a History of Idaho's Hispanic Elderly," in *Voces Hispanas*, an electronic report of the Idaho Commission on Hispanic Affairs, http://www2.state.id.us/icha/Events/voceshis.htm, 2-4 and 1-4 respectively. See also the oral history interviews of Victoria Archuleta Sierra, Juanita Zazueta Huerta, Felicitas Pérez García, and Rita Pérez, part of the collection of the Idaho Hispanic Oral History Project in *Voces Hispanas*, http://2222.state.id.us/icha/ Events/voceshis.html, 5-24. For women's voices of immigration and migration in California and the Southwest, see Vicki Ruiz, *From out of the Shadows: Mexican Women in Twentieth-Century America* (New York: Oxford University Press, 1999), 3-32.

47. For the earliest published interviews with Mexican contract laborers, see Manuel Gamio, *The Life Story of the Mexican Immigrant* (1931; reprint, New York: Dover Publications, Inc., 1971); and Manuel Gamio, *Mexican Immigration to the United States: A Study of Human Migration and Adjustment* (Chicago: University of Chicago Press, 1930).

48. Historian Erasmo Gamboa discusses the Hispanic presence in what is now the Pacific Northwest since the eighteenth-century colonial Spanish explorations in this region. See Erasmo Gamboa and Carolyn M. Guan, eds., *Nosotros: The Hispanic People of Oregon* (Portland: Oregon Council for the Humanities, 1995); Gamboa, "Notes toward a History of Idaho's

Hispanic Elderly"; Gamboa, *Mexican Labor and World War II: Braceros in the Pacific Northwest* (Austin: University of Texas Press, 1990); Gamboa, "The Mexican Mule Pack System of Transportation in the Pacific Northwest and British Columbia," *Journal of the West* 29 (January 1990): 16-26; and Carlos Gil, "Washington's Hispano American Communities," in *Peoples of Washington: Perspectives on Cultural Diversity*, eds. Sid White and S. E. Solberg (Pullman: Washington State University Press, 1989), 158-93.

49. "Los reenganchados a Kansas," in *Literatura Chicana, Texto y Contexto/Chicano Literature, Text and Context*, eds. Antonia Castañeda Shular, Tomas Ybarra-Frausto, and Joseph Sommers (Englewood Cliffs, NJ: Prentice-Hall, Inc., 1972), 222-23.

50. As quoted in Pérez, *The Decolonial Imaginary*, 79.

51. Felicitas Pérez García, *Voces Hispanas*, 5-6.

52. Pérez García, *Voces Hispanas*, 6.

53. Juanita Zazueta Huerta, *Voces Hispanas*, 7.

54. Victoria Archuleta Sierra, *Voces Hispanas*, 9-12, 11.

55. Rita Pérez, *Voces Hispanas*, 14-18.

56. Pérez, *Voces Hispanas*, 16

57. Ibid.

58. Pérez, *Voces Hispanas*.

59. Irene Castañeda, "Cronica personal de Cristal," in *Literatura Chicana, Texto y Contexto*, eds. Castañeda Shular, Ybarra- Frausto, and Sommers 27-30 and 243-49. First published in *El Grito*, Berkeley, 4, 1971. The published "Cronica" is excerpted from a personal letter Irene Castañeda wrote to her daughter Antonia in 1970.

60. Castañeda, "Cronica Personal de Cristal," 245.

61. White, *"It's Your Misfortune and None of My Own,"* 402-6; and Donald Worster, *Rivers of Empire: Water, Aridity, and the Growth of the American West* (New York: Pantheon Books, 1985).

62. For the voices of migrant farm workers in oral histories, autobiographies, and novels, especially of children and adults treating migrant life from the 1940s to the 1960s, see Frances Esquibel Tywoniak and Mario T. García, *Migrant Daughter: Coming of Age as a Mexican American Woman* (Berkeley: University of California Press, 2000); Elva Treviño Hart, *Barefoot Heart: Stories of a Migrant Child* (Tempe, AZ: Bilingual Press/Editorial Bilingue, 1999); Antonia I. Castañeda, "Language and Other Lethal Weapons: Cultural Politics and the Rites of Children as Translators of Culture," in *Mapping Multiculturalism*, eds. Avery F. Gordon and Christopher Newfields (Minneapolis: University of Minnesota

Press, 1996), 201-14; Helena María Viramontes, *Under the Feet of Jesus* (New York: Dutton, 1995); Fran Leeper Buss, *Forged under the Sun: The Life Story of María Elena Lucas* (Ann Arbor: University of Michigan Press, 1993); and Tomás Rivera, *Y no se lo Tragó la Tierra/And the Earth Did Not Part* (Berkeley: Quinto Sol Publications, 1970).

63. Camp Kennedy in Crystal City, TX, originally built to house German and Italian prisoners of war, became the camp to which Japanese and families of Japanese descent from Latin America, especially from Peru, were sent. See Seiichi Higashide, *Adios to Tears: The Memoirs of a Japanese-Peruvian Internee in US Concentration Camps* (Seattle: University of Washington Press, 1993); C. Harvey Gardiner, *Pawns in a Triangle of Hate: The Peruvian Japanese and the United States* (Seattle: University of Washington Press, 1981); and Roger Daniels, *Concentration Camps USA: Japanese Americans and World War II* (New York: Holt, Rinehart, and Winston, 1971).

64. Castañeda, "Crónica Personal de Cristal," 245.

65. Emilio Zamora, *The World of the Mexican Worker in Texas* (College Station: Texas A&M University Press, 1993); and Guadalupe San Miguel, *"Let All of Them Take Heed": Mexican Americans and the Campaign for Education Equality in Texas, 1910–1981* (Austin: University of Texas Press, 1987).

66. Castañeda, "Crónica Personal de Cristal," 27-28.

67. Irene R. Castañeda, interview.

68. John Steinbeck, *Grapes of Wrath* (New York: The Viking Press, 1939); Elizabeth Partridge, ed., *Dorothea Lange: A Visual Life* (Washington, DC: Smithsonian Institution Press, 1994); and Charles J. Shindo, *Dust Bowl Migrants in the American Imagination* (Lawrence: University of Kansas Press, 1997).

69. Abraham Hoffman, *Unwanted Mexican Americans in the Great Depression: Repatriation Pressures, 1929-1939* (Tucson: University of Arizona Press, 1974).

70. Richard Griswold del Castillo and Arnoldo de León, *North to Aztlán: A History of Mexican Americans in the United States* (New York: Twayne Publishers, 1996), 59- 82; Dennis Nodin Valdés, *Barrios Norteños: St. Paul and Midwestern Mexican Communities in the Twentieth Century* (Austin: University of Texas Press, 2000); Dennis Nodin Valdés, *Al Norte: Agricultural Workers in the Great Lakes Region, 1917-1970* (Austin: University of Texas Press, 1991); and Sarah Deutsch, *No Separate Refuge: Culture,*

Class, and Gender on an Anglo-Hispanic Frontier in the American South-west, 1880-1940 (New York: Oxford University Press, 1987).

71. Emma Pérez, interview.

72. Discussion of the documentary *Harvest of Shame* is revised from the initial publication of this article in *Frontiers: A Journal of Women's Studies*, 5, 22:3, 2001. See Byron Pitts, *"Harvest of Shame" 50 Years Later*," http://22 2.cbsnews.com/8301-18563_162-7087361.html. Accessed 5 January 2013. For discussion of the documentary *Poverty in the Valley of Plenty*, see Ernesto Galarza, *Spiders in the House and Workers in the Field* (Notre Dame: University of Notre Dame Press, 1970): 30-56.

CHAPTER 8

LANGUAGE AND OTHER
LETHAL WEAPONS

CULTURAL POLITICS AND THE RITES OF
CHILDREN AS TRANSLATORS OF CULTURE

Age 7: El Doctor[1]

"Dile que no puedo respirar—que se me atora el aire. Dile..." How do I say "atora"? (Tell him that I can't breathe that the air gets stuck. Tell him ...)

"Tell your mother that she has to stop and place this hose in her mouth and press this pump or else she will suffocate."

"Qué dice? Qué dice?" (What is he saying? What is he saying?)

He is sitting behind this big desk, and my mother was sitting beside me and holding on to my hand very tightly.

I... what does suffocate mean? How do I translate this? I don't have the words.

"Qué dice? Qué dice?" (What is he saying? What is he saying?)

"I... uh... Dice que... uh ... Dice que si no haces lo que te dice te mueres."

(He says... He says... He says that if you don't do what he says you will die.)

"Dile que cuando me acuesto por la noche que no puedo resollar." (Tell him that when I lay down at night, I can't breathe.)

"Resollar," what does that mean?

Her gasps came out quickly and sounded so awful: a croaking sound that seemed to hurt from deep inside her throat. I sit in front of the big desk remembering, hearing her sounds, and feel again the terror of last night and every time I heard her and could not help. I do not have the words to help her. She will die. And all I could do was sit there and hold her hand and listen to her gasp and gasp for air—for breath that would not reach her, her eyes popping out—and watch her die. She called me her *lengua*, her *voz*. If she dies, it would be my fault.

I tell the doctor she cannot breathe and will die. And he says something I cannot understand about asthmatics and how there is little he can do except give her this pump and that I should be sure to tell her not to panic.

Panic. What does that word mean? How do I say panic?

How does a 7-year-old girl, not yet in the second grade, translate the life and death words "atora," "suffocate," "resollar," "panic?" How does she explain and interpret words she does not know in either language, while knowing at the same time that her mother's life sits on her tongue and on what she does with the words given her? Where in her 7-year-old knowledge does she find the meaning of words that hold the life or death of the mother who calls her "mi lengua" —her tongue—the fleshy, movable organ attached to the floor of the mouth with which words are made? What cultural and linguistic rites are these in which a mother's life balances on a child's tongue?[2]

Age 8: La Cuenta

"Dile que no le podemos pagar toda la cuenta porque ha llovido mucho y no hemos podido pizcar. Pero que aquí están estos centavitos y luego

luego se la pagamos tan pronto que trabajemos... y que queremos llevar una poca comida hoy—que si nos extiende el crédito un poquito. Andale, dile."

He looks at me from behind his counter and says, "What? What'd she say?"

"My mother said we can't pay all the bill today—because of the rain we have not been able to work and we will pay the rest real soon, as soon as we work... and can we have a little more food on credit?"

He looks at me, then he looks at her, and we stand there in front of him. He starts to say something I cannot hear.

"Qué dice? Qué dice?" my mother asks. "Andale, dile que sí le pagamos —nomás que ahorita no hay trabajo." (What is he saying? What is he saying? Go on, tell that we will pay him but just now there is no work.)

I start to speak to him again. I look up to talk to him, and he stares down at me, and the look I see in his eyes tells me that he does not believe we will pay our bill. I have seen that same look on people's faces in town when we all get out of the back of the truck by the city park, and me and my friends walk down the street—in Toppenish—the people just stare at us and glare at us with eyes that tell us we do not belong there. It is the same look the man at the restaurant gave us—at that place where we stopped on our way from Texas—when he wouldn't sell us milk for the baby's bottle.

"Qué dice? Qué dice?" my mother asked.

"Nada mama. No dice nada. Mejor vámonos. No nos van a dar más crédito."

(Nothing mama. He is saying nothing. We best leave. They aren't going to give us any more credit.)

What cultural issues are at stake for child translators? How do they interpret for themselves the cultures they must translate for others? What are the politics they confront each time they translate cultures? How do they negotiate their culture of origin, which cannot protect them and in which the roles of parent and child are inverted as children become the tongues, the lifeline, the public voice of parents, family, and sometimes of communities? How do they negotiate the culture they must translate for their parents—the culture that assaults and violates them, their families, and their communities with its assumptions and attitudes about them as well as with its language and other lethal weapons?

Age 15: El Rifle

"Ay tocan a la puerta. Trae rifle. Ha de ser uno de esos gringos que cazan faisanes. Anda ver que quiere." (*Someone's at the door. He has a rifle. It must be one of those gringos who hunt pheasants. Go see what he wants.*)

I open the door to a man with a hunting rifle.

"Does Raaool Valhenzoola live here? Is he here? I want to talk to him."

"¿Qué dice? ¿Qué dice? ¿A quién busca? ¿Busca a Raúl?" (*What is he saying? What is he saying? Who is he looking for? Is he looking for Raul?*)

"Sí mamá, busca a Raúl. Quédate adentro. (*Yes, mama, he's looking for Raul. Stay inside.*)

"No, my brother's not home. He's working."

"Well, you tell your brother that I came here to order him to stay away from my daughter. You tell him I catch him anywhere near Janice, or even lookin' at her, he'll be sorry. You tell him I have friends, and they know who he is. You tell 'im, girlie, you tell 'im."

I look past him, past the lingering swirls of dust his truck tires had stirred up on the dirt road, and know what the people in the camp meant when they told us stories about the Texas Rangers.

"¿Qué dice? ¿Qué dice? ¿Qué quiere con Raúl?" my mother cries from somewhere behind me. (*What is he saying? What is he saying? What does he want with Raul?*)

I tell him to put the rifle down because he is scaring my mother and to please leave. I step back inside the house and close the door. What can I tell her that she doesn't already know?

Who are these children who speak in tongues and live in fire? What happens to them in educational and social systems that have historically committed psychological, cultural, and physical violence against children who speak languages other than English?[3] What happens to Chicano/Latina/o children whose schools devalue their home language and culture while they, and all children in the United States, are steeped in lessons about America as a classless, casteless society where equality and justice for all reign supreme, where merit and hard work are rewarded, and where education—which is free and available to all children is the key to success? What do we know about how working-class Chicano/Latina/o and other children—whose daily experiences of translating for family and community belie the national mythologies—negotiate the politics of cultures?[4]

What rites of passage are these in which children have to conceive the significance of construct, and interpret entire cultural universes for adults, universes that include every possible human experience, from the most traumatic to the most mundane? What rites are these in which childhood's boundaries are transgressed each time a child is required to translate—and thus mediate, negotiate, and broker adult realities across cultures? How do child translators understand the act of translating? What meaning do they give it?

These questions frame part of my project, a social history of Tejana farm workers who migrated with their families between the Rio Grande valley of south Texas and the Yakima and Skagit valleys of Washington State during the two decades after World War II, from 1945 to 1965. Based on interviews with women who lived in five labor camps in Washington, the study examines the lives of Tejanas who came of age during these two decades.[5] This excerpt is from the chapter on child translators.

Beginning in the 1920s and gaining momentum during the 1930s and 1940s, Tejano families, both nuclear and extended, began an annual migrant work cycle from Texas, to Arizona, to California, to Washington, to Oregon, to Idaho, and back to Texas. The children of these segregated south Texas communities, where generations of native-born children had often been denied even rudimentary education in English, were the girls and boys who scrambled onto the beds of tarp-covered flatbed trucks to migrate to las piscas, to live in labor camps, and work alongside their parents, older siblings, and other relatives in the row, field, and orchard crops of the Yakima, Skagit, and Wenatchee Valleys. For many, one aspect of their childhood reality in Washington was serving as translators for Spanish-speaking parents, families, and community. Ironically, Tejano child translators had to be bilingual, able to move back and forth between English and Spanish any time they were called upon to translate, but in the Texas educational system, with its monolingual ideology, Tejano children were prohibited from speaking Spanish in school, and suffered corporal punishment when caught doing so.[6]

In Washington, most migrant families lived in labor camps—some of which had communal showers, outside toilets, and communal laundries that consisted of large steel tubs with built-in washboards; others had neither showers nor laundries. Located at the end of long dusty roads or set far beyond groves of trees that hid the ramshackle structures from view, labor camps were not visible from the highway. Thus the camps, and their inhabitants, were rendered invisible to the local citizenry. Ostensibly, migrant farm workers did not exist.

What existed were inflammatory newspaper headlines decrying the threat that "illegal Mexican aliens" posed to local resources. McCarthyism and anticommunist hysteria denounced as foreign, subversive, and/or homosexual anyone even remotely suspected of harboring radical political sympathies and posing an internal threat to national security. What existed were INS roundups and deportations of Mexican workers, dubbed "Operation Wetback."[7] What also existed were Hollywood's countless renditions of the "West as America," which Chicano, Amerindian, Black, and Anglo children could see on Saturday afternoons at the segregated Liberty Theater in Toppenish, Washington—the heart of the Yakima Indian Reservation.[8]

Thus, for Tejanos, people of Mexican descent whose historical communities had existed under a state of siege since the end of the US war with Mexico in 1848, the repressive politics, policies, and culture of the 1950s were a postwar manifestation of long-lived patterns of repression, now further justified by nativist as well as racist arguments that Mexicans were foreigners. For the migrant farmworker families of the Tejanas interviewed for this study, the "keep America pure" ideology, the economic and political policy of containment, and the cultural and political repression of the 1950s conveyed the clear message that people of Mexican descent were un-American, subversive, and unwelcome except as temporary, seasonal agricultural laborers. Once the crops were in, they were to disappear.

During these postwar decades, the women whose stories begin and end this essay translated for their families and their communities. As children who translated in every possible situation, the question of how young Tejanitas experienced the act of translating is a critical political, and thus cultural, question. Their oral histories reveal that the act of translation occurs within, and is informed by, unequal relations of power. Translation usually occurs under conditions of stress and/or conflict. While the act of translating can be empowering to the child because she is helping her family, it is frequently traumatic, and the trauma is long-lasting. What, then, do we make of children translating cultures? How do we assess, analyze, theorize, and interpret this experience?

The scholarly literature on translation privileges the written word. It is produced by and directed to scholars who translate written texts in all literary genres. The non-academic literature on translation focuses on teaching businesses how to train workers to be translators and thus to digest "unassimilated diversity," to quote Angela Davis.[9] This work yields little of value for examining and understanding the experience of child translators who translate orally and on-the-spot.

In the late 1980s, social science scholars and practitioners—particularly sociolinguists, psychologists, anthropologists, teacher-education specialists, and social workers—began to examine and debate issues pertinent to children as translators. Generally, this scholarship casts the experience as a recent phenomenon specific to immigrant children and their families; it centers the debate on the psychological or linguistic "costs and benefits" to the individual child.[10]

One side argues that translating for parents and family is harmful to the child's psychological development and that, because children play an adult role while they are translating, they may grow up too quickly and resent or lose respect for their parents. This perspective is exemplified by Richard Rodriguez's undernourished *Hunger of Memory: The Education of Richard Rodriguez* (1981).[11]

Rodriguez accepted and internalized the tenets of a racist, classist society that deemed everything about him—the color of his skin, his language, his physiognomy, and his working-class origins—wrong, unacceptable, and un-American. He internalized these notions and relinquished his Mexican self, choosing erudite English over Spanish and a "public" Euro-American life over a "private" Mexican one.

The other side of the debate argues that translating can help children develop language skills and understand American institutions. Lowry Hemphill, a specialist in language development, argues that translating is not necessarily something that should be discouraged, since it is "part and parcel of the whole experience of being an immigrant child. People do what they have to do to get by."[12] Marjorie Faulstich Orellana, Professor of Education, who has conducted extensive studies on child translators in immigrant families, concludes that most children who serve as translators are comfortable in the role and that translating offers the opportunity for these children to improve their own literacy skills because "they have to make sense of words and ideas in one language and explain them in another." Student translators, she argues, draw on skills that are employed by good readers and writers. Interested in the strategies that Spanish-English bilingual children use when translating for immigrant parents, Faulstich Orellana's research offers unprecedented possibilities for understanding children's translation strategies, the effect and meaning of translating in their educational development as well as its significance in family dynamics.[13]

Similarly, in his autobiography *Barrio Boy: The Story of a Boy's Accul-turation* (1971), Ernesto Galarza reveals translating as empowering. The young Galarza learned very early to see himself in relation to his family, his community, and his class, and to understand and interpret the world in terms of power relations and class differences.[14] For Galarza, translating was a powerful, positive, and valuable skill that he first developed as a child translator, a skill he honed and applied to spoken, to written, and to cultural texts throughout his adult life as a scholar, a labor organizer, and a tireless advocate for economic and social justice.

Drawing on cultural anthropology's theories on translation, which focus on authority, power, and otherness, Galarza's acts of translation as an adult may be analyzed in terms of "the translator as social actor."[15] While translation studies and critical theory on translation conclude that "translation today is as much about the translation of cultural, political, and historical contexts and concepts as it is about language," the scholarship theorizes the act of translating literary and other written texts.[16] It does not analyze the translating acts or agency of children who translate the spoken word in situations and conditions not of their making, over which they have no control. So while children must read, translate, and interpret not only the spoken word, but also the text of bodies, attitudes, power relationships, space and movement of the translating moment, the new scholarship in translation studies has yet to analyze and theorize the universe of child translators.

Doctors and other medical professionals whose patients are recent immigrants, and who have medically diagnosed and/or treated a patient with a child serving as translator, have joined the debate over child translators. So too have some individuals who, as minor children, served as translators in medical situations.[17] Both groups concur that children have not the linguistic knowledge and skills to accurately translate complex medical concepts and terminology and to have a child translate is to put both the patient and child at risk. Still, some adults who were child translators interpret the act of translating as did Galarza, as part of familial responsibility which they gladly undertook, as empowering and transformative. In either case, I note that the current debate over child translators, and the state legislation that has been drafted to prevent children from providing language interpretation at hospitals, doctor's offices, and clinics responds to the reality of late twentieth and early twenty-first century immigration to the US.[18]

However, the issue of translating cultures, and specifically the experience of child translators, is a historical as much as a contemporary issue and experience. It is by no means solely or even principally an immigrant experience, at least not historically. Irrespective of which colonial power arrived on the shores of what Europeans named the North American continent, they had to communicate with the people living here. Europeans did not initially speak indigenous languages; somebody had to translate, and that somebody was often a child.[19] Beginning with Malintzín Tenepal, or La Malinche, as she is known—the fourteen-year-old girl whom the Chontal Maya coast gave to the Spaniards in 1519, along with fourteen other young women, and who became translator, lover, and tactical advisor to Hernán Cortés—the experience of translating cultures has been lived by native-born children and adolescents.[20]

Throughout the Spanish Mexican periods, both Amerindian and mestizo children and adolescents captured in war, raids, and slaving expeditions in the northern frontier of Mexico could find themselves translating cultures, as in the case of boys and young men who worked for the military as scouts, horse-breakers, or herders, and in that of young servant girls who worked in the homes of soldiers and settlers. Indian children, in particular, were often captured, traded, or sold into slavery by Spanish Mexican military forces as well as by settlers and, after the Euro-American conquest, by settlers and paramilitary groups.[21]

On another level, but also in terms of culture, children were at the center of the strategies employed by Spanish Mexicans as well as Euro-Americans to detribalize native peoples. Catholic missionaries and the Euro-American educational system went to great lengths to "denaturalize or deculturalize" native peoples through their children: in missions, in the case of the Jesuits and Franciscans, and in Indian boarding schools, in the case of Euro-American educators. In Texas, prior to the late 1960s, undemocratic language policies prohibited children of Mexican descent from speaking Spanish on the school grounds.[22] This is fundamentally what the contemporary English-only movement is all about.

Although Malintzín's narrative relating her experience is not available, we know that her acts of translation, as well as her sexuality, earned her the opprobrium of a Euro-centered, patriarchal Mexicano/Chicano history and culture, which portrays her—the symbolic mother of the mestizo peoples—as a traitor and a whore. In the past two decades, however, Native American and Chicana writers and scholars have reinterpreted the documentary record and inverted the spurious sexualized and racialized image of Malintzín, claiming her as our own, even as lesbian.[23]

Reinterpretations of Malintzín by Chicana and Native American scholars Adelaida del Castillo, Norma Alarcón, and Inés Hernández center on issues of subjectivities, translation, and agency. Del Castillo interprets Malintzín as a gifted linguist, a young woman who made well-considered choices based on her realities and those of her people. Alarcón examines La Malinche as a paradigmatic figure of Chicana feminism. Hernández draws upon the syncretic ceremonial dance tradition of the Concheros of "la Gran Tenochtitlán, in which La Malinche is the path-opener—the front(line) – the vanguard," to discuss how in the contemporary period we can choose to be Malinches in a political, social, and intellectual context.[24]

The Malinches of today, she states, are "all of the women who have accepted their role as 'tongues' and demanded that their voices be heard."[25] Including especially Rigoberta Menchú, who learned Spanish, the language of the oppressor—and made it her own, just as she learned and used the Bible as an organizing text and tool in her community; these women join their voices and their skills in the global struggle to end exploitation and oppression in all their forms.

With these very few exceptions, and linguist Frances Karttunen's *Between Worlds: Interpreters, Guides, and Survivors* (1994), which discusses the young translators Malintzín and Sacajawea within a global context and experience, scholars have yet to focus on the spoken word and the act of oral translation across unequal relations of power based on age, gender, race, class, and culture. Centering gender and the experience that women have had as child translators and examining the pressures, conflicts, and contradictions that arise when they must translate in a context of unequal power raises critical epistemological and theoretical questions for feminism, and for feminist scholars seeking to theorize history, politics, and culture.

What did a Tejanita of seven summers know and interpret as she broke through multilayered power differentials to translate for a mother facing racist male creditors, doctors, police, or school authorities? What did a teenage Mexican girl of fifteen understand about sexuality, race, and violence when she had to translate her family's needs to a storeowner who was close friends with the same white man with a hunting rifle who came to threaten her brother away from his daughter? How did these young Tejanas negotiate translating across two patriarchal cultures during the 1950s—their own, which sexualized them, and another, which sexualized and racialized them while disparaging their class origins? How did working-class Mexican girls live and interpret the cultural politics of the Cold War in which a pivotal ideological tenet was a domestic revival that centered the family, prescribed traditional gender roles, and prized marital stability?[26]

How did migrant farm-worker girls, adolescents, and young women assimilate, accept, resist, subvert, perform, and/or transform this experience in the post-World War II era?[27] What did they change, and how were they changed by the act of translating cultures across space, time, and circumstance? This study reveals that the rites of translating that Tejana and other child translators enacted as they interpreted adult realities from one adult to another and back again, challenge current theories of gender, childhood, class, power, language, translation, and the politics of culture in US history.

Age 10: La Escuela

"Dile que venimos con Doña Chelo para averiguar porqué espularson a Mariquita." (*Tell him we came with Doña Chelo to find out why they expelled Mariquita.*)

"Sí, y dile que…" (*Yes, and tell him that.*)

The door opened and the principal came out, asking, "Who is Mrs. Rowdríguez?"

I touched Doña Chelo's arm. She looked at me and stepped forward with her hand outstretched.

"We can't have all these Mexican kids disrupting our school…"

"Qué dice? Qué dice?" Doña Chelo asked.

"If this is Mawhría Rowdríguez's mother, tell her that her daughter bit the school nurse, and we had to expel her."

"Dile que Mariquita no tiene piojos. Que soy muy limpia—cada noche caliento tinas de agua y baño a todos mis muchachos y los mando muy limpiesitos a la escuela. Y a Mariquita le hago sus trenzas cada mañana. Por qué le echaron todo ese polvo tan apestoso? Dile que la asustaron y la humillaron."

"Doña Chelo says Mariquita does not have lice, her family is very clean. She heats water every night for baths and sends her children to school clean everyday. She braids Mariquita's hair every morning. Why did you pour that ugly powder on her? You scared Mariquita and hurt her."

"Tell her that we do this every year in March when all you kids from the camps start coming in. Tell her that the lice powder is not harmful and that the school nurse tries not to get it in their eyes or mouth. There was no reason for Mawhria to cry and scream like she did. And then when the nurse tried to hold her down, she screamed even louder and bit and kicked and hit our poor nurse. Tell her she should send her children to school clean and neat. And she should teach her children to behave —to respect school authorities."

"Qué dice? Qué dice? Cuándo puede regresar Mariquita a sus clases? Cómo puede aprender si la espulsan? Yo no quiero que se queden burros como nosotros, que no nos admitían a las escuelas en Tejas. Dile Nenita. Dile." (*What is he saying? What is he saying? When can Mariquita return to her classes? How can she learn if they expel her? I don't want them to remain ignorant like us because they wouldn't admit us in school in Texas. Tell him Nenita. Tell him.*)

"Les estoy diciendo, Doña Chelo. Les estoy diciendo." (*I am telling them, Doña Chelo. I am telling them.*)

Notes

1. The four translation stories in this essay derive from a larger study of Tejana farm workers based, in part, on oral histories. These stories are composites of translation stories related by the women I interviewed, and my own childhood experiences of translating. At issue is that with few exceptions, Tejano migrant families were Spanish-speaking US Citizens whose access to public education and instruction in English in pre-desegregation Texas was limited at best, when not outright denied.

2. For discussion of the ideology of monolingualism, which he terms anti-democratic linguistic ideology, see Otto Santa Ana, "Introduction: The Unspoken Issue of Silencing Americans," in *Tongue Tied: The Lives of Multilingual Children in Public Education*, ed. Otto Santa Ana (Lanham, MD: Rowman and Littlefield, 2004).

3. See Ruben Donato, *The Other Struggle for Equal Schools: Mexican Americans During the Civil Rights Movement* (Albany: State University of New York Press, 1997); David Wallace Adams, *Education for Extinction: American Indians and the Boarding School Experience, 1875–1928* (Lawrence: University Press of Kansas, 1997); Devon Mihesuah, *Cultivating the Rosebuds:The Education of Women at the Cherokee Female Seminary, 1851–1909* (Chicago: University of Illinois Press, 1997); Guadalupe San Miguel, *"Let All of Them Take Heed": Mexican-Americans and the Campaign for Educational Equality in Texas, 1910–1981* (Austin: University of Texas Press, 1987); Charles M. Wollenberg, *All Deliberate Speed: Segregation and Exclusion in California Schools, 1855–1975* (Berkeley: University of California Press, 1978).

4. See Teresa Palomo Acosta and Ruth Weingarten, *Las Tejanas: 300 Years of History* (Austin:University of Texas Press, 2003); Neil Foley, *The White Scourge: Mexicans, Blacks and PoorWhites in Texas Cotton Culture* (Berkeley: University of California Press, 1999); Rodolfo Acuña, *Occupied America: A History of Chicanos*, 3d ed. (New York: Harper and Row, 1988); Abraham Hoffman, *Unwanted Mexican Americans in the Great Depression* (Tucson: University of Arizona Press, 1974).

5. The women interviewed for this study lived in labor camps in Toppenish, Crewport, and Sunnyside in eastern Washington, and in Mt. Vernon and Lynden in western Washington.

6. See Miguel, *"Let All of Them Take Heed."*

7. Arnoldo de León, *Mexican Americans in Texas: A Brief History* (Arlington Heights, IL: Harlan Davidson, 1993); Juan Ramón García, *Operation Wetback: The Mass Deportation of Mexican Undocumented Workers in 1954* (Westport, CT: Greenwood Press, 1980).

8. See David Gutiérrez, "Significant to Whom? Mexican Americans and the History of the American West," *Western Historical Quarterly* (November 1993): 519–39. For representationand discussion of "the West as America" in art, see William H. Truettner, ed., *The West as America: Reinterpreting Images of the Frontier, 1820–1920* (Washington, DC: Smithsonian Institute Press, 1991).

9. Angela Y. Davis, "Gender, Class, and Multiculturalism: Rethinking 'Race' Politics," in *Mapping Multiculturalism*, eds. Avery F. Gordon and Christopher Newfield (Minneapolis: University of Minnesota Press, 1996), 40–8.

10. See Zita Arocha, "Like Most Children of Immigrants, I Suffer from a Split Psyche," *Los Angeles Times*, 27 October 1991; Lowry Hemphill, "For Immigrants' Children, an Adult Role," *New York Times*, 15 August 1991.

11. Richard Rodriguez, *Hunger of Memory: The Education of Richard Rodriguez* (Boston: David R. Godine, 1982). Omission of the accent in "Rodriguez" is consistent with the way the author of *Hunger of Memory* spells his family name.

12. Hemphill, "For Immigrants' Children, an Adult Role."

13. The quote is from Irasema Salinas-González, "Bilingual Students Gain Literacy Skills As Family Translators," *Catalyst* 15, no. 2 (October 2003), at: www.catalyst-chicago.org/arch/ 10-3/ l003researchprint.htm; see also Marjorie Faulstich Orellana, Lisa Dorner, and Lucila Pulido, "Accessing Assets, Immigrant Youth's Work as Family Translators or 'Paraphrasers'," *Social Problems* 50, no. 4 (November 2003): 482–504; Marjorie Faulstich Orellana, "Children's Responsibilities in Latino Immigrant Homes," *New Directions for Youth Development: Theory, Practice and Research: Special issue on Social Influences in the Positive Development of Immigrant Youth* 100 (2003): 25–39.

14. Ernesto Galarza, *Barrio Boy: The Story of a Boy's Acculturation* (Notre Dame: University of Notre Dame Press, 1971).

15. From proposal for "Translation and Ethnic Studies: Cultural and Historical Logics," translation symposium held at the University of Chicago, 14 February 2006. Raul Coronado to Antonia Castañeda, invitation to participate in translation conference, 15 June 2005, in possession of author.

16. The quote is from Eurozine Editorial, "The Politics of Translation," at: www.eurozine.com/articles/2004-01-16-eurozine-en.html; see also,

Antonio Sousa Ribeiro, "The Reason of Borders or a Border Reason? Translation as a Metaphor For Our Times," an extended and revised edition of a talk held at the 16th Meeting of Cultural Journals in Belgrade, Serbia and Montenegro entitled, "Europe and the Balkans: Politics of Translation," 24-27 October 2003, at: www.eurozine.com/authors/ribeiro.html.

17. See Glenn Flores, MD, Milagros Abreu, MD, and Sandra C. Tomany-Korman, MS, "Limited English Proficiency, Primary Language Spoken at Home, and Disparities in Children's Health and Healthcare: How Language Barriers are Measured," *Public Health Reports* 120, no. 4 (July/August 2005): 418–30; Glenn Flores, MD, "Language Barriers to Health Care in the United States," *Public Health Reports* (July/August 2005); Eurgenia Chen, "Child Medical Translators—At Grandpa's Bedside, Trying to Find Words for 'Defeat'," *Pacific News Service*, 23 November 2005, at: news.pacificnews.org/news/view_article.html.

18. See Elizabeth Weise, "Demand Surges for Translators at Medical Facilities," *USA Today*, 19 July 2006, at: www.usatoday.com/news/health/2007-07-19medical interpreters_x.htm; Thuy Ngo, "Translation Trouble – Children May be Barred from Interpreting for Parents," *New America Media*, 18 November 2005, at: www.news.newamericamedia.org/news/view_article.html ; Jonathan Kaminsky, "Working to End Use of Children as Translators," *North Gate News Online*, 19 November 2004, at: www.journalism.berkeley.edu/ngno/stories/003857_print.html.

19. For an important discussion of the politics of linguistic domination, and its centrality to the politics and policies of Spanish colonialism in Mexico, see Jorge Klor de Alva, "Language, Politics, and Translation: Colonial Discourse and Classic Nahuatl in New Spain," in *The Art of Translation: Voices from the Field*, ed. Rosanna Warren (Boston: Northeastern University Press, 1989), 143–62.

20. See Frances Karttunen, *Between Worlds: Interpreters, Guides, and Survivors* (New Brunswick, NJ: Rutgers University Press, 1994); Inés Hernández, "An Open Letter to Chicanas," in *Without Discovery: A Native Response to Columbus*, ed. Ray González (Seattle: Broken Moon Press, 1992), 153–66; Norma Alarcón, "Traductora, Traditora: A Paradigmatic Figure of Chicana Feminism," *Cultural Critique* (1990): 57–87; Norma Alarcón, "Chicana Feminism," *Cultural Studies* 4 (October 1990): 248–55; Adelaida del Castillo, "Malintzín Tenépal: A Preliminary Look into a New Perspective," in *Essays on La Mujer*, eds. Rosaura Sánchez and Rosa

Martínez Cruz (Los Angeles: Chicano Studies Center Publications, 1977), 124–49.

21. See James F. Brooks, *Captives and Cousins: Slaves, Kinship, and Community in the Spanish Borderlands* (Chapel Hill: University of North Carolina Press, 2002); Esteban Rael Gálvez, "Identifying Captivity and Capturing Identity: Narratives of American Indian Slavery," (PhD diss., University of Michigan, 2004); L. R. Bailey, *Indian Slave Trade in the Southwest: A Study of Slave-taking and the Traffic in Indian Captives* (Los Angeles: Westernlore Press, 1966).

22. See Santa Ana, *Tongue Tied*; Adams, *Education for Extinction*; Mihesuah, *Cultivating the Rosebuds*. For discussion about Jesuit and Franciscan strategies of using children to invert the lines of authority among native peoples, see Karen Anderson, *Chain Her By One Foot: The Subjugation of Native Women in Seventeenth-Century New France* (New York: Routledge, 1991), 159–61; Ramón Gutiérrez, *When Jesus Came, the Cornmothers Went Away: Marriage, Sexuality and Power in New Mexico, 1500–1846* (Stanford: Stanford University Press, 1991), 74–6.

23. See Deena J. González, "Malinche as Lesbian," *California Sociologist, Special Issue, Culture and Conflict in the Academy: Testimonies from the War Zone* 14 (Winter/ Spring, 1991).

24. Del Castillo, Malintzín Tenépal; Norma Alarcón, "Traductora, Traditora," *Cultural Studies* 4 (1990); Hernández-Avila, "Open Letter to Chicanas."

25. Hernández-Avila, "Open Letter to Chicanas."

26. See Elaine Tyler May, *Homeward Bound: American Families in the Cold War Era* (New York: Basic Books, 1988).

27. Marjorie Faulstich Orellana, who has conducted the most extensive research on child translators in immigrant families to date (see note 13), also works on the gendered nature of literacy practices but, to my knowledge, has not yet published on gender and child translators; see Marjorie Faulstich Orellana, "Texts, Talk, Tasks, and Take-up: Literacy as a Gendered Social Practice in Two Bilingual Classrooms," *Reading Research Quarterly* 30, no. 4 (1995): 674–708; Michelle Commeyras, Marjorie Faulstich Orellana, Bruce Bertram, and Lori Neilsen, "Why Feminist Theory and Literacy Research?: Four Responses," *Reading Research Quarterly* 31, no. 4 (1996): 458–68.

CHAPTER 9

LULLABIES Y CANCIONES DE CUNA

EMBODYING CHICANA HISTORY

I am interested in lullabies because the concepts, words, ideas, and emotions conveyed in these earliest, most basic forms of communication we hear as children, and that our mothers may have sung while we are still in the womb, form the subsoil of our own sense of being and, from earliest childhood, communicate, among many other sentiments, a sense of place, of identity, of memory. Here I work with lullabies, or cradle songs in English, *canciones de cuna* and *nanas* as they are known in Spanish, as a source of memory and history.

"The world's earliest archives or libraries were memories of women."[1] So observes noted film scholar Trinh T. Minh-ha. Memories, she continues, "patiently transmitted from mouth to ear, body to body, hand to hand. In the process of storytelling, speaking and listening refer to realities that do not involve the imagination alone. The speech is seen, heard, smelled, tasted, and touched. Every woman partakes in the chain of guardianship and transmission. Phrases like "I sucked it at my mother's breast, I heard it from our mother, I learned it on my mother's knee," to express what has been passed down, are commonplace"[2] and universal.

Who among us has not heard and savored those stories? Who among us has not drawn from that repository of women's memories and knowledge? What did those memories—transmitted in the form of stories, songs, rhymes, verses, and lullabies recount? Were they memories of family exploits and lore; creation stories of a people; ancestral tales of origin; histories of myriad migrations; of exile, of seeking sanctuary, of slavery and forced diasporas; of the 1830s Trail of Tears, narratives of loss of land, of deterritorialization; of internment camps, of forced relocation; of refugee life, of slavery on southern plantations—exemplary narratives of hard work, struggle and the promise of a better life? Were they humorous, nonsensical stories and verses to quiet a sleepless child in the long hours of the night, or to comfort a terrified child in the face of war and other conditions of brutal unspeakable violence—as in Iraq, Afghanistan, or crossing the Arizona-Sonora desert today?[3]

What are the stories that women weave into the larger historical fabric of a family, a community, a region, a nation? What constitutes those memories? What are the sources of knowledge archived in women's memories? How are they constructed?

Are they memories inscribed on the surface of the body, in its movements, voices, and tastes; memories of lived experience voiced on from generations before, and that continue to be passed on?[4] How do we access and use these archives? What meaning do we give to them? What value do we, who privilege the written word, the printed, documented word, attribute to the spoken, uttered, whispered, or sung archives of women's oral traditions? Do we use them as sources, as evidence in historical studies?

Though I have long studied women's historical experience with the tools of the historian's craft, more recently I am seeking to understand the significance of women's corporeal (physical) bodies as indelible sources of history.

As teachers often learn more from students than students from teachers, so I first learned about the meaning of women's bodies as the font, women's memories as the archives, and women's tongues as the instruments of transmission, from a student in a graduate seminar who was conducting oral history interviews for her research paper on the African American community of Brownwood, Texas.[5] Ramona Houston began her oral interview with the octogenarian Ms. Luella with questions about her mother and her family's history in Brownwood, a history that originated in slavery in the Texas of the 1850s.

"Ms. Luella, could you please tell me about your mother," Ms. Houston asked.

Ms.Luella quietly replied. "I don't know nothing about her. I didn't have no momma."

Thinking she had not asked her question clearly enough, Ms. Houston asked, "Ms. Luella, could you please tell me something about the history of your family?"

Again Ms. Luella responded, "I told you. I didn't have no momma."

Now believing Ms. Luella had not understood the question, that she was not just asking about her mother, but about other members of the family as well, Ms. Houston persisted. She needed this interview. Ms. Luella's family members were important stalwarts of the African American community in Brownwood—they were among the founders of the church and other community institutions. Once again Ms. Houston asked Ms. Luella about her family; again, the response was that she grew up without a mother.

Her mother's absence, Ms. Luella was telling us, meant that the store of knowledge about her own, her family, and therefore Brownwood's history was lost to her. She did not have a mother—the keeper and transmitter of memory—to tell her the stories. Consequently she did not know. She could not answer Ms. Houston's questions about the family or their part in Brownwood's early history. She did not have the locus of her mother's body with its own lived experience as the source of long-term historical memory or of more contemporary recent experiences upon which to draw and in turn, to pass on.

To further illustrate both the importance of women's memory, and of the forms in which women transmit the memory, I move from Ms. Luella's story of lost history to one of recovery—the story of Mary Moran, a woman born and raised in Georgia who traced her family's ancestry to Sierra Leone through a childhood song her mother, Amelia Dawley, taught her. In both Africa and the United States, the song was transmitted from mother to daughter over many generations of women giving, receiving, and passing it on.[6]

Moran learned that the song, a Mende funeral song, came with a woman or girl abducted from Sierra Leone in the eighteenth century and sold into captivity in Georgia. In Mende culture, funeral songs are women's songs because women traditionally preside over birth and death; the songs, which remember and connect the singer to her ancestors, are passed on from mother to daughter.

In the 1990s, Moran traveled to the village of Senehun Nglola, where she met Baindu Jabati, whose mother had taught her the same song, even though singing it was prohibited after Christianity came to her village. The song survived more than 200 years in Africa, it survived more than 200 years in the United States, and though the melody was somewhat different, the African words remained almost exact. Moran, who found family through this song, has taught it to her granddaughter; the song lives and continues.

Songs, one of the mainstays of women's oral traditions, are at the center of my current work on the history of women in colonial Alta California and the region that is now the US West and Southwest, including New Mexico, Texas, and Arizona. Like a significant majority of the world's women, the Spanish-speaking women who colonized New Mexico in 1598, Texas in 1718, and California in 1774, were not lettered. Nor were the indigenous and African descent women who, by servitude, captivity, enslavement, and in some cases by marriage, migrated northward with colonizing expeditions. With very few exceptions, women who came North with the imperialist Spanish colonial State, did not leave diaries, journals, travel accounts, autobiographies, captivity narratives, personal correspondence, or other written sources penned in their own hand. We do not have first-hand accounts from them of the landscape, the people, or their experiences of migration and colonialism, whether they came in private ventures as in New Mexico, or in those subsidized by the Department of War, as in Texas and California, or those annexed in the aftermath of the mid-nineteenth century war, as Tucson was in 1853. They did not leave written documents—the raw materials historians mine, select from, examine, analyze, and interpret in writing history—whether of a family, a community, or a nation.

Still, the paucity of written documents does not obviate the fact that women's lives and experiences shaped and were shaped in the history of this region—homeland to women from hundreds of diverse American Indian cultures: Chumash, Rumsien, Pueblo, Navajo, Apache (Mescalero, Jicarilla, Lipan), Caddo, Karankawa. Tohono O'dham (Tono-oohtam)

Spanish-speaking women, most of whom were impoverished mestizas (Indo-mestizas and Afro-mestizas), migrated to this remote borderlands of empire as members of soldier-settler, pueblo, artisanal, and convict families. To Alta California in the 1770s and 1780s, they migrated from other frontier presidios, pueblos, missions, and played-out mining towns of colonial Mexico, including Sinaloa-Sonora, Zacatecas, Tubac, Monclova, and Monterrey.

On northern frontier Borderlands, women colonizers not only came into contact with diverse Indian peoples, intent on protecting their homeland, but also with French, English, Russian, and later, Euro-Americans intent on expanding their national domain. Until the 1820s, the Europeans and Euro-Americans whom Mestizas and Indian women encountered on these outposts of empire, were males—priests, soldiers, seafarers, traders, trappers, adventurers, merchants, scientists, military men. In these remote landscapes, the reproductive labor of Mestiza and Indigenous women in all its forms—whether biological, economic, political, religious, or social —established the human, economic, socio-racial, and cultural basis of the cities in which we now live: Santa Fe, Albuquerque, San Antonio, El Paso, Tucson, San Diego, San Francisco, Los Angeles, San Bernardino.

Through our research in civil, military and ecclesiastical records, including census, mission, parish, and other documents, historians have reconstructed much about women's lives on the Spanish-Mexican-US borderlands. From civil, criminal, and ecclesiastical court and other records we reconstruct most aspects of women's families, their work, social, political, and religious lives, their contestations, struggles, actions, and agency in familial and other spaces.

Still, because women could not write their own statements, petitions, wills, or correspondence, their voices and words in these documents are not exactly their own. Rather, the voices of non-lettered mestiza, American Indian, and African descent women are mediated—filtered through the lens of male translators, interpreters, and scribes—the clergy, military, and civil authorities who wrote down women's words. If the woman was a Spanish speaker, her testament was mediated from the oral to the written word. If the woman's language differed from that of the person writing, her words were further mediated through the language of interpreters. The voices of Indian women were three times filtered: the women spoke in their own language, someone translated what they said into Spanish, and still someone else transcribed it. After the US-Mexican War the oral testimonies of Indian and Mexican women were further mediated by yet another translation, from indigenous language or from Spanish, and thence to the written English text.

In Hubert Howe Bancroft's collection of post-US invasion Spanish-Mexican archives, women's words were sometimes not collected as part of the written record at all specifically because the interpreter or scribe did not think women's words important enough to document or to reproduce. Thus Bancroft's scribes, in copying documents from the Spanish and Mexican archives, sometimes referred to a woman's testimony or statement with a cryptic notation that read, "unimportant, domestic matter. . ." and did not reproduce the document.

While I continue to work with written sources and documents, I also examine songs women sang, prayers they composed, and other extant forms of women's oral traditions as sources in writing Chicana history. Currently, I focus lullabies/canciones de cuna. My work on canciones de cuna draws on feminist theory, most specifically on the epistemological viewpoint based on the idea of knowledge as embodied, engendered, and embedded in the material context of place and space—what educational theorists similarly term somatic/embodied learning. In her essay "Feminist Theory and Social Science," Linda Martin Alcoff argues that reason has been defined in opposition to what have traditionally been considered feminine characteristics and that the mind-body dualism of Cartesian construct is a central feature of a masculinist formulation of reason.[7] Alcoff outlines four premises of a feminist theory of reason and knowledge:

- That the mind and body are not separable
- That mind has therefore never been separate from the body
- That our dominant ideas of reason are reflections of embodied ways of being
- That we therefore have to rethink the many assumptions which pervade social science that are based on the mind-body dualism of Cartesian constructs of knowledge

In the late 1980s, Chicana lesbiana feminist theorist and historian Emma Pérez centered gender, sexuality, race and class, in both corporeal and discursive terms, and elaborated the concept of *sitio y lengua*.[8] Chicana theorist writers and scholars Gloria Anzaldúa, Cherríe Moraga and Deena González further developed concepts of embodied knowledge within the framework of living Chicana theory.[9] More recently, Chela Sandoval argues that the theoretical project of US third world feminism insists on a standpoint, the theory and method of *oppositional consciousness*, based on situated knowledge.[10]

The fact that singers of lullabies, for the most part are women, enables me to explore ideas, concepts and knowledge transmitted through the corporeality of the situated body, its movements, sounds, smells, and textures. That women are most generally the singers and transmitters of lullabies has led me to explore the human experience women have in common, the strands of that which they share across cultures, races, genders, classes, sexualities, and languages. That is, the oral traditions they use to transmit ideas, experiences, and realities; the lullabies they sing to children; and often in their family histories. In this paper I focus on Spanish language lullabies that reflect and reveal representations of women on Spain and Mexico's geopolitical, military, and cultural frontiers.

What memories did women transmit about life on myriad frontiers, often the bloodied meeting grounds of diverse cultures, religions, languages, traditions? In the Americas, colonialist cultural frontiers included American Indian cultures, Iberian cultures, African, English, French, German, Dutch, Irish, Jewish, and the racial-cultural mixtures —mestizo, metis, creole, mixed-blood—that resulted from violent and other meetings and encounters.

What ideas and experiences might lullabies pass on about lives lived on frontiers that were often contested spaces—spaces of conflict, war, bloodshed, and resistance, as well as of negotiation, accommodation, adaptation, and cultural interchange. What memories might Dorotea Valdez have had in mind when she told her interviewer in 1874:

> My father. . . came to upper California with Captain Rivera. . . and afterwards emigrated to Monterey, where I was born in 1793. I have witnessed every event that has transpired since that time, but being a woman I was denied the privilege of mixing in politics or in business. My education has been very limited, yet my memory is good.[11]

Dorotea Valdez's life spanned three different political sovereignties on the California frontier. Born during Spanish colonial rule, she was twenty-eight when Mexico gained its independence from Spain in 1821, and in her mid-fifties at the end of the US-Mexican war and cession of half of Mexico's territory to the US with the Treaty of Guadalupe Hidalgo in 1848. At age eighty-one, she was nearing the end of her life when she narrated her history in 1874.

As a child of multiple Borderlands, Valdez's historical legacy, archived in lullabies and songs, included a repertoire that embraced Iberian/North African as well as North American realities. Like lullabies throughout the world, canciones de cuna, whether in the Iberian Peninsula or in the Americas, both instructed and entertained children being cradled, rocked, and soothed with rhythmic sounds and harmonious movement.

"The quality of a lullaby," states Leslie Daiken, "while married to its rocking rhythm, evokes different shades, or textures of feeling. They are as the play of light on different landscapes of our universe" even as they provide moral, religious, cultural and other life lessons pertinent to particular time and place.[12] Distinguishing between "Singing Inward" and "Singing Outward" Lullabies, Daiken describes the former as "joy rainbowed with grief; diffused with all the ups and downs of a mother's life troubles." "Singing inward," she continues, "is the moment when, into a song ostensibly to her child, a woman needs must inject disquiet. . . at the very zenith of tending the child she has borne. Every nuance of anxiety illumines the lullaby."[13]

Certainly women on global frontiers have had much about which to be anxious. Spanish lullabies and *romances fronterizos*, historical ballads of the Christian/Islamic frontier, wove the experience of raids, abduction, and captivity by both Christians and Muslims into the larger narrative of the protracted struggle for military and religio-political dominance of the Iberian Peninsula.[14] Much of this struggle occurred on remote frontiers as each side tried to hold fast to hard won territory.

Thus, some Spanish cradle songs of the fourteenth and fifteenth centuries taught and reminded Christian children of danger in the form of Muslims, represented as the enemy—or as the monster, the evil one, the Other—lurking outside their door, ready to take away a misbehaving, crying, or sleepless child.

"Duérmete niño" reflects cautionary elements:

> Duérmete, niño chiquito
> mira que viene la mora,
> preguntando en puerta e puerta
> cuar es er niño que yora
>
> Anda bete, morito
> ' a la morería
> que mi niño no entiende
> tu argarabía[15]

English Translation:

> Little one now close your eyes
> hark the Moorish woman's footsteps
> questioning from door to door
> who may be the child who cries?
>
> Go away little Moor
> to the Moorish quarter
> for my child does not understand
> your Arabic gibberish

Similarly, though Gypsies and Jews (Judaism), may not have posed the same religious or military threat to Christian Spain as did Islam, lullabies nevertheless also represented both Gypsies and Jews as "The Other," that is, as different, in this case, from the normative Christian self, and therefore as less than the self; as someone to be feared and rejected; as the enemy.

> Esta niña chiquita
> no tiene madre
> la parió una gitana
> y la echó a la calle[16]

Esta niña chiquita
no tiene madre
la cogió una gitana
y la echó a la calle[17]

English Translation:

This little girl child
is a motherless child
a gypsy gave birth to her
and threw her out on the street

This little girl child
is a motherless child
a gypsy woman grabbed her
and threw her out on the street

In these cradle songs, the threat to the Spanish Christian child being lulled to sleep is represented as a non-Christian woman, either Muslim or Gypsy. In one song, the Muslim woman is the monster who will abduct the sleepless child. The second lullaby, in two versions, represents the Gypsy as a bad mother—one who gives birth and discards her newborn, or as an abductress. Thus, in both cases, women of the group unlike ourselves, women who are part of the "Other," are disavowed, are constructed as abductresses, as bad mothers, as bad and evil women.

Abduction, specifically in the form of captivity, was a very real issue for women and children on the Christian/Islamic border. Thus, captivity is a recurring theme in both Spanish and Islamic poetry and in border ballads during the wars of the Reconquest, especially during the last two centuries of a conflict that lasted 800 years. Some of the *romances fronterizos*, like *Moriana Cautiva* (Moriana, the Captive) and *La Reina Xerifa Mora* (also known as Sisters: Queen and Captive) were fictionalized ballads of captivity that were sung at court as well as in homes.[18] Yet, during these 800 years, Christian, Muslim, and Jew also adapted to each other, adopted cultural elements from one another, and co-existed together. Sometimes, despite religious and cultural prohibitions against exogamous unions, they intermarried. And so, sometimes the woman singing the lullabies, or the children being lulled, were themselves captives, the children or grandchildren of captives, or had descended from an intermarriage in which one or another of the parents was the despised "Other."

From the late fifteenth through the late nineteenth centuries, the conflict, fear, and rejection of the religious, racial, military, and ethnic "Other" of European frontiers were recreated on the colonial borderlands of North America. Here the "Other" varied even more. Depending on time, place, and circumstance, the "Other" might be American Indian, Spanish, African, English, French, Russian, Euro-American, Mexican, Asian, or any mixture/mestizaje of the above. In colonial North America these groups each warred against Indians at times; and at other times, with their respective Indian allies, warred against each other on the borderlands frontiers of La Florida, Louisiana, Nuevo México, Tejas, Alta California, and later, Arizona. Here too, war and conflict revolved around acquiring, and then holding onto hard won territory. Here too, women and children were a historic and dynamic presence on the frontiers of newly forming multi-racial, multi-ethnic societies born of unions between women and men of the "Others," whomever the "Other" might be at any given time. Since colonialists of all stripes and American Indians alike took captives—whom each group might enslave, adopt, trade, sell, or kill —fear of the "Other" and of captivity remained a central issue on North American frontiers until the end of the nineteenth century.

Critically important historical studies on captivity, most recently by James Brooks and Estevan Raél Gálvez, detail the political economy, the experience, and the longevity of captivity in New Mexico. Accordingly, Brooks states that "Beginning with an indigenous tradition of captive taking, and intensified by Spanish military and economic exploitation, the captive-exchange system developed as one important component of a borderlands political economy that produced conflict and coexistence. . . In New Mexico, Spanish and Indian men found that even more horses, guns, or hides, their counterparts valued women and children; and they established some nominal agreement that these would serve as objects and agents of intersocial exchange. . . Despite the exploitative quality of the captive-exchange system," Brooks continues, "its victims found ways to exercise agency and achieve some measure of security and comfort for themselves and their descendants."[19] In his introduction to "Andele: The Mexican Kiowa Captive," Brooks notes that "by the 1860s, more than 4,000 indios gentiles (heathen Indians) resided in New Mexican households and villages, they were identified as *indios de rescate* (ransomed Indians); *indios genízaros* (slaves), *criados* (servants) or *huérfanos* (orphans) primarily through the artifice of 'ransom' by colonial officials, meaning that they were taken captive... estimates of Mexican and white captives (and their descendants) resident in southern Plains tribes suggest they numbered between 10 and 20 percent of tribal populations."[20]

Though English and later, Euro-American women, left written narratives of captivity, Spanish-speaking women left their experiences, including those of captivity, in the form of oral traditions, including lullabies, stories and games women and other family members sang, taught, and played with children.

I sang "Los Inditos," (the little Indians), one of the lullabies with which my Tejana mother rocked me to sleep, long before I understood that it was about frontier warfare and conflict on the eighteenth- and nineteenth-century Texas-Mexican Border.

> Hay vienen los Inditos
> por el carrizal
> Ay mamita! ay papito!
> Me quieren matar!
>
> Compónte tu chimal
> y vámonos a pasear,
> Me ves que estoy enfermo

y no me puedo levantar

English Translation:

The little Indians are coming
through the canebreak
Oh, mommy! Oh, daddy!
They want to kill me

Hold up your round shield,
and let's go for a walk
You can see that I am ill,
and that I cannot get up

The lullaby refers to the border conflict between the Comanches and Spanish-Mexican settlers on the Rio Grande.[21] Years later, I heard the renowned Tejano folklorist, Américo Paredes, who had learned it from his mother, sing it. In both our families the lullaby was sung and passed on for generations. Very similar versions of this lullaby have been found in New Mexico and in other parts of the Northern Mexican frontier. New Mexican versions are usually titled "El Comanchito."[22] While all people on the frontier may be subject to captivity, women and children, those who could be most easily adopted, or incorporated into a new culture, were more generally taken captive.

In the tradition of the *romances fronterizos* (frontier ballads) of the Spanish/Islamic frontier, but here transformed into a new genre, called "Inditas,"(literally Indian maiden), captivity remains a salient theme. In "La Indita de Plácida Romero/Indita Ballad of Plácida Romero," from Cubero, New Mexico, Romero narrates her experience of being taken captive by the Gileño Apaches in the 1880s.[23]

According to ethnomusicologists, folklorists, anthropologists, and literary historians, "Inditas" are "a broad genre of songs thematically and musically evocative of Indo-Hispano relations."[24] In a gendered analysis of the genre, ethnomusicologist Brenda Romero argues that the Indita genre reinforces the idea of a feminine personification of land, a sacred as well as fertile landscape, a metaphorical borderland that shapes identity.[25]

La Indita de Plácida Romero[26]

El día de San Lorenzo
era un día poderoso
que me llevaron cautiva
y mataron a mi esposo

El año de ochenta y uno
cerca de las diéz del día
así sería yo pienso
cuando esto nos sucedía

Adíos ya me voy
voy a padecer.
Adíos mis queridas hijas,
cuando las volveré a ver?

Adíos Rancho de la Cebolla,
por que te muestras esquiva?
Los palos, las piedras lloran
de verme salir cautiva

Adíos ya me voy
voy a padecer.
Adíos mis queridas hijas,
cuando las volveré a ver?

English Translation:

The day of Saint Lawrence
was a powerful day
when they took me captive
and they killed my husband

In the year of eighty one,
close to ten in the morning,

that was when it was I think
when this happened to us

Farewell, I'll be gone
gone into suffering.
Farewell, my beloved daughters,
when will I see you again?

Farewell, La Cebolla Ranch
why have you turned away?
The trees, the rocks are weeping
to see me go into captivity

Farewell, I'll be gone
gone into suffering.
Farewell, my beloved daughters,
when will I see you again?

In addition to border conflict, lullabies also inscribe other dimensions of frontier realities, including interracial and intercultural unions not rooted in abduction and captivity. I have been unable to determine whether "Cimarroncita"/"Little Cimarron Child," a tender affirmation of racial mixture, is an anonymous lullaby or had a historical composer. This lullaby which sounds as if it is from a tropical region, or originates perhaps on the Florida or Louisiana frontier, was also among the lullabies my mother sang and passed on to me.

En una mañana de cocoteros
en una mañana del mes de abril
Me mecieron en un hamaca
hecha de plumas de colibrí

Mi padre era Mulato
mi madre Cheroqui
y yo una cimarroncita
desde que nací

English Translation:

In a morning of coconut palms
In a morning of April month
I was rocked in a hammock
made of hummingbird feathers

My father was Mulato
my mother, Cherokee
And I a little Cimarron child
since I was born

Was this the child of one of the maroon community that existed along the Spanish-English colonial frontiers? My research has yet to yield the origins of this lullaby.

Similarly, in "Duerme Duerme, Negrito," an African American mother lulls her child with promises of the tasty dishes she will bring him and with harsh dimensions of her daily work life. This lullaby, compiled by Argentinean folk singer Atahualpa Yupanqui, infused in African rhythms, is sung and passed on throughout the Americas, whose history of African and Indian slavery binds us as Americans.[27]

Duerme, duerme, negrito
Que tu mama está en el campo,
Negrito
Duerme, duerme, negrito
Que tu mama está en el campo,
negrito

Te va'traer codornices para ti,
Te va'traer rica fruta, para ti
Te va'traer muchas cosas para ti,

Y si negro no se duerme
viene el diablo blanco
Y zas, le come la patita

Chacapá, chacapá, chacapá

Duerme, duerme, negrito
Que tu mama está en el campo,

Trabajando duramente, trabajando
Trabajando y no le pagan, trabajando

Trabajando y va tosiendo, trabando

Duerme, duerme, negrito
Que tu mama está en el campo, negrito

Duerme, duerme, negrito
Que tu mama está en el campo, negrito

English Translation:

Sleep, sleep, little black one
For your mama is in the fields, little
black one

Sleep, sleep, little black one
For your mama's in the field, little
black one

She's going to bring quail for you
She's going to bring fresh fruit for you
She's going to bring many things for you

And if little black one does not go to sleep,
The white devil will come
And zap! He'll eat your little foot off
Chacapá, chacapá, chacapá

Sleep, sleep, little black one
For your mama's in the fields,

Working, working hard, working
Working, and they don't pay her, working

Working, and she is coughing, working

Sleep, sleep, little black one
For your mama's in the fields, little black one

Sleep, sleep, little black one
For your mama's in the field, little black one

Women's experiences on American frontiers and borderlands, and the
oral traditions within which historical memory is often embedded, offer us
another way of examining and understanding the history of the Americas
writ large. I have but recently returned to this research project on lullabies
and oral traditions on the Spanish-Mexican-US Borderlands that I began
several years ago. My effort is to take a comparative approach, incorporating lullabies and songs of women on the Islamic/Christian/Judaic
borderlands of medieval Spain and the US-Mexico borderlands in the
nineteenth century—as different cultures encountered each other under
conditions of war and conflict as well as those of cooperation and collaboration on frontiers of invasion, conquest, and re-conquest.

I close where I began, with the words of Trinh T. Minh-ha and the
opening lines her grandmother chanted before embarking on a story.
"Tell me and let me tell my hearers what I have heard from you, who
heard it from your mother and your grandmother, so that what is said
may be guarded and unfailingly transmitted to the women of tomorrow,
who will be our children and the children of our children."[28]

NOTES

1. Trinh T. Minh-ha, *Woman, Native, Other: Writing Postcoloniality and Feminism* (Bloomington: Indiana University Press, 2009), 121
2. Ibid.
3. The Sonoran Desert, where between 125-150 migrants crossing on foot to the US die annually, is an arid region covering 120,000 square miles in southwestern Arizona and southeastern California, as well as most of Baja California and the western half of the state of Sonora, Mexico. Subdivisions of this hot, dry region include the Colorado and Yuma deserts. Irrigation has produced many fertile agricultural areas, including the Coachella and Imperial valleys of California. www.desertusa.com/du_sonoran.html 7 June 2006.
4. Elizabeth Grosz, "Bodies and Knowledge: Feminism and the Crisis of Reason," in *Feminist Epistemologies*, eds. Linda Alcoff and Elizabeth Potter (New York: Routledge, 1993): 187-216 (188). See also: Diana Taylor, *The Archive and the Repertoire: Performing Cultural Memory in the Americas* (Durham: Duke University Press, 2003).
5. Ramona Houston, (1995) "Women Did it All: 19th Century Black Women in Brown County."(Unpublished)
6. Keith Cartwright, *Reading Africa into American Literature: Epics, Fables, and Gothic Tales* (Lexington: University of Kentucky Press, 2004): 40-41. See also: "The Language You Cry In: Story of a Mende Song," Inko, Audiovisual Productions, http://www.terra.es/personal/inkoak/entlyci.htm. Accessed 26 September 2008; "A Gullah Song in Mende," from Joseph A. Opala, *The Gullah: Rice, Slavery, and the Sierra Leone-American Connection*, http://www.yale.edu/glc/gullah/11.htm. Accessed 26 September 2008.
7. Linda Martin Alcoff, "Feminist Theory and Social Science: New Knowledge, New Epistemologies," in *Body Space: Destabilizing Geographies of Gender and Sexuality*, ed. Nancy Duncan (London and New York: Rutgers University Press, 1996): 13-27.
8. Emma Pérez, "Sexuality and Discourse: Notes from a Chicana Survivor," *Chicana Lesbians: The Girls Our Mothers Warned Us About*, ed. Carla Trujillo (Berkeley: Third Woman Press, 1989).
9. Deena J. González, "Speaking Secrets: Living Chicana Theory," in *Living Chicana Theory*, ed. Carla Trujillo (Berkeley: Third Woman Press, 1998):

46-72; Gloria Anzaldúa, *Borderlands/La Frontera: The New Mestiza* (San Francisco: Spinster/Aunt Lute Press, 1987); Cherríe Moraga, *Loving in the War Years: lo que nunca pasó por sus labios* (Boston: South End Press, 1983).

10. Chela Sandoval, *Methodology of the Oppressed* (Minneapolis: University of Minnesota Press, 2000).

11. Dorotea Valdez, Reminiscences, Monterey County, 27 June 1874. CE 65:8. California Pioneers, no. 8. Bancroft Library.

12. Leslie Daiken, *The Lullaby Book* (London: Edmund Ward, Ltd., 1959), 10.

13. Ibid., 13. and Brooks, "Introduction," in *Andele: The Mexican Kiowa Captive,* ed. J. J. Methvin (Albuquerque: University of New Mexico Press, 1996), 5

14. David William Foster, *The Early Spanish Ballad* (New York: Twayne Publishers, Inc., 1971), 94-95.

15. Marcelino J. Canino Salgado, *La Canción de Cuna en la Tradición de Puerto Rico* (San Juan, PR: Instituto de Cultura Puertorriqueña, 1970), 30. Translated by the author.

16. Ibid., 22.

17. Ibid., 100.

18. *"Moriana Cautiva,"* in *Flor Nueva de Romances Viejos,* 5th ed., ed. Ramón Menéndez Pidal, (Buenos Aires and Mexico City: Espasa-Calpe Argentina, 1943) 233-235; *"La Reina Xerifa Mora"* (*el Conde Flor o Hermanas Reina y Cautiva*) in *Romancero Judo-Español de Marruecos,* Paul Bénichou (Madrid: Editorial Castalia, 1968), 221.

19. James F. Brooks, "This Evil Extends Especially. . .to the Feminine Sex': Negotiating Captivity in the New Mexico Borderlands," in *Women and Gender in the American West,* eds. Mary Ann Irwin and James F. Brooks (Albuquerque: University of New Mexico Press, 2004), 160-182; quote p. 181. Estevan Rael-Gálvez, "Identifying Captivity and Capturing Identity: Narratives of American Indian Servitude, Colorado, and New Mexico, 1776-1934," (PhD diss., Ann Arbor, 2004). See also: James F. Brooks, *Captives and Cousins: Slavery, Kinship, and Community in the Southwest Borderlands* (Williamsburg: Omohundro Institute of Early American History and Culture, 2002).

20. Brooks, "This Evil Extends Especially... to the Feminine Sex," 164.

21. Américo Paredes, *A Texas-Mexican Cancionero: Folksongs of the Lower Border* (1976; reprint Austin: University of Texas Press, 1995).

22. Ibid.

23. "La Indita de Plácida Romero," in *Tesoros del Espíritu: A Portrait in Sound of Hispanic New Mexico*, eds. Enrique R. Lamadrid, Jack Loeffler, and Miguel Gandert, (Embudo, NM: El Norte/Academia Publications (1994), 31-33.

24. Enrique Lamadrid and Miguel A. Gandert, *Hermanitos Comanchitos: Indo-Hispano Rituals of Captivity and Redemption* (Albuquerque: University of New Mexico Press, 2003).

25. Brenda M. Romero, "The Indita Genre of New Mexico: Gender and Cultural Identification," in *Chicana Traditions: Continuity and Change*, eds. Norma E. Cantú and Olga Nájera Ramírez (Urbana and Chicago: University of Illinois Press, 2002), 56-80.

26. Excerpted from "La Indita de Plácida Romero," in *Tesoros del Espíritu: A Portrait in Sound of Hispanic New Mexico*, eds. Lamadrid, Loeffler and Gandert, 31-33.

27. Excerpted from "Duerme, Duerme Negrito," in Mercedes Sosa, *30 Años* (Argentina: PolyGram Discos, 1993), 18.

28. Minh-ha, *Woman, Native, Other.*

CHAPTER 10

"La Despedida"

"*Se murió Doña Chelo,*" I heard my mother say when Doña Fina opened the door.

"*Noooo. ¿Cómo? Ay, Virgen santísima. ¿Y la criatura. . .?*"

"*La salvaron.*"

"*¿Pero cómo, si todo iba bien? Todavía andaba trabajando en el jape. Le faltaba otra semana para aliviarse. ¿Qué pasó?*"

"*No sé. Doña Lupe está furiosa. Que la pobre de Chelo estaba hecha garras con tanto embarazo. Lupe culpa a Don Juan—que no le tuvo compasión. Pos, ya sabes. . .hombres brutos.*"

"*¿Y el entierro?*"

"*No sé. Están haciendo los arreglos. Vamos. Hay que ayudarle a Doña Lupe con preparar a Chelo para el velorio esta noche antes de que se la lleven a la funeraria. Tráete trapos limpios y alcohol si lo tienes. Ya les pedí sábanas a Zenaida y a Rosario. Diamantina mandó tres botellas de Agua Florida.*"

That was not the first time I saw death, who was not an infrequent visitor to the camp. Don Macedonio keeled over in the hop yard; Beto,

Martina's brother, died from a ruptured appendix soon after they arrived from Texas; Juanita's baby was stillborn. But it was the first time I saw the preparation of a body.

None of the families in camp had a table large enough to lay out Doña Chelo. My mother took me to ask the *mayordomo* to loan us the table from the cutting shed. It was big and crude, ten feet long with heavy square posts for legs. The top was full of deep cuts—gouged out over the years by women twine cutters.

"It's piled high with twine," the *mayordomo* said. "It's gritty and grimy. You can't possibly use it to lay her out."

"Dile que nosotros sabemos cómo la limpiamos, y que sí, sí la podemos usar," my mother instructed me.

She sent Don Tomás and my dad to hose the table down, to scrub it, and carry it to Doña Chelo's. They set it in one of the three rooms of her family's living quarters, where other hands had placed two big tubs of ice on a raised platform. The men set the table over the ice, which was to serve as refrigeration for Doña Chelo's body. They brought in two small tables and set one on each side of the twine-cutting table.

Doña Lupe walked in from the back room. She unfolded and smoothed two white sheets over the table, turned and nodded to the two men. All three walked into the back room.

My mother came in carrying four wash basins, towels, and bottles of alcohol in an asparagus crate. She covered the two little tables with towels, brought boiling water from the *tina* bubbling on the wood stove and nearly filled each basin. Slowly, she unwrapped several large bars of Ivory soap and set out the other items—the bottles of alcohol and *Agua Florida*, two boxes of *salarete*. She looked up and saw I was still in the room and quietly said:

"Anda vete pa' la casa. Vamos a preparar a Doña Chelo y no quiero que te asustes."

"No me asusto, mamá. Apoco no he visto muertitos. Me quiero quedar contigo. No molesto. Déjame que me quede. . . "

She looked at me for a while and finally said, "Anda, corre con la Luisa y dile que nos faltan toallas, que nos mande las que tenga. . . y otra sábana también."

I ran out the door to la Luisa's, who lived at the other end of the camp, to get more towels and another sheet. Big Luisa trailed behind me as I ran back with the towels. She wouldn't hear of my coming back by myself.

"Your mother shouldn't let you see such things," Luisa said. "What's the matter with her?"

We knocked on the door and walked in to see four women bent over Doña Chelo, laid out on her back, her long black hair cascading over the head of the table. The sound of quiet voices filled the room.

My mother turned, set down her wet cloth, and came toward me to take the basket of towels. She looked at me for a long hard minute then told me to sit quietly at the other end of the room; she would call me if she needed my help. The other women did not look up.

"Trae más agua," Doña Lupe said to Rosario, "y pónle más salarete a este bacín. Hay que lavarle bien las manos y los pies, hasta debajo de las uñas. Irene, báñate las manos y los brazos con alcohol antes de que empieces a lavarla, y bañen a esa niña también."

Doña Lupe silently handed Luisa and me large, square dishtowels to wrap our hair, like the other women, and said something to her. Luisa took a large-toothed comb, a hair brush, and several fingernail files out of the paper sack she was carrying and handed them to Doña Lupe. The bright pattern on my flour sack dishtowel was faded out, almost gone. I had an underslip my mother had made for me out of the same cloth. Luisa wrapped my head in the towel, then wrapped her own.

"Anduve pidiendo limas para las uñas por todos rumbos, pero sólo encontré tres," Luisa said to no-one in particular. She motioned me to come with her to bathe our hands and arms in alcohol. The alcohol was cool. It stung. Afterwards, I went to sit on the only chair in the room, and Luisa went to the table.

I looked at Doña Chelo laid out, arms now at her sides. The women surrounded the table so Doña Chelo was not completely visible to me. She was nude except for her genitals and breasts. These were covered with dishtowels which I recognized as my mother's because they were crocheted, edged in intricate spider web designs. The edges hung over the sides of the table, casting delicate shadows against the snowy white sheets.

My mother, Doña Irene, and Zenaida were on either side of Doña Chelo. They bathed her genitals, torso, arms, and hands. Doña Rosario bathed her legs and feet, Doña Fina her neck, face, and head. La Luisa would comb her hair when they finished washing the body. Doña Lupe moved among the four, supervising.

"Ay Chelo," said Zenaida, as she slightly wrung out the soft cotton cloth, leaned over and began, with gentle stroking motions, to bathe the upper left chest, "que la Virgen te acompañe. Como te vamos a echar de menos."

"Ay sí," someone else murmured. "Quién nos va a contar chistes cuando andemos empinadas en los surcos?"

"Miren como se le cicatrizó la cortada que se dió con el cuchillo cuando andábamos podando el *jape* el año pasado," my mother commented.

"N'ombre, no fue el año pasado, fue el antepasado," Rosario retorted. "Yo me acuerdo porque todavía no nacía mi Lula. Fue antes de salir pa' la pisca de la fresa."

And so I watched and listened as the five bathed Doña Chelo's body and mapped her life, and their own, by the physical traces of her scars, the dirt under her fingernails, the swollen breasts of childbirth, the calloused skin of poorly shod feet, the allure of swaying hips at a dance. I heard tears and laughter, rage at life and death, beauty in everyday truths, unknown depths of love and friendship in voices sometimes loud, sometimes barely audible.

In the silence of their touch and the deliberateness of their cleansing strokes I learned the ways of these Tejanas. I learned from these women of the *pueblos*, of "pueblos arrumbados... que Díos y la historia han olvidado," as my mother spoke of our south Texas homeland. Donna, Merced, Edinburg, Kingsville, Mission, Raymondville, Harlingen, Weslaco, McAllen—pueblos mapped on red ribbons of highway, the blood streams of migrant families. Pueblos of no work, pueblos of constant migration.

I was sent on an errand when they were about to clean Doña Chelo's genitals and to dress her. I came back in time to watch La Luisa brush her wavy hair in long, even strokes. There was some discussion about whether or not to apply make-up. They finally decided to do so since "Chelo era muy mona, siempre muy bien arreglada, con lipstick y todo." I was sent out again, this time to ask Juana for some *colorete* and lipstick that she would be willing to give up since it would have to be discarded.

The family sent a pretty print dress for Doña Chelo. It fit tight around her stomach, which was still bloated. Luisa braided Doña Chelo's hair, wound the two thick braids around her head, and arranged them neatly in place with large black *orquillas* she held between her teeth. She then applied a very light touch of rouge and lipstick. Someone had removed the half-dollar coins used to keep her eyes closed. As Luisa finished Doña Fina brought out a beautifully embroidered sheet to wrap Doña Chelo.

"Ay Fina," someone cried, "te costó tanto trabajo esa sábana, es la más bonita de todas y la vas a perder."

"Si, ya sé," she responded. "Pero a Chelo le gustaba mucho lo bonito." Then in an afterthought, she smiled, "Es que Chelo siempre me admiraba esta sábana."

They wrapped Doña Chelo tightly in Doña Fina's finely embroidered sheet. Then my mother brought out still another sheet for final covering, its edges, like those of the dishcloths, intricately crocheted. I remembered the sheet flapping in the morning breeze and how carefully my mother cleaned the clothesline with a wet cloth so it did not leave rust or dirt stains on the sheet when she hung it up to dry, when I heard Doña Lupe say

"Ya acabamos. Sólo nos queda recoger todo, limpiar el cuarto muy bien, y traer las sillas."

Doña Fina and Rosario each grabbed a handle of the galvanized metal washtub containing all the water used to bathe Doña Chelo and carried it outside as I helped my mother pack up the empty bottles of alcohol, the boxes of *salarete*, and all but one of the basins. La Luisa swept and mopped the floor while Zenaida cleaned the little tables and replaced the towels with white crocheted doilies. She put large white candles on small ceramic plates and set them on the two tables.

When all was cleaned to Doña Lupe's satisfaction, the women gathered around Doña Chelo. My mother motioned me to join her. We stood silently for a while, until Doña Lupe reached behind her for the basin with *Agua Florida*, the scented water used for spiritual cleansings, in which leaves of *yerba buena* were floating. She handed the basin to Rosario, put her hands over it, made the sign of the cross over the water and, dipping her right hand in it, begin to walk around, inside our circle, sprinkling Doña Chelo with one motion of her hand, and the women gathered around her with another motion. When she finished she put the basin, still over half full, on the floor under the table and rejoined the circle. My mother, who had a large paper sack in her hand, opened it and brought out the heavy cloth estampa of the Virgin of Guadalupe that hung on our wall. She laid it on the sheet, across Doña Chelo's chest. It covered the upper half of her body. We stood silently. Soon Doña Lupe began to intone the Ave María, to which all responded. After the prayer, Doña Lupe began singing the farewell song to the Guadalupana, her clear lilting voice filling the room. The women waited while she sang her farewell to Doña Chelo, then one by one they joined the song until they ended in unison.

Adíos o virgen de Guadalupe.

Adíos o madre del redentor.

Desde que niña nombrarte supe.

Eres mi vida, eres mi vida,

Mi gran amor.

Adíos madre querida,

Adíos, Adíos, Adíos

"Ya está lista Chelo," said Doña Lupe. "Traigan las sillas. Irene, por favor avísale a la familia que todo está en orden, y diles que aquí estamos para el velorio a la noche. Las rezadoras ya saben a qué hora llegar. Díganles a las vecinas que traigan bastante comida, arroz con comino, mole, frijoles de la olla, y café con leche condensada. A Chelo le gustaba mucho comer y hay que despedirla con buenos sabores. Coman fuerte porque mañana hay que madrugar y trabajar doble para poder ir al entierro el sábado. Si no sacamos todos esos surcos, no va a haber quien acompañe a Chelo."

I walked out with my mother into the late afternoon sunlight. Across the roadway, dancing shadows of heavily laden twining vines darkened the furrows of the hop yard. The pungent smell of ripening hops filled our nostrils, reminding us that the harvest was about to begin.

Conclusion to Three Decades of Engendering History

At UC, Berkeley in the 1970s, fewer than 500 Chicanos and Chicanas, graduate and undergraduate, attended the university—a university whose reputation was both liberal and trendsetting. Often, underrepresented minorities were able to find one another because we were so few. In most graduate departments, we were the first Mexican-origin admitted; on the entire campus, there was one pre-tenured faculty member. Stanford University was not in any better shape, as Antonia Castañeda would recite to our gatherings; other campuses in northern California were just awakening to the strange disjuncture between the state's honored Spanish-Mexican heritage and its failures to provide that ethnic group upward mobility through education. In the more Latino populated areas of southern California, and at UCLA where Emma Pérez received her undergraduate degree and enrolled in a graduate program, the gaps were also evident between our presence in academe and the demographic realities outside the university. As graduate students and undergraduates, we were forced to deal with this reality in whatever unstructured ways we could; organizing seemed a logical outcome.

Honestly, when we began meeting as a small cohort of Chicanas, when we began plotting strategy for completing what seemed like interminable graduate programs; when we began envisioning a re-articulation of our Chicana/mestiza pasts, we did not see a path to demonstrable results as an achievement for all of that hard work. Currently, we count well over forty-five dissertations on Chicanas in the field of history alone, plus many others in literature, education, the social sciences, and a few in the arts. Until 1987, book titles solely dedicated to Chicanas numbered *all of four*, in the 1970s, by Marta Cotera and Irene Blea, and in the late 1980s, by Gloria Anzaldúa and Vicki Ruiz. Where few books lined shelves, today more than fifty books are available on topics that cite and explore specifically the Chicana experience. Antonia Castañeda and I edit the current twenty-volume series, *Chicana Matters*, for the University of Texas Press. In an academic context, the books in the series are blockbuster sellers; some have sold out in three months, unheard of for academic audiences unless the writers have been Pulitzer Prize winners and the like.

Chicanas and other Latinas occupy more positions of influence than ever before which may or may not be saying much; in state legislatures, courtrooms, classrooms, university boards, corporate headquarters, Chicanas are still too few in number. If in the halls of Congress women will have to wait 500 years to achieve parity, at the current rate of growth, I shudder to think what Chicanas will have to wait to achieve equity in institutional life in the US. Yet we do not wait, we fight to create change. Our gains have not been dramatic, but they have been persistent. And the small but persistent gains are important celebratory junctures, and the writings and scholarly productivity of one is a testament to the work of all. Thus, these chapters and the remarks preceding each reflect the state of the field that Dr. Castañeda helped engineer and nurture across a near-half century career as an academic and as a practicing historian.

Antonia and I met on a summer day in Santa Barbara, at the apartment of a Chicana Stanford scholar on a dissertation fellowship at UCSB, one of the few, one of the first. This political scientist delighted in introducing Chicanas belonging to the small clubs of three or four (three in anthropology, perhaps four in history graduate programs in the entire country). I had followed up on the dissertation fellow's invitation to stop by on my way from the Bay Area to New Mexico. I was recently divorced and leading a fast life in San Francisco, coming out, leaving behind, and in general, doing what all my twenty-something friends at the time were doing—exploring myself. There were no lap top computers, no cell phones, no Facebook, and we had just begun to use answering machines connected to our telephones. Everything was clunky, our shoes, our technology, and our work.

To this chaotic, messy but progressive and transgressive environment, Antonia Castañeda's vision about history's purpose afforded elegance as well as a higher political goal, one of community and of affirming our support for one another's larger goals. Antonia began many of her conversations with the personal voice; it was, and is today, her passion. The preamble we drafted for our MALCS organization in the early 1980s opened with her stirring vision: "We are the daughters of Chicano working class families involved in higher education. We were raised in labor camps and barrios, where sharing our resources was the basis of survival."

Some of us were not from working class families, but our political values underscored solidarity, as did our support of the UFW, CISPES, and many other grassroots community organizations and movements. We were not one, coherent body, as the essays in this volume might suggest about those from the past, because we have never been of "one mind." But the generation from which Antonia Castañeda derived believes in examining and naming the points of departure, whether these fall within western US history, Chicano history, or US women's history. As the essays indicate, not being of a single or singular stance does not mean that historically, and as a group, we were or had not been singularly erased, universally rendered mostly invisible.

Unless as a *soldadera* (actually a *pistolera,* or gun-toting woman), or a prostitute, women of Mexican origin appeared only in the breach, within scandal, as intrigue, or as the saintly mother of a nation lying just to the south of the US-Mexico border. Rarely did the image of a full person, a human being with contradictions or complexity, emerge. And so much of Antonia's work, as with the work of others from our generation, was the work of excavation—excavation of women's lives and women's resistance. Antonia's essays set out to remedy one-dimensional and stereotyped portrayals of Chicanas, and to offer examples of women resisting victimization.

Recognizing them as victims proved an important step in many cases because of colonial/historical erasure. But like so many of us, Antonia Castañeda refused to leave them at that door. Instead, stories of the resisters' lives, stories of their efforts to make sense of racism and sexism, to move beyond social, political, and economic barriers, let alone cultural and religious ones, were woven into her many examples located in archives across the country, from the Bancroft to the Benson collections.

Hundreds of dissertations, books, volumes, anthologies, chapters, presentations, and MA theses later, we can trace this route toward greater visibility of Mexican-origin women directly back to Antonia Castañeda's pen and voice. Serving on juried prize committees, as she did, on journal and project boards, as she has, on theses' committees, or in PBS specials, her quest has been to never miss the Chicana voice, small though it might be in these important arenas. As we know today among the younger class of the professoriate and among young professionals, the costs of a PhD, an advanced professional degree, or of a job, are considerable. In the case of Professor Castañeda, the cost came in the form of completing a single-author book. Many giants in other fields have no sole-authored book, but have instead many essays and publications, short stories and published lectures, and seem not to miss the pinnacle of one's academic script. As paean, the authored monograph measures accomplishment, but it is also a status symbol. As the articles herein attest, it is sometimes not necessary because other times the contributions across varied fields, sub-fields, and arenas outweigh what a particular work accomplishes. In this case, the essays embody and symbolize life, that of an academic, that of a scholar-teacher, that of a mentor, that of a devoted agent of change and a seeker of historical justice.

These essays, without exaggeration, toil the fields. Just as Antonia Castañeda and her family did in the late 1940s and early 1950s, as members of migrant labor caravans and agricultural field workers, the goal of these articles is to turn the soil, pick the ripe vegetables and fruit. To this day, Castañeda hates cucumbers, they being some of the most difficult vegetables to harvest. To this day, as these essays reflect, that labor of recovering the voices of people closest to the soil remains a consistent thread in her work, whether of women working the missions of California or the children translating for their parents in official institutional settings the heavy vocabularies of the law or of science, as she did for her mother and for the other workers in the camps where they lived. How do you say, "If she does not use her inhaler, she might choke?" The translation into Spanish instead told the mother in this case that if she did not take the medicine, she would die. The fear or terror of seeing people in distress and far from a medical center that might save a life engendered in Professor Castañeda an abiding interest in people's humanity and survival, but also in the part of the story that lay untold, missing altogether. In the mission system of Alta California, for example, the focus in previous histories might fall on the number of candles produced by the indigenous women, or the mission gardens and food preparation. The friars retained excellent ledgers. But, Castañeda reminded us, that was just the beginning of the story. Who were these women? What did they suffer, endure, and survive? Refusing to portray them as victims, Castañeda also refused to ignore their victimization, their terror, or fright. As the basis of their political acumen, their survival instincts and community-driven spirit kept many indigenous women, and later, Spanish-Mexican, mixed-race women alive in the face of organized colonization.

The essays suggest a method: to tell a full or better story, we must walk in the shoes of these ancestors and imagine their struggles, victories, and grief, as well as their humor and commiseration. The whole human being, not just the political or laboring one, not just the gendered one, not just the rich or poor one, not just the worshipping or non-worshipping one, nothing less is important to the history Antonia Castañeda seeks to reveal. Because the essays are not just path-breaking but also part of her legacy, I have chosen to render a conclusion by naming her purpose. An historian's motives are rarely of much deep interest: to right the record, to insert into the record, to say we were present; to be sure, all are admirable and motivational. But to pursue a vision based on what is missing or misunderstood is a far more difficult task than simply restoring Chicanas to history. Chicanas were never really lost to or in history; their ancestors were awaiting discovery or unmasking more than anything. The archives in almost all regions of the southwest, far west, and other areas of the country are filled with cases, mention, and documentation about women's presence, extending as far back as some of the earliest sketches drawn when Europeans first arrived on these continents. Malinche, or Malintzín Tenepal, the woman interpreter to Cortés and Moctezuma, is depicted exactly in the middle between the two playing out a role as translator, her children certified as "of Spanish blood."

Our ability to reason with Chicana absence in its earliest written forms, to square it away against so many books about men and their heroics, was something Professor Castañeda's initial and later work remedied. The pattern this collection details is enviable and applicable across many terrains, as recovery projects and methodologies increasingly take up an important place at historians' gatherings. One purpose of the recovered stories or documents is to share them so that the field grows and changes; as more is known about women in colonial or postcolonial California, or New Mexico, Texas, Colorado, or Arizona, for example, more grants and funding will presumably allow for even greater explorations. The work is not done—our work is not done.

The key to this exploration, recovery, and historical analysis lies in support—in having money and time, particularly for travel and for research assistance in the academy. Many of us, from my generation— from Antonia's generation—have devoted our time to the recruitment and teaching of undergraduates; this is important work. Yet the work of exploration, recovery and analysis is incomplete, and the support for accomplishing the task remains inadequate. Only with a large and funded cadre of individuals devoted to the restoration of Chicanas to history, as Antonia Castañeda argues in these essays, will a story worthy of its principals emerge. And so the battles continue, for support, for resources, to excavate, decolonize, "write Chicanas into history." We have faith in the next generation to continue the work, as we all struggle for the resources to write the stories.

Deena J. González

Loyola Marymount University

PERMISSIONS ACKNOWLEDGMENTS

The editors gratefully acknowledge the following presses for their kind permission to reprint the works below:

Castañeda, Antonia. "The Political Economy of Nineteenth Century Stereotypes of Californianas." In *Between Borders: Essays on Mexicana/ Chicano History,* ed. Adelaida R. Del Castillo. Los Angeles: Floricanto, 1990. Republished by permission of Floricanto Press/Inter American Development Corporation.

Castañeda, Antonia. "Women of Color and the Rewriting of Western History: The Discourse, Politics and Decolonization of History" *Pacific Historical Review* Vol. 61, No. 4, Western Women's History Revisited (Nov., 1992): 501-533. © 1992 by the Regents of the University of California. Republished by permission of the University of California Press.

Castañeda, Antonia. "Sexual Violence in the Politics and Policies of Conquest: Amerindian Women and the Spanish Conquest of Alta California," *Building with Our Hands: New Directions in Chicana Studies* edited by Adela de la Torre, Beatríz M. Pesquera. University of California Press: Berkeley, 1993 (15-33). © 1994 by the Regents of the University of California. Republished by permission of the University of California Press.

Castañeda, Antonia. "Engendering the History of Alta California, 1769-1848: Gender, Sexuality and the Family," *California History,* Vol. 76, No. 2/3, Contested Eden: California before the Gold Rush (Summer–Fall, 1997): 230–259. © 1997 by the Regents of the University of California. Republished by permission of the University of California Press.

Castañeda, Antonia. "Gender, Race, and Culture: Spanish-Mexican Women in the Historiography of Frontier California." *Frontiers: A Journal of Women Studies* 11 (1990): 8–20. Republished by permission of the University of Nebraska Press.

Castañeda, Antonia. "'Que Se Pudieran Defender': Chicanas Regional History and National Discourses." *Frontiers: A Journal of Women Studies* Vol. 22, No. 3 *Women's West* (2001): 116–142. Republished by permission of the University of Nebraska Press.

Castañeda, Antonia. "Language and Other Lethal Weapons: Cultural Politics and the Rites of Children as Translators of Culture." In *Mapping Multiculturalism*. Edited by A.V. Gordon and C. Newfield. Minneapolis, MN: University of Minnesota Press, 1996. Republished by permission of the University of Minnesota Press.

Castañeda, Antonia. "La Despedida," *La Voz de Esperanza*, 18 no. 9 (November 2005): 5-7. Republished by permission of *La Voz de Esperanza*, Esperanza Peace and Justice Center, San Antonio, Texas.

Castañeda, Antonia. "Malinche, Calafia y Toypurina: Of Myths, Monsters and Embodied History." In *Feminism, Nation and Myth: La Malinche*. Eds. Rolando Romero and Amanda Harris. Houston, Tex.: Arte Público Press, 2005. Republished by permission of Arte Público Press, Houston, Texas.

BIBLIOGRAPHY

ARCHIVES:

Archives of the State of California

    Records of the Land Grant Commission

Bancroft Library, Berkeley, California

    Archives of California, 63 vols.

    Archivo General de la Nación, Provincias Internas

    Bale Family Papers

    California Pioneers

    Copias de varios documentos en la Parroquia de Monterrey, Parroquia de Monterrey

    Provincial State Papers, Benicia Military

    Memorias de Doña Apolinaria Lorenzana

    M. G. Vallejo Collection

    Rosalia Vallejo de Leese, "History of the Bear Flag Party"

Mission of San Carlos Borromeo, Monterey, California

Mission of Santa Barbara, Santa Barbara, California

Office of the Monterey County Clerk, Salinas, California,

    Mexican Archives, Civil Records, 1821-1848

    Mexican Archives of Monterey County, Criminal Court Records

INTERVIEWS:

Castañeda, Antonia I., Emma Pérez and Deena González. Pasadena, California, March 2011. Interview by Luz María Gordillo.

Castañeda, Antonia I. Crystal City, Texas. November, 2011. Interview by Luz María Gordillo.

Castañeda, Antonia I. and Tomás Ybarra-Frausto. San Antonio, Texas, November, 2011. Interview by Luz María Gordillo.

Castañeda, Irene R., Romana Raquel Rodríguez's daughter. Union Gap, Washington. March, 1976. Interview by Antonia Castañeda.

Sierra, Victoria Archuleta, Juanita Zazueta Huerta, Felicitas Pérez García, and Rita Pérez, part of the collection of the Idaho Hispanic Oral History Project. In *Voces Hispanas,* http://2222.state.id.us/icha/ Events/ voceshis.htm.

Gamboa, Erasmo. "The Roots of Mexican American History," and "Notes Toward a History of Idaho's Hispanic Elderly," In *Voces Hispanas,* an electronic report of the Idaho Commission on Hispanic Affairs. http://www2.state.id.us/icha/Events/voceshis.htm.

BOOKS, ARTICLES, DISSERTATIONS, PAPERS:

Abascal, Anita. "Parteras, Llaveras y Maestras: Women in Provincial California." paper presented at the Conference of the West Coast Association of Women Historians, Los Angeles, California, May, 1976.

Acosta, Teresa Palomo and Ruth Weingarten. *Las Tejanas: 3000 Years of History.* Austin:University of Texas Press, 2003.

Acuña, Rodolfo. *Occupied America: The Chicano's Struggle Toward Liberation.* San Francisco: Canfield Press, 1972.

———."The Struggles of Class and Gender: Current Research in Chicano Studies." *Journal of American Ethnic History* 8 (Spring 1989) 134–38.

Adams, David Wallace. *Education for Extinction: American Indians and the Boarding School Experience, 1875–1928.* Lawrence: University Press of Kansas, 1997.

Adams, Henry. *Historical Essays*. New York: Charles Scribner's Sons, 1891.

Agonito, Rosemary. *History of Ideas on Women: A Sourcebook*. New York: Perigee Brooks, 1977.

Alarcón, Norma. "Chicana Feminism: In the Tracks of 'The' Native Woman." *Cultural Studies* 4 (October, 1990): 248–256.

———. "Traductora, Traditora: A Paradigmatic Figure of Chicana Feminism." *Cultural Critique* (1990): 57–87.

Alberro, Solange. "Herejes, brujas, y beatas: Mujeres ante el Tribunal del Santo Oficio de la Inquisición en la Nueva España." In *Presencia y transparencia*. Ed. Escandón. México: El Colegio de México, 1987.

Albers, Patricia. "Autonomy and Dependency in the Lives of Dakota Women: A Study in Historical Change." *Review of Radical Political Economics* 17 (Fall 1985): 109-134.

Albers, Patricia, and Beatrice Medicine, eds. *The Hidden Hay: Studies of Plains Indian Women*. New York: University Press of America, 1983.

Alcoff, Linda Martin. "Feminist Theory and Social Science: New Knowledge, New Epistemologies." In *Body Space: Destabilizing Geographies of Gender and Sexuality,* ed. Nancy Duncan. London and New York: Rutgers University Press, 1996.

Allen, Paula Gunn. *Spider Women's Granddaughters: Traditional Tales and Contemporary Writing by Native American Women*. New York: Fawcett Columbine, 1989.

———. *Grandmothers of the Light: A Medicine Woman's Sourcebook*. Boston: Beacon Press, 1991.

———. *The Sacred Hoop: Recovering the Feminine in American Indian Traditions*. Boston: Beacon Press, 1992.

Allen, Barbara and Thomas J. Schlereth. *Sense of Place: American Regional Cultures*. Lexington: University of Kentucky, 1990.

Alloula, Malek. *The Colonial Harem*. Trans. Myrna Godzich and Wlad Godzich. Minneapolis: University of Minnesota, 1986.

Almaguer, Tomas. *Interpreting Chicano History: The "World-System" Approach to 19th Century California,* Working Paper Series 101, Institute for the Study of Social Change, Berkeley, Calif., 1977.

Alonso, Ana María. *Thread of Blood: Colonialism, Revolution, and Gender on Mexico's Northern Frontier.* Tucson: University of Arizona Press, 1955.

Alvarez, Roberto Jr. *Familia: Migration and Adaption in Baja and Alto California, 1800-1975.* Berkeley Los Angeles, London: University of California Press, 1987.

Anderson, Benedict. *Imagined Communities: Reflections on the Origin and Spread of Nationalism.* London: Verso Press, 1983.

Anderson, Karen. *Chain Her By One Foot: The Subjugation of Native Women in Seventeenth-Century New France.* New York: Routledge, 1991.

Anzaldúa, Gloria. *Borderlands/La Frontera: The New Mestiza.* San Francisco: Aunt Lute Press, 1987.

———. ed. *Making Face, Making Soul: Haciendo Caras.* San Francisco: Aunt Lute Books,1990.

Apodaca, Maria Linda. "The Chicana Woman: An Historical Materialist Perspective." *Latin American Perspectives* 4 no.1/2 (Spring 1977): 70-89.

Armitage, Susan. "Women and Men in Western History: A Stereotypical Vision." *The Western Historical Quarterly* 16 (October 1985): 381–95.

Armitage, Susan, and Elizabeth Jameson, eds. *The Women's West.* University of Oklahoma, 1987.

Aroyo, Laura E. "Industrial and Occupational Distribution of Chicana Workers." *Aztlán* 4 no.2 (Fall 1973): 343-382.

Arrom, Sylvia M. *The Women of Mexico City, 1790–1857.* Stanford: Stanford University Press, 1985.

Ashcroft, Bill, Gareth Griffiths, and Helen Tiffin, eds. *The Empire Writes Back: Theory and Practice in Post-Colonial Literatures.* New York: Routledge, 1989.

Asian Women United of California, ed. *Making Waves: An Anthology by and about Asian American Women.* Boston: Beacon Press, 1989.

Ayers, Edward L. et al. *All over the Map: Rethinking American Regions.* Baltimore: Johns Hopkins University Press, 1996.

Bacon, Walter. "Value of a Historical Society." *Historical Society of Southern California Publications* 4 (1899): 237–42.

Bailey, L. R. *Indian Slave Trade in the Southwest: A Study of Slave-taking and the Traffic in Indian Captives.* Los Angeles: Westernlore Press, 1966.

Bancroft, Hubert Howe. *California Pastoral, 1769–1848.* San Francisco: The History Company, 1888.

———. *History of California.* San Francisco: H. H. Bancroft & Company, 1885.

Bannon, John Francis. *The Spanish Borderlands Frontier, 1531–1821.* New York: Holt, Rinehart, and Winston, 1970.

———. *Herbert Eugene Bolton: The Historian and the Man.* Tucson: University of Arizona Press, 1978.

Barrera, Mario. *Race and Class in the Southwest.* Notre Dame: University of Notre Dame Press, 1979.

Barton, Bruce Walter. *The Tree at the Center of the World: A Study of the California Missions.* Santa Barbara: Ross-Erickson Publications, 1980.

Bataille, Gretchen M., and Kathleen Mullen Sands, eds. *American Indian Women: Telling Their Lives.* Lincoln: University of Nebraska, 1984.

Beasley, Delilah L. *The Negro Trail Blazers of California.* 1919; New York: Book Jungle, 1969.

Beeler, Madison S., ed. *The Ventureno Confesionario of José Senan, O. EM. U of California Publication in Linguistics* 47. Berkeley: University of California, 1967.

Beesley, David. "From Chinese to Chinese American: Chinese Women and Families in a Sierra Nevada Town." *California History* 67 (1988): 168-179.

Behar, Ruth. "Sex and Sin, Witchcraft, and the Devil in Late Colonial Mexico." *American Ethnologist* 14 (February 1987): 34-54.

———. "The Visions of a Guachichil Witch in 1599: A Window on the Subjugation of Mexico's Hunter-Gatherers." *Ethnohistory* 34 (Spring 1987): 115-138.

Beilharz, Edwin A. *Felipe de Neve: First Governor of California.* San Francisco: California Historical Society, 1971.

Bénichou, Paul. *Romancero Judo-Español de Marruecos.* Madrid: Editorial Castalia, 1968.

Billington, Ray Allen. *America's Frontier Heritage.* New York: Holt, Rinehart, and Winston, 1966.

Billington, Ray Allen, ed. *The Frontier Thesis: Valid Interpretation of American History?* 1966. Reprint, New York: Robert E. Krieger Publishing Company, 1977.

Blackmar, Frank W. *Spanish Institutions in the Southwest.* 1891. Reprint, Glorieta, N.M.: Rio Grande Press, 1976.

Blackwell, Maylei. *¡Chicana Power! Contested Histories of Feminism in the Chicano Movement.* Austin: University of Texas Press, 2011.

Blackwood, Evelyn."Sexuality and Gender in Certain Native American Tribes: The Case of Cross-Gender Females." *Signs: Journal of Women in Society and Culture* 10 (1984): 27-42.

Bobb, Bernard E. *The Viceregency of Antonio María Bucareli in New Spain, 1771-1779.* Austin: University of Texas Press, 1962.

Bolton, Herbert Eugene. *The Spanish Borderlands: A Chronicle of Old Florida and the Southwest.* New Haven, Conn.: Yale University Press, 1921.

———. Trans. and ed. *Anza's California Expeditions,* 5 vols. Berkeley: University of California Press, 1930.

———. Trans. and ed. *Font's Complete Diary: A Chronicle of the Founding of San Francisco.* Berkeley: University of California Press, 1931.

———. *Wider Horizons of American History.* 1930. Reprint, New York: D. Appleton-Century Company, 1939.

———. "The Epic of Greater America." *American Historical Review* 38 (April 1933): 448-74.

Bouvier, Virginia Marie. *Women and the Conquest of California, 1542-1840: Codes of Silence.* Tucson: University of Arizona, 2001.

———. "Women, Conquest, and the Production of History: Hispanic California, 1542-1840." Ph.D. diss., University of California, Berkeley, 1995.

Boxer, Marilyn J. "For and about Women: The Theory and Practice of Women's Studies in the United States." In *Feminist Theory: A Critique of Ideology*, eds. Nannerl O. Keohane, Michelle Z. Rosaldo, and Barbara C. Gelpi. Chicago: University of Chicago Press, 1982.

Brady, Victoria, Sarah Crome, and Lyn Reese. "Resist! Survival Tactics of Indian Women," *California History* 63 (1984):140-149.

Brinckerhoff, Sidney B. and Odie B. Faulk. *Lancers for the King: A Study of the Frontier Military System of Northern New Spain, with a Translation of the Royal Regulations of 1772.* Phoenix: Arizona Historical Foundation, 1965.

Brook, Barbara. *Feminist Perspectives on the Body.* London and New York: Longman, 1999.

Brooks, James F. *Captives and Cousins: Slaves, Kinship and Community in the Spanish Borderlands.* Chapel Hill: University of North Carolina Press, 2002.

———. "'This Evil Extends Especially. . .to the Feminine Sex': Negotiating Captivity in the New Mexico Borderlands." In *Women and Gender in the American West*, eds. Mary Ann Irwin and James F. Brooks. Albuquerque: University of New Mexico Press, 2004.

Brown, Dee. *The Gentle Tamers: Women of the Old Wild West.* New York: Bantam Books, 1974.

Brown, Kathleen M. "Brave New Worlds: Women's and Gender History." *William and Mary Quarterly* 50 (April 1993): 311-328.

Brownmiller, Susan. *Against Our Will: Men, Women and Rape.* 1975. Reprint, New York, London: Bantam Books, 1976.

Broyles-González, Yolanda ed. *Re-Emerging Native Women of the Americas: Native Chicana Latina Women's Studies.* Dubuque IA: Kendall/ Hunt Publishing Company, 2001.

Buhle, Mari Jo, Ann D. Gordon and Nancy Schrom. "Women in American Society: An Historical Contribution." *Radical America* 5 (July-August 1971): 3-66.

Buss, Fran Leeper. *Forged under the Sun: The Life Story of Maria Elena Lucas.* Ann Arbor: University of Michigan Press, 1993.

Butler, Anne M. *Daughters of Joy, Sisters of Misery: Prostitutes in the American West, 1865-90.* Urbana: University of Chicago Press, 1987.

———."Still in Chains: Black Women in Western Prisons, 1865-1910." *Western Historical Quarterly* 20 (1989):19-36.

Butler, Jonella. "Difficult Dialogues." *Women's Review of Books* 6 (February 1989): 16.

Callcot, George. *History in the United States, 1800–1860: Its Practices and Purpose.* Baltimore and London: The John Hopkins Press, 1970.

Camarillo, Albert. *Chicanos in a Changing Society: From Mexican Pueblos to American Barrios in Santa Barbara and Southern California, 1848–1930.* Cambridge: Harvard University Press, 1979.

———. *Chicanos in California: A History of Mexican Americans in California.* San Francisco: Boyd and Fraser Publishing Company, 1984.

Campbell, Leon G. "The First Californios: Presidial Society in Spanish California, 1760-1822." In *The Spanish Borderlands: A First Reader*, ed. Oakah L. Jones, Jr. Los Angeles: Lorrin L. Morrison, 1974.

Candelaria, Cordelia. "La Malinche, Feminist Prototype." In *Chicana Leadership: The Frontiers Reader*, eds. Yolanda Flores Niemann, et al. Lincoln and London: University of Nebraska, 2002.

Carby, Hazel V. "White Woman Listen: Black Feminism and the Boundaries of Sisterhood." In Center for Contemporary Cultural Studies, *The Empire Strikes Back: Race and Racism in Seventies Britain.* London: Hutchinson, 1982.

Carmichael, Stokley. *Black Power: The Politics of Liberation in America.* New York: Vintage, 1967.

Carpenter, Virginia L. *The Ranchos of Don Pacifico Ontiveros.* Santa Ana, Calif.: Friis Pioneer Press, 1982.

Carroll, Berenice A., ed. *Liberating Women's History: Theoretical and Critical Essays.* Urbana: University of Chicago Press, 1976.

Cartwright, Keith. *Reading Africa into American Literature: Epics, Fables, and Gothic Tales.* Lexington: University of Kentucky Press, 2004.

Casas, María Raquél. *Married to a Daughter of the Land: Spanish-Mexican Women and Interethnic Marriage in California, 1820-1880.* Reno: Nevada, 2007.

Castañeda, Antonia. "Comparative Frontiers: The Migration of Women to Alta California and New Zealand." In *Western Women: Their Land, Their Lives,* eds. Lillian Schlissel, Vicki L. Ruiz, and Janice Monk. Albuquerque: University of New Mexico, 1988.

———. "The Political Economy of Nineteenth Century Stereotypes of Californianas." In *Between Borders: Essays on Mexicana/ Chicano History,* ed. Adelaida R. Del Castillo. Los Angeles: Floricanto, 1990.

———. "Gender, Race, and Culture: Spanish-Mexican Women in the Historiography of Frontier California." *Frontiers: A Journal of Women Studies* 11 (1990): 8-20.

———. "Sexual Violence in the Politics and Policies of Conquest: Amerindian Women and the Spanish Conquest of Alta California." In *Building with Our Hands: New Directions in Chicana Studies,* eds. Adela de la Torre and Beatriz M. Pesquera. Berkeley: University of California, 1993.

———. "Language and Other Lethal Weapons: Cultural Politics and the Rites of Children as Translators of Culture." In *Mapping Multiculturalism,* eds. A. V. Gordon and C. Newfield. Minneapolis: University of Minnesota Press, 1996.

———. "Engendering the History of Alta California, 1769-1848: Gender, Sexuality, and the Family." In *Contested Eden: California before the Gold Rush,* eds. Ramón A. Gutiérrez and Richard J. Orsi. Berkeley: University of California, 1997.

———. "Witchcraft on the Spanish-Mexican Borderlands." In *The Reader's Companion to U.S. Women's History*, eds. Wilma Mankiller, et al. New York: Houghton Mifflin Company, 1998.

———."'Que Se Pudieran Defender': Chicanas Regional History and National Discourses." *Frontiers: A Journal of Women Studies* 22, no. 3 Women's West (2001): 116-142.

———. "Comino Chronicles: A Tale of Tejana Migration." *Chicana/Latina Studies* 9 no. 1 (Fall 2009).

———. "Marriage: The Spanish Borderlands." In *Encyclopedia of the North American Colonies*, eds. Jacob Ernest Cooke, et al. 3 vols. New York: Charles Scribner's Sons, 1993.

———. "Presidarias y Pobladoras: Spanish-Mexican Women in Frontier Monterey, Alta California, 1770-1821." Ph.D. diss., Stanford University, 1990.

———. "Amazonas, Brujas, and Fandango Dancers: Women's Sexuality and the Politics of Representation on the Borderlands." Paper presented at the American Historical Association Annual Conference , January 1995.

Castañeda, Antonia, Tomás Ybarra-Frausto, and Joseph Sommers, eds. *Literatura Chicana: texto y contexto*. Englewood Cliffs: Prentice-Hall, 1972.

Castañeda, Irene. "Cronica de Cristal"/Chronicle of Cristal." *El Grito* 4, no. 2 (Winter 1971): 42-52.

Castillo, Edward D., ed., *Native American Perspectives on the Hispanic Colonization of Alta California, Spanish Borderlands Sourcebook 26*. New York: Garland, 1991.

———. Trans. and ed. "The Assassination of Padre Andres Quintana by the Indians of Mission Santa Cruz in 1812: The Narrative of Lorenzo Asisara." *California History* 68 (fall 1989): 117-25.

Caughey, John W. "Herbert Eugene Bolton." In *Turner/Bolton/Webb: Three Historians of the American Frontier*, ed. Wilbur Jacobs, John W Caughey, and Joe B. Frantz. Seattle: University of Washington Press, 1965.

Caughey, John W."The Insignificance of the Frontier in American History." *Western Historical Quarterly* 5 (1974): 6-15.

Chai, Alice Y. "Toward a Holistic Paradigm for Asian American Women's Studies: A Synthesis of Feminist Scholarship and Women of Color's Feminist Politics." *Women's Studies International Forum* 8 (1985): 59-66.

Chapman, Charles E. *A History of California: The Spanish Period.* New York: The Macmillan Company, 1930.

Chartkoff, Joseph L. and Kerry Kona Chartkoff. *Archaeology of California.* Stanford: Stanford University Press,1984.

Chávez-García, Miroslava. *Negotiating Conquest: Gender and Power in California, 1770s to 1880s.* Tucson: University of Arizona Press, 2004.

———. "The Interdisciplinary Project of Chicana History: Looking Back, Moving Forward." *Pacific Historical Review* 82, no. 4 (Nov. 2013): 542-565.

Chávez, John. *The Lost Land: The Chicano Image of the Southwest.* Albuquerque: University of New Mexico Press, 1984.

Cheng, Lucie and Edna Bonacich, eds. *Labor Immigration under Capitalism: Asian Workers in the United States before World War II.* Berkeley: University of California Press, 1984.

Chilcote, Ronald H. *Dependency and Marxism: Towards a Resolution of the Debate.* Boulder, CO: Westview Press, 1982.

Chilcote, Ronald H., and Joel C. Edelstein, eds. *Latin America: The Struggle with Dependency and Beyond.* New York: John Wiley and Sons, 1974.

Chow, Esther Ngan-Ling. "The Feminist Movement: Where Are All the Asian American Women?" In *Making Waves: An Anthology of Writings by and about Asian Women,* ed. Asian Women United of California. Boston: Beacon Press, 1989.

Christian, Barbara. "The Race for Theory." *Feminist Studies* 14 (1988): 67–70.

Clappe, Louise A. K. S. (Dame Shirley). *The Shirley Letters. 1854–1855;* reprint Santa Barbara and Salt Lake City: Peregrine Smith, Inc., 1970.

Clark, Harry. "Their Pride, Their Manners, and Their Voices: Sources of the Traditional Portrait of Early Californians." *California Historical Review* 52 (Spring 1974): 71-82.

Clark, Sydney A. *Golden Tapestry of California.* New York: Robert M. McBride and Company, 1937.

Clifford, James. *The Predicament of Cultures.* Cambridge: Harvard University Press, 1988.

Cohen, Roberta, and Francis M. Deng, eds. *The Forsaken People: Case Studies of the Internally Displaced.* Washington DC: Brookings Institution Press, 1998.

Commeyras, Michelle, et al. "Why Feminist Theory and Literacy Research?: Four Responses." *Reading Research Quarterly* 31, no. 4 (1996): 458 68.

Committee on Women Historians. *Guidelines on Hiring Women Historians in Academia.* 3rd ed., Washington, D.C.: American Historical Association, 1990.

Conrad, Susan Phinney. *Perish the Thought: Intellectual Women in Romantic America, 1830-1860.* New York: Oxford University Press, 1976.

Cooey, Paula M. *Religious Imagination and the Body: A Feminist Analysis.* New York and Oxford: Oxford University, 1994.

Cook, Sherburne F. *The Population of the California Indians, 1769-1970.* Berkeley: University of California Press, 1976.

———. *Conflict between the California Indian and White Civilization.* Berkeley and Los Angeles: University of California Press, 1976.

Cook, Sherburne F., and Woodrow Borah. *Essays in Population History: Mexico and the Caribbean.* 3 vols. Berkeley: University of California Press, 1971-1979.

Córdova, Teresa, et al., eds. *Chicana Voices: Intersections of Class Race, and Gender 1986.* Albuquerque: University of New Mexico Press, 1990.

Corwin, Arthur. "Mexican American History: An Assessment." Pacific Historical Review 42 (August 1973): 269-308.

Cotera, María. Epilogue to *Caballero: A Historical Novel*, by Jovita González and Eve Raleigh. College Station: Texas A&M University Press, 1996.

Craver, Rebecca McDowell. *The Impact of Intimacy: Mexican-Anglo Intermarriage in New Mexico, 1821-1846*. El Paso: Southwestern Studies, 1982.

Crawford, Kathleen. "María Amparo Ruíz de Burton: The General's Lady." *Journal of San Diego History* 30 (Summer 1984): 198–211.

Creed, Barbara. *The Monstrous Feminine: Film, Feminism, Psychoanalysis*. New York: Routledge, 1993.

Cronon, William, et al. "Women and the West: Rethinking the Western History Survey Course." *The Western Historical Quarterly* 17 (July 1986): 269–90.

Czarnowski, Lucille K. *Dances of Early California Days*. Palo Alto: Pacific Books, 1950.

Daiken, Leslie. *The Lullaby Book*. London: Edmund Ward, Ltd., 1959.

Dakin, Susanna Bryant. *Rose, or Rose Thorn? Three Women of Spanish California*. Berkeley: The Friends of the Bancroft Library, 1963.

———. ed. *A Scotch Paisano: Hugo Reid's Life in California, 1832–1852*. Berkeley: University of California, 1939.

———. *The Lives of William Hartnell*. Stanford, CA: Stanford University Press, 1949.

Dana, Richard Henry Jr. *Two Years Before the Mast*. New York: Harper & Brothers, 1840. Reprint, New York: Airmont Publishing Company, 1965.

Daniel, Cletus E. *Bitter Harvest: A History of California Farmworkers, 1870-1941*. Ithaca, N Y: Cornell University Press, 1981.

Daniels, Roger. *Concentration Camps USA: Japanese Americans and World War II*. New York: Holt, Rinehart, and Winston, 1971.

Davis, Angela Y. *With My Mind on Freedom: An Autobiography*. New York, 1974.

———. *Women, Race, and Class*. New York: Random House, 1981.

———. "Gender, Class, and Multiculturalism: Rethinking 'Race' Politics." In *Mapping Multiculturalism*, eds. Avery F. Gordon and Christopher Newfield. Minneapolis: University of Minnesota Press, 1996.

Davis, W. N., Jr. "Will the West Survive as a Field in American History?" *Mississippi Valley Historical Review* 50 (1964):672-685.

de la Torre, Adela, and Beatriz Pesquera. *Building with Our Hands: New Directions in Chicana Scholarship.* Berkeley: University of California, 1993.

de Lauretis, Teresa. *Technologies of Gender: Essays on Theory, Film, and Fiction.* Bloomington: Indiana University Press, 1987.

———, ed. *Feminist Studies/Critical Studies.* Bloomington: Indiana University Press, 1986.

de León, Arnoldo. *Mexican Americans in Texas: A Brief History.* Arlington Heights, IL: Harlan Davidson, 1993.

———. *They Called them Greasers: Anglo Attitudes toward Mexicans in Texas, 1821-1900.* Austin: University of Texas Press, 1983.

———. "Whither Borderlands History? A Review Essay." *New Mexico Historical Review* 64 (1989): 349-360.

de Montalvo, Garcí Ordóñez. *Las Segos Del Muy Esforzado Caballeo Esplandián.* In *Biblioteca de autores españoles, Libros de caballerías,* ed. Don Pascual de Gayangos vol. 40. 1857; reprint, Madrid: M Rivadeneyra, 1874/1880.

Del Castillo, Adelaida R., ed. *Between Borders: Essays on Mexicana/Chicana History.* Encino: Floricanto Press, 1990.

———. "Malintzín Tenepal: A Preliminary Look into a New Perspective." In *Essays on La Mujer*, eds. Rosaura Sánchez and Rosa Martínez Cruz. Berkeley: University of California, Chicano Studies Center Publications, 1977.

Del Castillo, Richard Griswold. *The Los Angeles Barrio, 1850-1890: A Social History.* Berkeley: University of California Press, 1979.

———. *La Familia: Chicano Families in the Urban Southwest, 1848 to the Present.* Notre Dame, University of Notre Dame Press, 1984.

———. *The Treaty of Guadalupe Hidalgo: A Legacy of Conflict.* Norman: University of Oklahoma Press, 1990.

———. "The del Valle Family and the Fantasy Heritage." *California History* 59 (Spring 1980): 2 15.

———. "Neither Activist Nor Victim: Mexican Women's Historical Discourse—The Case of San Diego, 1820-1850." *California History* (Fall 1995): 230-43.

———. "The U.S. Mexican War: Contemporary Implications for Mexican Americans Civil and International Rights." In *Culture y Cultura: Consequences of the U.S. Mexican War, 1846-1848,* eds. Iris H. W. Engstrand et al. Los Angeles: Autry Museum of Western Heritage, 1998.

Del Castillo, Richard Griswold and Arnoldo de León. *North to Aztlán: A History of Mexican Americans in the United States.* New York: Twayne Publishers, 1996.

Deloria, Vine. *Custer Died for Your Sins: An Indian Manifesto.* New York: Macmillan, 1969.

Deutsch, Sarah. *No Separate Refuge: Culture, Class, and Gender on an Anglo-Hispanic Frontier in the American Southwest, 1880-1940.* New York: Oxford University Press, 1987.

Deutsch, Sarah, et al. "Historical Commentary: The Contributions and Challenges of Western Women's History—Four Essays by Sarah Deutsch, Virginia Scharff, Glenda Riley, and John Mack Faragher." *Montana, the Magazine of Western History* 41(Spring 1991):57-73.

Devens, Carol. *Countering Colonization: Native American Women in the Great Lakes Missions, 1630-1900.* Berkeley: University of California,1992.

Diao, Nancy. "From Homemaker to Housing Advocate: An Interview with Mrs. Chang Jok Lee." In *Making Waves: An Anthology of Writings by and about Asian Women,* ed., Asian Women United of California. Boston: Beacon Press, 1989.

Dillard, Heath. *Daughters of the Reconquest: Women in Castilian Town Society, 1100-1300.* New York: Cambridge University Press, 1984.

———. "Women in Reconquest Castile: The Fueros of Sepulveda and Cuenca." In *Women in Medieval Society*, ed. Susan Mosher Stuard. Philadelphia: University of Pennsylvania Press, 1976.

Dippie, Brian. "The Winning of the West Reconsidered." *Wilson Quarterly* 14 (Summer 1990): 70-85.

Donato, Ruben. *The Other Struggle for Equal Schools: Mexican Americans During the CivilRights Movement.* Albany: State University of New York Press, 1997.

DuBois. Ellen Carol and Vicki L. Ruiz, eds. *Unequal Sisters: A Multicultural Reader in US. Women's History.* New York: Routledge, 1990.

Ducille, Anne. "Othered Matters: Reconceptualizing Dominance and Difference in the History of Sexuality in America." *Journal of the History of Sexuality* 1 (1990): 102–127.

Duffin, Lorna. "Prisoners of Progress: Women and Evolution." In *The Nineteenth Century Woman: Her Cultural and Physical World*, eds. Sara Delamont and Lorna Duffin. NewYork: Barnes and Noble Books, 1978.

Dunn, Alvis E. "A Cry at Daybreak: Death, Disease, and Defense of Community in a Highland Ixil-Mayan Village." In *Women, Power, and Resistance in Colonial Mesoamerica*, spec. issue *Ethnohistory* 42, no. 4 (Autumn 1995): 595-606.

Dysart, Jane. "Mexican Women in San Antonio, 1830–1860: The Assimilation Process." *The Western Historical Quarterly* 7 (October 1976): 365-75.

Eldredge, Zoeth Skinner. *History of California*, 5 vols. New York: The Century Company, 1915.

Emmerich, Lisa. "Civilization and Transculturation: Field Matrons and Native American Women, 1891-1938." Paper presented at the conference, "The Women's West: Race, Class, and Social Change," San Francisco, Calif., Aug., 1987.

Emparan, Madie Brown. *The Vallejos of California.* San Francisco: Gleeson Library Association, 1968.

Erdrich, Louise. *Love Medicine.* New York: Harper Perennial, 1984.

Etienne, Mona and Eleanor Leacock, eds., *Women and Colonization: Anthropological Perspectives.* New York: Greenwood, 1980.

Farnham, Thomas Jefferson. *Travelers in California and Scenes in the Pacific Ocean.* New York: Saxton & Miles, 1844; reprint ed., Oakland: Biobooks, 1947.

Few, Martha. "Women, Religion, and Power: Gender and Resistance in Daily Life in Late-Seventeenth-Century Santiago de Guatemala." In *Women, Power, and Resistance in Colonial Mesoamerica,* spec. issue *Ethnohistory* 42, no. 4 (Autumn 1995): 627–637.

Fields Victor M., and Victor Zamudio Taylor, eds. *The Road to Aztlán: Art from the Mythic Homeland.* Los Angeles: Los Angeles County Museum of Art, 2001.

Fischer, Christine, ed. *Let Them Speak for Themselves: Women in the American West, 1849–1900.* New York: E. P. Dutton, 1977.

Flores, Glenn. "Language Barriers to Health Care in the United States. *Public Health Reports* (July/August 2005).

Flores, Glenn, et al. "Limited English Proficiency, Primary Language Spoken at Home, and Disparities in Children's Health and Healthcare: How Language Barriers are Measured." *Public Health Reports* 120: 4 (July/August 2005): 418–30.

Foley, Neil. *The White Scourge: Mexicans, Blacks and Poor Whites in Texas Cotton Culture.* Berkeley: University of California Press, 1999.

Foote, Cheryl J., and Sandra K. Schackel. "Indian Women of New Mexico, 1535-1680." *New Mexico Historical Review* 65 (1991): 1-16.

Forbes, Jack. *Apache, Navaho, and Spaniard.* Norman: University of Oklahoma, 1960.

Forbes, Jack D. *Aztecas del Norte: The Chicanos of Aztlán.* Greenwich, CT: Fawcett Publications, 1973.

———. "Frontiers in American History." *Journal of the West* 1 (1962): 63-73.

———. "Black Pioneers: The Spanish-Speaking Afroamericans of the Southwest." In *Minorities in California History,* eds. George E. Frakes and Curtis B. Solberg. New York: Random House, 1971.

———. "Hispano-Mexican Pioneers of the San Francisco Bay Region: An Analysis of Racial Origins." *Aztlán* (Spring 1983): 175-189.

Ford, Tirey L. *Dawn and the Dons: The Romance of Monterey*. San Francisco: A. M. Robertson, 1926.

Foster, David William. *The Early Spanish Ballad*. New York: Twayne Publishers, Inc., 1971.

"Founding Statement: Latin American Subaltern Studies Group." *Boundary 2* 20, no. 3 (Fall 1993): 110-21.

Gailey, Christine Ward. "Evolutionary Perspectives on Gender Hierarchy." In *Analyzing Gender: A Handbook of Social Science Research*, eds. Beth B. Hess and Myra Marx Ferree. Newbury Park: Sage Publications, 1987.

Galarza, Ernesto. *Spiders in the House and Workers in the Field*. Notre Dame: University of Notre Dame Press, 1970.

———. *Barrio Boy: The Story of a Boy's Acculturation*. Notre Dame: University of Notre Dame Press, 1971.

Gálvez, Esteban Rael. "Identifying Captivity and Capturing Identity: Narratives of American Indian Slavery." PhD dissertation, University of Michigan, 2004.

Gamboa, Erasmo. *Mexican Labor and World War II: Braceros in the Pacific Northwest*. Austin: University of Texas Press, 1990.

———. "Braceros in the Pacific Northwest: Laborers on the Domestic Front, 1942-1947." *Pacific Historical Review* 56, no. 3 (Aug. 1987): 378-398.

———. "The Mexican Mule Pack System of Transportation in the Pacific Northwest and British Columbia." *Journal of the West* 29 (January 1990): 16-26.

Gamboa, Erasmo and Carolyn M. Guan, eds. *Nosotros: The Hispanic People of Oregon*. Portland: Oregon Council for the Humanities, 1995.

Gamio, Manuel. *Mexican Immigration to the United States: A Study of Human Migration and Adjustment*. Chicago: University of Chicago Press, 1930.

———. *The Life Story of the Mexican Immigrant.* 1931. Reprint, New York: Dover Publications, Inc., 1971.

Gándara, Patricia. "Chicanos in Higher Education: The Politics of Self-Interest." *American Journal of Education* 95, no. 1. *The Education of Hispanic Americans: A Challenge for the Future* (Nov., 1986): 256-272

García, Alma M., ed. *Chicana Feminist Thought: Basic Historical Writings.* New York: Routledge, 1997.

García, Alma. "Studying Chicanas: Bringing Women into the Frame of Chicano Studies." In *Chicana Voices: Intersections of Class, Race, and Gender,* eds. Teresa Cordóva, et al. Austin: Center for Mexican American Studies, 1986.

García, Juan Ramón. *Operation Wetback: The Mass Deportation of Mexican Undocumented Workers in 1954.* Westport: Greenwood Press, 1980.

García, Mario T. *Desert Immigrants: The Mexicans of El Paso, 1880-1920.* New Haven: Yale University, 1981.

———. "The Chicana in American History: The Mexican Women of El Paso, 1880–1920: A Case Study." *Pacific Historical Review* 49 (May 1980): 315–37.

García, Richard A. "Turning Points: Mexican Americans in California History: Introduction to the Special Issue." *California History* 74, no. 3 (Fall, 1995): 226-229.

Gardiner, C. Harvey. *Pawns in a Triangle of Hate: The Peruvian Japanese and the United States.* Seattle: University of Washington Press, 1981.

Garner, Bess Adams. *Windows in an Old Adobe.* 1939. Reprint, Claremont, CA: Bronson Press, 1970.

Gates, Henry Louis Jr., ed. *Race, Writing, and Difference.* Chicago: University of Chicago, 1986.

Gibson, Charles, ed. *The Black Legend: Anti-Spanish Attitudes in the Old World and the New.* New York: Alfred A. Knopf, 1971.

Giddings, Paula. *When and Where I Enter: The Impact of Black Women on Race and Sex in America.* Toronto: William Morrow Paperbacks, 1984.

Gil, Carlos. "Washington's Hispano American Communities." In *Peoples of Washington: Perspectives on Cultural Diversity,* eds. Sid White and S. E. Solberg. Pullman: Washington State University Press, 1989.

Giraud, Francois. "Mujeres y Familia en Nueva España." In *Presencia y transparencia: La mujer en la historia de México,* ed. Carmen Ramos Escandón. Mexico, D.F.: Colegio de Mexico, 1987.

Glenn, Evelyn Nakano. *Issei, Nisei, War Bride: Three Generations of Japanese American Women in Domestic Service.* Philadelphia: Temple University, 1986.

———. "Racial Ethnic Women's Labor: The Intersection of Race, Gender, and Class oppression." *Review of Radical Political Economics* 17 (Fall 1985): 86-108.

Goldman, Marion S. *Gold Diggers and Silver Miners: Prostitution and Social Life in the Comstock Lode.* Ann Arbor: University of Michigan Press, 1981.

Goméz-Quiñones, Juan, and Luis L. Arroyo, "On the State of Chicano History: Observations on its Development, Interpretations and Theory, 1970-1974." *Western Historical Quarterly* 7 (April 1976): 155-185.

González, Deena. *Refusing the Favor: The Spanish-Mexican Women of Santa Fe, 1820-1880.* New York: Oxford University Press, 1999.

———. "The Widowed Women of Santa Fe: Assessments on the Lives of an Unmarried Population, 1850-80." In *On Their Own: Widows and Widowhood in the American Southwest, 1848-1939,* ed. Arlene Scadron. Chicago : University of Illinois Press, 1988.

———."Malinche as Lesbian." *Culture and Conflict in the Academy: Testimonies from the War Zone,* 14 spec. issue *California Sociologist* (Winter/Summer 1991): 90-97.

———. "Speaking Secrets: Living Chicana Theory." In *Living Chicana Theory,* ed.Carla Trujillo. Berkeley: Third Woman Press, 1998.

———. "Lupe's Song: On the Origins of Mexican/Woman-Hating in the United States." In *Race in 21st Century America,* eds. Curtis Stokes, Theresa Meléndez, Genice Rhodes-Reed. East Lansing: Michigan State University Press, 2001.

———. "Juanotilla of Cochin, Vecina and Coyota: Nuevomexicanas in the Eighteenth Century." In *New Mexican Lives: Profiles and Historical Stories*, ed. Richard Etualain. Albuquerque: University of New Mexico, 2002.

———. "Gender on the Borderlands: Re-textualizing the Classics." *Frontiers* 24 (2003): 15-29.

———. "The Spanish Mexican Women of Santa Fe: Patterns of Their Resistance and Accommodation, 1820–1880." PhD diss., University of California, Berkeley, 1985.

———. "The Spanish-Mexican Women of Santa Fe: Mocking the Conquerors." Paper presented at the Writing on the Border Conference, Claremont Colleges, 1989.

———. "A Resituated West: Johnson's Re-gendered, Re-racialized Perspective." In *A New Significance: Re-envisioning the History of the American West*, ed. Clyde Milner III. Berkeley: University of California, 1998.

González, Jovita. *Caballero: A Historical Novel*, ed. Jose Limon and Maria Cotera. College Station: Texas A&M University Press, 1996.

Gordillo, Luz María. *Mexican Women and the Other Side of Immigration: Engendering Transnational Ties*. Austin: University of Texas Press, 2010.

Gosner, Kevin and Deborah E. Kanter, eds. *Women, Power, and Resistance in Colonial Mesoamerica*, spec. issue of *Ethnohistory* 42 (Fall 1995).

de Graaf, Lawrence B. "Race, Sex, and Region: Black Women in the American West, 1850-1920." *Pacific Historical Review* 60 (1980): 285-313.

Green, Rayna. "The Pocahontas Perplex: The Image of Indian Women in American Culture." *Massachusetts Review* 16 (1975):698-714.

———. "Native American Women." *Signs* 6 (1980): 248-267.

———. ed. *Native American Women: A Contextual Bibliography*. Bloomington: Newberry Library Center for the History of the American Indian, 1983.

Gressley, Gene M. "The West: Past, Present, and Future." *Western Historical Quarterly* 17 (1986): 5-23.

Griswold, Robert L. *Family and Divorce in California, 1850–1890.* Albany: State University of New York Press, 1982.

Grosz, Elizabeth. *Volatile Bodies: Toward A Corporeal Feminism.* Bloomington and Indianapolis: Indiana University Press, 1994.

———. "Bodies and Knowledges: Feminism and the Crisis of Reason." In *Feminist Epistemologies*, eds. Linda Alcoff and Elizabeth Potter. New York, London: Routledge, 1993.

Guinn, J. M. *A History of California and an Extended History of Los Angeles and Environs Also Containing Biographies of Well Known Citizens of the Past and Present.* 3 vols. Los Angeles: Historic Record Company, 1915.

Gutiérrez, David G. "Significant to Whom?: Mexican Americans and the History of the American West." *Western Historical Quarterly* 24 no.4 (Nov. 1993): 519-539.

Gutiérrez, Ramón A. *When Jesus Came, the Corn Mothers Went Away: Marriage, Sexuality, and Power in New Mexico, 1500-1846.* Stanford: Stanford University, 1991.

———. "Marriage and Seduction in Colonial New Mexico." In *Between Borders: Essays on Mexicana/Chicana History*, ed. Adelaida R. Del Castillo. Los Angeles: Floricanto Press, 1990.

———. "From Honor to Love: Transformations of the Meaning of Sexuality in Colonial New Mexico." In *Kinship Ideology and Practice in Latin America*, ed. Raymond T. Smith. Chapel Hill: University of North Carolina Press, 1984.

———."Honor Ideology, Marriage Negotiation, and Class-Gender Domination in New Mexico, 1690-1846." *Latin American Perspectives* 44 (Winter 1985): 81–104.

———. "Unraveling America's Hispanic Past: Internal Stratification and Class Boundaries." *Aztlán* 17 (1986): 79-101.

———. "Ethnic and Class Boundaries in America's Hispanic Past. In *Social and Gender Boundaries in the United States*, ed. Sucheng Chan. Lewiston, NY: Mellon Studies in Sociology, 1989.

———. "Community, Patriarchy and Individualism: The Politics of Chicano History and the Dream of Equality." *American Quarterly* 45, no. 1 (March 1993): 44-72.

———. "Sexual Mores and Behavior: The Spanish Borderlands." In *The Encyclopedia of the North American Colonies*, vol. 2, eds. Jacob Ernest Cooke, et al. New York: Charles Scribner's Sons, 1993.

———. "Marriage, Sex, and the Family: Social Change in Colonial New Mexico, 1690-1846." PhD diss., University of Wisconsin–Madison, 1980.

Guy, Donna J., and Thomas E. Sheridan. "On Frontiers: The Northern and Southern Edges of the Spanish Empire in the Americas." In *Contested Ground: Comparative Frontiers on the Northern and Southern Edges of the Spanish Empire*. Tucson: University of Arizona Press, 1998.

Haas, Lisbeth. *Conquest and Historical Identities*. Berkeley: University of California Press, 1995.

Hagen, William T. "How the West Was Lost." In *Indians in American History*, ed. Frederick E . Hoxie. Arlington Heights, Illinois: Harlan Davidson, Inc., 1988.

Hanke, Lewis. *The Spanish Struggle for Justice in the Conquest of America*. Philadelphia: University of Pennsylvania Press, 1949.

Hanke, Lewis, ed. *Do the Americas Have a Common History? A Critique of the Bolton Theory*. New York: Alfred A. Knopf, 1964.

Hanmer, Jalna and Mary Maynard, eds. *Women, Violence and Social Control*. New Jersey: Humanities Press International, 1987.

Harjo, Joy and Gloria Bird, eds. *Reinventing the Enemy's Language: Contemporary Native American Women's Writings of North America*. New York: W. W. Norton, 1998.

Harjo, Suzan Shown. "Western Women's History: A Challenge for the Future." In *The Women's West*, eds. Susan Armitage and Elizabeth Jameson. Norman: University of Oklahoma,1987.

Hart, James. *American Images of Spanish California*. Berkeley: Friends of the Bancroft Library, 1960.

Hart, Elva Treviño. *Barefoot Heart: Stories of a Migrant Child.* Tempe, AZ: Bilingual Press/Editorial Bilingue, 1999.

Hauptman, Laurence M. "Congress, Plenary Power, and the American Indian, 1870 to 1992." In *Exiled in the Land of the Free: Democracy, Indian Nations, and the U.S. Constitution,* eds. Oren Lyons, et.al. Santa Fe: Clear Light Publishers, 1992.

Heizer, Robert F. "A California Messianic Movement of 1801 among the Chumash." *American Anthropologist* 43 (1941; reprint, 1962): 128-29.

Heizer Robert F. and Albert B. Elsasser. *The Natural World of the California Indians.* Berkeley: University of California Press, 1980.

Hernández-Avila, Inés. "An Open Letter to Chicanas: On the Power and Politics of Origin." In *Without Discovery: A Native Response to Columbus,* ed. Ray Gonzales, Seattle: Broken Moon, 1992.

Hernández, José, Leo Estrada, and David Alvírez, "Census Data and the Problem of Conceptually Defining the Mexican American Population." *Social Science Quarterly* 53 (1973): 671-687.

Hernández, Patricia. "Lives of Chicana Activists: The Chicano Student Movement (A Case Study)." In *Mexican Women in the United States: Struggles Past and Present,* eds. Magdalena Mora and Adelaida R. Del Castillo. Los Angeles: Chicano Studies Research Center, 1980.

Hernández, Salomé. "No Settlement without Women: Three Spanish California Settlement Schemes, 1790-1800." *Southern California Quarterly* 72 (Fall 1990): 203-33.

———. "Nueva Mexicanas as Refugees and Reconquest Settlers, 1680-1696." *New Mexico Historical Review* 65 (1991):17-40.

Hietala, Thomas R. *Manifest Design: Anxious Aggrandizement in Late Jacksonian America.* Ithaca, NY, and London: Cornell University Press, 1985.

Higashide, Seiichi. *Adios to Tears: The Memoirs of a Japanese-Peruvian Internee in U.S. Concentration Camps.* Seattle: University of Washington Press, 1993.

Higham, John. History: *Professional Scholarship in America.* New York: Harper and Row, 1965.

Higham, John. *Writing American History: Essays on Modern Scholarship.* Bloomington: Indiana University Press, 1970.

Hinojosa, Gilberto Miguel. *A Borderlands Town in Transition: Laredo, 1775-1870.* College Station: Texas A&M, 1983.

Hirata, Lucie Cheng. "Free, Indentured, Enslaved: Chinese Prostitutes in Nineteenth-Century America." *Signs: Journal of Women in Culture and Society* 5 (1979): 3-29.

Hittell, Theodore S. *History of California,* 4 vols. San Francisco: The History Company, 1897.

Hoffman, Abraham. *Unwanted Mexican Americans in the Great Depression: Repatriation Pressures, 1929-1939.* Tucson: University of Arizona Press, 1974.

Hofstadter, Richard. *Social Darwinism in American Thought.* 1944. Reprint, New York: George Braziller, Inc., 1959.

———. *The Progressive Historians: Turner, Beard, Parrington.* New York: Alfred A. Knopf, 1968.

hooks, bell. *Ain't I a Woman: Black Women and Feminism.* Boston: South End, 1981.

———. *Talking Back: Thinking Feminist, Thinking Black.* Boston: South End, 1984.

———. *Feminist Theory: From Margin to Center.* Boston: South End, 1984.

———. *Black Looks: Race and Representation.* Boston: Beacon Press, 1992.

Hori, Joan. "Japanese Prostitution in Hawaii during the Immigration Period." In *Asian and Pacific American Experiences: Women's Perspectives,* eds. Nobuya Tsuchida, et al. Minneapolis: Asian/Pacific American Learning Resource Center, 1982.

Horn, Marlon K. *Songs of Gold Mountain: Cantonese Rhymes from San Francisco Chinatown.* Berkeley: University of California, 1987.

Horsman, Reginald. *Race and Manifest Destiny: The Origins of Racial Anglo Saxonism.* Cambridge and London, 1981.

Houston, Ramona. "Anglo Americans, African Americans and Mexican Americans in the Desegregation of Texas, 1946-1957." PhD diss., University of Texas at Austin, 2000.

Hubbard, Henry D. *Vallejo.* Boston: Meador Publishing Company, 1941.

Hunt, Lynn, ed., *The New Cultural History.* Berkeley: University of California, 1989.

Hurtado, Albert. *Indian Survival on the California Frontier.* New Haven: Yale University Press, 1990.

———. *Intimate Frontiers: Sex, Gender, and Culture in Old California.* Albuquerque: University of New Mexico Press, 1999.

———. "Sexuality in California's Franciscan Missions: Cultural Perceptions and Sad Realities." *California History* 71 (Fall 1992): 370-85.

Hutchinson, C. Alan. *Frontier Settlement in Mexican California: The Hijar-Padres Colony and Its Origins,1769-1835.* New Haven: Yale University Press, 1969.

Ichioka, Yuji. *The Issei: The World of the First Generation Japanese Immigrants, 1885-1924.* New York: Macmillan, 1988.

———. "Amerika Nadeshiko: Japanese Immigrant Women in the United States, 1900-1924." *Pacific Historical Review.* 40 (1980): 339-357.

Jackson, Hunt. *Ramona: A Story.* Boston: Roberts Brothers, 1892.

Jameson, Elizabeth. "Toward a Multicultural History of Women in the Western United States." *Signs: Journal of Women in Culture and Society* 13 (1988): 761-791.

Jeffrey, Julie Roy. *Frontier Women: The Trans-Mississippi West. 1840-1880.* New York: Hill & Wang, 1979.

Jensen, Joan and Gloria Ricci Lothrop. *California Women: A History.* San Francisco: Boyd and Fraser, 1987.

Jensen, Joan M. and Darlis A. Miller. "The Gentle Tamers Revisited: New Approaches to the History of Women in the American West." *Pacific Historical Review* 44 (May 1980): 173-213.

Johnson, Susan Lee. "A Memory Sweet to Soldiers: The Significance of Gender in the History of the American West." *Western Historical Quarterly* 24, no.4 (Nov. 1993): 495-517.

―――. *Roaring Camp: The Social World of the California Gold Rush.* New York: W.W. Norton, 2000.

Jone, Reverend Heribert. *Moral Theology, Englished and Adapted to the Laws and Customs of the United States of America by Reverend Urban Adelman.* Westminster, MD: Newman Press, 1960.

Jones, Oakah L., Jr. *Los Paisanos: Spanish Settlers on the Northern Frontiers of New Spain.* Norman: University of Oklahoma Press, 1979.

Jones, Oakah L., Jr, ed. *The Spanish Borderlands: A First Reader.* Los Angeles: Lorrin L. Morrison, 1974.

Josephy, Alvin M., Jr., ed. *Red Power: The American Indians' Fight for Freedom.* New York: American Heritage Press, 1971.

Kamen, Henry. *Inquisition and Society in Spain in the Sixteenth and Seventeenth Century.* Bloomington: Indiana University Press,1985.

―――. "Notes on Witchcraft, Sexuality, and the Inquisition." In *The Spanish Inquisition and the Inquisitorial Mind,* ed. Angel Alcalá. Boulder, CO: Social Science Monographs, 1987.

Karttunen, Frances. *Between Worlds: Interpreters, Guides, and Survivors.* New Brunswick: Rutgers, 1994.

Katz, William Loren. *The Black West: A Documentary and Pictorial History.* Seattle: Touchstone, 1987.

Keating, AnaLouise, and Gloria Anzaldúa. "Writing, Politics, and Las Lesberadas: Platicando con Gloria Anzaldúa." *Frontiers: A Journal of Women Studies* 14, no. 1 (1993):105-130.

Kelly Gadol, Joan. "The Social Relation of the Sexes: Methodological Implications of Women's History." In *Sex and Class in Women's History,* eds. Judith L. Norton, Mary P. Ryan, and Judith Walkowitz. London: Routledge and Kegan Paul, 1983.

Kelsey, Harry, ed. *The Doctrina and Confesionario of Juan Cortés.* Altadena: Howling Coyote, 1979.

Kenneally, Finbar, O.F.M., trans and ed. "Refutation of Charges, Mission of San Carlos of Monterey, June 19, 1801." In *Writings of Fermín Francisco de Lasuén*, 2 vols. Washington, D.C.: Academy of American Franciscan History, 1965.

Kerber, Linda K. *Women of the Republic: Intellect and Ideology in Revolutionary America*. 1980. Reprint New York: W. W. Norton & Company, 1986.

Kessler-Harris, Alice. *Women Have Always Worked*. New York: The Feminist Press, 1981.

Kidwell, Clara Sue. "Indian Women as Cultural Mediators." *Ethnohistory* 39 (Spring 1992): 97-107.

Kikumura, Akeme. *Through Harsh Winters: The Life of a Japanese Immigrant Woman*. Novato: Chandler and Sharp, 1981.

Klein Laura F. and Lillian A. Ackerman, eds. *Women and Power in Native North America*. Norman: University of Oklahoma, 1995.

Klor de Alva, Jorge. "Language, Politics, and Translation: Colonial Discourse and Classic Nahuatl in New Spain." In *The Art of Translation: Voices from the Field*, ed. Rosanna Warren. Boston: Northeastern University Press, 1989.

Kolodny, Annette. *The Land before Her: Fantasy and Experience of the American Frontiers, 1630-1860*. Chapel Hill: University of North Carolina, 1984.

Korn, David A. *In Exodus within Borders: An Introduction to the Crisis of Internal Displacement*. Washington DC: Brookings Institution Press, 1999.

Kraus, Michael and Davis D. Joyce. *The Writing of American History*, rev. ed. Norman: University of Oklahoma Press, 1985.

Lacy, James H. "New Mexico Women in Early American Writings." *New Mexico Historical Review* 34 (1959): 41-51.

Lamadrid, Enrique R., et al. *Tesoros del Espíritu: A Portrait in Sound of Hispanic New Mexico*. Embudo, NM: El Norte/Academia Publications, 1994.

Lamadrid, Enrique and Miguel A. Gandert. *Hermanitos Comanchitos: Indo-Hispano Rituals of Captivity and Redemption.* Albuquerque: University of New Mexico Press, 2003.

Lamar, Howard and Leonard Thompson, eds. *The Frontier in History: North America and Southern Africa Compared.* New Haven: Yale University Press, 1981.

Lang, Sabine. *Men as Women, Women as Men: Changing Gender in Native American Cultures.* Austin: University of Texas Press, 1998.

Langum, David J. *Law and Community on the Mexican California Frontier: Anglo-American Expatriates and the Clash of Legal Traditions, 1821-1846.* Norman: University of Oklahoma Press, 1987.

———. "California Women and the Image of Virtue." *Southern California Quarterly* 59 (Fall 1977): 245-250.

———. "Californios and the Image of Indolence." *The Western Historical Quarterly* 9 (April 1978): 181–96.

LaPérouse, Jean-Francois de Galaup. *A Voyage Round the World in the Years 1785, 1786, 1787 and 1788,* ed. M. L. A. Milet Mureau, 3 vols. London: J. Johnson, 1798.

Lapp, Rudolph M. *Afro-Americans in California.* 2d ed. San Francisco: Materials for Today's Learning, 1987.

Laslett, Barbara. "Household Structure on an American Frontier: Los Angeles, California, in 1850." *American Journal of Sociology* 81 (January 1975): 109-28.

Lavrín, Asunción. *Latin American Women: Historical Perspectives.* Westport, CT: Greenwood Press, 1978.

———. "Women in Convents: Their Economic and Social Roles in Colonial Mexico." In *Liberating Women's History: Theoretical and Critical Essays,* ed. Berenice A. Carroll. Urbana: University of Illinois Press, 1976.

———. "La vida feminina como experiencia religiosa: Biografía hagiografía en Hispanoamérica colonial." *Colonial Latin American Review* 2 (1993): 27-52.

———. "Lo Feminino: Women in Colonial Historical Sources." In *Coded Encounters: Writing, Gender, and Ethnicity in Colonial Latin America,* eds. Francisco Javier Cevallos-Candau, et al. Amherst: University of Massachusetts Press, 1994.

Lavrín, Asunción, ed. *Sexuality and Marriage in Colonial Latin America.* Lincoln: University of Nebraska Press, 1989.

Lavrín, Asunción, and Edith Couturier. "Dowries and Wills: A View of Women's Socioeconomic Role in Colonial Guadalajara and Puebla, 1640–1790." *Hispanic American Historical Review* 59 (May 1979): 280 304.

———. "Las mujeres tienen la palabra: Otras voces en la historia colonial de México." *Historia Mexicana* 31 (1981): 278-313.

Leacock, Eleanor Burke. *Myths of Male Dominance: Collected Articles on Women Cross-Culturally.* New York: Monthly Review Press, 1981.

———. "Women, Development, and Anthropological Facts and Fictions." *Latin American Perspectives* 4 (Winter-Spring 1977): 8-17.

———. "Women in Egalitarian Societies." In *Becoming Visible: Women in European History,* eds. Renate Bridenthal and Claudia Koonz. Boston: Cengage Learning, 1977.

Leacock, Eleanor, and Richard Lee, eds. *Politics and History in Band Societies.* Cambridge: Cambridge University, 1982.

LeCompte, Janet. "The Independent Women of Hispanic New Mexico, 1821-1846." *Western Historical Quarterly* 12 (January 1981): 17-35.

Lentin, Ronit. "Introduction: (En)gendering Genocides." In *Gender and Catastrophe,* ed. Ronit Lentin. New York: Zed Books, 1997.

Leonard, Irving. *Romances of Chivalry in the Spanish Indies.* Berkeley: University of California, 1933.

———. *Books of the Brave: Being an Account of Books and of Men in the Spanish Conquest and Settlement of the Sixteenth Century New World.* 1949; Berkeley, Los Angeles: University of California, 1992.

Lerner, Gerda. *The Majority Finds Its Past: Placing Women in History.* New York: Oxford University Press, 1979.

———. *The Creation of Patriarchy.* New York and Oxford: Oxford University Press, 1986.

Lester, Julius. *Revolutionary Notes.* New York: Richard W. Barron, 1969.

Levin, David. *History as Romantic Art: Bancroft, Prescott, Motley and Parkman.* Stanford, Calif.: Stanford University Press, 1959.

Limerick, Patricia. *The Legacy of Conquest: The Unbroken Past of the American West.* New York, 1987.

Limón, José E. *Dancing with the Devil: Society and Cultural Poetics in Mexican-American South Texas.* Madison: University of Wisconsin, 1994.

Lockhart, Katharine Meyer. "A Demographic Profile of an Alta California Pueblo: San Jose de Guadalupe, 1777-1850." PhD diss., University of Colorado, 1986.

Lowenberg, Bert James. *American History in American Thought.* New York: Simon and Schuster, 1972.

Luchetti, Cathy and Carol Olwell. *Women of the West.* St. George, Utah: Antelope Island, 1982.

Lynch, Henry. "Six Families: A Study of the Power and Influence of the Alvarado, Carrillo, Castro, de la Guerra, Pico, and Vallejo Families in California, 1769-1846." Master's thesis, California State University, Sacramento, 1977.

Lyons, Oren, et al. *Exiled in the Land of the Free: Democracy, Indian Nations, and the U.S. Constitution.* Santa Fe: Clear Light Publishers, 1992.

McClain, Charles J., et al., eds. *Entry Denied: Exclusion and the Chinese Community in America, 1882-1943.* Philadelphia: Temple, 1991.

McClure, Charlotte S. *Gertrude Atherton.* Boston: Twayne Publishers, 1979.

MacKinnon, Catharine A. "Feminism, Marxism, Method, and the State: An Agenda for Theory." In *Feminist Theory: A Critique of Ideology,* ed. Nannerl et al. Chicago: The University of Chicago Press, 1982.

McKittrick, Myrtle. *Vallejo: Son of California.* Portland, OR: Bindfords and Mort Publishers, 1944.

McWilliams, Carey. *North from Mexico: The Spanish Speaking People of the United States.* 1948. Reprint, New York: Greenwood Press, 1968.

———. *Factories in the Fields: The Story of Migratory Farm Labor in California.* Santa Barbara: Peregrine Publishers, 1971.

Mallon, Florencia E. "The Promise and Dilemma of Subaltern Studies: Perspectives from Latin American History." *American Historical Review* 99 (1994): 1491-1515.

Malone, Michael P., ed. *Historians and the American West.* Lincoln: University of Nebraska Press, 1983.

Marcos, Sylvia, ed. *Gender/Bodies/Religions.* Cuernavaca, Mexico: ALER Publications, 2000.

Mariscal, George. "The Role of Spain in Contemporary Race Theory." *Arizona Journal of Hispanic Cultural Studies* 2 (1998): 7-22.

Massey, Doreen. *Space, Place and Gender.* Minneapolis: University of Minnesota Press, 1994.

Martínez-Alier, Verena. *Marriage, Class, and Color in Nineteenth-Century Cuba: A Study of Racial Attitudes and Sexual Values in a Slave Society.* Cambridge, England: Cambridge University Press, 1974.

Mata, Jennifer. "Creating a Chicana Narrative: Writing the Chicanas at Farah into Labor History." Ph.D. diss., Washington State University, 2004.

May, Elaine Tyler. *Homeward Bound: American Families in the Cold War Era.* New York: Basic Books, 1988.

Medicine, Beatrice and Patricia Albers, eds. *The Hidden Half: Studies of Plains Indian Women.* Lanham: University of America, 1983.

Meier, Matt A. and Feliciano Rivera. *The Chicanos: A History of Mexican Americans.* New York: Hill and Wang, 1972.

Merk, Frederick. *A Reinterpretation of Manifest Destiny and Mission in American History.* New York: Alfred Knopf, 1963.

Messinger Cypess, Sandra. *La Malinche in Mexican Literature: From History to Myth.* Austin: University of Texas Press, 1991.

Methvin, J. J. *Andele: The Mexican Kiowa Captive.* Albuquerque: University of New Mexico Press, 1996.

Meyer, Doris L. "Early Mexican American Responses to Negative Stereotyping." *New Mexico Historical Review* 53 (January 1978) 75-91.

Mihesuah, Devon. *Cultivating the Rosebuds:The Education of Women at the Cherokee Female Seminary, 1851–1909.* Chicago: Universityof Illinois Press, 1997.

Miller, Darlis A. "Cross-Cultural Marriages in the Southwest: The New Mexico Experience, 1846-1900." *New Mexico Historical Review* 57 (1982): 335-359.

———. "Foragers, Army Women, and Prostitutes." *New Mexico Historical Review* 65 (1991): 141-168.

Minh-ha, Trinh T. *Woman, Native, Other.* Bloomington: Indiana University, 1989.

Mink, Gwendolyn, et al. *The Reader's Companion to U.S. Women's History.* New York: Houghton Mifflin Harcourt, 1998.

Miranda, Gloria E."Gente de Razón Marriage Patterns in Spanish and Mexican California: A Case Study of Santa Barbara and Los Angeles." *Southern California Historical Quarterly* 63 (1981): 1–21.

———. "Hispano-Mexicano Childrearing Practices in Pre American Santa Barbara." *Southern California Historical Quarterly* 65 (1983): 307–20

———. "Racial and Cultural Dimensions of Gente de Razón Status in Spanish and Mexican California." *Southern California Quarterly* 70 (1988): 265-278.

———. "Family Patterns and the Social Order in Hispanic Santa Barbara, 1784-1848." PhD diss., University of Southern California, 1978.

Mirikitani, Janice. *Awake in the River.* San Francisco: Isthmus Press, 1978.

———. *Shedding Silence.* Berkeley: Celestial Arts,1987.

Mohanram, Radhika. *Black Body: Women, Colonialism and Space.* Minneapolis and London: University of Minnesota Press, 1999.

Mohanty, Chandra. "Under Western Eyes: Feminist Scholarship and Colonial Discourses." *Boundary 2: A Journal of Lost Modern Literature and Culture* 12 (Spring/ Fall 1984): 333-358.

Mohanty, Chandra P., and Saya P. Mohanty. "Review: Contradictions of Colonialism." *Women's Review of Books* 8 (March 1990): 19-21.

Mohanty, Chandra Talpade, Ann Russo, and Lourdes Torres, eds. *Third World Women and the Politics of Feminism.* Bloomington: Indiana University Press, 1991.

Monroy, Douglas. *Thrown among Strangers: The Making of Mexican Culture in Frontier California.* Berkeley: University of California Press, 1990.

Montejano, David. *Anglos and Mexicans in the Making of Texas, 1836–1986.* Austin: University of Texas Press, 1987.

Montrose, Louis. "The Work of Gender in the Discourse of Discovery." *New World Encounters*, ed. Stephen Greenblatt. Berkeley: University of California, 1993.

Moore, Shirley Ann. "Not in Somebody's Kitchen: African-American Women Workers in Richmond, California, 1910-1950." Paper presented at the Huntington Library, Seminar in Women's Studies, San Marino, Calif., 1991.

Moorhead, Max L. *The Presidio: Bastion of the Spanish Borderlands.* Norman: University of Oklahoma Press, 1975.

Moraga, Cherríe. *Loving in the War Years: lo que nunca pasó por sus labios.* 1983. 2nd ed. Cambridge: South End Press, 2000.

Moraga, Cherríe, and Gloria Anzaldúa, eds. *This Bridge Called My Back: Writings by Radical Women of Color.* Watertown: Persephone Press, 1981.

Morner, Magnus. *Race Mixture in the History of Latin America.* Boston: Little, Brown, 1967.

Morrison, Toni. *Beloved.* New York: Knopf, 1987.

Mujeres Activas en Letras y Cambio Social. "June 1983 MALCS Declaración," Mujeres Activas en Letras y Cambio Social. Accessed January 6, 2011.http://malcs.net/.

Mujeres en Marcha. *Chicanos in the 80s: Unsettled Issues.* Berkeley: Chicano Studies Library, 1983.

Murphy, Lucy Eldersveld. "Autonomy and the Economic Roles of Indian Women of the Fox-Wisconsin Riverway Region, 1763-1832." In *Negotiators of Change: Historical Perspectives on Native American Women,* ed. Nancy Shoemaker. New York: Routledge, 1995.

Myers, Sandra L. *Westering Women and the Frontier Experience, 1800-1915.* Albuquerque: University of New Mexico Press, 1982.

———."Mexican Americans and Westering Anglos: A Feminine Perspective." *New Mexico Historical Review* 57 (1982): 414-430.

———. "Women in the West." In *Historians and the American West,* ed. Michael Malone. Lincoln: University of Nebraska Press, 1983.

———. "What Kind of Animal Be This?" *Western Historical Quarterly* 20 (1989): 5-17.

Myers, Sandra L., ed. *Ho for California: Women's Overland Diaries from the Huntington Library.* San Marino: Henry E. Huntington Library and Art Gallery, 1980.

Nash, Gerald D. "Where's the West?" *Historian* 49 (1986): 1-9.

Nelson, Edna Deu Pree. *The California Dons.* New York: Appleton-Century-Crofts, 1962.

Ngai, Mae M. *Impossible Subjects: Illegal Aliens and The Making of Modern America.* Princeton and Oxford: Princeton University Press, 2004.

Nichols, Roger L., ed. *American Frontier and Western Issues: A Historiographical Review.* Westport, CT, 1986.

Nicholson, Linda J. *Gender and History: The Limits of Social Theory in the Age of the Family.* New York: Columbia University Press, 1986.

Norman, Lucia . *A Popular History of California from the Earliest Period of Its Discovery to the Present Time.* 1867. Reprint San Francisco: A. Roman, AGT, Publisher, 1883.

Norton, Mary Beth. "The Evolution of White Women's Experience in Early America." *The American Historical Review* 89 (June 1984): 593–619

Nugent, Walter. "Western History: Stocktaking and New Crops." *Reviews in American History* 13 (1985): 319-329.

Nuttall, Donald A."The Gobernantes of Upper California: A Profile." *California Historical Quarterly* 51 (Fall 1972): 253 80.

Offiong, Daniel. *Imperialism and Dependency: Obstacles to African Development.* Washington, D.C.: Howard University Press, 1982.

Okihiro, Gary T., ed. *In Resistance: Studies in African, Caribbean and Afro-American History.* Amherst: University of Massachusetts Press, 1986.

O'Meara, Walter. *Daughters of the Country: The Women of the Fur Traders.* New York: Harcourt, Brace, and World, 1968.

Ord, Angustias de la Guerra. *Occurrences in Hispanic California.* Trans. Francis Price and William Ellison. Washington, D.C.: Academy of Franciscan History, 1956.

Orellana, Marjorie Faulstich. "Texts, Talk, Tasks, and Take-up: Literacy as a Gendered Social Practice in Two Bilingual Classrooms." *Reading Research Quarterly* 30: 4 (1995): 674 70.

———. "Children's Responsibilities in Latino Immigrant Homes." *New Directions for Youth Development: Theory, Practice and Research: Special Issue on Social Influences in the Positive Development of Immigrant Youth* 100 (2003): 25 39.

Orellana, Marjorie Faulstich, et al."Accessing Assets, Immigrant Youth's Work as Family Translators or 'Para-phrasers'." *Social Problems* 50, no. 4 (November 2003): 482 504.

Orozco, Cynthia. "Sexism in Chicano Studies and the Community." In *Chicana Voices: Intersections of Class, Race, and Gender*, eds. Teresa Cordóva, et al. Austin: Center for Mexican American Studies, 1986.

———. "Mexican Elite Women in the 19th-Century: Work, Social Life, and Intermarriage," paper presented at "Mexicana/Chicana Women's History Symposium." Santa Monica, California, March 1982.

Ortiz, Roxanne Dunbar. "Toward a Democratic Women's Movement in the United States." In *Mexican Women in the United States: Struggles Past and Present*, eds. Magdalena Mora and Adelaida R. Del Castillo. Los Angeles: Chicano Studies Research Center, 1980.

Oshana, Maryann. "Native American Women in Westerns: Reality and Myth." *Frontiers: A Journal of Women Studies* 6 (Fall 1981): 46-50.

Ots y Capdequi, José María. *Instituciones.* Barcelona: Salvat Editores, S.A., 1959.

———. *Historia del derecho español en America y del derecho indiano.* Madrid: Ediciones S.A. de Aguilar, 1967.

Padilla, Genaro. *My History, Not Yours: The Formation of Mexican American Autobiography.* Madison: University of Wisconsin Press, 1993.

———. "Yo Sola Aprendí: Mexican Women's Personal Narratives from Nineteenth-Century California." In *Revealing Lives: Autobiography, Biography, and Gender,* eds. Susan Groag Bell and Marilyn Yalom. New York: State University of New York Press, 1990.

———. "Discontinuous Continuities: Remapping the Terrain of Spanish Colonial Narrative." In *Reconstructing a Chicana/o Literary Heritage: Hispanic Colonial Literature of the Southwest,* ed. María Herrera-Sobek. Tucson: University of Arizona Press, 1993.

Pardo, Mary. "Honoring and Remembering One of the First Chicana Historians: Shirlene Soto." *Noticias de NACCS* December 2009, pp. 2, 15.

Paredes, Américo. *A Texas-Mexican Cancionero: Folksongs of the Lower Border.* 1976. Reprint Austin: University of Texas Press, 1995.

Paredes, Raymond A. "The Mexican Image in American Travel Literature, 1831-1869." *New Mexico Historical Review* 52 (January 1977): 5-59.

———. "The Origins of Anti-Mexican Sentiment in the United States." *New Scholar* 6 (1977): 139-165.

Parks, Marion. "In Pursuit of Vanished Days: Visits to the Extant Historic Adobe Houses of Los Angeles County," Part 1, *Historical Society of Southern California Annual Publications* 14 (1928): 7–63.

Partridge, Elizabeth, ed. *Dorothea Lange: A Visual Life.* Washington, D.C.: Smithsonian Institution Press, 1994.

Pascoe, Peggy. *Relations of Rescue: The Search for Female Moral Authority in the American West, 1874-1939.* New York: Oxford University Press, 1990.

———. "At the Crossroads of Culture." *Women's Review of Books* 7 (February 1990): 22-23.

———. "Gender, Race, and Intercultural Relations: The Case of Interracial Marriage." *Frontiers: A Journal of Women's Studies* 12 (1991): 5-18.

Paul, Rodman W. *A Victorian Gentlewoman in the Far West: The Reminiscences of Mary Hallock Foote.* San Marino: The Huntington Library, 1980.

Paul, Rodman W. and Michael P. Malone. "Tradition and Challenge in Western Historiography." *Western Historical Quarterly* 16 (January 1985):27-53.

Pawn, Frederick Logan. *The Last American Frontier.* New York: The Macmillan Company, 1910.

Peffer, George Anthony. "Forbidden Families: Emigration Experiences of Chinese Women under the Page Law, 1875-1882." *Journal of American Ethnic History* 6 (Fall 1986): 28-46.

Pérez, Emma. *The Decolonial Imaginary: Writing Chicanas into History.* Bloomington: Indiana University Press, 1999.

———. "Sexuality and Discourse: Notes from a Chicana Survivor." In *Chicana Lesbians: The Girls our Mothers Warned Us About*, ed. Carla Trujillo. Berkeley: Third Woman Press, 1991.

Pérez, Erika. "Colonial Intimacies: Interethnic Kinship, Sexuality, and Marriage in Southern California, 1769-1885." Ph.D. diss., University of California, Los Angeles, 2010.

Peterson, Charles S. "The Look of the Elephant: On Seeing Western History." *Montana, the Magazine of Western History* 39 (Spring 1989): 69-73.

Phillips, George Harwood. *Chiefs and Challengers: Indian Resistance and Cooperation in Southern California.* Berkeley: University of California, 1975.

Pidal, Ramón Menéndez. *Flor Nueva de Romances Viejos.* Buenos Aires y México: Espasa-Calpe Argentina, 1943.

Pierce, Richard A. *Resanov Reconnoiters California: A New Translation of Resanov's Letters, Parts of Lieutenant Khvostov's Log of the Ship Juno, and Dr. Georg von Langsdorff's Observations.* San Francisco: The Book Club of San Francisco, 1972.

Pitt, Leonard. *The Decline of the Californios: A Social History of the Spanish-Speaking Californians, 1846-1890.* Berkeley: University of California Press, 1970.

Polk, Dora Beale. *The Island of California: A History of the Myth.* Spokane: The Arthur H. Clark Company, 1991.

Pomeroy, Earl. "The Changing West." In *The Reconstruction of American History*, ed. John Higham. London: Hutchinson & Co., 1962.

Powell, Lawrence Clark. *California Classics: The Creative Literature of the Golden State.* Los Angeles: Word Ritchie Press, 1971.

Powell, Phillip Wayne. *Tree of Hate: Propaganda and Prejudice Affecting United States Relations with the Hispanic World.* New York and London: Basic Books, 1971.

Power, Eileen. *Medieval Women*, ed. M. M. Postan. London, New York, Melbourne: Cambridge University Press, 1975.

Poyo, Gerald E. and Gilberto M. Hinojosa. "Spanish Texas and Borderlands Historiography in Transition: Implications for United States History." *Journal of American History* 75 (1988): 393-416.

Prakash, Gyan. "Subaltern Studies as Postcolonial Criticism." *American Historical Review* 99 (1994): 1475-90.

Price, Glen W. *Origins of the War with Mexico: The Polk-Stockton Intrigue.* Austin: University of Texas Press, 1967.

Price, Janet and Margrit Shildrick, eds. *Feminist Theory and the Body: A Reader.* New York and London: Routledge, 1999.

Rawls, James J. *Indians of California: The Changing Image.* Norman and London: University of Oklahoma Press, 1984.

Reagan, Bernice Johnson. "Forward: Nurturing Resistance." In *Reimaging America: The Arts of Social Change*, eds. Mark O'Brien and Craig Little. Philadelphia: New Society Publications, 1990.

Rebolledo, Tey Diana and Eliana S. Rivero, eds. *Infinite Divisions: An Anthology of Chicano Literature.* Tucson: University of Arizona, 1993.

Rendón, Armando B. *Chicano Manifesto*. New York: Macmillan, 1971.

Reyes, Barbara O. *Private Women, Public Lives: Gender and the Missions of the Californias*. Austin: University of Texas, 2009.

Reyna, Sergio. Introduction to *The Woman Who Lost Her Soul and Other Stories*, by Jovita González. Houston: Arte Público, 2000.

Richman, Irving Berdine. *California under Spain and Mexico, 1535-1847*. Boston: Houghton Mifflin, 1911.

Ridge, Martin. "The American West: From Frontier to Region." *New Mexico Historical Review* 64 (1989): 125-142.

Riley, Denise. *Am I That Name? Feminism and the Category of "Women" in History*. Minneapolis: University of Minnesota Press, 1988.

Riley, Glenda. *Women and Indians on the Frontier, 1825-1915*. Albuquerque: University of New Mexico, 1984.

———. "Images of the Frontierswoman: Iowa as a Case Study." *Western Historical Quarterly* 8(1977): 189–202.

———. "Frontier Women." In *American Frontier and Western Issues: A Historiographical Review*. Ed. Roger L. Nichols. New York: Greenwood Press, 1986.

Rischin, Moses. "Continuities and Discontinuities in Spanish-Speaking California," in *Ethnic Conflict in California History*, ed. Charles Wollenberg. Los Angeles: Tinnon-Brown Publishers, 1969.

Risling, Lois. "Native Women in California." Paper presented at the Huntington Library Seminar in Women's Studies, San Marino, Calif., 1991.

Rivera, Tomás. *Y no se lo Tragó la Tierra/And the Earth Did Not Part*. Berkeley: Quinto Sol Publications, 1970.

Robbins, William G."Western History: A Dialectic on the Modern Condition." *Western Historical Quarterly* 20 (1989): 429-449.

Robinson, Alfred. *Life in California*. New York: Wiley & Putnam, 1846. Reprint, Santa Barbara: Peregrine Press, 1970.

Robinson, Cecil. *With the Ears of Strangers: The Mexican in American Literature*. Tucson: University of Arizona Press, 1963.

Robinson, W. W. *Land in California.* Berkeley: University of California Press, 1949; paperback edition, 1979.

Rock, Rosalind Z. "'Pido y Suplico': Women and the Law in Spanish New Mexico." *New Mexico Historical Review* 65 (1991):145-160.

Rodríguez, Richard and Gloria L. Rodríguez. "Teresa Urrea: Her Life as it Affected the Mexican-U.S. Frontier." *El Grito* 5 no.4 (Summer 1972): 48-68.

Rodriguez, Richard. *Hunger of Memory: The Education of Richard Rodriguez.* Boston: David R. Godine, 1982.

Rojas Muñoz, Mary Virginia. "'She Bathes in a Sacred Place': Rites of Reciprocity, Scratching Sticks and Prestige in Alta California." Master's thesis, University of Santa Barbara, 1997.

Romero, Brenda M. "The Indita Genre of New Mexico: Gender and Cultural Identification." In *Chicana Traditions: Continuity and Change,* eds. Norma E. Cantú and Olga Nájera Ramírez. Urbana and Chicago: University of Illinois Press, 2002.

Romo, Ricardo. *East Los Angeles: History of a Barrio.* Austin, University of Texas Press, 1983.

———. "Southern California and the Origins of Latino Civil-Rights Activism." *Western Legal History* 3 (1990): 379-406.

Rose, Gillian. *Feminism and Geography: The Limits of Geographical Knowledge.* Minneapolis: University of Minnesota Press, 1993.

Ruiz, Ramon Eduardo, ed. *The Mexican War: Was It Manifest Destiny?* New York: Holt, Rinehart and Winston, 1963.

Ruiz, Vicki L. *Cannery Women, Cannery Lives.* Albuquerque: University of New Mexico, 1987.

———. *From Out of the Shadows: Mexican Women in Twentieth-Century America.* New York: Oxford University Press, 1999.

Ruiz, Vicki L. and Leisa D. Meyer. "'Ongoing Missionary Labor': Building, Maintaining, and Expanding Chicana Studies/History, an Interview with Vicki L. Ruiz." *Feminist Studies* 34 no. 1/2 (Summer 2008): 23-45.

Ruiz de Burton, María Amparo. *The Squatter and the Don.* Houston: Arte Público Press, 1992.

Ryan, Mary P. *The Empire of the Mother: American Writing about Domesticity, 1830–1860.* New York: Harrington Park Press, 1985.

Salas, Elizabeth. *Soldaderas in the Mexican Military.* Austin: University of Texas Press, 1990.

Salgado, Marcelino J. Canino. *La Canción de Cuna en la Tradición de Puerto Rico.* San Juan Puerto Rico: Instituto de Cultura Puertorriqueña, 1970.

Salinas-González, Irasema. "Bilingual Students Gain Literacy Skills As Family Translators." *Catalyst* 15, no. 2 (October 2003).www.catalystchicago.org/arch/ 10-3/ l003researchprint.htm.

Sánchez, Nellie Van de Grift. *Spanish Arcadia.* San Francisco: Powell Publishing Company, 1929.

Sánchez-Ortega, María Helena "Woman as a Source of 'Evil' in Counter-Reformation Spain." In *Culture and Control in Counter-Reformation Spain, Hispanic Issues 7,* eds. Anne J. Cruz and Mary Elizabeth Perry. Minneapolis: University of Minnesota, 1992.

Sánchez, Rosaura. *Telling Identities: The California Testimonios.* Minneapolis: University of Minnesota Press, 1995.

———. "The History of Chicanas: Proposal for a Materialist Perspective." In *Between Borders: Essays on Mexicana/Chicana History,* ed. Adelaida del Castillo. Los Angeles: Floricanto Press, 1990.

Sánchez, Rosaura, Beatrice Pita, and Barbara Reyes, eds. "Nineteenth Century Californio Testimonials." *Crítica: A Journal of Critical Essays.* University of California, San Diego: Critica Monograph Series, Spring 1994.

Sandos, James. "Levantamiento! The 1824 Chumash Uprising." *The Californians* 5 (January-February 1987): 8-11.

Sandoval, Chéla. *Methodology of the Oppressed.* Minneapolis and London: University of Minnesota Press, 2000.

———. "U.S. Third World Feminism: The Theory and Method of Oppositional Consciousness in the Postmodern World." *Genders* 10 (Spring
1991): 1-24.

Sangari, Kukum, and Sudesh Vaid, eds. *Recasting Women: Essays in Indian
Colonial History.* New Brunswick, NJ: Rutgers, 1990.

San Miguel, Guadalupe. *"Let All of Them Take Heed": Mexican Americans
and the Campaign for Education Equality in Texas, 1910–1981.* Austin:
University of Texas Press, 1987.

Santa Ana, Otto, ed. *Tongue Tied: The Lives of Multilingual Children in
Public Education.* Lanham, MD: Rowman and Littlefield, 2004.

Sarris, Greg. *Keeping Slug Woman Alive: A Holistic Approach to American
Indian Texts.* Berkeley: University of California, 1993.

———. Mabel McKay: *Weaving the Dream.* Berkeley: University of California, 1994.

———."'What I'm Talking about When I'm Talking about My Baskets:
Conversations with Mabel McKay." In *De/Colonizing the Subject: The
Politics of Gender in Women's Autobiography,* eds. Sidonie Smith and
Julia Watson. Minneapolis: University of Minnesota Press, 1992.

Saveth, Edward. *American Historians and European Immigrants, 1875–
1925.* New York: Russell and Russell, 1965.

Saveth, Edward N., ed. *American History and the Social Sciences.* London:
The Free Press of Glencoe, 1964.

Scadron, Arlene, ed. *On Their Own: Widows and Widowhood in the American Southwest, 1848-1939.* Chicago: University of Illinois, 1988.

Schlissel, Lillian. *Women's Diaries of the Westward Journey.* New York:
Schocken Books, 1982.

Scott, Joan Wallach. *Gender and the Politics of History.* New York, 1988.

———. "Gender: A Useful Category of Historical Analysis." *American Historical Review* 91 (December 1986): 1053-75.

Secrest, William B. *Juanita: The Only Woman Lynched During Gold Rush
Days.* Fresno: Saga-West Publishing Company, 1967.

Seed, Patricia. *To Love, Honor, and Obey in Colonial Mexico: Conflicts over Marriage Choice, 1574–1821.* Stanford: Stanford University Press, 1988.

Segura, Denise. "Chicanas and Triple Oppression in the Labor Force." In *Chicana Voices: Intersections of Race, Class, Gender,* eds. Teresa Córdova, et al. Albuquerque: University of New Mexico, 1990.

Servín, Manuel Patricio. "California's Hispanic Heritage: A View into the Spanish Myth." *The Journal of San Diego History* 19 (1973): 1–9.

Shapiro, Ann-Louise, ed. *Feminists Re-Vision History.* New Brunswick: Rutgers University Press, 1994.

Shaler, William. *Journal of a Voyage between China and the Northwestern Coast of America Made in 1804 by William Shaler.* Claremont, Calif.: Saunders Studio Press, 1935.

Sheffield, Carole J. "Sexual Terrorism: The Social Control of Women." In *Analyzing Gender: A Handbook of Social Science Research,* eds. Beth B. Hess and Myra Marx Ferree. Newbury Park: Sage Publications, 1987.

Shindo, Charles J. *Dust Bowl Migrants in the American Imagination.* Lawrence: University of Kansas Press, 1997.

Shinn, Charles Howard. "Pioneer Spanish Families in California." *The Century Magazine* (new series) 5, no. 19 (1891): 377-89.

Shoemaker, Nancy, ed. *Negotiators of Change: Historical Perspectives on Native American Women.* New York: Routledge, 1995.

Sicherman, Barbara. "Review Essay: American History." *Signs: Journal of Women in Culture and Society* 5 (1975): 461-485.

Silko, Leslie Marmon. *Yellow Woman and a Beauty of the Spirit: Essays on Native American Life Today.* New York: Simon & Schuster, 1996.

Silverblatt, Irene. *Moon, Sun, and Witches: Gender Ideologies and Class in Inca and Colonial Peru.* Princeton: Princeton University, 1987.

–––."Interpreting Women in States: New Feminist Ethnohistories" In *Gender at the Crossroads of Knowledge: Feminist Anthropology in the Postmodern Era,* ed. Micaela di Leonardo. Berkeley, Los Angeles, Oxford: University of California Press, 1991.

Simmons, Marc. *Witchcraft in the Southwest: Spanish and Indian Supernaturalism on the Rio Grande*. Lincoln: University of Nebraska Press, 1980.

Smith, Barbara. "Racism in Women's Studies." In *All the Women are White, All the Men are Black, But Some of Us Are Brave*, eds. Gloria T. Hull, Patricia Bell Scott, and Barbara Smith. New York: The Feminist Press, 1982.

Smith, Sherry L. "A Window on Themselves: Perceptions of Indians by Military Officers and Their Wives." *New Mexico Historical Review* 64 (1989): 447-462.

Smith Rosenberg, Carroll. *Disorderly Conduct: Visions of Gender in Victorian America*. New York and Oxford: Oxford University Press, 1985.

Sobek, Maria Herrera, ed. *Santa Barraza, Artist of the Borderlands*. College Station: Texas A&M University Press, 2001.

Solórzano y Pereyra, Juan de. *Politica indiana*, 5 vols. Buenos Aires: Compañía Ibero-Americana de Publicaciones, 1972.

Sosa-Riddell, Adaljiza. n.t. *El Grito* 7. no.1 *Chicanas en la Literatura y el Arte* (Sept. 1973): 76.

———. "Chicanas en el Movimiento. *Aztlán* 5 (1974): 155-165.

Soto, Shirlene. "Tres Modelos Culturales: La Virgen de Guadalupe, La Malinche y la Llorona." *Fem* 10 (1986): 13-16.

Spivak, Gayatri Chakravorty. "The Rani of Simur: An Essay in Reading the Archives." *History and Theory* 25 (1985): 247-72.

———. "Can the Subaltern Speak?" In *Marxism and the Interpretation of Culture*, eds. Cary Nelson and Lawrence Grossberg. Urbana: University of Illinois Press, 1988.

Steinbeck, John . *Grapes of Wrath*. New York: The Viking Press, 1939.

Stephenson, Tory E. "Tomas Yorba, His Wife Vicenta, and His Account Book." *The Quarterly Historical Society of Southern California* 23 (March 1944): 126-55.

Stone, J. A. "He's the Man for Me." In *The Songs of the Gold Rush*, eds. Richard A. Dwyer and Richard E. Lingenfelter. Berkeley: University of California Press, 1964.

Stull, Holt W. *Historical Scholarship in the United States and Other Essays.* Seattle: University of Washington Press, 1967.

Swagerty, William R. "Marriage and Settlement Patterns of Rocky Mountain Trappers and Traders." *The Western Historical Quarterly* 49 (1980): 159–80.

Takaki, Ronald. *Iron Cages: Race and Culture in 19th-Century America.* New York: Alfred A. Knopf, 1979.

———. *Strangers from a Different Shore: A History of Asian Americans.* New York: Little, Brown and Co.,1989.

Talamantez, Inés. "Images of the Feminine in Apache Religious Tradition." In *After Patriarchy: Feminist Transformations of the World Religions*, eds. William R. Eakin, et. al. Orbis Books, 1991.

Tamez, Margo. "Nádasi'né' ndé' isdzáné begoz'aahí' shimaa shiní' gokal gowa goshjaa ha'áná 'idlí texas-nakaiyé godesdzog: Returning Lipan Apache women's laws, lands, & power in El Caladoz Ranchería, Texas-Mexico border." Ph.D. diss., Washington State University, 2010.

Tan, Amy. *The Joy Luck Club.* New York: Penguin, 1989.

Taylor, Diana. *The Archive and the Repertoire: Performing Cultural Memory in the Americas.* Durham: Duke University Press, 2003.

Taylor, George Rogers. *The Turner Thesis: Concerning the Role of the Frontier in American History.* Lexington: D.C. Heath and Company, 1956.

Temple, Thomas Workman II. "Toypurina the Witch and the Indian Uprising at San Gabriel" *Masterkey* 32 (September–October 1958): 136-152.

Thomas, Alfred Barnaby. *Teodoro de Croix and the Northern Frontier of New Spain, 1776-1783.* Norman: University of Oklahoma Press, 1941.

Tiebesar, Antonine, ed. *The Writings of Junipero Serra*, 4 vols. Washington, D.C.: Academy of Franciscan History, 1955-66.

Tjarks, Alicia V. "Comparative Demographic Analysis of Texas, 1777 1793." *Southwestern Historical Quarterly* 77 (January 1974): 291–338.

———. "Demographic, Ethnic, and Occupational Structure of New Mexico, 1790." *The Americas* 35 (July 1978): 45-88.

Todorov, Tzvetan. *The Conquest of America: The Question of the Other.* Trans. Richard Howard. New York: Harper and Row, 1982.

Trafzer, Clifford E. and Joel R. Hyer, eds. *Exterminate Them!: Written Accounts of the Murder, Rape, and Enslavement of Native Americans during the California Gold Rush.* East Lansing: Michigan State University, 1999.

Trexler, Richard C. *Sex and Conquest: Gendered Violence, Political Order and the European Conquest of the Americas.* Ithaca: Cornell University Press, 1995.

Truettner, William H., ed. *The West as America: Reinterpreting Images of the Frontier, 1820–1920.* Washington: Smithsonian Institute Press, 1991.

Trulio, Beverly. "Anglo American Attitudes Toward New Mexican Women." *Journal of the West* 12 (1973): 229-239.

Tsuchida, Nobuya, Linda M. Mealey, and Gail Thoen, eds. *Asian and Pacific American Experiences: Women's Perspectives.* Minneapolis: University of Minnesota, 1982.

Tuhiwai Smith, Linda. *Decolonizing Methodologies: Research and Indigenous Peoples.* New York and London: Zed Books Ltd., 1999.

Turner, Frederick Jackson. *The Frontier in American History.* 1920. Reprint, New York: Robert E. Krieger Publishing Company, 1976.

Tuthill, Franklin. *The History of California.* San Francisco: H. H. Bancroft and Company, 1866.

Tywoniak, Frances Esquibel and Mario T. Garcia. *Migrant Daughter: Coming of Age as a Mexican American Woman.* Berkeley: University of California Press, 2000.

Valdés, Dennis Nodin. *Al Norte: Agricultural Workers in the Great Lakes Region, 1917-1970.* Austin: University of Texas Press, 1991.

———. *Barrios Norteños: St. Paul and Midwestern Mexican Communities in the Twentieth Century.* Austin, University of Texas Press, 2000.

Vancouver, George. *Vancouver in California, 1792–1794: The Original Account of George Vancouver, Early California Travel Series,* Nos. 9, 10, and 22. Ed. Marguerite Eyer Wilbur. Los Angeles: Glen Dawson, 1953 54.

Van Kirk, Sylvia. *Many Tender Ties: Women in Fur-Trade Society, 1670-1870.* Norman: University of Oklahoma, 1980.

Van Kleffens, E. N. *Hispanic Law.* Edinburgh: Edinburgh University Press, 1968.

Viramontes, Helena Maria. *Under the Feet of Jesus.* New York: Dutton, 1995.

Waldman, Carl. *Atlas of the North American Indian.* New York: Facts on File Publications, 1985.

Ware, Carolyn. Introduction to *Class, Sex and the Woman Worker,* eds. Milton Cantor and Bruce Laurie. Westport, CT: Greenwood Press, 1979.

Weber, David J. *The Mexican Frontier, 1821-1846: The American Southwest under Mexico.* Albuquerque: University of New Mexico Press, 1982.

———."Mexico's Far Northern Frontier: Historiography Askew." *Western Historical Quarterly* 7 (July 1976): 279–93.

———. "Here Rests Juan Espinosa: Toward a Clearer Look at the Image of the 'Indolent' Californios." *The Western Historical Quarterly* 10 (January 1979): 61–68.

Weber, David J., ed. *New Spain's Far Northern Frontier: Essay on Spain in the American West, 1540–1821.* Albuquerque: University of New Mexico Press, 1979.

———."Turner, the Boltonians, and the Borderlands." *American Historical Review* 91 (February 1986): 66-81.

———. "John Francis Bannon and the Historiography of the Spanish Borderlands: Retrospect and Prospect." *Journal of the Southwest* 29 (1987): 331-363.

———. David Weber, ed. *Foreigners in Their Native Land: Historical Roots of Mexican Americans.* Albuquerque: University of New Mexico Press, 1973.

Weckmann, Luis. *The Medieval Heritage of Mexico,* trans. Frances M. Lopez-Morillas. New York: Fordham University, 1992.

Welter, Barbara. *Dimity Convictions.* Athens: Ohio University Press, 1976.

———. "The Cult of True Womanhood." *The American Quarterly* 18 (1966): 151-174.

West, Cornel. "Minority Discourse and the Pitfalls of Canon Formation." *Yale Journal of Criticism* 1 (Fall 1987): 173-200.

White, Richard. *"It's Your Misfortune and None of My Own": A New History of the American West.* New York: Norton, 1993.

———. "Race Relations in the American West." *American Quarterly* 38 (1986): 396-416.

White, Richard and John M. Findlay, eds. *Power and Place in the North American West.* Seattle: University of Washington Press, 1999.

Whitenack, Judith. "Conversion to Christianity in the Spanish Romance of Chivalry, 1490-1524." *Journal of Hispanic Philology* 13 (Autumn, 1988): 13-39.

———. "Don Quijote y La Maga: Otra Mujer Que `No Parece.'" In *La Mujer y su representación en las literaturas hispánicas, Actas Irvine-92: Asociación Internacional de Hispanistas,* ed. Juan Villegas. Irvine: Regents of the University of California, 1994.

Wittig, Monica. *The Straight Mind and Other Essays.* Boston: Beacon Press, 1992.

Wollenberg, Charles M. *All Deliberate Speed: Segregation and Exclusion in California Schools, 1855–1975.* Berkeley: University of California Press, 1978.

Womack, John Jr. "Who Are the Chicanos?" *The New York Review of Books* 19 (August 1972): 12-18.

Worster, Donald. *Rivers of Empire: Water, Aridity, and the Growth of the American West.* New York: Pantheon Books, 1985.

———. "New West, True West: Interpreting the Region's History." *Western Historical Quarterly* 18 (1987): 141-156.

Yung, Judy. *Chinese Women of America: A Pictorial History.* Seattle: University of Washington 1986.

Zamora, Emilio. *The World of the Mexican Worker in Texas.* College Station: Texas A&M University Press, 1993.

Zinn, Maxine Baca. "Political Familism: Toward Sex Role Equality in Chicano Families." *Aztlán* 6, no.1 (Spring 1975): 13-26.

INDEX

abortion, 71, 235–236
accommodation, 126, 179, 356
Acuña, Rodolfo, 22, 56, 130, 134, 322, 345
adaption, 183
Africa, 118, 140, 352, 368
African American, 108, 113–114, 126, 128, 142, 282, 351, 365
agency, 66, 115, 117, 120, 126, 230, 232, 241, 291, 306, 320, 339, 341, 354, 361
Alarcón, Norma, 21, 66, 80, 87, 128, 130, 138, 140, 288, 341, 347–348
Albers, Patricia, 84–85, 121, 138, 141, 264, 266
Alcoff, Linda Martin, 81, 355, 368
Allen, Paula Gunn, 86, 117, 139, 264, 325
Alloula, Malek, 118, 140
Alonso, Ana María, 76, 86, 229–230, 262, 272
Alta California, 3, 14, 19, 49, 66, 70–71, 75, 80, 83–84, 86–87, 146, 161, 166, 169, 181, 197–198, 201, 206, 209, 215–216, 220, 229, 238, 241–243, 245–246, 251–252, 256, 260–262, 265, 267, 270, 324–326, 352–353, 360, 383, 387
Alvarez, Roberto, 166, 183
Amazons, 66–70
American Historical Association, 133, 154, 176, 262, 327
Amerindian, 71, 80, 83, 87, 145, 152, 161, 163–164, 167–169, 181, 197, 201–202, 208, 211, 214, 217–218,

Amerindian (*continued*), 221–222, 225, 235, 240–242, 245, 249, 259–260, 262, 325, 337, 340, 387
Anglo Men, 39, 136, 163–164, 168, 314
Anglo Women, 49, 115, 162–164, 314
Año Nuevo Kerr, Luisa, 11–12
Anza, Juan Bautista de, 146, 205, 243, 252–253
Anzaldúa, Gloria, 11, 19, 22, 25, 32–33, 66, 80, 87, 117, 131–133, 139, 285, 288, 355, 369, 380
Apodaca, Linda María, 10–11, 22, 179
Arballo, María Feliciana, 251–252, 254–255
archives, 31, 60, 67, 184–185, 223, 225–226, 263, 267–268, 271–272, 279, 288–289, 349–351, 354, 382, 384
Arguello, José, 145
Arguello, Concepción, 145
Armitage, Susan, 20, 129–130, 134–135, 138–140, 164, 180–181
Arrom, Sylvia, 166, 184, 228, 264, 271
Asian, 105, 108–109, 113–114, 116–119, 122, 125–126, 128, 130–135, 138–139, 141–142, 299, 360
Asian American women, 108–109, 117, 122–123, 125, 130–132, 134
assimilation, 52, 62, 109, 133, 165, 169, 182

Atherton, Gertrude, 158, 177
Aztlán, 9, 21–22, 81, 131, 268–269, 321, 329

Baca, Judith F., 77, 87, 241, 267
Baca Zinn, Maxine, 22
Bancroft, Hubert Howe, 58, 143, 168, 172, 247, 270, 354
baptism, 184
Barrio Boy: The Story of a Boy's Acculturation, 339
Bear Flag Revolt, 116
Behar, Ruth, 76, 85–86, 239, 264, 266
Beilharz, Edwin A., 206, 224–226
berdache, 73
Bernal, Josefa, 259
Between Borders: Essays in Chicana/ Mexicana History, 1
birth rate, 153
Black Legend, 145, 152, 173
Blackmar, Frank W., 152, 175
Blackwell, Maylei, 2, 8, 18, 20–21
Blea, Irene, 380
Bolton, Herbert Eugene, 70, 100, 159–162, 171, 175, 177–178, 223, 270, 281
Boltonians, 129, 160–161, 178
Brooks, Dudley, 30, 188
Brooks, James, 360
Bourbon Reforms, 232
Brownmiller, Susan, 181, 216, 226–227
Broyles, Yolanda Julia, 6, 321
brujas, 85, 262, 266, 305, 327
Bucareli, Antonio María, 201, 224
Building with Our Hands: New Directions in Chicana Studies, 80, 83, 181, 198, 262, 325, 387
Butler, Anne, 115, 132, 134–136,

Butler, Anne (*continued*), 139, 272

Calafia, 13, 35–36, 65–68, 70, 72, 81, 325, 388
Californiana, 42–43, 49–50, 53–54, 70, 269, 301
California Pastoral, 147, 172–174, 270
Californio, 149, 164, 182, 199, 245, 247, 249, 259–260, 268–269
Callis, Eulalia, 145, 161, 173, 251, 253–256, 271
Calmecac, 30, 33, 192–193
Camarillo, Albert, 10, 22, 56, 100, 166, 183, 323
camps, 5, 90, 94, 189, 191, 193, 305, 314, 329, 335–336, 344–345, 350, 381, 383
Canciones de Cuna, 14, 291–293, 349, 355, 357
canon law, 232, 259
Cantú, Norma, 6, 132, 288, 370
capitalism, 10–11, 38, 47, 49, 119, 121, 142
captivity, 302, 348, 352–353, 357, 359–362, 364, 369–370
Carrillo, Teresa, 6
Casas, María Raquél, 2, 18, 82, 201
Castañeda, Antonia, xi–xii, 1–2, 5, 12–13, 16, 19, 22–23, 25–28, 31–34, 89–90, 98, 188, 196, 273–275, 278, 290, 293, 328, 346, 379–383, 385, 387–388
Castañeda, Carlos, 7
Castañeda, Irene R., xiii, 188, 317–318, 327, 329
Castañeda, José, 314
Castillian, 145, 157, 160
Cea, Helen Lara, 5, 58, 140
Chan, Sucheng, 100, 122–124, 134, 138, 141

Chávez-García, Miroslava, 1–2, 8, 11, 18, 20

Chelo, Doña, 343–344, 371–376

Chicana Feminist, 7–9, 20–21, 101, 130, 198

Chicana historians, 2, 7, 12, 15, 22–23, 26, 32, 197, 275, 278, 280, 289

Chicana Lesbians: The Girls Our Mothers Warned Us About, 19, 132, 198, 272, 368

Chicana Matters, 26, 380

Chicana/Mexicana History Conference, 276–277

Chicana/o Movement, 7–8

Chicana/o Studies, xii, 2–3, 6–7, 9, 12, 16–17, 66, 188, 280, 282, 288, 292

Chicano history, 9–10, 13, 20, 22, 56, 59–60, 78, 83, 132, 143–144, 166, 276, 278, 281, 286, 298, 341, 381, 387

child translators, 293, 333, 335–336, 338–340, 342–343, 348

children, 14, 29, 47, 67, 72, 74, 77, 121, 148, 165, 167–168, 187, 190, 203–204, 206, 233, 235–236, 241, 245, 247, 250, 254, 291–292, 312, 314–316, 319, 328, 331, 334–341, 343–349, 356–357, 359–362, 367, 383–384, 388

Chinese, 40, 108, 115, 122–124, 134–135, 139, 141–142, 155, 300, 308

Chinese Exclusion Laws, 122

Christianity, 67, 75, 82, 207, 222, 239, 352

Christians, 357

Chumash, 75–76, 85–86, 238–240, 266–267, 353

Chumash Woman, 75

Chumash visionary, 76, 85, 239–240

Chupu, 75, 238–239

Catholic, xiii, 68, 193, 205, 207, 209, 221, 232, 242, 255–256, 260, 341

Cimarroncita, 364

class, 3, 5, 7, 19, 29, 33, 37–39, 42–54, 56–59, 61–62, 91, 100, 103–108, 110–114, 116, 118, 120, 122, 125–129, 131–136, 138, 140, 142–143, 153, 156–159, 163, 165, 168–169, 178–179, 184, 191, 196, 210, 215, 217–220, 227–228, 230, 269, 278, 281–282, 286–287, 291, 295–297, 299, 301, 303, 320, 330, 335, 338–339, 342–343, 346, 355, 381–382

class oppression, 105–106, 128

Club Las Hijas de Cuauhtémoc, 8

colonialism, 75–76, 79–80, 85–86, 105, 110, 118–119, 121–122, 126–127, 140, 230, 239–240, 260, 262, 266, 325–326, 347, 353

Color of Privilege, The, 198

community, 13, 20, 22–23, 26, 28–32, 43, 56, 75, 85, 91, 94, 99, 112, 126, 128, 132, 135, 141–142, 148, 160, 188, 193–194, 238, 248, 256, 269, 275, 301, 305, 315, 335–336, 339, 342, 348, 350–351, 353, 365, 369, 381, 383

conquest, 4, 10–11, 14, 18, 35–36, 45–47, 51–52, 54, 65, 67, 69–70, 73, 80–83, 87, 99–100, 110–111, 114–116, 118, 120, 128, 139–140, 147, 155, 157, 161, 164–165, 168–169, 176, 181, 197–198, 201–202, 206–207, 216–222, 224, 227–228, 233, 240, 242, 245, 257, 260, 262, 265–266, 269, 293, 295–296, 303–304, 322–326, 341, 367, 387

conquest of California, 52, 80, 87, 155, 202, 207, 324
conquest of Mexico, 67, 69, 228
contract labor, 123–124, 306
converts, 67, 206, 208, 244
convicts, 161, 243
Cook, Sherburne F., 86, 136, 206, 223–226, 267–268
Córdova, Teresa, 5–6, 19–20, 132, 135, 196
corridos, 193, 306–307
Cortés, Hernán, 68–69, 78, 82–83, 340, 384
Cotera, Marta, 11, 21, 380
court records, 116, 167–168, 185, 272
Craver, Rebecca, 135, 165, 182
Crystal City, 28, 32, 34, 89–90, 97, 189, 305, 311, 314–315, 317, 329
Cuádraz, Gloria, 5–6
cult of true womanhood, 38, 47, 50–51, 57, 59–60
cultural diversity, 109–110, 328
culture, xii, 8, 10, 12, 14, 18, 23, 27, 35, 39, 43, 45, 47, 53–54, 57, 73, 82–83, 86–87, 99–100, 104, 107, 110–113, 117–118, 120, 122–123, 125–126, 131–133, 136–139, 141, 143–144, 153, 155, 158, 163, 165, 168–169, 179, 193–194, 198, 215–216, 230, 235, 263, 266, 269–270, 281, 290–292, 294, 302, 304, 322–323, 325–326, 328–329, 331, 334–335, 337, 341–343, 345, 348, 352, 362, 369, 387–388

Daiken, Leslie, 357, 369
Dana, Richard Henry, 36, 39–40, 58, 149, 165
danza del jale, 29, 90
Davis, Angela, 106, 132, 337

Dawley, Amelia, 352
Decierdo, Margarita, 5–6
decolonize, 127, 385
Decolonial Imaginary, 81, 287, 292, 321–322, 326–328
de la Guerra y Noriega, María Teresa, 149
de la Perouse, Jean Francois Galaup, 152, 175
de la Torre, Adela, 5–6, 80, 83, 130, 181, 198, 262, 325, 387
Del Castillo, Adelaida R., 12, 16, 21, 23, 83, 87, 130, 322, 387
Del Castillo, Richard Griswold, 278
Deng, Francis M., 302, 324–325
diaspora, 296
DiGiorgio Corporation, 319
disease, 85, 301
dispossession, 51, 54, 57, 247, 291, 300–303, 320
divorce, 74, 121, 167, 180, 222, 235, 254
domesticity, 47, 49, 147, 173
Doña Irene, 314–316, 374
double standard, 9, 48, 233
DuCille, Ann, 111
Duerme Duerme, Negrito, 365, 370
dust bowl migration, 316, 319
Dysart, Jane, 165, 182

Eastern Washington, 92, 189–192, 194, 310, 345
ecclesiastical court, 167, 354
economic production, 47
economy, 1–2, 12–13, 16, 35–39, 49, 51, 74, 83, 114–115, 122–123, 125, 134, 137–139, 169, 172, 174, 181, 235, 246–247, 252, 257, 269–270, 290, 301, 307, 322, 325, 360, 387
education, 5, 7–8, 10, 91, 130, 148,

education (*continued*), 190, 290, 314–315, 319, 329, 335–336, 338, 345–346, 348, 356, 379–381
Edwards, Anne, 181, 216, 227
El Grito, 3, 8–9, 19, 21, 328
Eldredge, Zoeth Skinner, 143, 172–173
embodied knowledge, 306, 355
enlightenment, 299
Encuentro Feminíl, 8, 21
Erdrich, Louise, 117, 139
eugenicist, 153
Euro-American men, 114, 116, 149, 167
Euro-American women, 6, 101, 109, 111, 137, 155, 163, 361
expansionism, 112, 116, 125, 153
exploitation, 96, 105–106, 115–116, 159–160, 207, 213, 220–221, 342, 360

Facio, Elisa, 6
Fages, Pedro, 75, 208, 213, 225–226, 238, 254, 271
family, xiii, 3–4, 14, 27, 29, 40, 43, 49, 53, 58, 61, 77, 79, 83, 91, 96, 114, 122, 124, 126, 136, 144–146, 148, 155, 158, 162–163, 166–168, 171, 177–178, 180, 183, 185, 188–189, 191, 197–199, 204, 209, 216, 222, 227–229, 232–233, 241–242, 246–248, 250–252, 254–256, 259–260, 262, 270, 291–292, 298–299, 305, 307–309, 311–312, 314–315, 317–320, 326, 334–335, 337–339, 342–343, 346, 350–353, 356, 361, 372, 375, 383, 387
fantasy Spanish heritage, 154, 157
farm workers movement, 191–192
feminist historians, 127, 162, 199

feminist scholars, 105, 111, 127, 164, 198, 227, 303, 342
feminists of color, 11, 106
Farnham, Thomas Jefferson, 36, 39, 41–43, 50, 58–59, 62
Font, Pedro, 205, 252
Forbes, Jack, 81, 125, 129, 140, 268, 321
Foreign Miner's Tax, 300
foundlings, 245
Franciscan priests, 72, 237
Frausto, Tomás Ybarra, 3, 16, 19, 27, 30, 98, 187–189, 196, 328
Frémont, John C., 149
Friars, 207, 383
Frias, Lupe, 5
frontier, 14, 19, 21, 23, 50, 57, 62, 66, 83, 99, 107–108, 112, 119–120, 128–129, 132–133, 135, 137–140, 143–144, 146, 153–160, 162–164, 166–169, 171–172, 174, 176–182, 198, 206, 209–210, 213, 215–216, 221, 224–226, 228–229, 244, 249, 254, 256, 262, 267–271, 281, 290, 322–325, 330, 340, 346, 353, 356–357, 361–362, 364, 387

Gabrielinos, 77, 241
Galarza, Ernesto, 7, 330, 339–340, 346
Gálvez, Estevan Raél, 348, 360, 369
Gamboa, Lupe, 192
García, Alma M., 6, 8, 20–21
García, Felicitas Pérez, 306–307, 327–328
Gender on the Borderlands, 18, 20–23, 277, 290
gender oppression, 5, 104, 106
gender roles, 47, 342
genocide, 10, 302
gente de razón, 243, 246, 250,

gente de razón (*continued*), 255–256
gentle tamers, 38, 57, 62, 100,
    103–104, 107, 110–111, 113, 116,
    130, 133, 137, 155, 176, 179–180
germ theory, 151, 153–154
girls, 19, 65, 96, 132, 146, 191, 198,
    205, 208, 211, 229, 245, 249, 256,
    272, 304, 336, 340, 342–343, 368
Gobernadora, 253–254, 256
gold rush, 18, 41, 45, 52–53, 55,
    62, 83, 88, 144, 158, 164, 168,
    300–302, 304, 324, 326–327, 387
Gómez Quiñones, Juan, 1, 16, 276,
    281
Gonzales, Tanya, xii, 2
González, Deena, xi–xii, 2, 5–6, 12,
    15–16, 18–20, 23, 26–27, 31, 66,
    100, 122, 125, 137, 165, 273–275,
    278, 290, 292, 298, 304, 355
González, Jovita, 7, 20, 323
González, Rosalinda Méndez, 119,
    140
graduate students, 1, 10, 192, 277,
    280, 379
Great Depression, 159, 310, 316,
    329, 345
great migration, 124
growers, 98, 191
Gutiérrez, Ramón, 11, 72, 118, 166,
    179, 184, 230, 237, 269, 326, 348
Gypsy, Gypsies, 359

Hall, Stuart, 307
Harjo, Suzan Shown, 103, 129
Harvest of Shame, 319, 330
Hemphill, Lowry, 338, 346
Hernández, Inés, 66, 78, 80, 341, 347
Hernández-Avila, Inés, 66, 80, 348
heterosexuality, 232
Hijar-Padres expedition, 245
Hispanophobia, 44, 160

historical analysis, 120, 125, 168,
    178–179, 198–199, 272, 299, 302,
    384
historiography, 14, 23, 57, 79, 83,
    99–100, 103–104, 107, 111, 118,
    128–129, 132, 137, 143, 150, 153,
    159, 162–163, 171–172, 174–175,
    189, 270, 281, 290, 295, 297, 299,
    322, 387
Hittell, Theodore, H., 143–144, 148,
    150, 172, 174
Hofstadter, Richard, 155, 176
homophobia, 283–285
honor, 76–77, 122, 166, 184,
    219–220, 228, 230, 233, 239,
    251–252, 254–255, 263, 265
hop, 89, 310, 313, 315, 318, 371, 377
Houston, Ramona, 20, 269, 323, 351,
    368, 388
Huerta, Dolores, 106, 132
Huerta, Juanita Zazueta, 306, 308,
    327–328
Hurtado, Aída, 198
Hurtado, Albert, 2, 87, 121, 139,
    164, 240, 324

Iberian, 242, 356–357
imperialism, 47, 51, 55, 105, 131,
    139, 153
immigrants, 22, 98, 134, 153, 173,
    175–176, 183, 300–301, 339, 346
immigration, 15, 18, 23, 26, 33, 79,
    122–126, 135, 142, 153, 249, 298,
    327, 340
Indian, 35, 42, 51, 53, 65–66, 69–73,
    75, 77–79, 82, 84–86, 108, 113,
    116–117, 131–132, 134–141,
    160, 164, 181, 201, 203, 206–211,
    213–214, 217, 221, 223, 225, 231,
    236–237, 239–240, 245, 262,
    264–267, 301, 305, 316, 323–325,

Indian (*continued*), 337, 340–341,
    348, 353–354, 356, 360, 362, 365,
    369
Indian boarding schools, 341
indigenous., 3, 10, 13–14, 33,
    36, 65–66, 73–74, 78, 81, 105,
    109–110, 119, 131, 197–198, 217,
    230, 232, 235, 237, 240, 243–244,
    246, 286, 301, 321, 340, 352–354,
    360, 383
indios, 361
infanticide, 71, 235–236
interdisciplinary, 1, 8–11, 15, 18, 20,
    22, 118, 126, 232, 280
intermarriage., 58, 60, 62, 112, 126,
    135, 161–162, 165, 169, 182, 208,
    224, 242–243, 245–247, 249, 360
internal migration, 296, 300–302,
    306, 319–320
interracial marriage, 109, 112, 125,
    133, 138, 164–165, 167–168, 224
Islam, 358

Jabati, Baindu, 352
Jackson, Helen Hunt, 157, 177
Japanese, 108, 122, 124, 134–135,
    138, 141–142, 314, 316, 329
Japanese women, 122, 124
Jeffrey, Julie Roy, 57, 62, 163, 180
Jensen, Joan, 57, 62, 102–104,
    107–108, 110–112, 114, 130,
    133–134, 142, 155, 176, 179–181,
    267
Jews, 358
Johnson, Susan Lee, 2, 18, 272
Jones, Oakah, 171, 178, 215, 226,
    271
Josefa of Downieville, 52, 62
Juncosa, Domingo, 203

Karttunen, Frances, 58, 78, 87, 342,

Karttunen, Frances (*continued*), 347
Kolodny, Annette, 135, 139, 163,
    181

labor, xi, xiii, 5, 9, 11, 13, 16, 18,
    21, 28–29, 33, 72, 91–94, 109,
    123–126, 128, 142, 166, 169,
    189–190, 192, 196, 206, 221, 236,
    278, 293, 300–301, 305–306,
    309, 312, 314–316, 319, 323, 328,
    335–336, 339, 345, 353, 381, 383
labor camp, 29, 91, 189–190,
    315–316
La Colectiva, 7, 275
Land Grant Commission, 168, 185
language, 14, 69, 78, 104, 110–112,
    122, 150, 159, 178, 190–191, 240,
    252, 291–293, 297, 301–302, 306,
    314, 325, 328, 331–332, 334–335,
    338–343, 347, 354, 356, 368, 388
Langum, David, 44–45, 57–59, 62,
    164–165, 177, 182, 269
land grants, 49, 61, 167–168
Las Sergas de Esplandián, 67, 69, 81
Lasuén, Fermín Francisco de,
    221–222, 224–225, 228
Latin American history, 12, 81, 263,
    280–281, 283, 298
Laws of the Indies, 216, 220
LeCompte, Janet, 44–45, 48, 57,
    59–60
Lerner, Gerda, 164, 174, 181, 216,
    226–228
lesbian, 87, 106, 277, 283–285, 341,
    348
lesbian caucus, 284–285
liberalism, 104
liberation movements, 104–105,
    131, 196
Lim, Shirley Geok-Lin, 117, 132,
    140

Limerick, Patricia, 119, 128, 140, 176, 181, 322–324
Limón, José, 7, 12, 20
Life in California, 39, 42, 58–62, 141, 171, 174, 223, 265
Literatura Chicana: Texto Y Contexto, 3, 19, 98, 188, 196, 328
Lockhart, Katharine Meyer, 249–250, 270
Lorenzana, Apolinaria, 185, 245, 256–257, 268, 271
Loyola Marymount, xi, 287, 385
Luella, Ms., 351
Lugo, María Antonia Isabela de, 246
Los Inditos, 361
lullabies, 14, 291–293, 349–350, 355–358, 360–361, 364, 367
Lupe's Song, 303–304
Lyzárraga, Sylvia, 5

McCloud, Janet, 106, 132
McWilliams, Carey, 157, 177, 301, 323
Macías, Ana, 12
Maestas, Roberto, 192
Malinche, 8–9, 13, 21, 35–36, 65–67, 69–72, 78–79, 87, 325, 340–341, 348, 384, 388
Malintzín, 8, 21, 78, 87, 340–342, 347–348, 384
Manifest Destiny, 10, 36–37, 46, 57, 151, 172, 174, 292, 327
Mallon, Florencia, 81, 251, 263, 270
Malone, Michael, 128–129, 156, 175–176, 179
maquiladoras, 79
marriage, 18, 43–44, 49, 51, 54, 60, 62, 67, 74, 85, 109, 112–114, 121, 125, 133, 136–138, 146, 161,

marriage (*continued*), 164–168, 179, 182–184, 208, 215, 222, 224, 227–228, 232–235, 242, 245–250, 256, 262, 264–266, 270, 348, 352
Marxist, 105–106, 118
Mata, Jennifer, 2, 18
Mende, 352, 368
memory, 18, 76–77, 79, 241, 272, 338, 346, 349, 351–352, 356, 367–368
menstruation, 74
mestiza, 3, 10–11, 13–14, 22, 36, 65–66, 71, 77, 79–80, 82, 99–100, 118, 135–136, 139, 169, 197, 230, 239, 241, 251, 256–257, 259–260, 353–354, 369, 379
mestizo, 2, 50, 53, 61, 78, 147, 160, 165, 243, 246, 249–250, 340–341, 356
mestizaje, 109, 112, 126, 360
Methodology of the Oppressed, 76, 80, 327, 369
Mexican American, 56–57, 63, 112, 128, 137, 182, 196, 269, 301–303, 306, 316, 327–328
Mexican-American War, 37, 40, 44, 50–51, 53, 55–56, 166
Mexican independence, 249
Mexican men, 148–149, 174
Mexican rule, 49, 245, 247, 259
Mexican War, 66, 144, 149, 152, 162, 172, 247, 299–300, 303–304, 322, 354, 357
Mexican women, 12, 14–15, 18–19, 23, 26, 33, 38–56, 58–60, 79–80, 83, 87, 99, 108–109, 113–116, 120, 122, 130, 132, 134, 136–137, 140, 142–143, 146–150, 153, 155, 158, 161–165, 167–168, 171, 179, 182, 224, 262–263, 270–271, 276, 281, 287, 290, 304, 314, 316, 322,

Mexican women (*continued*), 327, 354, 387
midwives, 305
migrant worker, 91, 291, 320
Mihesuah, Devon, 100, 345, 348
military, 50, 61, 70–71, 85, 114, 135, 160, 164, 167, 169, 202, 206–211, 213–215, 217, 221, 225, 235, 242, 246, 248–249, 256–257, 266, 271, 295–296, 303, 340–341, 353–354, 356–358, 360
Miller, Darlis, 57, 62, 102–104, 107–108, 110–112, 114, 130, 133–136, 155, 165, 176, 179–182, 267
Minh-ha, Trinh T., 131, 140, 349, 367–368, 370
Minnesota, 3, 80–82, 84, 189, 263–264, 266, 286, 319, 326–328, 346, 369, 388
Miranda, Gloria, 58, 138, 166, 183–184, 248–250, 268, 270
Mirikitani, Janice, 106, 132
miscarriage, 254
miscegenation, 111–112, 114, 138, 162
missionaries, 72, 152, 161, 167, 203, 207–208, 213, 221–222, 236, 241, 341
missionization, 202–203, 205
Mission Santa Barbara, 75, 184, 238
Mission San Diego, 210, 257
Mission San Gabriel, 71, 75, 202, 210, 225, 236–237
Mission San Luis Obispo, 203
Mission Santa Cruz, 72, 76, 86, 236, 240, 266
Mohanty, Chandra, 112, 119, 131, 326
monigote, 71–72, 236
monjero, 72, 222, 236, 257

Monroy, Douglas, 269, 278, 323
Monterey, 19, 41, 60–61, 140, 146, 177, 179, 185, 202–203, 205, 223–226, 228, 244–245, 249, 256, 262, 267–268, 270–272, 356, 369
Mora, Magdalena, 12, 23, 130, 359, 369
Moraga, Cherríe, 3, 19, 131, 369
Moran, Mary, 352
Moriana Cautiva, 359, 369
Moore, Shirley Ann, 100, 124, 142
Morrison, Toni, 117, 139
Mujeres Activas en Letras y Cambio Social (MALCS), xii, 4–7, 12–13, 16, 19, 31, 33, 282–285, 290, 381
Mujeres en Marcha, 5, 7, 131
mulato, 147, 160, 246, 364–365
multiculturalism, 100, 107, 111, 133, 328, 346, 388
Muñoz, Mary Rojas, 73–74, 84–85
Muslim, 69, 359
Myres, Sandra L., 128, 135, 139, 163–164, 179–181

narratives, 4, 8, 32, 40, 43, 51, 54, 59, 76, 91, 168, 240, 247, 259–260, 269, 302, 348, 350, 353, 361, 369
National Association for Chicano Studies (NACS), 5–7, 19
National Association for Chicana and Chicano Studies (NACCS), xi, 13, 16, 19, 22, 27, 31, 274, 283–285, 290
National Defense Education Act, 190
nationalism, 79, 105, 150–151, 160, 322
Native American, 74, 83–86, 108–109, 113–114, 118, 121, 125–126, 128, 132–139, 141, 241,

Native American (*continued*),
    264–267, 301–303, 324–325, 341
nativism, 155
neocolonial, 105
neophyte, 75, 222, 238, 257, 268
*New Mexico Women: Intercultural
    Perspectives*, 134, 163, 179, 267
Neve, Felipe de, 204, 206, 210–214,
    221, 224–226
New Spain, 72, 152, 166, 171, 182,
    208, 211, 216, 218, 220, 224–226,
    228, 230, 237, 271, 347
NietoGómez, Anna, 8
Northwest., xii–xiii, 15, 28, 68,
    98, 156, 189–190, 192, 194, 196,
    305–306, 310, 312, 315, 319, 325,
    327–328
novelas de caballería, 36, 66, 68

Occupied America, 10, 22, 56, 59,
    130, 322, 345
Olbes , Father, 72, 236
Operation Wetback, 336, 346
oppositional consciousness, 20, 117,
    139, 306, 355
oral testimonies, 354
oral traditions, 241, 350, 352,
    355–356, 361, 367
Orellana, Marjorie Faulstich,
    338–339, 346, 348
Orozco, Cynthia, 6, 58, 132

Pacific Northwest, 15, 28, 98, 156,
    189, 192, 196, 305–306, 310, 315,
    319, 325, 327–328
Padilla, Genaro, 259, 269, 272
Pomona College, 287
Panagua, Francisco, 210
Paredes, Américo, 362, 369
Pascoe, Peggy, 109, 133, 136

patriarchal family, 166–167,
    198–199, 222, 232, 242, 251, 260
patriarchal society, 219–220
patriarchy, 7–8, 20, 22, 84, 106, 169,
    181, 226–228
Pattie, James Ohio, 162
Paul, Rodman, 153
Paxson, Frederic L., 155, 176
Peffer, George, 123–124, 142
Pérez, Emma, 5, 12, 16, 19, 27, 31,
    73, 81, 132, 272–275, 277–278,
    290, 296–298, 319, 321–322, 330,
    355, 368, 379
Pérez, Erika, 2, 18
Pérez, Rita, 306, 308, 327–328
Pescador, Juan Javier, xi, 26–27
Pesquera, Beatriz, 5, 130, 325
Pitti, Steve, 280
pláticas, 2, 13, 15–16, 25, 28, 32
poblador, 50, 161, 252
politics, 4, 14, 19–20, 22, 28, 33,
    70, 78–80, 83–84, 87, 99–100,
    103–104, 107, 112, 114, 118,
    120, 125, 128, 130–131, 133,
    136, 139, 141, 147, 155, 168–169,
    181, 197–198, 201, 206, 216, 262,
    264–265, 272, 291, 296, 302–304,
    321–322, 325–328, 331, 334–335,
    337, 342–343, 346–347, 356,
    387–388
popular histories, 143–144, 152, 158
postcolonial, 100, 250, 263, 384
Poverty in the Valley of Plenty, 319,
    330
presidio(s), 61, 145, 160, 202, 204,
    209, 211–212, 225, 248–249
priests, 71–72, 76, 152, 198, 203,
    205, 207, 212–213, 220, 229,
    236–237, 240, 242, 353
primary sources, 39, 147, 150, 152,
    157–158, 298–299

procreation, 67, 71–72, 233, 236–237, 260
prostitution, 58, 62, 109, 115, 124, 134–135, 141–142, 164, 257, 259
purity of blood, 217, 246

Quabajay people, 205
Quintana, Andres, 76, 86, 240, 266
Quiñones, Juan Gómez, 1, 16, 56, 276, 281

race, xii, 5, 10, 14, 19, 23, 29, 38–39, 41–43, 46–48, 51–53, 56–59, 61–62, 79–80, 82–83, 98–100, 104–106, 108, 110–114, 116, 118, 120, 124–126, 128–129, 131–133, 135–138, 142–145, 147, 151, 153–155, 158, 161, 163–169, 171–172, 174, 191, 196, 215–219, 224, 227–228, 230, 246, 270, 278, 281–282, 284–285, 287, 290, 295, 297, 314, 322, 326–327, 342, 346, 355, 383, 387
racial discrimination, 91
racially mixed, 145, 152, 160–161, 215, 239, 242, 245
racial purity, 43, 54
Ramona, 63, 157, 177
rancherias, 75, 201, 210, 238
rape, 88, 164, 181, 203–204, 207, 211–214, 216–217, 226, 257, 259, 324
Rebolledo, Tey Diana, 87, 198
Reconquest, 69, 134, 179, 217, 227–228, 242, 267, 359
refugees, 134, 179, 267, 301–302
Refusing the Favor, 18, 80, 83, 140–141, 263, 287
regional history, 14, 291, 295–297, 300, 305, 320–321, 388
Regulations, Echeveste, 209

Reid, Hugo, 71, 141, 223, 236, 265
Reina Xerifa Mora, La, 359, 369
religion, 68, 76, 85, 126, 145, 217–219, 228, 239, 266, 302
reproduction, 72, 79, 236
reproductive labor, 353
Resanov, Nickolai Petrovich, 145–146, 173
resistance, 4, 10, 14, 26, 29–30, 35–36, 66, 73, 76–77, 79, 84–85, 90–91, 120–121, 126, 130, 133, 140, 169, 178–179, 189, 192, 194, 198, 203, 216, 223, 232, 236–237, 240–241, 245, 251, 256, 259–260, 264, 266, 272, 356, 382
revisionist frontier historians, 155
Reyes, Bárbara O., 2, 18, 269
Rodriguez, Richard, 338, 346
Riley, Glenda, 128, 135, 163, 179–181
Rivera y Moncada, Fernando de, 209
Robinson, Alfred, 36, 39, 42, 58, 60, 149, 174
Robinson, Cecil, 44, 56, 59, 165, 182
Rocha, Vera, 77, 86, 241, 267
Rodríguez, Romana Raquel, 305, 311
romances fronterizos, 357, 359, 362
Romero, Brenda, 362
Romero, Yolanda, 11
Romo, Ricardo, 10, 22, 100, 137, 166, 183, 278
Rubio Goldsmith, Raquel, 12
rugged individualism, 154
Ruiz, Vicki L., 9, 19, 21, 86, 130, 267
Russia, 146

San Antonio, 27–28, 30, 33, 90, 182, 189–190, 194, 243, 267, 274, 277, 290, 313, 319, 354, 388

Sánchez, George I., 7
Sánchez, Nellie Van de Grift, 157, 177
Sánchez, Rosaura, 12, 80, 87, 179, 263, 269, 347
Sandoval, Chela, 76, 117, 139, 306, 327, 355, 369
santa patrona de las lesbianas, 284
secularization, 167, 240, 247
Seed, Patricia, 166, 184, 265
segregation, 98, 207, 211, 345
Segura, Denise, 5–6, 196
Serra, Junipero, 184, 201–205, 207–210, 213, 215, 223–226, 234, 242–243, 262, 267–268
Servín, Manuel, 152, 175, 271
settler, 50, 145–146, 161, 169, 199, 215–216, 242–243, 245, 268, 353
sex, 4, 10, 18, 22, 37–38, 46–47, 51–52, 57–59, 62, 74, 80, 85, 87, 107, 118, 120, 123–124, 138, 142–143, 147, 153, 163, 165, 168, 179, 181, 198–199, 206–208, 216–220, 222, 227–228, 235, 250, 257, 262, 266, 304, 325–326, 369
sexism, 9, 45, 52, 132, 174, 382
sexual assault, 164
sexual morality, 219, 227–228
sexual violence, 4, 14, 83, 87, 116, 139, 164, 181, 197–198, 201–202, 208, 213, 215–217, 221–222, 226, 228–229, 240, 257, 259, 262, 325–326, 387
sexuality, 4, 12, 14, 18–19, 65–66, 71–74, 78–79, 83, 85–86, 90, 93, 99, 104, 106, 114, 118, 120–121, 123–126, 132, 136–137, 139, 141, 169, 179, 197–198, 219, 228–233, 235–237, 240, 242, 257, 259–260, 262–264, 266, 272, 281–282, 284, 297, 303–304, 325–327, 341–342,
sexuality (continued), 348, 355, 368, 387
Shoemaker, Nancy, 73, 84, 264–265
Sierra, Victoria Archuleta, 306, 308, 327–328
Sierra, Chris, 275
silences, 30, 73, 288, 292
sitio y lengua, 5, 283, 355
soldado de cuera, 161
Sommers, Joseph, 3, 19, 98, 192, 196, 328
soldier, 145–146, 161, 169, 202–203, 208, 213, 215–216, 242–246, 268, 353
Sonoma, 149
Sosa Riddell, Adaljiza, 21, 131
Soto, Shirlene, 11–12, 21–22, 211–212
Spain, 32, 40, 70, 72, 82, 86, 145–146, 152–153, 156–160, 166, 169, 171, 182, 198, 208, 211, 216–218, 220, 224–226, 228, 230, 237, 242, 246, 249, 256, 266, 271, 347, 356–358, 367
Spanish borderlands, 83, 85, 129, 144, 159–161, 166, 171, 177–178, 225–226, 262–265, 271, 279–281, 298, 348
Spanish colonialism, 75, 347
Spanish conquest, 10, 80–81, 83, 87, 181, 197, 201, 221, 262, 325, 387
Spanish-Mexican women, 18–19, 23, 80, 83, 108, 120, 122, 132, 137, 140, 142–143, 146, 155, 162, 165, 167–168, 171, 179, 182, 224, 262–263, 270–271, 322, 387
Stanford, 19, 136, 140, 171–172, 179, 184, 224, 228, 262, 264–265, 275–277, 280, 282, 298, 322, 348, 379–380
stereotypes, 1–2, 4, 10, 13, 16,

stereotypes (*continued*), 35–39,
43–46, 48, 51–57, 59, 83, 99–100,
111–114, 137–139, 143, 146–150,
153, 155, 157, 164–165, 169, 172,
174, 177, 180–182, 269–270, 322,
325, 387
stories, 4, 7, 11, 20, 28, 32, 74, 80,
157–158, 293–294, 297, 299, 307,
328, 334, 337, 345, 347, 350–351,
361, 382, 384–385
subaltern, 81, 100, 232, 250–251,
263, 270, 299, 305
sugar beets, 308

Talamantes, Inés, 73
Tamez, Margo, 2, 18
Tan, Amy, 117, 139
Teatro del Piojo, El, 194
Tejanos, 7, 30, 189, 194, 301, 337
Tejas, 3, 70, 96, 190–191, 193–194,
277, 310, 344, 360
testimonios, 80, 263, 293
Teutonic Historians, 150–152
Texas, 11, 15, 18, 20, 22–23, 26–28,
33, 56, 87, 89, 98, 129, 182–183,
189–190, 196, 224, 250, 266, 270,
286, 290, 296, 300, 304–305, 311,
313–317, 319, 321, 323, 328–329,
333–336, 341, 344–346, 351–353,
361, 369, 372, 375, 380, 384, 388
Text and Context, 3, 188, 196, 328
They Wait for Us, 149, 174, 304, 327
third-world feminists, 118–119
third-world liberation, 104–105
This Bridge Called My Back, 11, 19,
21, 131–132
*To Love Honor and Obey in Colonial
Mexico*, 166, 184, 265
tongue, 254, 332, 345, 348
Torres, Edén, 286

Toypurina, 13, 35–36, 65, 75–77, 79,
198, 210–211, 225, 237–241, 325,
388
translating cultures, 337, 340, 343
*Travels in California and Scenes in
the Pacific Ocean*, 39, 41
True Woman, 147
Trujillo, Carla, 19, 132, 198, 272, 368
Two Years Before the Mast, 39–40,
58–60, 62
Turner, Frederick Jackson, 100, 108,
129, 153–154, 156, 159, 176, 178
Turner thesis, 100, 176

UC Berkeley, 275, 379
UCLA, 23, 276–279, 285, 298, 379
undergraduates, 192, 278, 379, 384
United Farm Workers (UFW), 132,
192, 381
United Farm Workers Organizing
Committee, 192
University of Texas, 11, 18, 20,
22–23, 26, 33, 56, 87, 183, 190,
224, 266, 286, 313, 323, 328–329,
345, 369, 380
University of Texas Press, 18, 22,
26, 33, 56, 87, 183, 224, 266, 323,
328–329, 345, 369, 380
University of Washington, 175, 178,
190, 192–193, 286, 303, 321, 326,
329

Valdez, Dorotea, 185, 356–357, 369
Vallejo, Rosalía, 60, 116, 185
Vallejo, Ygnacio Vicente Ferrer, 246
Verger, Rafael, 201–202, 223
violence, 4, 11, 14, 29, 36, 52, 54,
66, 73, 79–80, 83, 87, 99–100,
116–117, 121–122, 125, 139,
145, 164, 167, 169, 181, 197–198,
201–208, 213–217, 220–222,

violence (*continued*), 226–229, 237, 240, 257, 259, 262, 292, 300–303, 325–326, 335, 342, 350, 387
virtue, 40–44, 46, 48, 51–53, 57–59, 62, 147, 164, 182, 220, 222, 239
Voces Hispanas, 308, 327–328

war, 8, 19, 37, 40, 44–48, 50–57, 66, 70, 76–77, 87, 100, 115–117, 121, 134, 141–142, 144–145, 147, 149–153, 155, 162, 166, 169, 172, 189, 204–205, 210, 216–218, 241, 247, 299–301, 303–304, 322, 324, 328–329, 335, 337, 340, 342–343, 348, 350, 353–354, 356–357, 360, 367, 369
warfare, 117, 121, 204, 210, 229, 361
Western civilization, 216–217
Western History, 2, 14, 99–100, 102–103, 117, 127–129, 180, 255, 272, 322, 387
Western Women: Their Land, Their Lives, 19, 86, 130, 134, 163, 180–181, 267
westward expansion, 39, 108
When Jesus Came the Corn Mothers Went Away, 136, 166, 179, 184
witch, 85, 225, 266

witchcraft, 69, 76, 85–86, 239–240, 266
white women, 76, 104–106, 110–112, 115–116, 121, 163, 173, 282, 285, 303
white supremacy, 10, 13
women of color, 13–14, 19, 21, 31, 76, 99–100, 102–108, 110–118, 122, 125–128, 131–133, 139, 272, 275, 322, 387
Women of Mexico City, 1790–1857, The, 166, 184
Women Singing in the Snow, 198
women's liberation, 104–105
Women's studies, 105–106, 278, 282–283, 286, 330
Women's West, The, 129, 163, 180

Yakima Valley, 30, 190–192, 310
Yankee, 40–41, 149, 163, 304
Ybarra-Frausto, Tomás, 3, 19, 30, 98, 188–189, 196, 328
Young, Judy, 100
Yuma rebellion, 243
Yumas, 204
Yurok, 73–74

Zavella, Patricia, 5